Lancelot An… s

1555 –

Teacher an… …st
Reformatio… …urch

Some catechetical lectures and … …s of Lancelot Andrewes

Introduced and edited
by Marianne Dorman

Train up a child in the way he should go and when he is old he will not depart from it.
Proverbs 22.6

Lancelot Andrewes: Teacher and Preacher in the Post Reformation Church

Published by Wheatmark™
610 East Delano Street, Suite 104, Tucson, Arizona 85705 U.S.A.
www.wheatmark.com

ISBN-13: 978-1-58736-639-0
ISBN-10: 1-58736-639-8
LCCN: 2006924770

AD MAJOREM DEI GLORIAM

IN MEMORY OF MICHAEL ROWETT

My dear friend
May he rest in peace and joy.

"The last and great feast indeed, when all destroyers and all destruction will cease and come to an end for evermore, and we hear that joyful voice, *Transi in gaudium Domini*, 'Passover into the joy of the Lord,' the joys of Heaven, joy not mingled with any leaven as this world's joy is, but pure and entire; not transient as that of this world, and ever flitting and forsaking us then soonest when we think we have best hold of them, but permanent and abiding still. A Passover that will never be passed over, but last and continue as feast to all eternity."

—From Andrewes' Easter Day Sermon for 1612

CONTENTS

PREFACE

In preparing this work for publication there are three people to whom I owe my sincere thanks. The first is Dr. Richard Palmer, Librarian and Archivist of Lambeth Palace Library. It was he who first told me of this manuscript just before the library purchased it in 1994 (now Ms. 3707 together with Ms. 3708). As I was using this manuscript when researching for my doctrinal thesis on Lancelot Andrewes as the mentor of Reformed Catholicism, I realised just how valuable this would be for historians and theologians working in the post-Reformation period in the English Church. During those many visits to Lambeth Palace Library to type the text on my computer and follow up research, I received much encouragement, help and support from Dr. Palmer and his staff.

The second is a dear friend, Mr. Michael Rowett, who spent many, many hours in proof reading, and helping me with the Greek. As he said, "it was a labour of love", but one very much appreciated. Unfortunately Michael died before seeing this manuscript in print.

The third is Mr. David Baxter, the previous owner of both manuscripts. After I completed my work on Ms. 3707 he shared with me his own reflections and research on this manuscript, some of which have been included in this book, and more extensively on Ms. 3708. The notes on that manuscript in the Appendix, I owe almost entirely to him.

I would also like to thank the Trustees of Lambeth Palace Library for permission to publish this book and to the Principal, Fellows and Scholars of Jesus College, Oxford for permission to use their portrait of Lancelot Andrewes on the front cover.

A note about text, spelling and punctuation in the manuscript. Scriptural references are mainly from the Authorized Version, although we know that Andrewes mostly used the Genevan Bible. Many of the biblical references are abbreviated, while some are inaccurate. I have endeavoured to complete and correct where necessary. There are also quotations from the bible incorporated into the text without any reference. These I have added in parenthesis.

As there were no spelling rules in Andrewes' time, there are sometimes different spellings for the same word in the manuscript. For example *sin* is spelt *sin, sinn* and *sinne*, and *son* spelt *son, sone* and *sonne*. Sometimes the *e* is dropped from the end of words, e.g. *preserv, serv, beelev*. In some words ending with the suffix *ness* the last *s* is omitted, and at other times an *e* is added to the suffix *ness*, such as in *happinesse, holinesse* and *witnesse*. Other words ending with a suffix have the *e* sometimes omitted from the first syllable such as in *houshold, wholsome*, and *falshood*. Some pronouns have an extra *e* such as *yee, mee, hee* and *shee*. Verbs such as *go, do, posses* are often spelt with an *e* added. A few words are spelt with a double *l* at the end, such as *historicall, doctrinall, eternall* and *gospell*. Many plural words are spelt with *es*, such as *bookes* and *workes*. Our modern words such as *burden* and *murder* are spelt as *burthen* and *murther; heretic* and *catholic* as *heretique* and *catholique;* and words like *vanity* are spelt with an *ie*. *Then* is spelt as *than*. There are the occasional archaic spellings such as *thorow* or *throw* for *through*. As will be obvious many words were abbreviated in the text, as was the word *and*, except when beginning a sentence. *Capital letters, full stops* and *commas* are used indiscriminately, which I have adhered to mostly. One major exception is the name of *Christ*, which I have always spelt with a capital. The *apostrophe* is seldom used to show ownership or even abbreviation, but note *its* as a possessive pronoun is sometimes spelt as *it's*.

Andrewes we know always wrote in various languages, and this manuscript is no exception with its inclusion of Greek, Latin and Hebrew. [For the last of these I have used modern Hebrew for publishing purposes.] Mostly he gave the meaning or a paraphrase of these in the next sentence, but when it has not been given, the translation has been provided.

It would seem that Andrewes always quoted from memory, and so at times some of his references are inaccurate. I have endeavoured to correct these in footnotes.

Ash Wednesday, 2006.

ABBREVIATIONS AND BIBLIOGRAPHY

Andrewes	*The Works of Lancelot Andrewes*, eds. J. Bliss & J. P. Wilson, 11 Vols (L.A.C.T., Oxford, 1841–54).
Apos. Sacra	*Apospasmatia Sacra: Or A Collection of posthumous and orphan Lectures: Delivered at St. Pauls and St. Giles his Church by the Right Honourable and Reverend Father in God Lancelot Andrews, Lord Bishop of Winchester* (London, 1657).
Aquinas	T. Aquinas, *Summa theologiae, 'Sacra Doctrina ist Scientia'* (London, Blackfriars, 1964).
Blackstone	B. Blackstone (ed.), *Ferrar Papers: Containing A Life of Nicholas Ferrar, The Winding-Sheet, A Collection of Short Moral Histories, A Selection of Family Letters* (Cambridge, 1938).
Briefe View	J. Harington, *A Briefe View of the State of the Church of England, As it stood in Q. Elizabeths and King James his Reigne to the Yeere 1608* (London, 1653).
Brightman	*The Preces Privatæ of Lancelot Andrewes*, trans. and introd. by F. E. Brightman (London, 1903).
Brigtman, *Manual*	*The Manual for the Sick of Lancelot An-*

	drewes, ed. and introd. by F.E. Brightman (London, 1909).
Cassan	S. H. Cassan, *The Lives of the Bishops of Winchester: From Birinus, The first Bishop of the West Saxons to the Present Time*, 2 Vols (London, 1827).
Chambers	D. Chambers, "A Catalogue Of The Library Of Bishop Lancelot Andrewes (1555 – 1626)", *Transactions Of The Cambridge Bibliographical Society*, Vol. 5 (1970), pp. 99 – 121.
Chamberlain	*The Letters of John Chamberlain*, ed., N. E. McClure, 2 Vols (Philadelphia, 1939).
Chrysostom	John Chrysostom, *Homily No. 75. ch. 3 on St. John's Gospel*, Nicene and Post-Nicene Fathers, Series I, Vol. XIV (Edinburgh, 1988).
Clement	Clement, *Letter to the Corinthians*, The Ante-Nicene Fathers, Vol. 1 (Edinburgh, 1993).
Cosin	*The Works of the Rt. Reverend Father In God John Cosin, Lord Bishop of Durham*, ed., J. Sanson, 5 vols (Oxford, 1843 - 55).
Cyprian	Cyprian, *The Treatises of Cyprian* Vol. V. Ante-Nicene Fathers, (Edinburgh, 1995).
De Civitate	Augustine, *De Civitate Dei*, 2 vols (London, 1945).
Dering	E. Dering, *M. Derings workes, More at large than ever has heere-to-fore been printed in any one volume* (London, 1597).
Oxford Dictionary	F.E. Cross and E.A. Livingstone, Ed., *The Oxford Dictionary of the Christian Church* (Oxford, 1997).
Donne	J. Donne, *The Sermons of John Donne*, eds.,

	E. M. Simpson, & G. R. Potter, 10 Vols (Berkeley, 1955 - 62).
Gouk	P. Gouk, *Music, Science and Natural Magic in Seventeenth Century* (New Haven), 1999).
E.P.	*The Works of Richard Hooker*, ed., J. Keble, and revised by R. W. Church, and F. Paget, 3 Vols, 7th edition (Oxford, 1878).
Episcopacy	*Of Episcopacy. Three Epistles of Peter Moulin Doctor and Professorof Divinity. Answered By the Right Reverend Father in God Lancelot Andrews, Late Lord Bishop of Winchester* (London, 1647).
Eusebius	Eusebius, *Church History*, Series II, Vol. I, Nicene and Post-Nicene Fathers (Edinburgh, 1989).
Green	I. Green, "'For Children in Yeeres and Children in Understanding': The Emergence of the English Catechism under Elizabeth and the Early Stuarts", *Journal of Ecclesiastical History*, Vol. 37 No. 3 (July, 1986), pp. 397 – 425.
Green, *Clergy*	I. Green, "'Reformed Pastors' and Bons Curés: The Changing Role of the Parish Clergy in Early Modern Europe," *Studies in Church History: The Ministry: Clerical and Lay*, Vol. 26 (Oxford, 1989), pp. 249 - 286.
Hippolytus	Hippolytus, *The Refutation of all Heresies*, Vol. 5 (Ante-Nicene Fathers, Edinburgh, 1995).
Inst. Piæ	H. Isaacson, *Institutiones Piæ, or Directions to Pray* (London, 1630).
Gregory of Nanzianus	Gregory of Nanzianus, Series II, Vol.VII,

	Nicene and Post- Nicene Fathers (Edinburgh, 1989).
John of Damascus	Damascene, *An Exact Exposition of the Orthodox Faith*, Bk. 2, Ch. 3, Series II, Vol. IX. (Nicene and Post-Nicene Fathers, Edinburgh 1989).
Johnson	P. Johnson, *A history of Christianity* (Penguin, Hammondsworth, 1976).
L.A.C.T.	Library of Anglo-Catholic Theology.
Laud	*The Works of The Most Reverend Father in God William Laud D.D. Sometime Lord Archbishop of Canterbury*, eds. J. Bliss and W. Scott, 9 Vols (L.A.C.T. Oxford, 1847-1860).
Learned Disc.	*A Learned Discourse of Ceremonies; Retained and used in Christian Churches, written By Right Reverend Father in God Lancelot Andrewes Late Bishop of Winchester a little before his Death: At the Request of an Eminent Person that desired satisfaction therein,* introduced by E. Leigh (London, 1653).
Lossky	N. Lossky, *Lancelot Andrewes the Preacher (1555-1626),* trans. by A. Louth (Oxford, 1991).
Mathew	A. H. Mathew, *A True Historical Relation of The Conversion of Sir Tobie Matthew to The Holy Catholic Faith with the Antecedents and Consequences Thereof* (London, 1904).
Ms. 3707	Lambeth Palace Library Ms.3707.
Ms. 3708	Lambeth Palace Library Ms. 3708.
McGrath	A. E. McGrath, *Reformation Thought* (Oxford, 1993).

M.L.E.	*The Morall Law Expounded ... The long-expected and much desired Work of Bishop Andrewes upon The Ten Commandments: Being his Lectures many yeares since in Pembroch-Hall Chappell, in Cambridge* (London, 1642).
Morgan	J. Morgan, *Godly Learning: Puritan Attitudes towards Reason, Learning and Education, 1560 - 1640* (Cambridge, 1988).
Moseley	H. Moseley, *The Private Devotions of ... Lancelot Andrewes* (London, 1647).
P.C.D.	*A Patterne of Catechisticall Doctrine. Wherein many profitable Questions touching Christian religion are handled. And the whole Decalogue succintly and judiciously expounded* (London, 1641), as in Andrewes, Vol. 6.
P.C.D. (1650)	*The Pattern of Catecheticall Doctrine at Large: or, A learned and pious exposition of the Ten Commandments* (London, 1650).
Pearson	J. Pearson, *Exposition of the Creed* (Cambridge 1867).
Perkins	*The Works of that famous and worthie Minister of Christ, in the Universitie of Cambridge, Mr. W. Perkins*, 3 Vols (Cambridge, 1608).
Plutarch	Plutarch, *Moralia* (London, 1657).
Porter	H. C. Porter, *Reformation and Reaction in Tudor Cambridge* (Cambridge, 1958).
Procatechesis	Cyril of Jerusalem, Series II, Vol. VII, Nicene and Post-Nicene Fathers (Edinburgh, 1989).
Preces Quotidianæ	Andrewes, Vol. 9 in L.A.C. T. collection.
P.R.O.	Public Record Office.

Rowell	G. Rowell (ed.), *The English Religious Tradition and the Genius of Anglicanism* (Wantage, 1992).
Sargeaunt	J. Sargeaunt, *Annals of Westminster School* (London, 1898).
Scala Coeli	L. Andrewes, *Scala Coeli: Nineteene Sermons Concerning Prayer* (London, 1611).
Scrin. Res.	J. Hacket, *Scrinia Reserata: A Memorial offr'd to the great deservings of John Williams D.D* (London, 1693).
Socrates	Socrates, *The Ecclesiastical History*, Series II, Vol. II Nicene and Post-Nicene Fathers (Edinburgh, 1989).
Stokes	D. Stokes, *An Appendix to the Directions For Private Devotions and Retirements* attached to *Verus Christianus* (Oxford, 1668).
S.P.	State Papers.
Taylor	*The Whole Works of the Right Rev. Jeremy Taylor D. D. Lord Bishop of Down, Connor, and Dromore* ed., C. P. Eden, 10 Vols (London, 1847 - 1853).
Tertullian	Tertullian, *De præscriptio adversus hæreticos,* Vol. III, The Anti-Nicene Fathers (Edinburgh, 1993).
True Religion	H. Grotius, *True Religion Explained and Defended* (London, 1632).
Tyacke	N. Tyacke, "Lancelot Andrewes and the Myth of Anglicanism" in *Conformity and Orthodoxy* (Woodbridge, 2000).
Walton	I. Walton, The Lives of Mr. Richard Hooker, Mr. George Herbert, & Dr. Robert Sanderson (London, 1947).

Welsby	P. A. Welsby, *Lancelot Andrewes* (London, 1958).
Whitgift	J. Whitgift, *The Works of John Whitgift*, ed. J. Ayres, 3 Vols (Parker Society, Cambridge, 1851 - 53).

INTRODUCTION

The purchase of two manuscripts, lots 3 and 4, by the Friends of Lambeth Palace Library with the help of the V. and A. Purchase Grant Fund, at a public sale at Southerby's on 19th July, 1994 is of immense importance for scholars interested in Lancelot Andrewes' theology and piety. They have been catalogued as Mss. 3707 and 3708 respectively in Lambeth Palace Library.

Ms. 3707 is a small, calf-binding manuscript with transcriptions at both ends. One has catechetical lectures preceded by *Manductio ad theologiam polemicam*, while the other end contains six sermons. Neither end has an introduction nor any mention of the author. However it would seem there is a common authorship of the lectures and sermons. That author, I suggest, is Andrewes. Anyone familiar with his works would recognise his signature throughout. Why? There is too much common material with other works of his, as footnotes in appropriate places in this book reveal, while the style, phraseology and the constant appeal to the Fathers are distinctly his. Furthermore the beginning of the opening lecture expresses the same sentiment that appears on the motto of Andrewes' Episcopal ring, "Who is sufficient worthy?" of undertaking such pastoral responsibility.[1]

Ms. 3707 was transcribed by an unknown hand, c.1650, as it includes quotations from Grotius' commentaries that were not published until 1642 and 1650. Whoever it was, it would seem that he believed, as others did at the time, that Andrewes' piety and teaching were an inspiration during those bleak years of the

---

1 Ms. 3707, p.12. The exact inscription engraved on the Episcopal ring on his appointment as bishop of Chichester is "And who is sufficient for these things?"

Interregnum. Previously privately owned[2] these lectures support what was stated by editors of Andrewes' works such as *The Morall Law Expounded,*[3] *The Private Devotions of …Lancelot Andrewes,*[4] *An Appendix*: *To the Directions for Private Devotions and Retirements*[5] that there were various manuscripts of this divine in circulation during his life time and afterwards.

This book is a transcription of Ms. 3707 with introduction and notes to thirteen complete lectures (one lecture has only a heading), and six sermons, one of which is mainly in note form. It would seem that the lectures belong to a course of catechetical lectures, parts of which probably date from as early as 1578 as there is much common material with those catechetical lectures Andrewes gave in Pembroke Chapel, Cambridge after his appointment as Catechist in 1578.

There were various editions of these lectures published in the first half of the seventeenth century, beginning in 1630. This edition, known as *A Patterne of Catechisticall Doctrine. Wherein many profitable Questions touching Christian religion are handled. And the whole Decalogue succintly and judiciously expounded,* provided the bare text only; and so the next edition in 1641 "revised and

---

2 The owner was David Baxter who had purchased them from Shakespeare Head bookshop, Cambridge, c. 1963. Their whereabouts before this date is unknown.

3 The title-page explained that these were the lectures given "many years since in Pembroch-Hall Chappell, in Cambridge", and since those days "have ever since passed from hand to hand in Manuscripts, and been accounted one of the greatest Treasures of private Libraries." M.L.E., title page and Dedicatory.

4 Moseley, in the preface wrote, "I must clearely confesse, when these Copies came first to my hand, I resolved to imprint them in my own heart … then one of my profession, and withall that there were divers manuscripts dispersed abroad, and the Church might be deprived of this genuine Edition … I thought this publication absolutely necessary. … I thought good not to keep wrapt up in a napkin from the public, ... the memory of the devout Author." Moseley, A5.

5 David Stokes, a student at Westminster School in Andrewes' time, in this Appendix makes various references to "papers" of Andrewes. He explained how to help his readers to follow in the pattern of this beloved bishop, he had made "use of, such choice Papers of his, as may be found out; which is as good, as the *observing the light of his Candle*". Later on he remarked "I have seen an imperfect Copy of another confession", and "These Two last meditations, I find thus rendered in the Learned Bishop's Greek Papers, with some advantage, and enlargement." Stokes, pp.5, 13, 17.

amended" these notes.[6] A year later in 1642, *The Morall Law Expounded* was published in which the title-page drew attention that this volume contained those lectures given "many years since in Pembroch-Hall Chappell, in Cambridge". The editor, John Jackson, described Andrewes as "a man both at home and abroad of great fame for his clerk-ship and of a good fame for his regular and strict life." To *The Morall Law Expounded,* were appended the Temptation and Prayer Sermons, first published in 1592 and 1611 respectively. Another edition was printed in 1650, entitled *The Pattern of Catechistical Doctrine at large: or, A learned and pious exposition of the Ten Commandments,* which the editor claimed would replace "a rude imperfect draught" compiled from those notes of lectures of Andrewes "which had passed through diverse hands". This edition is "the Author's own Copy, revised and compared with diverse other manuscripts", and therefore it was supposedly purged of the "many thousands of errors, defects and corruptions" of the "imperfect Draught formerly Published."[7] However in this fuller version, the editor, as intimated, has added other extracts, notably from the Court Sermons of Andrewes, and at times it would seem, has given a liberal expansion of previous publications.

Of all these publications, it is *The Morall Law Expounded* that these lectures share the most common material. Does this also tell us that *The Morall Law Expounded* is not a vastly expanded version of *A Patterne of Catechisticall Doctrine* as claimed by some scholars such as Dr. Tyacke, and it is therefore a more accurate account of Andrewes' teachings than previously considered?[8] The lectures also have common material with the Temptation and Prayer Sermons, and the lectures on Genesis and Sermons in *Apospasmatia Sacra* published in 1657. There is also common material shared with various editions of the *Preces Privatæ,* and *A Manual for the Sick,* both first published in 1648 by Richard Drake, a chaplain of Andrewes and a Fellow of Pembroke Hall.

These lectures also contain some identical or similar mate-

6 This is the version that appears in the Library of Anglo-Catholic Theology.

7 P.C.D. (1650), Title Page.

8 Tyacke, p. 8.

rial with other works of the period. The first of these is Hooker's first Five Books of *Ecclesiastical Polity* published before his death in 1600. This poses some interesting questions. Did Hooker have access to Andrewes' manuscripts in circulation, and incorporated text from them into his *Ecclesiastical* Polity? We know that they were friends, and we also know that Andrewes sent a copy of a manuscript that he had prepared for Whitgift to Hooker, which he never returned.[9] Hooker's teaching on the Sabbath in Book Five is similar to Andrewes' teaching in the Catechetical lectures given at Pembroke long beforehand. Is this mere co-incidence or was Hooker influenced by Andrewes on this subject?[10] Or did Andrewes or the transcriber interpolate appropriate texts from Hooker into this manuscript? Of all the common material in this manuscript, only one is acknowledged as Hooker's. This is in Lecture No. 1 when Hooker is referred to as the "Judicious Hooker".[11] Isaac Walton revealed that King James always prefaced any reference to Hooker by this adjective.[12] So if Hooker was acknowledged for one quotation why not for the others if either Andrewes or the transcriber lifted work from *Ecclesiastical Polity*? If it is Andrewes' interpolation it is out of character as he consistently acknowledged the writings of others as evident in these lectures. And if it were the transcriber why would he acknowledge Grotius when interpolating his comments and not Hooker's? So it leaves the possibility that Hooker used Andrewes' writings when compiling *Ecclesiastical Polity.*

This leads to the second batch of identical or similar material, no other than with Grotius' *De Veritate Religionis Christinae*, pub-

---

9 Presumably this writing was of an anti-Calvinist tone as Chamberlain wrote of Andrewes' concern about its whereabouts at the time when Grotius was trying to gain the support of Andrewes in the Arminian struggle against the Calvinists just prior to the Synod of Dort. Andrewes added that although Hooker "promised to return it but never did". Chamberlain, Vol. 2, pp. 110-11.

10 E.P., 5.70.9.

11 Ms. 3707.p. 14.

12 Walton, p. 151. Sir William Cowper erected a memorial to Hooker in which he referred to him as "judicious Hooker" in epitaph. When the completed works of Hooker were eventually published in 1662 by John Gauden they were titled Ecclesiastical Polity as The Works of Mr. Richard Hooker (that learned, godly, judicious and eloquent divine) ... in Eight Books of Ecclesiastical Polity. ... Ibid., p. 161.

lished in 1627 and translated into English by 1632 as *The True Religion*. We know Grotius was anxious to have Andrewes' friendship, recognition and support in the Arminians' disputes against the Calvinists in the Low Countries. Grotius had spent time in England in 1613 during which he visited and dined at Andrewes' table on two separate occasions. The latter specifically related that no communication passed between them "at the table". However it would seem that Grotius sought, almost desperately, for Andrewes' support, and so his version of their meeting was different as he described conversing with the bishop. He also intimated that he had received letters from this prelate "in countenance of theyr cause". We know he wrote to Andrewes at the end of October, 1617, before the Synod of Dordt, and from prison afterwards. But Andrewes failed to reply to either of the letters or indeed any others.[13] Nevertheless it is possible that Grotius gained access to some of the bishop's manuscripts. Accordingly in Grotius' *The True Religion*, Book One on God proving that there is a God who is one and eternal, and the cause of all things; Book Two on how "True Religion agrees to Christian Religion"; Book Three on authority, authenticity, and veracity of Holy Scripture and its writers and Book Four on how some Pagan religions came to recognise that there is one God, and that Christianity was approved by the wisest of Pagans, all contain identical passages with Ms. 3707. Although the material of Books Five and Six do not feature in Ms. 3707, they do in *The Morall Law Expounded* and *The Pattern of Catechetical Doctrine* (1650).[14]

Thirdly, Cosin who regarded Andrewes as one of his mentors (the other was Overall) followed his teaching on the strict observance of the Lord's Day as a day of rest for worship and works of spiritual mercies.[15] Furthermore his undated sermons on the Temptation contain material taken from Andrewes' Temptations Sermons, parts of which appear in this manuscript.[16]

---

13 Chamberlain, Vol. 2, pp. 111, 141.

14 M.L.E., pp. 158 -64, P.C.D. (1650), pp. 37- 42.

15 Cosin preached at least two sermons on the strict observance of Sunday, one of which was in St. Brandon, Brancepath, 1633. Cosin, Vol. 1, pp. 153 - 189.

16 Cosin patched together seventy-five sentences or parts of sentences from Andrewes' *Seven Sermons on the Temptations of Christ* in two undated sermons of his own. Ibid., pp. 58-83.

Fourthly, John Pearson lifted some of Andrewes' text from his lecture on *Creation* into the first article on *God, Maker of Heaven and Earth*, in his *Exposition of the Creed*, first published in 1659.

> To whom and when were these lectures delivered? I like to think that this series of lectures was given at Westminster School when Andrewes was Dean or Abbot of Westminster Abbey from 1601 - 1605. The opening words of Lecture One suggest a place like Westminster Abbey: "Being injoyned by my superiors (to whose care and descretion the furniture of this place is committed) to appeare here upon this occasion; I may call this Duty a work of meer Obedience, and so a matter of necessity rather than of choice."[17]

The lectures form a little *Summa* of Catholic theology. Like Aquinas, Andrewes saw religion as a science, and so it could not be "rightly delivered and profitably learned unles some Grounds be laid"[18] in the principles of it, which come from divine revelation through Scripture and creation.[19] The lectures are therefore arranged in a logical order for catechising and reflect this divine's aim to teach the essential beliefs of the Christian faith according to the Fathers to the young, and to encourage them to live godly and virtuous lives. Hence the lectures also have a strong moral tone as most of them end with some advice on how to apply Christian teachings in their lives. He reminded them too of the privilege to have instruction in the Christian faith, to be taught to know right from wrong, and how to commit their lives to Christ whilst they were young.

It would also seem that in undertaking these catechetical lectures Andrewes had in mind that many of the boys would go up to Cambridge,[20] which, doctrinally at the beginning of the seventeenth century, was predominantly Calvinist with a strong em-

---

17 Ms. 3707, p. 12.

18 Ibid., p. 118.

19 Thomas Aquinas had stated, "Christian theology should be pronounced to be a science." Aquinas, 1a.1.2.

20 Scholarships were available to the scholars at Trinity College, Cambridge and also Christ Church, Oxford.

phasis on double predestination and covenantal theology. As he was still Master of Pembroke College he knew well the religious climate. Accordingly in the course of these lectures he constantly emphasised love and mercy as being God's prime attributes in His plan for man's redemption. Mercy has "the pre-eminence over all his works", even over His justice. Above all the "originall and foundacion of all his mercyes to mankind was the Incarnacion of his sonne." Such expressions are similar to those found in Sermon Three where He described mercy as "incomprehensible, ... that boundles, bottomles fountain of all His favours, the best link in the golden chain of salvacion, the whole and sole cause of all our happinesse". Mercy and love were the indissoluble links in God's "golden chain".[21] This description would seem to be an obvious attack on William Perkins' work on election and reprobation, entitled A *Golden Chaine.*[22] He obviously had no love for the promotion of the doctrine of double predestination by making clear that God "hath no pleasure in the death of the wicked".[23]

The introduction to these lectures is similar to those given at Pembroke Hall. Both emphasise the importance of catechising over preaching in communicating the Christian faith. Like Cyril of Jerusalem he viewed catechising unlike "homilies or sermons, for of them if we misse one, we may redeem it by another, but if we misse this exercise there will be a chasme."[24] He also believed that catechising was essential "for the preservation and safety of both Church and State". "Where there is no knowledge of the true God, there can be no true church", while a commonwealth cannot be truly just and moral without its members being faithful Christians. "If judgment and opinion be not right biased, all will be amisse in our Actions." Education could be regarded in the same light as a custom which "hath such power and influence upon the soul, and doth so modell and frame the whole man that 'tis a 2nd Nature," stated Andrewes.[25]

---

21 Ms. 3707, pp. 56, 87, 156.

22 This was first published in 1591.

23 Ms. 3707, p. 118.

24 Ibid., p. 24.

25 Ibid., pp.19-20.

The lectures end abruptly as the lectures on the *Heavenly Offices of Christ* are incomplete. Either Andrewes failed to lecture on the all proposed five headings or the transcriber did not complete his task. There is one lecture, number Seven, with only its heading *Of Gods Providence* and the text reference. There are clearly other lectures he gave or intended to give, as evident in Lecture Five where he stated that he will content himself at this time to speak in general on the attributes of God, as at some other "text" he will deliver "severall lectures" on these.[26]

These lectures unfold just how extensive Andrewes' reading and learning was as they are filled with quotations not only from the early Fathers such as Basil and Augustine and medieval theologians like Bernard and Anselm but also from the pagan writers of the pre-Christian era such as Plutarch, Tacitus, Livy, Pliny and Aristotle. By quoting from them he illustrated his belief that all men are endowed with natural grace and reason to discern the existence of God, as well as emphasising his teaching that the early Church adopted many of the heathen practices for their worship, and converted temples into churches.

Above all the lectures are important in assessing Andrewes' theology as they clearly set out his doctrinal beliefs on many topics not readily defined in other sermons, such as original sin, angelogy, covenantal theology, the heavenly offices of Christ and the nature of the Church.

The six sermons probably date from the late 1580's onwards into the early 90's. Sermon Two was in all probability preached at Easter, 1589 as there are references to victory over the Spanish Armada, as there are also in the next one.

> In times of distraction, warrs and fightings when we have to doe with subtle and powerfull enemies, what better newes, than newes of a victory and that victory absolute, and that over ordinary, but potent enemies, such as flesh and blood could not encounter with.[27]

---

26 Ibid., p. 56.

27 Ms. 3707, p. 142.

This sermon also refers to Perkins' *A Golden Chaine*, first published in Latin in 1590, and in English the following year. Where were they preached? - probably in Cambridge at Christmas and Easter. If the sermons have been scribed in chronological order it may well be that the first sermon on the Nativity was in 1588, the second in 1589 and the rest in the early nineties.

These sermons share much common material with the Court Sermons. For example the Third Sermon, much in note-form text, is an abbreviation of the Passion of Christ that appears in the Sermon for Good Friday, 1604, whilst Sermon Four too has common material with this one. Sermon One, with its teaching on orthodoxy against various heresies, is similar to the Christmas Sermon of 1611 preached at Court.

Ms. 3707 also reveals that Andrewes was a gifted teacher (see separate chapter). It is also important in analysing his theological beliefs in his early days. As much of the text is as old as those Catechetical Lectures at Pembroke it manifests that his beliefs changed very little over fifty years. They further uphold his statement to Walsingham in 1589 that his years of learning, especially in the Patristics, had taught him that their teaching was the way to follow, and his conscience would not allow him to do otherwise.[28] It also cements my belief that it is Andrewes, not Hooker, who was the most influential divine in presenting and upholding the reformed Catholic faith, and passing it on to those who sat at his feet and took notes on his lectures and sermons.

This manuscript also unveils Andrewes as a pastor who cared for the souls under his authority. He left no doubt in the minds of his auditors what were the consequences of sin, but on the other side of the coin he taught them that God desperately wanted them to repent of their sins and experience His abundant love and mercy. God "had rather his Trees should be for fruit than fuell."[29]

Ms. 3707 reveals too his concern for reverend worship. The young were constantly being admonished to be more reverent at worship, to remember God's special presence in His house, and to

---

28 *Briefe View*, p. 143.

29 Ms. 3707, p. 118.

listen attentively like the small Samuel in order to hear God and His word being spoken to them. Furthermore he stressed the importance of the whole person, that is, both soul and body to be active in worship. "'Tis the soul that worships God, but 'tis the Body that lifts up the eye and bowes the knee to him. 'Tis the soul that is charitable, but the hand gives Almes. 'Tis the soul that is fed in the sacrament, but the mouth that receiveth bread and wine."[30]

The other manuscript, Ms. 3708 is a transcription of Andrewes' *Preces* by Gilbert Sheldon for the Shirley household around the mid seventeenth century. Notes and an extract of Ms. 3708 are attached as an Appendix. As stated in the Preface its content is not a result of my research, only of my patience in reproducing it, but that of David Baxter, the previous owner of this manuscript.

Both manuscripts are also important in the light that nothing has survived in Andrewes' own handwriting. As Laud and Buckeridge had the royal prerogative to pursue and publish his works, it would seem that his writings were severely censored. They published only those that suited their agenda and presumably the rest were destroyed, or at least they hoped so. Evidence for this censorship is illustrated in 1627 when Laud prevented the distribution of Michael Sparke's reprint of *Seven Sermons on the wonderfull combate betweene Christ and Sathan*, first published in 1592. Laud, when he wrote to Bishop Montaigne of London requesting its withdrawal, claimed that its publication would interfere with "the printing of the whole of the late Bishop's works" which had been commanded by Charles 1.[31] Yes, it would interfere, as some of Andrewes' views expressed in these sermons were not exactly those held by Laud.[32] There was for example an uncomplimentary remark about bishops:

> Who would not tread hard there, and take upon him, being in such a place? where if a man will be carried away with example, he may see Ananias the high-priest renting his clothes at the

30 Ibid., p. 150.

31 P.R.O. S.P. 16/140/15, 16/800/48.

32 Andrewes himself had refused two sees (Salisbury and Ely) under Queen Elizabeth, as it would have meant agreeing to alienation of church income to the Sovereign.

hearing of things that sounded like blasphemy, and yet buying his bishopric for money.[33]

It would also seem from Andrewes' remarks that he preached a series of sermons on the Commandments in his parish church of St. Giles, Cripplegate in 1591/2. Laud published two, those on the second and third commandments. As illustrated in his catechetical lectures any sermon on the fourth commandment would not be acceptable to Laud, who supported the *Declaration of Sports*, first issued by James I in 1618 and re-issued by Charles I in 1633.[34] Andrewes insisted Sunday was a day for worship and abstaining from any recreation and unnecessary work.

The publication of so much material of Andrewes after 1640 also manifested how selective Laud was. Fortunately manuscripts survived Laud's scrutiny. These include those that Andrewes personally gave to others, those transcribed by others from his manuscripts and those based on notes taken by students whilst attending Andrewes' lectures, as already seen in Jackson's editing of *The Morall Law Expounded* in 1642.

Other manuscripts, surviving the axe of Laud were also published during the Interregnum. When Richard Drake, a fellow of Pembroke, first published Andrewes' *Private Devotions* in 1648[35] he explained his motive in a letter to John Ferrar in 1647. With "the great declining of Christianitie, which our eyes have seen with tears", Andrewes' devotions would be an asset to "keep our soules". Then when this stormy time is passed "all our losses [will] be gaines in the end."[36] In the same year Drake also published *A Manual for Direction of the Sick*, a manual An-

33 Andrewes, Vol. 5, p. 515.

34 This allowed recreation in the form of games and sport after Evensong on Sundays.

35 The first publication of Andrewes' Private Devotions was in the previous year, undertaken by the publisher Humphrey Moseley under the title of *The Private Devotions of the Right Reverend Father in God Lancelot Andrewes, late Bishop of Winchester*. Andrewes, Vol. 11, p. 227. Drake commented in the epistle dedicatory to his translation of 1648 of this publication having "some broken parcels, miserable defaced by a careless press."

36 Blackstone pp. 299 - 30.

drewes had used "in his ordinary Visitation of the Sick, when he was Vicar of St. Giles Cripplegate". Seven years later there was another edition published.[37]

The year before in 1647 Drake published two of Andrewes' very early sermons and his correspondence with the French Calvinist, Pierre Du Moulin in 1619 on episcopacy so that "in these sad calamitous distractions" they may be used "to their great advantage." These were published as *Sacrilege a Snare, Of the Right of Tithes,* and *Of Episcopacy* under the general title of *Three Learned and Seasonable Discourses.* Commenting on the substance of these and other sermons, Drake declared that Andrewes, whom he described as that "*Precious Father of our Church*", had a "divinely piercing ey[e], . . . into the then growing mischiefs of these times", and therefore Drake believed it was not presumptuous to conclude "that the *Spirit*, by which He spake was no othere then *Prophetical*."[38]

A fourth edition of *Institutiones Piæ*, first published in 1630 by Isaacson, Andrewes' amanuensis, was republished in 1655. It was a manual on how to pray, based on extracts from Andrewes' papers. The editor revealed how originally he had compiled this anthology "for my own private use", but then realised how "every good thing is the better for being communicated". Hence he had this work published "for the publique use of them ... to perform those Duties, which are contained in it."[39] Isaacson also wrote the first biography on Andrewes, published in 1650.

In 1653 *A Learned Discourse of Ceremonies Retained and used in Christian Churches, &c.* was published in which the editor remarked, "I would the Church of God had more such Bishops."[40] *Apospasmatia Sacra* was published in 1657, which contained the series of lectures Andrewes gave on each verse of chapters one to four on Genesis, firstly in St. Paul's Cathedral in the academ-

---

37 Andrewes, Vol. 11, p. 172.

38 Episcopacy, Dedicatory.

39 Inst. Piæ, pp. A 3 - 4.

40 *Learned Disc.*, A4. Perhaps this remark was just as much a criticism of the ineffectualness of bishops during the Interregnum.

ic years of 1590-2 and then continued five years later in 1597/8 at St. Giles' Cripplegate, his parish church in London. Sermons he preached here were also included. The editor referred to him as "*both a* faithfull *and* able Steward, *rightly* using *the* Key of knowledge, *religiously* opening the Mysteries of God, [and] 'bringing forth out of his Treasures things new and old.'" He commented on how he had collected notes from some of the scholars who had sat at Andrewes' feet. "*We caught them out of his* mouth *by* sleight *of* hand, *in such a manner as we were* able, *that recollecting in our memories the excellent* Lessons *which we had* heard, *we might be* able *the more effectually* to lay them up *in our* Hearts." He noted that Andrewes' whole purpose in teaching was not to win "*man's* applause; *but was* wholly intent *upon this very thing, That he might* benefit *his Hearers* by all he spake. He *was so* powerfull *and* mighty *in what he taught us out of the* Pulpit, *as* to carry *our* affections *which way he pleased*." [41]

In this quotation the editor revealed from his own experience the impact Andrewes had on his life and that of others. He was a true "Pastor [who] took *carefull* heed . . . to his flock, over which the holy-Ghost had made him Overseer." Thus in those disillusioned days his teaching and example gave strength and comfort to be faithful until that time when God will "raise up *such* able Pastors to goe in and out before his People, and to keep his Remnant from being carried *from* Jerusalem to Bethel, *from* Bethel *to* Babel, and from Babel to Babylon; *That he will* binde *up the* Breaches, *and* wipe *off* the Stains, repair *the* Glory *and* Reputation, *of his* afflicted, defiled, disgraced Spouse."[42]

These two manuscripts in Lambeth Palace Library stand in this tradition.

---

41 Apos. Sacra, Preface.

42 Ibid., On the authenticity of *Apospasmatia Sacra*, a noted modern scholar on Lancelot Andrewes, Donald Allchin, writes, "Certainly their style is less highly wrought than in the case of the great sermons, and the patristic quotations are less numerous. But the substance of the doctrine is identical and it is interesting to see how positions characteristic of Andrews' later teaching are here advanced in the last years of the sixteenth century." Rowell, p. 147.

ANDREWES AS TEACHER

Ms. 3707 reveals how seriously and conscientiously Andrewes taught the Christian faith. The lectures are arranged in a logical order, flowing from one into the other as he began each by recalling what he had taught previously, and then outlining its logical continuation. For example the first lecture on Christ as Mediator, he began by reminding students that he had previously taught them what was "the Nature of sin, the severall sorts and divisions of sin" and the consequences of that sin: "Guilt, and stain, and Punishment." Now he was going to expand a little on the last of these before showing them the remedy for those consequences from sin.[43]

Similarly on the lecture *Of Christ's Kingly Office*, he began:

> Having spoken heretofore of the Humanitie and Divinity of our Saviour, that he is true God and perfect man, of the distinction of his natures, and of the union of his Natures in one person, Christ Jesus; We proceed now from the person to the Office of our Redeemer, his Mediatourshipp betwixt God and man, whereby he was appoynted to discharg all that was requisite for the reconcileing of us to God, and the perfecting the work of our salvation. And here we shall show

1. What 'tis to be a Mediatour.
2. That we have only one Mediatour.
3. That Christ is this Mediatour in both natures.

---

43 Ms. 3707, p.87.

4. Offices of our mediat[our]: King, Pr[iest] and Prophet.[44]

It is obvious from these lectures that Andrewes regarded catechising as very important, evident in this statement.

> It hath such power and influence upon the soul, and doth so modell and frame the whole man that 'tis a 2nd Nature.
>
> And therefore it hath been the care and practice of all civil Nacions, as well Pagan as Christian to season the tender yeares of their youth with wholsome Principles of piety and morality, to lay good foundacions in their younger yeares, that they might reape the benefit of it in their riper Age. That is the reason which Solomon gives us in this Hebrew Proverb - Train up [a child in the way he should go and when he is old he will not depart from it].[45]

He stated that teaching was very ancient as it would seem that Noah had instructed his children, after whom Abraham, Moses, the Prophets and Levites did likewise until the time of our Lord. After him it continued in the Apostolic and early Church, clearly evident in the School at Alexandria.[46]

This divine obviously saw education as a precept from God.

> We have God's command for it, Deut: 4.9; so soon as the Law was given, God commanded that they should teach it [to] their children. These words which I command thee this day, shall be in thine heart, and thou shalt teach them diligently to thy children, Deut: 6.7. And again, yee shall teach them [to] your children, speakeing of them when thou sittest in thy house, when thou walkest by the way, when thou lyest down, and when thou risest up. Deut: 11.19.[47]

---

44 Ibid., p. 96.

45 Ibid., p.12.

46 Ibid., pp. 15-6.

47 Ibid., p. 18.

This precept was also evident in the ministry of Christ himself who appointed some to be teachers whilst He Himself gave the example of how to teach. For example when teaching a child it should be:

> according to his capacity, bring him on by little and little according to the practice of our Saviour, who did (as 't were) lipse unto the people in their own language, teach them with country rhetorique, in Parables and similitudes of merchants and Husbandmen and vine-dressers, as they were able to bear it.[48]

It was also important that the young learnt to differentiate between truth and lies, honest and deceitful persons.

> This knowl[edge] of Grounds and Principles is requisite to assure unto us the Truth, and to sanctifie unto us the use of all our Graces; as 1. Faith, for unles we know, whom we beleeve, we may beleeve a lye, and instead of the substance, (as the Author to the Hebrewes terms faith) embrace a shadow. 2. Hope, for except we know upon what Rock, and how to fasten the Anchor of our hope, that Anchor will fail us, and that hope make us ashamed. 3. Zeal, for tis only true know[ledge] which can keep that from runing out into fury; without which the zeal of God may lead us from God, being nothing else but a corrupt and unruly passion.[49]

Andrewes insisted that without true knowledge it was easy to succumb to the prevalent atheism or heresy in their midst and so he warned the young "not to lose the Truth in the great and fatall rubbish of errors and heresies." Of course Atheism was not the sole ownership of disbelievers, as even in the pious there were traces of it. "Every man hath much Atheism in his heart by nature, but such desperate stupiditie doth wonderfully improve it," and even "in the best of God's servants" there were "some degrees of Atheisme," declared Andrewes.[50]

---

48 Ibid., p. 13.

49 Ibid., p. 19.

50 Ibid., pp. 47, 52.

For this reason it would seem, next to holiness, the most important virtue to possess for him was knowledge. "Knowledg, as 'tis the beauty and ornament, so 'tis the delight and desire of the soul. … all men by nature love to be knowing." He explained how God has given keys to unlock this true knowledge that leads to Heaven. One is "the creacion of the World"[51] and the other in the revelation of Himself through the Word. Accordingly this divine encouraged his auditors to be aware of the world of nature around them that would teach them aspects of the faith such as the resurrection from the new shoots of spring. He also emphasised that when the scholars were in Church how important it was to be attentive to hear God's word.[52] Another advantage from learning true knowledge was to understand the purpose "of Piety, vertue and goodnesse" in shaping one's life so that in later years they could spend "their lives comfortable" and without fear of death or reproach.[53]

Catechising and true knowledge were also necessary for making the young conscientious citizens. No civil establishment could hope to function properly without Christian precepts.

> Catechiseing and teaching principles of Religion [are] necessary to be used in every church and commonwealth, for the preservation and safety of both church and state; for 1st where there is no knowledge of the true God, there can be no true church. 2. the course of politique affaires, cannot in any good sort goe forward, without fit instruments and that which fitteth and qualifieth them is their vertues. So Politie must acknowledge itself indebted to religion; Godlinesse being the chiefest top and originall, the wellspring of all true vertues. So naturall is the

---

51 Cp. with "If then wee intend to get knowledg, and with that key to open Heaven dores, and to see the glorious Majestie of God, let us take this book in hand (i.e. Genesis), which hath in it both leaves at large, both the knowledge of the Creation of all Gods works, and the knowledge of the wisdome and the true word of God." *Apos.* Sacra p. 659.

52 Ms. 3707, pp. 12, 47, 60, 149.

53 Ibid., p. 20.

> union of Religion with justice; that we may bodily deem, there is neither where they are not both.[54]

According to Andrewes no one could know too much, and so for him a true scholar would spend his morning in prayer and study. Yet learning and scholarship were not to be pursued for their own ends but in order to know Christ and His teaching as based on the Scriptures, decreed by the early Ecumenical Councils and taught by the Fathers. Above all it was to know that true way to heaven. As he said in his 1615 Gowrie Sermon, "what is it to live out the full compass of man's uttermost age, if he live not so in this life, as after this he may live for ever?"[55]

---

54 Ibid.

55 Andrewes, Vol. 4, p. 116.

ANDREWES AND WESTMINSTER SCHOOL

As I believe these catechetical lectures were given to students at Westminster School by Andrewes, I thought it appropriate to include a short chapter about the School. Unlike the other great schools such as Eton and Winchester, Westminster School was an integral part of the Collegiate Church of St. Peter's, Westminster with the Dean or Abbot as head of both. The School was completely dependent upon the Chapter, as it had not any revenue of its own. The Elizabethan Charter issued on the 12th May, 1560 for the Chapter and School of St. Peter's, Westminster differed very little from that of Henry VIII. The Dean, twelve prebendaries, two schoolmasters, forty scholars and other officials were re-appointed. William Bill was its first dean, but was quickly followed by Gabrielle Goodman whose incumbency lasted forty years (1561 - 1601). Andrewes was thus Elizabeth's third appointment. He was installed on the 4th July 1601 after having been a prebendary (11th stall) of the Abbey since 1597. However his association with Elizabeth went back to the mid-eighties when he was appointed one of her chaplains and was a preacher at her Court.

Westminster School evolved from the school attached to the Benedictine Monastery, refounded by Edward Confessor in the eleventh century. When it first started is not known but by the late fourteenth century we know that it was small, taking in between eighteen to twenty-four students, mostly from the immediate neighbourhood. These were taught by the *Magister Scholarum* who was paid 26s 8d yearly and was given a gown. In 1421 the School House was rebuilt, but in 1461 it was abandoned when a new school was built within the precincts to the east side of what is now the Dean's Yard. Under Henry VIII the School with the

Abbey was given a new charter when he dissolved the monastery. From henceforth the students were known as the King's Scholars. Alexander Nowell, Head Master from 1543 to 1555, gave the School a solid foundation. The School continued during the time of Mary under Udall, even though the monastery was restored briefly. On its dissolution in 1560 the buildings were incorporated into the school: the monks' dormitory became the classroom, the granary, the boys' dormitory, and the abbot's dining hall, the college hall.

Just as Elizabeth took great pains to maintain the standard of worship at the Abbey, so she was determined to be the founder of a great school of learning, and she visited the School often. The statutes were similar to those of Eton, with one notable difference. The study of Greek was to be an essential part of the timetable from the fourth form. The Statutes also specified that all boys spend two hours a week with the Choristers' Master at a charge of 6d. The School also had a choral foundation in order to train singing clerks.[56] As well as the forty boarding scholars, according to the foundation, "town boys" could also attend the School. Under the Statutes they were allowed to win a number of scholarships each year, provided they had already spent a year there. Westminster was one of the three Royal Colleges: the others being Christ Church, Oxford and Trinity, Cambridge. It was to these two colleges that annual scholarships were awarded to the top students to continue their education.

The school day commenced at 5.00 a.m. when one of the dormitory monitors announced *Surgite!* On rising, the boys knelt to say the collect for grace, followed by a form of Morning Prayer (similar to the Prayer Book). Then came the domestic chores of making beds and sweeping, and ablutions in the cloisters. At 6.00 a.m. the students reported to the Second Master for more prayers, after which he took the lower forms, whilst the upper school reported to the Head Master at 7.00 am. At the end of this hour of learning, the Master set a proposition or passage in Latin to be translated by the Fourth Form, controverted by the Fifth and versified by the Sixth and Seventh. The Lower Forms had briefer passages. The Statutes did not provide a time for breakfast, but the hour from 8 to 9 was not spent in school. The time from nine to noon was devoted to lessons in Latin. At noon,

---

56 Gouk, p. 40.

after grace, the boys had dinner with members of the Chapter during which a boy read a passage from the Old Testament at the discretion of the Dean. Between 1-2 p.m. the boys were under the supervision of the Second Master. Lessons then continued until 6.00 p.m. For the Upper School this meant studying Greek or Hebrew. Supper was taken at 6.00 p.m. and at 7.00 p.m. the School Monitors took the various forms to teach translation from English into Latin. At 8.00 p.m. the boys said evening prayers in the dormitory collectively, and concluded with their own private prayers. Sometimes the boys would work late into the night on a dissertation or translation, and were allowed the following day, if sleepy, to seek permission to drop the head upon the desk. Friday was a day of correction and repetition, as was Saturday morning. Examinations were also held on this morning.

On Saturday afternoons two or three students were chosen by the Head Master to discourse on some subject in the hall. Sunday (*Dies Dominica*), as stated in the Statutes was distinct from Saturday (*Dies Sabbati*) when the boys said the Litany and read psalms and scripture readings in the dormitory. During the day they attended the services in the Abbey, and afterwards all were expected to make a summary of the sermons. For the Upper Forms this was expected in Latin, and for the Lower in English. Saints' Days were a holiday or play-day. Performing plays became one of the characteristics of Westminster School, to which Elizabeth often attended.

Under Goodman and Andrewes there was a close link between the Abbey and School. When Andrewes first came to the Abbey as a prebendary, the Headmaster was the antiquary and historian, William Camden.[57] He had been appointed through his close association with Goodman in 1593, eighteen years after his appointment as Second Master in 1575. One of his lasting contributions to the School was *Institutio Graecæ Grammatics Compendiaria*, his Greek grammar for the boys.[58] He resigned in 1599 and was succeeded by Richard Ireland[59] who had been a student at the School from 1582 –1587.

---

57 He is probably best known for the translations of *Britannia* and his *Annales* of Elizabeth 1.

58 Camden after he resigned from the School, held the office of Clarenceux King of Arms and continued to live in the precincts.

59 Little is known of Ireland, except when he resigned in 1610 he joined the Church of

It is thus Ireland for whom Andrewes sometimes filled in as acting Head Master, and it is known that at least on one occasion he overruled Ireland. This was in connection with latter's decision to close the School when an outbreak of severe plague hit London in the summer of 1603. The Dean insisted that the Head Master, those seniors "who were to be major candidates at the next election" and five servants must stay. This "enforced idleness" would only disadvantage the boys, Andrewes believed.[60]

Gauging from the comments made in later life by some of the students present in Andrewes' time, this divine must have given a considerable amount of his time in teaching and pastoral care to the boys. As well as catechising, he taught Greek and Hebrew to the seniors. Brian Duppa, later a bishop, was so appreciative of Andrewes' tuition that he had inscribed on his monument in Westminster Abbey that this divine taught him Hebrew.[61]

John Hacket who went on to become bishop of Lichfield at the Restoration spoke of this divine in glowing terms. He was "the first who planted me in my tender Studies and water'd them continually with his Bounty. ... In my opinion [he] was the most Devout that ever I saw when he appeared before God; of such a Growth in all kinds of Learning." From Hacket we also know that the Dean took some of the boys with him on his daily walks to Chiswick.[62] No doubt on these trips he shared with them his love of nature and how it not only mirrored God's loveliness but also unfolded the truths of many Christian doctrines. Hacket expressed these and other thoughts about Andrewes to Bishop Williams who, after his appointment as Dean of the Abbey in 1620, consulted him about how he could emulate Andrewes in his "advanced Learning in the School".[63]

Andrewes left the Abbey and School in October 1605 after his

Rome and went to France. He returned at some point as by 1624 he was living in London as a Roman Catholic priest.

60 Sargeaunt, p. 67.

61 Cassan, Vol. 2, p. 166.

62 Chiswick House was the residence for the prebendary of Chiswick at St. Paul's Cathedral. Goodman who held this prebend whilst Dean, procured its tenancy for the School. It became a holiday home for the boys.

63 *Scrin. Res.*, p. 44.

appointment by James 1 to be bishop of Chichester. He was consecrated bishop on the 3rd November by Archbishop Bancroft, assisted by Dr. Richard Vaughan, Bishop of London, John Jegon, Bishop of Norwich, Dr. Thomas Ravis, Bishop of Gloucester, and Dr. William Barlow, Bishop of Rochester. He took his seat in the House of Lords, the day designed for the Gunpowder Plot, that is, the 5th November. Yet he never lost contact with many of the boys as Hacket verified when he was an undergraduate at Trinity. He continued to encourage them in their studies through his generous giving of money, books and friendship. He always remembered the School in his private devotions when he prayed for "the West monastery".

This great inspirer to learning and holiness of living ended his life as Bishop of Winchester, and died on 25th September, 1626. On this day Laud wrote in his diary, "Monday, About 4 o'clock in the morning, died Lancelot Andrews, the most worthy bishop of Winchester, the great light of the Christian world."[64] How appropriate it is that the Revised Calendar in the English Church commemorates him on this day. He was buried in St. Maries Ovaries, now Southwark Cathedral.

---

64 Laud, Vol. 3, p. 196.

PART I

THE LECTURES

LECTURE ONE

INTRODUCING THE CATECHETICAL LECTURES

Andrewes prefaced the first catechetical lecture with his own feeling of inadequacy for such an important task of instructing the young in the Christian faith. It was a task not to be taken lightly by the catechist or for that matter by the catechized who, if they missed a lecture, would have "a chasme" in their instruction. Much of this lecture is identical to passages in *A Patterne of Catechisticall Doctrine* and *The Morall Law Expounded*. They all stressed the necessity of attending the complete set of lectures, "for unless we have all, we can make no profitable building", and so "we must not any way excuse our absence".[65]

Catechising, both public and private, was very popular in the post Reformation Church, but none stressed its importance more than Andrewes.[66] He showed that in regular and structured catechising, the young could be taught the faith in such a way that they thirsted to know more. He compared students to plants needing water to grow, but in order to grow the plants must first make firm roots. Those firm roots for young Christians are to know those doctrines necessary for salvation.

The importance of catechising, he believed, was illustrated by its antiquity. It was even older than Abraham's instruction to his family, as evident in Seth and Japheth's covering of their father (Gen. 9.23). Later

---

65 P.C.D., p. 10.

66 Ian Green gave the figure of over 280 different catechetical forms printed between 1549 and 1646, and if larger works were included, the total came to over 350. Green, pp. 399 - 400, 414 - 5, 417; Green, *Clergy*, p. 253.

on Moses was a great teacher who was followed by Levites, prophets, teachers of Israel during the time of our Lord, and then by the likes of Theophilus, Apollos and Timothy in the Apostolic Church. Catechising continued in the early Church, especially in the great centres of learning such as Alexandria and Antioch. The need of catechising had also been recognised by pagan teachers who taught their "sacred rememberances" by rote to their pupils.[67]

Catechising therefore should begin as soon as a child is capable of learning, in order to ensure a secure foundation to grow up in "Piety and Honesty", as a weapon to fight against sin and the devil, and also for the preservation of "church and commonwealth". Andrewes had no illusions of what man is like without grace, and how he succumbs to the temptations of Satan so easily. Sin and the need to overcome it featured prominently in all these lectures as it did in all his preaching. Accordingly he outlined the path that leads to becoming a hardened sinner. It begins at first with "fear and reluctacion" and a pang of conscience but gradually it becomes a "custom" so that the conscience is numbed until sinners become so gratified by sin that there is no taming it.[68] He returned to this theme in his lecture on *Sin*. Yet to live without sin ruling one's life will give peace of mind, especially in old age.

One of Andrewes' favourite metaphors for promoting sound catechising was a building. Not only does it feature in this lecture but also in the third, and in his introduction to the Pembroke catechetic lectures. Just as a building needs a solid foundation, so the Christian must have a firm base for his belief in God and His precepts. With a sound foundation a Christian is able to refute heresy and to give an answer to those who "undermine the very foundation" of Christianity by stating that "there is no God".[69]

As Andrewes was "a lover of books" it is not surprising that he began these lectures by emphasising the necessity of knowledge—it is "the beauty and ornament", "the delight and desire of the soul". "All men by nature love to be knowing" and "account . . . it a thing desirable." It is the key that gives a reason for our faith, and a hope of things to come, eternal life in Christ Jesus by revealing the kingdom of God as

---

67 Ms. 3707, p. 18.

68 Ibid., pp. 13, 21-2.

69 Andrewes, P.C.D., p. 13.

taught by Christ.[70] But many, he believed, did not desire knowledge in order to know Him who said "*Ego sum Veritas*" He made it clear that knowledge sought for itself is of little avail; it must lead to Truth, that is, Christ, the eternal *Logos*. "There is no truth at all in human learning or philosophy that thwarteth any truth in Divinity." As he preached to Elizabethan courtiers on Good Friday, 1597, "the perfection of our knowledge is Christ; and the perfection of our knowledge in or touching Christ, is the knowledge of His Cross and Passion". Later on at Easter 1610 he extended this knowledge to include the sacraments when he preached before James 1 that "we shall be nearer our *scio*" when "'we taste and see ... how gracious the Lord is'" in the Sacrament.[71]

Yet this divine felt many had a predestinarian attitude towards knowledge. These wanted to sit in "Moses's chair" before sitting "at the feet of Gamaliel" which was contrary to both Christ and Paul's teaching to have "milk" before "meat". "He that would safely climb this Jacob's Ladder must begin at the lowest round." He also warned against misguided knowledge given by those who wanted to swim before wading in the waters of Scripture. Thus many drowned in "deep waters" as "they utter, they know not what." This they call an "overflowing of the spirit", but in truth they are "tossed to and fro with the wind of every doctrine." Although "great is the numbers of Preachers; but how many speak into the air" with their "untruthes",

70 Ms. 3707, p.12; Mathew, p. 93; *Apos. Sacra* pp. 23, 657. Cp. this with "*Omnes homines naturâ scire desiderant*, 'all men even by nature love to be knowing.' The philosopher hath made it his ground, and set it in the front of his metaphysics. So saith philosophy. And even to this day, saith divinity, doth the 'true knowledge' still work in the sons of Eve; we still reckon the attaining of knowledge a thing to be desired, and be it good or evil, we love to be knowing, all the sort of us. Knowing but what? Not such things as every one knoweth that goeth by the way, vulgar and trivial; tush, those are nothing. But metaphysics that are the arcana of divinity; such as few besides are admitted to; those be the things we desire to know. We see it in the Bethshemites, they longed to be prying into the Ark of God, they were heathen. We see it in the people of God too, they pressed too near the mount; rails were fain to be set to keep them back. It is because it is held a point of deep wit to search out secrets, as in Joseph. At least of special favour to be received so far, as V*obis datum est nosse mysteria.* All desire to be in credit." So preached Andrewes in his Christmas Sermon, 1607, when he was elucidating on the great mystery of the Incarnation. Andrewes, Vol. 1, p. 33.

71 Ibid., Vol. 2, pp. 122,159, 268.

a theme he would harp on in many a sermon. Having in mind those ministers who followed their own devices he warned scholars against those who preferred "zeal" to "knowledge" in preaching. Preachers should be "zealous according to knowledge" and not to "passion", but what was ascertained from many pulpits was anything "else but a corrupt and unruly passion." On the other hand the good teacher would follow "the good ancient way of laying down at first, elements and grounds of religion."[72]

This lecture also reflected another of Andrewes persistent teaching, the attaining of perfection. He informed students that they should "proceed by little and little" in their learning "till they come to the period of perfection." Some twenty years on, at Pentecost 1621 he was still preaching on the Christian's pilgrimage towards perfection. "As to go on still forward is the perfection of a traveller, to draw still nearer and nearer to his journey's end. To work to-day and to-morrow as Christ said, and the third day to be perfect, perfectly perfect."[73]

Andrewes concluded with what is also an introduction to his next lecture, that Scripture is the foundation for all Christian teaching.

As our ministers are of this day and as they have beene in the church of God for now above 140[0] years, for if we may believe Polydor Virgil[74], so long time since the first constituencies of Parochial churches.[75]

---

72 Ms. 3707, pp. 12-13, 23; Andrewes, Vol. 3, pp. 273, 286 -7.

73 Ibid., p. 367; Ms. 3707, p.13.

74 He was born in Urbino c. 1470 and buried in its cathedral in 1555. Vergil attended both the universities of Padua and Bologna before being ordained in 1496. He came to England in 1502 when his protector and kinsman Hadrian Castellensis was appointed bishop of Hereford, and shortly afterwards to the see of Bath and Wells. He himself received various appointments, including the archdeaconry of Wells and prebend of Oxgate, St. Paul's Cathedral. It is said that Henry VII approached him to write a history of England from its beginning to the present day. Accordingly *Anglicae Historiae* was first published in 1534 at Basle and then a revised edition in 1546 in England. In the first book on England's early history, Vergil commented on the early coming of Christianity to the island. It is probably this reference to which Andrewes or the scribe is alluding, and therefore the author wrote mistakingly 140 years rather than 1400.

75 It was not until Theodore of Tarsus, Archbishop of Canterbury summoned the Council of Hertford in 672 that diocesan and parochial life was given a definite structure.

Being injoyned by my superiors (to whose care and descretion the furniture of this place is committed) to appeare here upon this occasion; I may call this Duty a work of meer Obedience, and so a matter of necessity rather than of choice.

I am conscious to my self of my small gifts and weake endownments, and so unfitt for such an employment, and indeed πὰς πρὸς ἱκανὸς ταῦτα [who is sufficiently worthy].[76] But haveing put my hand to the Plough, I may not looke back; and so as far as my imperfections will permitt (the condicion of this prophane age requireing it, so full of Impeity and Atheism) I shall endeavour to lay down some Principles of Christianity and shall pitch upon that Hebrew Proverb for my preliminary discourse;

This text you may read ...

Prov. 22.6. *Train up a child in the way he should goe: and when he is old he will not depart from it.*

Knowledg,[77] as tis the beauty and ornament, so tis the delight and desire of the soul. The Philosopher hath made it his ground, and set it in the front of his metaphysickes, πάντες τοῦ εἰδέναι ὀρέγονται φύσει, all men by nature love to be knowing; as our first Parents, so all their Posterity, have an itching desire and a thirst after the tree of knowledg. Be it grace or nature, nay be it good or evill, we account the knowl[edge] of it a thing desirable.

Now as the Philosopher hath his *Arcana Philosophiæ,* so the Divine his *mysteria Theologiæ,* as his Principles, so his mysteryes of Divinity: and such is our pride and overhastines, that passing by those grounds; those mysteryes we first and principally desire to know. But too many would sit in Moses's chair, before they sit

76 As explained in the Introduction when Andrewes was appointed bishop of Chichester he had this same sentiment engraved "about the seal of his Bishopric, those words of St. Paul, *Et ad hæc quis idoneus?* 'And who is sufficient for these things?' (2 Cor 2:16)." Andrewes, Vol. 11, p. xxiv.

77 This text reappears almost identically in the Christmas Day Sermon for 1607, Andrewes, Vol. 1, p. 33. In M.L.E. the seeking of knowledge is described as "the fulnesse of perswasion, a settled beliefe which we call faith. ... Our knowledge in this life but a taste of that which will be blessed in the life to come." Therefore "We cannot be without it" pp. 126 -7.

at the feet of a Gamaliel, would be Doctors in Israel, before they be taught their first Principles, which is as preposterous, as if they should desire to be born, not children but perfect men and to be fed at first, not with such meates as are agreeable to the tendernes of their age, and the weaknes of their nature, but with such as are fit only for men of riper yeares and strong constitucions. But we cannot so learn Christ *μακρὸς κὰι ὄρθιος ὃμος ἐπὶ αὐτήν*,[78] what the Poet said of vertue, is true of this Knowledge, tis not to be attained all at once, but by partes and degrees; He that would safely climb this Jacob's ladder must begin at the lowest round. *Præpropera consilia,* overhastines doth not agree with that of the Prophet, Esa: 28.16 He that beleeveth shall not make hast. A man is not to ground his faith upon presumptions and presupposeings, but by little and little goe forward till he come to the rock.[79] In scripture as we read of perfect men in Christ Jesus, so of Babes in Christ,[80] 1Cor. 3.1 and as of *ὀυσνόητα* things hard to be understood, so of elementary knowledg, of *γάλα* as well as *βρῶμα*, milk as strong meat. This is the method which St. Paul used in converting and confirming his Proselites 1Cor: 3.2. I have fed you with milk and not with meate. And this is the same method that Solomon prescribes to us in this Text. Train up [a child in] the way he should goe, or as 'tis in the originall *hhanokh lana'ar al piy darku gam kiy yazqiyn lo yasur minenah.*[81] *Super os via suæ,* put such meat into his mouth as he is able to digest, teach him according to his capacity. Train up a child in the way he should [go and he will not depart from it].

In the Text we have

1. An exhortacion or a Precept; Train up, or as in the margine,[82] catechise.

---

78 Translated it means "long and steep is the road to it."

79 Identical to M.L.E., p. 24; Cp. also with P.C.D., p. 22.

80 In M.L.E. this is expounded, "for all things whereof they are capable, it is better even from their childhood to accustome them thereunto but by little & little." p. 2.

81 I owe this translation and the two others in this manuscript in modern Hebrew to Jeff Benner of the Ancient Hebrew Research Centre.

82 An indication of how Andrewes constantly revised his lectures.

2. The reason or ground of that Precept when he is old, he will not depart from it. (i.e.) the seasoning of youth with Principles of true Religion, will much further and confirm Piety and goodnesse in riper years.

In the precept observ
(corner of page torn off)
1. The
2. The
3. How ...
way, (i.e.) ...

age is capable of ... *instilla puero doctrinæ ... aetatis.* ...[83] teach him according to his capacity, bring him on by little and little; according to the practice of our saviour, who did (as 'twere) lipse unto the People in their own language, teach them with country Rhetorique, in Parables and similitudes of Merchants and Husbandmen and vine-dressers,[84] as they were able to bear it, Mar. 4.33.[85] So the words here are a Metaphor, taken from things Temporall, and applyed to those that are spirituall. *Superfluam humoris copiam angustiora vasa respuunt* (Quintill[ian]).[86] When you are to fill a Bottle with a narrow mouth; you doe it by degrees, least you shed more, than your powr in; and when Nurses feed their children, they do it with minced meat and small morsells, such as they are able to swallow and digest; so they that would make spirituall Proficiency in matters of Religion, must doe it by graduall accesses, and proceed by little and little till they come to the period of perfection.

(I shall not speak at present of each particular in the order proposed but from the words thus opened draw this conclusion).

Con[clusion]: That tis not only expedient but necessary, that all men be taught so soon as capable of knowl[edge], the too much neglected Principles of Piety and Honesty

---

83 Translated it means "instil into boys those doctrines for eternal life."

84 Andrewes used the same image in Lecture Twelve.

85 The Authorised Version has "to hear it".

86 A rhetorician of the first century in Rome (35-96AD). Quintillian believed that rhetoric showed "a good man speaking well."

PAGE TORN

The …Practice ... of … All, or later times ... creation of the world, ... our Saviour. The later since ... the flesh into this present. Againe the former may be divided into three Periods; the 1st from Adam unto Abraham, the 2nd from Abraham to Moses, the 3rd from Moses to our saviour Christ.

1. For the Religion of that Age which went before Abraham 'twas very imperfect and obscure; and some are of opinion; that men did not then act so much by set lawes and the Precepts, as by the judgement of right Reason. Abell brought an offering unto the lord of the firstlings and the fat of the flock, Gen.4.4 *ἄλλ᾽ οἴκοθεν κὶ παρὰ τȏυ συνειδ᾽ολοι διδαχθεὶς*,[87] Chry[sostom] he did this, not by vertue of any Law or command given, injoyning such dutyes; but he was led unto it by the dictate of his conscience, and the light of reason; And Justin Martyr (in his Dialogue against Tripho, the Jew) is of the same mind *σὐδεὶς τῶν θυσάντων τὰ ἄλογα* none of those sacrifices, which were offered before Moses were in obedience to any divine command; for in his History of those times, we doe not read of any generall Precept to that purpose. Indeed we may gather *a posteriori* from God's accepting of Abell's Offering in Gen. 4.4, and Noah's sacrifices Gen. 8.21, that such services were agreeable to his will, and so his servants might be encouraged in their performance of such Dutyes.[88]

Now (I say) tho' we read of no expresse Precepts either concerning Religion, or life and conversacion, yet 'twould not be difficult to collect such from some passages of scripture; as from that speech of God to Cain Gen: 4.7, where he dehorts[89] him from envy and wrath, exhorts him to bridle and subdue his unruly affections, and to do that which is just and right. With such admonicions as these and by apparicions of God 'tis probable the men of those times were instructed to beleeve there was a God, and that this God was to be religiously worshipped, feared and reverenced. After the Flood 2 Lawes were given, th' one ceremoni-

---

87 Translated it means "but learning of his own accord and by his conscience."

88 M.L.E. added "*Caine* and *Abel* sacrificing must needs have learned of their father this duty." p. 5. Refer also to P.C.D., p. 8.

89 It means "dissuades".

all, forbidding to eat blood; the other morall, forbidding to shed man's blood, Gen. 9. 4,6. I call the former cermoniall, bec[ause] (as Judicious Hooker L.4. Eccl. Pol) they were not of perpetuall observacion, but only necessary in respect of the conveniency and fitnesse for the present state of the church.[90]

And further from the Practice of Noah and his sonnes, we may infer that they knew Parents were to be reverenced and obeyed; otherwise Noah could not justly have cursed Ham; nor had S[h]em and Jaspet[h] known their Duty to cover their Father's nakedness.[91] And that they were not ignorant of the 7th commandment we may gather from the storyes of Pharaoh and Abimilech; they accounted Adultery a great sin, and thought it utterly unlawfull to take another man's wife, Gen: 20.9.

2ly. For the Times from Abraham to Moses; Knowledg of true Religion was only to be found in Abraham and his Family. God was pleased to enter into a league of amitie with him to chuse him for his friend, Esa: 41. 8. How often did he appear unto him and how clearly in respect of former times did he reveal his mind unto him? both in respect of Precepts and Promises Gen: 26.5, Abram obeyed my voyce, kept my charg, my commandments, my statutes, and my lawes. And therefore Abram shall be called Abraham the Father of many Nacions, Gen: 17.5. And God did not deal so with any Nacion as with his; they had the knowledg of his lawes, and right and title to his promises.[92]

Now for the propagacion of Religion in these 2 periods of time, 'twas by Tradicion from Parents to their children and Families. For 1. of Abraham, God hims[elf] tells us, that he was a catechist in his Family, Gen: 18.19.[93] I know him that he will command his children and houshold after him, and they shall keep the way of the Lord, to doe justice and judgement. 2ly, Untill the solemn institution of Priesthood, the First-born in every Family did supply that office, as is clear from Numb: 3.41 where the Levites were appoynted to the service of the Altar, instead of the first-born as their

90 A direct quote from E.P. 4.11.5.

91 Genesis 9.23, 25.

92 This paragraph is very similar to M.L.E., p. 5.

93 Appears in P.C.D., p. 8 and M.L.E., p.5.

λύτρον[94] or price of Redemption. Thou shalt take the Levites for me, (saith Lord) instead of all the First-born of the children of Israel. So Adam, and after him, every first born, ruled their Families as Kings, instructed them as Prophets and sacrificed for them as Priests. So Noah is called a Preacher of Righte[ousness], 2Pet 2.5, and Tertull[ian] in his book *de cultu faeminarum*, tells us how Enoch commanded his sonne Methusulah, faithfully to deliver to his posterity, the knowledg of those things which he had read from his Ancestors: 'Tis not to be doubted therefore, but this counsell of Solomon in the Text was practised in those early times of the world, from Adam to Abraham and from Abraham to Moses.

3ly. For the next period, from Moses untill the comeing of our Saviour in the flesh, for the propagation of Religion and learning what care was taken to erect and what provision was made to maintain Naiothes and Bethells, houses of Prophetts and Prophetts children[95] is clear and evident to any acquainted with the scriptures.

1. God commanded that 48 cities with their suburbs should be given to the Levites Numb. 35.7. And as we may read Jos: 21 those citties were appoynted to them out of all the Tribes of Israel, so that the Levites were scattered throughout the whole land, to this end, that the People might be taught in the law of the lord, and instructed in the Principles of true Religion.

2. And that there were such Nurseries of learning for young scholars to be trained up in, in the knowl[edge] of the true God, in very bad times; and that men famous for Piety, learning, sobriety, were set over them, we may gather from the stories of Samuel, who was visitor of Naioth in Rama;[96] and Elijah and Elisha, who were successively Heads and governours at the Colledge of Jericho, 2K: 4.38 and chapter 6.1. Their schollers were termed *filii Prophetarum*, children of the Prophets; by reason of which relacion, the prophet sometimes is called a Father, so Elisha called Elijah, my Father 2K: 2.12.

3. After Malachi, when Prophesie ceased, then the office of

---

94 Translated it means "ransom".

95 1Samuel 19.20.

96 1Samuel 19.18, 22 - 3.

expounding scripture, was more common, yet appropriated to expositors which we may call Teachers of Israel Joh: 3.10. They are reduced to three severall sorts, and all comprised by the Apostle 1Cor: 1.20. Wisemen, Scribes, Disputers, Where is the wise? where is the scribe? where is the disputer? And that there were such Teachers of Israel in our Saviours time, we may gather 1st from Luc: 2. 46, 47, where 'tis said that the Parents of our Saviour when he was but twelve yeares old, found him in the Temple, sitting in the midst of the Doctors, both heareing them and asking them questions: so the custome then was *proponere et explorandi profectûs causa interrogare* (Grotius) [com. on Luke 2: 46-7] to propose Questions out of the Law and Prophetts, thus he to the Doctors, and to examine their schollers to try their proficiency, thus they to him, and the Auditors were astonished at his Answers. 2ly, St. Paul was sent from the citty Tarsus to Jerusalem, there to be brought up, and instructed in the law of his Fathers under that great Doctor of the Law, Gamaliel, Acts. 22.3. I am verily a man which am a Jew, born in Tarsus, a city in Cilicia, yet brought up in this city at the feet of Gamaliel, and taught according to the perfect manner of the law of the Fathers. And if we beleeve the Jewish story,[97] there were above 400 Synagogues in Jerusalem, which were as publique schooles, and in which were placed men able and eminent for variety of Knowledg, for publique teaching and propagateing their Religion to Posterity.

Thus much of the former Times, from the Creacion of Adam untill the Incarnacion of our Saviour, how constantly and carefully this Precept of Solomon was practised.

Now for the later times, since the Incarnation of our saviour, which the Apostle calls the Ends of the world, 1Cor: 10.11 which is the same with the fulnes of times, Eph: 1.10 (i.e.) such times after which no new lawes, no greater Prophesie, no greater manifestacion of God is to be expected untill the end of the world. God in former times spoke to our Fathers in a world of Tropes and shadowes, Types and figures, their light was but candle-light, but *vespertina cognito*, in comparison of ours, whom the day hath

97 It is in "the book of antiquities that there is an act for Jewish children thirteen years to be catechised." The same figure for schools is also in M.L.E., p. 6.

visited sprung from on high, Luc: 1.78.[98] So in respect of the full knowl[edge] of divine Truth, so full as we are capable of in this life, these days are called the last dayes.

And for planting and propagateing the Truth of the Gospell, if we begin at the kalends[99]of Christianity, we shall find, 'twas by way of Catechisme. That this was the practice of the prim[itive] Christian church … we have warrant in these three persons, Theophilus, Apollos, Timothy. [Acts] Luc: 1.4 It seemed good to mee haveing had perfect understanding of things from the very first, to write unto thee in order (most excellent Theop[hilus]) that thou mightest know the certainty of those things, *ἵνα ἐπιγνῷς περὶ ὧν κατηχήθης λόγωυ τὴν ἀσάλειαν*, wherein thou hast been catechized. So Act. 18.25.[100] And a certain Jew named Apollos, born at Alexandria, an eloquent man and mighty in the Script[ures]: And how came he to the height of that perfection? It followes *οὗτος ἦυ καταηχημένος τὴν ὁδὸν τοῦ Κμρίου*, this man was taught, trained up, instructed in the way of the Lord. And the same is said of Timothy, that of a child he had known the holy Scriptures, 2Tim: 3.15. And mention is made both of the Catechist and Catechumeni, Gal: 6.6 where the Apostle desires, that provision should be made for them, that they should be encouraged by a liberall maintenance, *κοινωείτω ὁ κατηχοὺμενος τῷ κατηχόυτι*. Let him that is taught in the word, communicate unto him that teacheth, in all good things.[101] And the Author of the Epistle to the Hebrewes tells us of the Heads of the Apostles Catechisime Heb: 6.1,2. Repentance from dead works, faith tow[ards] God,[102] doctrine of Baptisme, laying on of hands, Resurrection of the dead, and Eternall judgements.

After the Apostles' time, Euseb[ius] lib. 6. c.3.12.16 is very larg in setting down the Number and succession of Catechists, in Alexandria,[103] the first, St. Mark, the evangelist; after him

98 This idea reappears in the Nativity Sermon for 1612, Andrewes, Vol. 1, p. 105.

99 This is the first of the month in the ancient Roman calendar.

100 In the Authorized Version this is 18.24.

101 This is identical to M.L.E., p. 6. Cp. also with P.C.D., p. 9.

102 Cp. also with P.C.D., p. 7 and M.L.E., p.5.

103 The Alexandrian school was one of the great centres of Christian learning, along

Pantænus,[104] then Clemens Alexandrinus,[105] then Origen,[106] Didymus,[107]Dionysius,[108] Athenodorus.[109] And as in Alexandria, so in Antioch, Jerusalem and Carthage, this method of teaching was practised, and at Rome in her Puritie as Hierom *de viris illustribus*.

The Catechumeni, or those to be instructed were of 2 sorts. 1. the Proselyte - Jews or Gentiles which were comed to years of

---

with Antioch until its demise in the fifth century. Originally it was designed for instructing catechumens but soon became a theological school. At first it had one teacher, but later there were two or more. Andrewes did not give a strict chronological order of its heads. St. Jerome states that there have always been teachers from the time of St. Mark in the first century, but the first teacher of any certainty was Pantænus c. 180 until 190 when he was followed by his pupil Clement who held that post until the persecution under Severus in 202. The position was then filled by the young and brilliant Origen who stayed probably until 231 before being forced to leave by the bishop, Demetrius, and moving to Caesarea where he opened a school. Heracles who was co-teacher with Origen took over for a short time before being elected bishop of Antioch in 233. He was succeeded by Dionysius until he became bishop in 248. After him there probably followed Theognostus, Pierius, Pomphilus and Peter during the persecution of Diocletian. Didymus was probably the last head. Cp. with that in M.L.E., p. 6.

104 A converted stoic philosopher, he died in c.190. His teachings and writings greatly influenced Clement who succeeded him. It is thought that he also undertook missionary work in India.

105 In his *Pædagogus* Clement stated that the prime aim of the teacher is to "improve the soul, not to teach and to train it up to a virtuous, not to an intellectual life." This comes later. Ch. 1. Besides this work he also wrote *The Exhortation to the Heathens,* and *Stromata.* To Clement we owe the oldest surviving Christian hymn in praise of the Logos.

106 Many of his theological works have not survived, partly because of later condemnation of his teachings. As a biblical scholar his most famous work was the *Hexapla*, an edition of the Old Testament with six or more parallel versions. There was also the *Tetrapla,* a four-fold version.

107 Although blind, of immense erudition, he was entrusted by St. Athanasius as head of the school. Amongst his scholars were Jerome and Rufinus. He died c. 395.

108 He was bishop of Alexandria until 265. During the Decian persecution c.250 fled from the city, but returned, only to be banished during the persecution of Valerian.

109 He was not a head of the Alexandrian school. He was the brother of Gregory Thaumaturgus (wonderworker). Both were pupils of Origen in Caesarea, and both became bishops in the region of the Pontus. Eusebius included both of them as amongst "the illustrious Bishops of that time." Gregory was bishop of neo-Caeserae, but we do not know Athenodorus' see. All that Eusebius tells us they "were presiding over churches in Pontus." Eusebius, Bk. 7, chs. 14.1 and 28.1.

discretion; and those were taught or made Disciples before they were baptized, according to that command of our saviour, Math: 28.19 Goe teach all nations, baptizeing them in the name of the Father, [and of the Son and of the Holy Ghost]. 2ly, children of Beleeving Parents and those were taught after their Baptisme. The former sort were first called Catechumeni, whiles they were learning, their grounds and Principles. 2ly, when they desired to be received into the bosom of the ch[urch] by the sacrament of Baptisme, *συναιτοῦτες*, Petitioners. 3ly, After they were Baptized *ποιτέυοντες*, Beleevers. This custome, and this order was observed in the ch[urch] by the Prim[itive] Fathers; and by this diligent instructing of the ch[urch] (if we will beleeve an ancient writer)[110] then was no known commonwealth in any part of the inhabited world, but within 40 yeares after our saviours' Passion, received a great shakeing of their heathenish Religion,[111] were brought out of darknes into the marvelous light, from the slavery of Sin and Satan called into the glorious liberty of the sonnes of God.

And *fas est ab hoste doceri*, we may learn the benefit of this kind of teaching, from the practice of the subtillest enimy that ever the ch[urch] had, Julian the Apostat,[112] who the easier to root out Christian Religion, suppressed all Christian schooles, all places of catechizeing;[113] the readiest way to dry up the streames, was to stop the fountaines; to reduce all to a chaos of darknes, to put out the lights; The wolves in Libanius would make a league with the shepherds upon condicion they would kill their Doggs; And what can we expect, but that all should be outspread with error and heresie; that ignorance should get the upper hand, if learning be discouraged, and the meanes of knowledge removed; if the blind lead the blind, you know the event wil be, both must [fall into the ditch]. So Lord remove not these candles of divine and humane knowledg from us, and give us any famine, but of thy word. And

110 This is Eusebius. Refer also to M.L.E., p. 7.

111 From "This Custome to Religion" appears exactly in M.L.E., p.7.

112 Although a just ruler, in the fourth century Julian tried to remake the Roman world pagan. In his *Against the Galileans* he attempted to undo Constantine's legalising of Christianity in the Roman Empire.

113 From "subtillest … to catechizeing" appears exactly in M.L.E., p. 7.

this much for the proof of the poynt by way of Practice, how the church of God for the endles good of all her children, hath provided and endeavoured that they should be instructed in the fear and knowledg of God.[114]

And here we might look over the Pale and see how this exercise of Catechizeing was used among the Heathen.[115] They had their *ἱεραὶ ὑπομνήσεις*, sacred remembrances,[116] which they were to learn, when they were boyes. And Caesar Lib 6. commentary tells us of the Gaules Druides, their Magi [or] or Priests, *sine scripto docebant*, such things as concerned the know[ledge] and worship of their Gods, they taught not by writeing, but word of mouth, least their catechumeni, should trust more to their bookes, then their memories, and forget that which was their duty to remember. And Ar[isto]t[l]e lib.7. c.17. Pol. *εὔλογον ἀιῶν ἀπολαύειν*,[117]fit it is that youth be restrained, both from heareing and seeing of things unlawfull;[118] but *πάντα ὅσα δυνατὸν ἐθίζειν*,[119] for all good things whereof they are capable, 'tis better even from their childhood to accustome themselves to the practice of them. And how Pharaoh, an heathen Prince, esteemed the Teachers and Professors of his divinity, we may gather from the care he had of their Lands, Gen: 47.22. In that great extremity of famine, which forced the Ægyptians to part with their mony, their cattell, their lands, their libertyes, their ch[urch] and colledge lands, the lands of the Priests were kept from alientacion, free from Tribute and contribucion for v. 26, the fifth part of all the lands of Ægypt became

---

114 Cp. with E.P., 5.18. 2. Although this paragraph has two similar quotes from E.P. i. "for the endless good of her children" and ii. "be instructed in the fear … of God", the two meanings are opposites. E.P. claims that catechising is the work of the Church only.

115 Andrewes differs with Hooker over this. The latter believed that the Church had a monopoly on catechising, but the Church for Hooker also included the Jews. E.P., 5.18. 2,3.

116 M.L.E. tells us that this quotation is from Solon. p. 2.

117 Translated it means "to enjoy a reasonable life". Andrewes translation is a free gloss on this.

118 Identical to M.L.E., p. 2; Cp. also with P.C.D., p. 4.

119 Translated it means "to be accustomed to as many good things as possible." Cp. this with Andrewes' translation.

Pharaoh's, except the land of the Priests only, which became not his.[120]

But to return. Besides the Practice of all sorts of men, both within and without the church; we have God's command for it, Deut: 4.9; so soon as the Law was given, God commanded that they should teach it [to] their children. These words which I command thee this day, shall be in thine heart, and thou shalt teach them diligently to thy children, Deut: 6.7.[121] And again, yee shall teach them [to] your children, speakeing of them when thou sittest in thy house, when thou walkest by the way, when thou lyest down, and when thou risest up. Deut: 11.19.[122] Tremelius[123] reades it, acute *ingeres* or *exacues*, thou shalt diligently whet them upon thy children; a Metaphor taken from warriours, who whet and sharpen their weapons that they may do the better execution: so they were to fit and apply the knowledg of these Precepts, that they might make the deeper impression in the minds and hearts of the hearers. And as under the Law, so under the Gospell, our blessed saviour haveing overcomed the sharpnes of death, and being ready to be taken up into heaven; his charg to Peter, and in him to all the Apostles, and in them to all their successors, which was his last charg, was *pasce agnos*, then *pasce oves*, Joh: 21. 15-6, feed my lambs, then feed my sheep; whereupon St. Aug[ustine] observes, that the prospering of the Lords sheepfold dependeth upon the good feeding of the lambes. Parallel to my Text, Train up [a child in the way he should goe]. And hence is that command of St. Paul, Eph: 6.4 that Parents should provide as well spirituall as corporall, nourishment for their children, *ἐκτρέψειν ἐν παιδεία*,

---

120 Buckeridge related in his Funeral Oration for Andrewes how the latter had said, "I will not be made a Bishop, because I will not alienate Bishops' lands." This referred to his being offered the sees of Ely and Salisbury by Elizabeth but she wanted him to alienate some of the bishoprics' wealth. Andrewes, Vol. 5, p. 292.

121 Identical with M.L.E., p.6; also P.C.D., p. 9.

122 Cp. with E.P., 5. 18.3.

123 He lived from 1510 –1580. In 1541 he was converted from his Jewish faith to Catholicism, but a year later he embraced Protestantism. He was a noted Hebrew scholar, and his greatest work was the translation of the Old and New Testaments into Latin from Hebrew and Syriac.

bring them up in the knowledge, nurture and admonicion of the Lord.[124]

And the necessity of this exercise we may gather Prov. 22.6 Train up a child [in the way he should go; and when he is old, he will not depart from it].

What is commonly said of Custome, is most true of Educacion, it hath such power and influence upon the soul, and doth so modell and frame the whole man that 'tis a 2nd Nature.

And therefore it hath been the care and practice of all civil Nacions, as well Pagan as Christian to season the tender yeares of their youth with wholsome Principles of piety and morality, to lay good foundacions in their younger yeares, that they might reape the benefit of it in their riper Age. That is the reason which Solomon gives us in this Hebrew Proverb - Train up [a child in the way he should go and when he is old he will not depart from it].

Out of which words.

IIIly, Necessity.

1. From that order, which Christ hath ordained in his church Eph: 4.11. He gave some Apostles, some Prophets, some Evangelists, and some Pastors and Teachers; so Pastors and Teachers are as necessary, as Evangelists and Proph[ets], those to inform the head in matter of opinion, as these to worke upon the affections for matter of practice; for if the head be sick, the heart cannot be well; if judgment and opinion be not right biassed, all will be amisse in our Actions.

2. This knowl[edge] of Grounds and Principles is requisite to assure unto us the Truth, and to sanctifie unto us the use of all our Graces; as 1. Faith, for unles we know, whom we beleeve, we may beleeve a lye, and instead of the substance, (as the Author to the Hebrewes terms faith) embrace a shadow. 2. Hope, for except we know upon what Rock, and how to fasten the Anchor of our hope, that Anchor will fail us, and that hope make us ashamed.[125] 3. Zeal, for tis only true know[ledge] which can keep that from runing out into fury; without which the zeal of God may lead us

---

124 This is exactly as in M.L.E. except it is linked with its text "children are to be brought up in the feare of the Lord." Ps. 34.11, p. 3. Cp. also with P.C.D., p. 5.

125 Cp. with Ms. 3708, pp. 8 -9; and Andrewes, Vol. 11, pp. 261- 2.

from God, being nothing else but a corrupt and unruly passion. For as Fire (tho' it be of all other creatures, one of the most comfortable and usefull, while it abides in its proper place) yet when it once exceeds those limitts and getts to the house topp, 'tis most mercylesse and overrunning: so this passion of Zeal (tho' of excellent service, for the heating and enlivening of vertue, for adding edge and spirit to all good undertakeings) yet if it once flye out beyond it's bounds and be not sub[ject] to the lawes of right Reason, there is nothing more tumultuous and tyranicall.[126] As Bias[127] said of the Tongue, that it was the best and the worst part of the sacrifice; so we may say of this affection, 'tis the best servant, if subordinate to knowledg,[128] but the worst that be without it. Tis a Rule generally true; Things most usefull and excellent in their regularitie, are most dangerous in their abuse; and the best way to regulate this, and to prevent the inconveniences that may follow upon it, is to be zealous according to knowledge. Where was it the Prophet [i.e. Elisha] cast in his salt 2K: 2.21, not into the channell but the spring-head, for if the fountain be redressed or healed (as the prophet) the streames cannot be faulty or unwholesome, if the Foundacion be good, the building will be firm and strong. And this brings in a

3rd. Reason; Religion is compared to a Building; and the Teachers to Maister-builders, 1Cor. 3.10.[129] Now if we build upon the sand, or if the foundacion be not well layd, what can we expect but that the whole fabrick should fall? We are termed Plants, Math: 15.13. And accordingly St. Peter bids us grow in grace, 2 ep: 3.18. But what growth is to be looked for, from those Plants

126 Cp. with *Apos. Sacra*, pp. 25, 35; Andrewes, Vol. 5, p. 534, and with Hooker, "Zeal, unless it be rightly guided, when it endeavoureth most busily to please God, forceth upon him those unseasonable offices which please him not. … Zeal, except it be ordered aright, when it bendeth itself unto conflict with things either in deed, or but imagined to be opposite unto religion, useth the razor many times with such eagerness, that the very life of religion itself is thereby hazarded." E.P., 5.3.1

127 A mythological character who wanted to marry the fair lady Pero and was required to provide for a dowry the cattle of Iphicles which eventually his brother Melampus obtained for him.

128 Cp. with Andrewes, Vol. 2, p. 39.

129 This is expressed fuller in M.L.E., p. 14. Cp. also with P.C.D., p. 191.

that have no root? We are to presse forward toward the mark, but 'tis fitt that we be first in the right way, otherwise every step we make, will make us more amisse, and we shall have further to return back and a longer journey to goe.

4. As no Arts nor sciences can be rightly delivered or profitably learned unles some Grounds be laid which are now called the Principles of that Art. The Physitian hath his Aphorismes, the Lawyer his Institucions, the Philosopher his *κύριαι δόζαι,*[130] cheif sentences;[131] so with Religion it fareth as with other sciences. 1. Delivery of the Elements according to the capacity of young beginners; unto which manner of teaching Principles in Christianity, the Apostle doth allude, Heb: 6.1. For this cause, *Agenda, Precanda et credenda,*[132] we find drawn as three Heads. 1. those things we ought to doe summarily comprized in the Decalogue; 2. whatsoever we should request or desire in the Lords Prayer; 3. either by the Apostles; or at leastwise out of their writeings we have the substance of Christian belief compendiously drawn into 12 Articles, commonly called the Apostles Creed; to the end that the weaknes of no man's wit, might either altogether hinder the knowledg or excuse the utter ignorance of things needfull to be known.[133]

5. Catechiseing and teaching principles of Religion is necessary to be used in every church and commonwealth, for the preservation and safety of both church and state; for 1st where there is no knowledge of the true God, there can be no true church. 2. the course of politique affaires, cannot in any good sort goe forward, without fit instruments and that which fitteth and qualifieth them is their vertues. So Politie must acknowledge itself indebted to religion; Godlinesse being the chiefest top and originall, the well-spring of all true vertues. So naturall is the union of Religion with justice; that we may bodily deem, there is neither where they are not both. In breif; if Religion did possesse syncerely and sufficiently the hearts of all men, there would need no other restraint from

---

130 Translated it means literally "principal opinions."

131 This is identical to P.C.D., p. 7 and M.L.E., p.5.

132 Translated it means, "things must be prayed for and believed."

133 Most of this text is identical to that in E.P., 5.18.3.

evill. This doth not only give life and perfection to all endeavours wherewith it concurreth, but what events soever ensue, it breedeth, if not joy and gladnesse, yet allwayes patience, satisfaction and contentment of mind. Whereupon 'tis set down as an axiome of good experience; That all things religiously taken in hand, are prosperously ended, Psal: 1.3 because whether men in the end have that which Religion did allow them to desire, or that which it teacheth them contentedly to suffer; they are in neither event unfortunate. And this breed content, peace, and so preservation of church and state.[134]

6. For matter of practice; they that would have the latter part of their lives comfortable, must have their tender years seasoned with principles of Piety, vertue and goodnesse. Job tells us that the wicked man's bones are full of the sinnes of his youth, Ch: 20. v.11. Every man when he is young comitts sin enough, to fill his bones when he is old; and therefore (St. Paul) fly youthfull lusts, 2Tim: 2.22. Old age hath his proper lusts and so hath youth too. These are speciall sinnes following the constitucion of the Body; and there are speciall sinnes hanging about our relationships. The bones of some are full of the sinnes of their condicions and callings. The bones of not a few are full of the sinnes of the place, time and age wherein they live. The bones of many are full of that speciall age of their lives, their youth; there is a stock or treasure of their youthful sinnes, laid up, not only in their bones, but in their hearts; and as God makes them to possesse the sinnes of their youth in punishments; so they do possesse the sinnes of their youth, if not in practice, yet in affection and pleasing contemplacion. Tho' a sinner be an 100 yeares old, he calls to minde the sinnes of his youth with delight; and acts them over again, when he cannot act them, as youthfull, as when he first comitted them. He periwiggs his age with wanton behaviour; he boasts of what he cannot act; and would be more sinfull if he could; and is so, because he would. It is a sad contemplacion, a lamentable thing to consider, how men startle at sin in their tender yeares, and how they venture by degrees and engage themselves: how fearfull they are at first; how indiscreet

134 This text is also in E.P., 5. 1.2.

afterwards; how familiar within awhile, and then how they are settled and hardened in it at the last.

We usually say custome is a second Nature; and indeed it followes and imitates naturall motion; it is weake in the beginning, stronger in the progresse, but most strong in and violent towards the end; *Transit in violentiam voluntas antiqua tibi* (Aristotle)[135] That which we will often, we will with eagernesse and violence. Our first onset in sin is with fear and reluctacion; we then venture further and proceed with lesse regret; we move forwards with delight; Delight continues the motion, and makes it customary; and Custome at last drives and binds us to it,[136] as to our center; *vitia insolentiora renascuntur* (Seneca).[137] Sin growes more insolent by degrees; first flatters, then commands, after enslaves, and then betrayes us: first, gaines consent, afterwards works delight; at last ἀναισχυντίαν, a shamelessnesse in sin; were they ashamed saith God by his Prophet Jer: 6.15, and he answers himself, they were not ashamed; nay to goe one step yet further this custome of sinning begets ἀναισθηοί αν, a senslessnesse and stupidity in sin; and Caligula's ἀδιατρεψία, a stubbornesse and perversnesse of disposicion, which will not let us turn from sin. For by neglecting a timely remedy, for want of being acquainted with the wayes of God in our youth, *vitia mores fiunt*, our evill wayes become our manners and common deportment, and we looke upon them, as upon that which becomes us; upon an unlawfull act, as upon that which we ought to doe; and upon all others as fooles or men of no spirits, that will not run with us to the same excesse of riot. Nay yet further, *Peccatum fit lex*, sin which is the transgression of the law,[138] is made a lawe it self; I find a law in my members (Apostle) warring against the law of my mind [Rom: 7.23]; and St. Aug[ustine] calls it so, Confessions lib.8. c.6 *lex peccati est violentia consuetudinis*, That law of sin which carries us with that violence to sin, is nothing else but the force of

---

135 Translated it means, "your ancient voluntary will grow into violence."

136 Cp. the similarities with P.C.D., p. 285; M.L.E., p .848.

137 A native of Rome (4B.C. - A.D.65): writer, statesman and tutor. For a time a political adviser to Nero until he fell from favour and was forced to commit suicide on a charge of conspiracy.

138 Refer for more details to lecture on *Original and Actual Sin*.

long custome and continuance in sin. For sin by custome gains a kingdome in our soules, and having taken her seat or throne there, shee commands not as a Tyrant, but haveing gained dominion over us, shee finds us willing subjects; shee holds us captive, and we call our captivity our liberty.[139] Her poyson is as the poyson of the Aspick; shee bites us, and we smile and die, and feel it not. How highly then doth it concern us all to prevent this custome of sining, by accustoming ourselves to the wayes of Piety and vertue, by walking according to those rules, which we have lively drawn in the word of God; that so when we come to the declining of our age, we may look upon our life past, as a constant and continued motion towards heaven; this will fill our consciences with peace, make the close of our lives more comfortable, and death which to others is the greatest of terrors, not so much a punishment as a passage to our eternal happinesse.

7. The necessity of this duty of acquainting ourselves with the wayes of God in our younger yeares, may be drawn from the shortnesse of our lives; for alas! what is our life? 'tis but a vapour that appeares for a little while and then vanisheth, [James 4.14] like the crackling of thorns under a Pot [Eccl: 7.6], or the blaze of a brush faggot no sooner in but out.[140] The Greek word ἄω which signifies to live or breath, consists but of two letters, the first and the last of the Greek alphabet and α[Alpha] doth no sooner beginn it; but ω [Omega] concludes it, without the interposicion of any other letters, or so much as an aspiracion to prolong the sound; which intimates unto us the shortnesse of our lives, they are no sooner begun but they are at an end; Here we are alive at this present; but who knowes how

139 In the next lecture Andrewes intimated how the Athenians in Paul's time could not be convinced of their "thraldome to sin". Cp. this with remarks Andrewes made about the domination of sin on Whitsunday 1614. In his sermon *Of the keys*, Andrewes pointed out there is a release from the fetters or captivity of sin in *Remiseritis* and *Remittuntur*, that is by sacramental confession. Andrewes, Vol. 3, p. 228, Vol. 5, p. 88.

140 This simile reappears in Andrewes' Nativity Sermon for 1610 when he is preaching about fleeting joy. Ibid, Vol.1, p. 72.

soon he shall goe down into silence, or whose turn shall be first.[141]

And this consideracion should make us very frugall and thrifty of our time, and so to number our dayes that we may apply our hearts unto wisdome; being every day mindfull of our last day, and of that strict account which we much one day give of all our Actions, of all those opportunityes of learning and instruction, which we have here afforded us.

The Jewes relate of Ben Syra, that whiles he was yet a child he often desired his Tutor to instruct him in the wayes of Gods commandments, and his Tutor as often put him off, telling him that he was but a child, and so not fit to be entred into the study of that sacred science; Oh, but sayes he, I have been in the churchyard, and there I find by many graves that I have layn down by and measured and found shorter than my selfe, that many have dyed younger than I am; and if I should dye before I were acquainted with God and his commandments, oh what would become of me then master (for tis pitty but this story should be true). For the application of it is very obvious, to teach us to remember our creator in the dayes of our youth; to make hast to learn to know and serv God; and to think, that we can never possibly begin that lesson too soon, which can never be learned too well; And withall to use all speed and diligence; least so, as children have usually tore their bookes, we have ended our lives before we have learned our lesson; Let us therefore translate all our care from earth to heaven, cut off all superfluous expences of time, that we may afford to be more liberall towards heavenly and spirituall exercises; least if we let much water goe besides the mill, spend much time besid the main businesse, what was reported of Demonsthenes that his breath was too short for his periods, happen to us in a matter of the greatest moment and concernment; that the period of dayes be ended before we come to the period of our desires, the comfortable assurance of God's favour here, and everlasting glory hereafter.

Lastly, as in Scripture there are places where every Lamb

141 Cp. with Ibid.,Vol. 2, p. 96.

may wade, so where elephants may swim;[142] And tis dangerous, nay folly and madnesse to venture at first to swim in those waters, before we learn to wade; we may see, nay we feel, the sad events of such preposterous proceedings, in the blasphemies and prodigious opinions of such as have been drowned in these deep waters, both themselves in high mysteryes of Religion; Father forgive them - - they utter, they know not what; which they call or rather miscall, overflowing of the spirit. Hence 'tis (we need not goe into the wildernesse to see it) for alas we may see everywhere, many Reeds shaken with the wind, [Math: 11.7] tossed to and fro with the wind of every doctrine [Eph: 4.14]. Now whence proceed so many mishapen errors, such strange uncoth and unheard of untruthes, but amongst other defects from this; that the good ancient way of laying down at first, elements and grounds of Religion, is laid aside, as out of date and useles; But too many there are, (God knowes) who have no more knowledge of God and Christ, but the bare names. Great is the number of Preachers; but how many speak into the air [1Cor: 14.9]; they speak indeed unto men, but (as the Apostle), no man understandeth them; they hear a noyse, but know not the meaning of the voyce; so by reason of their want of elementary knowledge, he that speaketh is no better than a Barbarian [1Cor: 14.11].[143]

And to prevent this inconvenience, and that all sorts of persons might be set in the right way, instructed and trained up in the knowledg of God; it were to be wished, that catechiseing and teaching fundamentalls of Religion, were more practised than 'tis, not only in this place, but everywhere else in the land; that the Primitive Discipline might be restored and men taught, 1st to stand, then to goe, and then with patience to run the race that is set before them. Questionles this would make more for the peace of the church and the benefit of their own soules.

I shall therefore in my ensuing discourses, not confine my-

---

142 In M.L.E. scripture references are given as 2Pet.3.18, 1Cor.4.20, Eph. 14.13. p. 5. Cp. also with P.C.D., p. 7.

143 Cp. with some of Andrewes' Pentecost Sermons, such as for 1616 and 1622. Also a similar comment about praying in Prayer Sermon on the 'Amen'. Andrewes, Vol. 3, pp. 274 – 5, 396, Vol. 5, p. 473.

self to any one particular point, but breifly and plainly lay down some Principall Heads and grounds of Christianity, such as are most moral and necessary to be known. And because only scripture teacheth all supernaturally revealed Truth, without the knowledge whereof; salvacion cannot be attained; and the main Principle whereupon our beleef of all things therein contained is, That the Scriptures are the oracles of God himself.[144] Therefore in the 1. place, I shall endeavour to maintain the Aut[h]oritie of those Books by Arguments and Reasons, such as unbeleevers themselves may think reasonable, if they judg thereof as they should.[145] 2. That those holy Bookes contain in them all things necessary to be known of any Christian for the eternall good and wisdome of his soul. 3. That the holy scriptures are the only Rule, according to which we are to square all our Actions, and the only *Judex Normalis* of all controversies, and so show the no necessity of unwritten Traditions. As for other matters, as that we are carefully to search the scriptures, diligently and reverently to read them and hear them read, and to practise what is commanded in them; these will fall in by way of use and Inferences.

And now in conclusion I must desire of you

1. That you would resort hither with alacritie and cheerfullnes, knowing that those houres which we bestow on this exercise; we bestow them on a thing most pleasing unto God: This Duty you heard was practised of the church in all Ages, and 'tis especially commanded by God Hims[elf]; we must therefore come cheerfully to it.[146]

---

144 This is identical to text in E.P., 3.8.13.

145 This is identical to text in E.P., 3:8.14.

146 In M.L.E. this paragraph and the rest of this lecture has been expanded. "For as much as we are children, we doe *imbibere errores*, drinke in errors. We must learne to put them off, while we are children, and have truth in their place.

The fruit of the first: that knowing that judgment waiteth for us, we must be carefull of our duties, and so to practise them.

Of the second commandment forasmuch as we see of the Church in all ages, that it is a thing especially commanded of the Lord we must know those houres which we bestow on this exercise we bestow them on a thing most pleasing to God. … We must therefore come cheerfully and when we come, so behave ourselves as it becometh, namely we must heare with attentive eares, and earnest hearts.

2. That you consider, that all this duty lieth not only on the speaker, for our saviour maketh it a matter of consequence to hear well, Luc. 8.18. *βλέπετε πῶς ἀκούετε*. Take heed how yee hear. And he inforceth it with this Reason; for to every one that hath to him shall be given; and whosoever hath not from him shall be taken even that which he seemeth to have. He that heareth well, God will reveal more unto him; and from him that heareth not well, shall be taken away that little which he had before. And therefore you are to hear with attentive eares, and earnest hearts not grudgingly and of necessity; for God loveth a cheerful hearer.[147]

3ly. Bec[ause] these Institucions are compared to a Building therefore Assiduity is required, that you fail not to be present, never to intermit this exercise: for as Cyrill of Jer[usalem] *οὐκ ἐρίν ἡ παιδάγωγὴ*, these Institucions are not as Homilies or Sermons, for of them if we misse one, we may redeem it by another; but if we once misse this exercise, there will be a chasme,

---

Paul, Rom: 6.21. What fruit had ye then in these things whereof ye are now ashamed? And secondly, in 22 verse, he setteth the fruit downe to be holinesse of life; ... unto holiness. And the heathen wisheth us in all our actions to aske this question, *Cur bono*, to what good; admonishing us to enquire what good cometh to us by our exercises. Even that which Paul setteth down 1Tim: 4. 8 For bodily exercise profiteth little, but godlinesse is profitable unto all things, ...

In this life, the fruit length of daies; as Deut: 11. 21 [That your days may be multiplied... .] In life to come Joh: 17. 3 [and this is] eternall life. Having seen the fruits we are to take care that those houres which we spend in this exercise, we misspend not, least we be deprived thereof. For as in naturall philosophy, it is a great absurdity, *ut quid frustra fiat;* that anything be in vaine; and in morall, *ut fiat* ...vaine desire. In divine things much more; 1Cor: 15. 14 Paul useth no other argument to prove that Christ is risen, then that, else his preaching and their hearing should be vaine Gal: 2. 2. I went up by revelation, and communicated unto them that Gospell [which I preach among the Gentiles, but privately to them which were of reputation, lest by any means I should run, or had run, in vaine].

Ratio, the reason - - lest by any meanes I should run, or had runne in vaine, 2Cor: 6.1 as he desired the Corinthians that they received not the grace of God in vaine: so we be like those (Jer: 6. 29) that let the bellows burne, and the lead consume in the fire, and the founder melt in vaine. The worde of the Lord is not in vaine, either in respect 1. of it selfe 2. Preacher 3. hearer ... great care then is to be taken how we behave ourselves in hearing." M.L.E., pp. 7 - 9.

147 This is a play on 2 Corinthians 9.7, "God loveth a cheerful giver." Cp. with P.C.D., p. 11.

we cannot have a perfect building; for if one parte be wanting,[148] then of necessity the whole fabrick is imperfect.[149]

148 Based on Cyril's words. "Study our teachings and keep them for ever. Think not that they are ordinary homilies; for though they also are good and trustworthy, yet if we neglect them to-day we may study them to-morrow. But if the teaching concerning the layer of regeneration delivered in a consecutive course be neglected to-day, when shall it be made right? ... Suppose, pray, that the Catechising is a kind of building: if we do not bind the house together by regular bonds in the building, lest some gap be found, and the building become unsound, even our former labour is of no use. But stone must follow stone by course, and corner match with corner ... ." *Procatechesis*, Ch. 11.

149 This paragraph appears exactly in M.L.E.. p. 8. Cp. also with P.C.D. p. 10. In M.L.E. and P.C.D. Andrewes concluded the section, The Duty of the Catechised, with the following quotation from Cyril. "*Meum est docere* 'tis my work to teach;' *vestrum auscultare* 'yours to learn;' *Dei perficere* 'God's to give a blessing to both.'" M.L.E., p. 13; P.C.D., p. 12.

LECTURE TWO

Of the Aut[h]oritie of the Scriptures - pt. 1

Introduction

It will become obvious in this and the next two lectures on the Scriptures that Andrewes would be described as a fundamentalist today. He believed that Moses wrote the Pentateuch, and what he wrote was true, including his account of creation. He took exception to those of his day who interpreted parts of the Scriptures as allegorical, as illustrated in this Genesis lecture at St. Paul's Cathedral: "There are with us and in our age which draw everything to a figurative sense", and as a result they turn "Gods Paradise" into a "fools Paradise". He maintained that this was certainly not the teaching of the Fathers such as Epiphanius and Chrysostom who opposed such allegorising of God's paradise. Here Andrewes overlooked the teaching of the Alexandrian school and the medieval tradition! Of course he was not the only one of his day to hold a fundamentalist view. His protégé, JohnCosin, commenting on the Garden of Eden declared, "that there was a tree, forbidden tree, whereof this woman did really eat; and that there was a serpent, a deceiving serpent, by whom she was really beguiled." However there are some of "licentious wits" who take all these as allegories. They have made "an imaginary doctrine of their own ... which came first either from the fancy of the heathen poets, ... or from Julian the apostate and his master Porphyry."[150]

---

150 *Apos. Sacra*, pp. 157 - 8; Cosin, Vol. 1, pp. 225 - 6.

Andrewes not only presented Moses as the author of the Pentateuch but also the oldest writer in the world, even older than Homer. Indeed he suggested that the latter and other ancient writers such as Solon, Pythagoras were "debtors" to Moses.[151] Furthermore although all Scripture was inspired by God, he maintained that there were some parts of it that were more inspired than others. He had already preached on this approach in his Spital Sermon on Easter Wednesday, 1588.[152]

For Andrewes as with Hooker[153] understanding of Scripture could never be separated from reason and enlightened knowledge, which "is a virtue of the reasonable part". The former stated, "as the sun giveth light to the body, so God hath provided light for the soul; and that is, first, the light of nature, ... from this light we have ... knowledge. ... With this light 'every one that cometh into the world' is enlightened." Through this enlightenment we can come to see that "the bible is the perfect rule of knowledge." This is not unlike what the Puritans called "inner light" which "makes us see in the Scriptures more cleere ... than we see the Sunne light with our own eyes." However for the Puritans this enlightenment always followed faith; it could never be given before. Hence they maintained that the heathens could not possess reason or true enlightenment.[154]

Not so, argued Andrewes, reason is a gift from God given to the "naturall man", and even in him it is not "so repugnant from Faith". This he believed was manifested in the "Heathenist Philosophers" who in their writings also acknowledged God as the creator of the universe. Thus reason is "an instrument which God useth" in bringing unbelievers to the Christian faith as well as confirming the believers. Therefore "reason is no enimy to Religion, to be ripen in faith is not to be raw in judgment."[155]

---

151 Ms. 3707, p. 27.

152 Andrewes, Vol. 5, pp. 3 - 4.

153 For Hooker's view, refer to E.P., 1.8.3.

154 Andrewes, Vol. 5, p. 319, Apos. *Sacra*, pp. 189, 631; Dering, sigs. G2; Morgan, pp. 56 - 8.

155 *Apos. Sacra*, p. 3; Ms. 3707, p. 27. Hooker had written in a similar vein. It is the "light of natural reason that shineth in [man] and maketh him apt to apprehend those

Antiquity "and universall Tradicion" Andrewes believed were a proof for its authenticity as it has stood the test of time. If there were any errors in the writings of Moses or of any others it was through "ignorance" and not "malice". In regards to the New Testament, the writers either knew Christ personally or knew those who did, and so their works were truly authentic. He therefore upheld the Scriptures as being the authority on God's creative, redemptive and sanctifying acts for His world and mankind, and indeed for all doctrine necessary for salvation. This he indicated had been the view of the early Church, and was even accepted by infidels such as Julian the Apostate.[156]

In this first lecture on the Scriptures Andrewes indicated that ever since antiquity, man has reached out for God, aspired for happiness and eternal life, all of which are now available through our blessed Saviour. Man perceives God's existence, His attributes and gifts through knowledge, of which there are two kinds: natural and revealed. The former, by the gift of reason given to all, man can be convinced or persuaded that God does exist.[157] With the latter, through the guidance of the Holy Spirit in reading Scripture and appreciating His creative acts, man can glean what God is like. Of the two, revealed knowledge is the more important as it tells us how God intervened in this world, firstly through His prophets, and secondly in His son, Jesus Christ who has given us the means for eternal life by His redemptive work and through forgiveness of sins and the sacraments.

So we all should be thankful that we no longer have "to worship sticks and stones" but a God who through the Scriptures has assured us that He will guide us to a "glorious and eternall kingdome".[158]

The Scriptures is often prefixed by *Holy*. Andrewes explained

---

things of God, which being by grace discovered are effectual to persuade reasonable minds and none other." E.P., 3.8.11

156 Ms. 3707, pp. 28 - 30.

157 In the Pembroke lectures Andrewes stated that if we only came to God "by knowledge ... and reason", then many would never know of God, as these ways are for the "learned". M.L.E., p. 19.

158 Ms. 3707, p. 31.

why this is so. It is "holy" because of 1. Its author, God; 2. The Penmen, "holy men of God"; 3. "The holy matter" contained; and 4. The expression of the "holy will ... of God". Its contents could be summarised as the Old Testament containing "those histories, Prophecies and doctrines ... delivered to our Fathers under the Law" and the New Testament as "the law revealed and laid open". All other writings in comparison are "dry and ju[i]clesse".[159]

The collection of books in the bible in the Old or New Testament was significant for Andrewes as "testament" denoted "the Covenant of grace, ... made between God and his church." Furthermore a testament or as it is sometimes called "a last will" unveils the mind of the testator. Hence these books revealed firstly, the testator, Jesus Christ; secondly, his legacies, life eternal; thirdly his heirs, his children; and fourthly, the seals, the sacraments. Both the testament and the covenant of grace were implemented when the testator died on the cross.[160]

Text 2 Timothy 3: 16 - 7.
All scripture is given by inspiracion of God and is profitable for doctrine, for reproof, for correction, for instruction in righteousnesse: That the man of God be perfect, throughly furnished unto all good works.

Blessednes and eternall glory were the ends for which man was made, and whereunto in his dayly thoughts he doth tend and aspire. For tho' men be much amisse in their judgment concerning good and evill, yet we find that of the Philosopher universally true. ἀγαθοῦ τινος εφίεσθαι δοχεῖ, every creature desires it's own good and preservacion; so there was never any man but did really desire his own happines. This being graunted, he that would chalk out the way, and lay down the meanes by which a man may become happy, deserves both our thanks and obedience: And our blessed Saviour hath done it. Joh: 17.3 This is life eternall [that

159 Ibid., pp. 25, 31. Andrewes at Pembroke had referred to the Law as "nothing else but the old gospel, so the gospel is nothing but the new Law; the Law *evangelium reconditum*, 'the gospel under the veil,' the gospel *lex revelata*, 'the law unveiled.'" P. C. D., p. 47.

160 Ms. 3707, p. 26.

they might know thee the only true God, and Jesus Christ, whom thou hast sent].

Now knowledge is 2fold 1. Naturall 2. Revealed; Natural knowl[edge] is so termed either 1st because it is naturally imprinted in every man's mind, stamped upon the soul of every reasonable creature; or 2ly, acquired by the meditacion and consideracion of the creatures; so the Heavens declare the glory; [and the firmament sheweth his handywork, Ps.19.1]. Nay we need not look so high - *quaelibet herba Deum,* every grasse pile we tread upon, may serv as a little Catechism to teach us a Diety. But this naturall knowl[edge] is not sufficient to salvacion, to make us eternally happy. For where the star of this know[ledge] shone the brightest, at Athens, 'twas dark night with them in respect of the knowledg of the true God;[161] they proclaimed their ignorance of him in that Inscription upon one of their Altars, *ἀγνῶστω Θεῷ*[162]Act:17.23. Many powerfull speakers they had, who by their wining Rhetorique were able to carry the crowd captive, to their own ends, but none of them were able to show them their thraldome to Sin and Satan and the meanes of their deliverance thence. And therefore.

2ly. Revealed knowl[edge] is necessary, i.e. the knowl[edge] of such Truthes as are revealed to us in God's Word, which we call the holy Scriptures. 1. the Scriptures *κατεζένην*[163] in regard of the Eminent, supereminent excellencie of them; all other scriptures are but dry and ju[i]celesse writeings in respect of these holy scriptures; which are 2ly call Holy, 1st in respect of the holy Author, G[od] Alm[ighty], 2. in respect of the holy Penmen - holy

---

161 Cp. this with Andrewes' glowing comment of Athenian art, government and philosophy in M.L.E. It is almost as glowing as that of the Fathers in regards to Theology. "It cannot be denied but that the chiefest wits concerning the knowledge of Arts and policy have been in them, and among them and in Philosophy their light hath shined most brightly; and we have all lighted our candles at their light, and yet as the wisest of us may wonder at them for nature and human knowledge, so may the simplest of us laught at them for the worship of God: so dim hath their light burned in the worship of God." M.L.E., p. 41. Refer also to Andrewes, Vol. 3, pp. 286 - 7.

162 Or as it was composed in the New Testament in capital letters, ΑΤΝΩΕΤΩ ΘΕΩ. Translated it means "to the unknown God."

163 Translated it means "received".

men of God 2Pet: 1.21, 3ly, in respect of the holy matter they contain, the holy will and councell of God. 4. In respect of their holy use, to make us wise unto salvation.

Again, these scriptures are called the Bookes of the Old and N[ew] T[estament] which 2 Testaments are one in substance, differ only in circumstances of Time and Persons, when, by whom and to whom they were delivered. As those bookes of the Old Testament are so stiled, because they contain those histories, Prophesies and Doctrines, which of old time were delivered to our Fathers under the Law. And the bookes of the N[ew] T[estament] are not so called *ex parte materiæ* in regard of any new matter therein contained, but *ex parte modi,* and *patefactionis voluntatis divinæ* in respect of the time and manner of their deliverance; the Gospell is but *Lex revelata,* the law revealed and laid open; Our Saviour came not to destroy but to fullfill the Law and the Prophets, Math: 5.17, in which regard, times of the Gospell are called the fullnes of time, Gal: 4.4, and the later days 1Tim: 4.1.

Lastly, the h[oly] scriptures are called the Bookes of the Old and N[ew] T[estament] by reason of that Analogie which the Covenant of grace, made between God and his church hath with a Testament, which Analogie consists in these Particulars.

1st. In a last will or Testament is declared the mind and will of the Testator: so the will and good pleasure of God to[wards] his creatures, is fully revealed in these bookes. 2ly, As to the makeing up of a Will are required 1. a testator, 2. legacies, 3. heirs, 4. writeings, 5. seales; So answerably we have all these in these bookes. 1. testator, Christ Jesus, 2. legacie, life Eternall, 3. heirs, his children and chosen, 4. writeings, the holy scriptures, 5. seales, which are the sacraments.[164] 3ly. As a will or Testament is of no force so long as the Testator liveth:[165] so this Test[ament] and covenant of grace is of full force by the death of the Testator, Christ Jesus.

These things being premised I shall now enter upon the Text,

---

164 In his Pentecost Sermon for 1613 Andrewes elaborated on this. "The outward seal should be a thing visible, to be shown; and the sacrament is the only visible part of religion, and nothing subject to that sense but it. This I find, that the schoolmen, when they numbered seven, those seven were the seven seals; so for seals they have ever been reputed." Andrewes, Vol. 3, p. 219.

165 Cp. with Hebrews 9.17.

All Scripture is given by inspiracion of God and is [profitable for doctrine, for reproof, for correction, for instruction in righteousness: That the man of God be perfect, thoroughly furnished unto all good works].

From whence we inferr these 3 conclusions.

1. That the h[oly] Scriptures, the bookes of the Old and N[ew] T[estament] are of divine Aut[h]oritie, the Word of G[od]. All Scripture is given by inspiracion.

2. The sufficiency of the h[oly] scripture, that all things necessary to be beleeved and practised are contained in the h[oly] script[ures]. They are able to make us wise to salvacion, to make the man of G[od] perfect througly furnished [unto all good works].

3. The Usefulnes of h[oly] script[ure], they are profitable for Doctrine, for reproofe, for correction, for instruccion in righteousnes.

To begin with the first. That the holy scriptures are the Oracles of God hims[elf Heb: 5.12], and so of Divine Aut[h]oritie, this is such a Principle, as in itself we cannot say is evident; for then all men, as well within as without the church, that hear it would acknowledge the truth of it; but we know the contrarie. And therefore there must be some former knowl[edge] presupposed, which does assure unto the hearts of all Beleevers the Truth of this poynt. This Question then being put;

By what means are we taught the truth of this, that all scripture [is given by inspiration by God]. To which we answer 1. Negatively, That no scripture can teach us the sacred Aut[h]oritie of Scripture; bec[ause] there is not any kind of science which leadeth us unto knowledg without presupposing a number of things already known. The first Principles in every science, are either taken as plain and manifest in themselves or as approved and graunted already some former knowl[edge] having made them evident. But

2ly, To the Q[uestion], Affirmatively 1. One meanes to know that the h[oly] scriptures are the word of G[od] is the <u>Antiquitie</u> of them, and <u>universall Tradicion.</u> As Namely that so we beleev bec[ause] both we from our predecessors and they from theirs, have so received. The ch[urch] of G[od] of all Ages, tho' disagreeing about many poynts yet all agreed in the profession of this Truth, that the scriptures were given by inspiracion of God.

2ly. The inward Motive, leading us so to esteem of the scripture as given by inspiracion of God, is the Testimony of God's Spirit, witnessing and proveing to the soul of every Beleever, that these h[oly] scriptures are the word of God. But

3ly. If Infidells or Atheists at any time chance to call this Truth in Question, this giveth us occasion to search and sift out what reason there is, whereby the outer Testimony of G[od]'s Ch[urch] and our own [many] perswasions concerning the Truth of the scriptures, may be proved a Truth infallible. In which case the Ancient F[athers] being often constrained to shew what warrant they had, so much to rely upon the scriptures, endeavoured still to maintain the Aut[h]oritie of those books, by Arguments and Reasons, such as none could deny, without denying some apparent Principle, such as all men acknowledg to be true.[166] So these are three good wayes, whereby we are taught this truth: 1. by the Antiquity of them and universall tradicion 2. by the inward Testimony of G[od]'s spirit. 3. by Arguments and Reasons to confirme Beleevers in the truth of that which they beleev; and to convince and (by the assistance of God's Spirit) to bring such as doe not beleev into the number of Beleevers. In which regard, Reason is of singular use, as an instrument which God useth to such purposes. The Apostle requireth Abilitie in Titus to convince Heretiques, Titus 1.9, 11. And can we think he judgeth it a thing unlawfull and not rather needfull, to use the Instrument of their conviction, the light of reason. Their mouthes must be stopt' (Apostle) and therefore 'tis fit the church should be furnished with Reasons to stop the mouthes of her Adversaries. Be ready to give a reason of the hope that is in you, 1Pet: 3.15. And therefore Reason is no enimy to Religion, to be ripe in faith is not to be raw in judgment.[167] But

1. To begin with that which I first proposed, the Antiquitie of the scriptures; in which poynt they have the preemincency of all other writeings in the world, not only in respect of their originall

166 This is very similar to what he said in the previous lecture with its closeness to E.P., 3.8.13-4.

167 Much of the last two pages are similar to Hooker. E.P., 3.8.4, 8,13-5.

copy, which was written without hands, but in respect of such a materiall writing as may be seen handled, read and understood by men. And here I would be understood, not of the body of the scriptures, as tis now compleated (for there are many bookes and writeings to be found, that bear a far more ancient date than that parte of the scripture which we call the N[ew] T[estament], yea possibly then any writeings of the Prophetts), but the Bookes and writeings of Moses, wherein the summe and substance of all the rest is comprised, they ly[e] many yeares nearer the foundacions of the world, than any writeings whatsoever. Justin Martyr, who lived within 130 yeares after our Saviour, in his *Paræmitique* [*Paroemitic*] to the Greekes, by compareing the times of all humane writers, Poets, Philosophers, Historians, Lawgivers, those that were esteemed the most ancient, he proves that Moses[168] and his writeings were extant in the world, before they were brought forth, or any of their writeings brought to the light. Yea further he there clearly shewes, that whatsoever Orpheus,[169] Homer,[170] Solon[171], Pythagoras,[172] Plato,[173] or any other of those ancient heathen writers wrote concerning God or divine matters with any savour or relish of truth, they were debtors to Moses for it, and borrowed

---

168 The preface for the Genesis lectures also states, "Moses was but the pen of that God did speak." *Apos. Sacra*, p. 659.

169 Perhaps a real person who founded Orphism in 7th century B. C. This mystical religion taught that there is a mixture of good and evil in every human who should strive to purge himself from the evil by ritual and moral purification throughout a series of reincarnations. The nobler thoughts of Orphism were taken up by Pindar and Plato.

170 Probably the author of the epic poems the *Iliad* and the *Odyssey*, written before 700B.C.

171 An Athenian statesman of the early sixth century B.C. whose constitutional reforms laid the foundations for democracy.

172 He lived c.582 - c.507B.C. Little is known of his life and writings but the Pythagoreans based in Croton, south Italy, claimed him as their founder. They taught that the soul is condemned to a cycle of reincarnation from which it perhaps could escape by attaining a state of purity.

173 He lived from 427- 348B.C. In his writings the *Republic, Symposium, Phaedo* and *Timaeus* he articulated that Virtue consists in the harmony of the souls with the universe of Ideas, which assure order, intelligence and pattern to a world in constant flux. Supreme is the idea of Good. Only the ruler who understood this harmony is capable of ruling the just State. Plato also believed that the soul is immortal.

their light in such things from the lamp of his writeings. Eusebius also, Lib 10. c.2.3. *de Præparacione Evang[elica]*[174] prosecutes the same Argument at larg, and from many places and passages and confessions, out of the best and most authentique Heathen Authors themselves,[175] clearly demonstrates that Moses was the most ancient of all writers that were known or named amongst them.[176]

But it may be here objected; is not sin and error almost of as ancient standing as the world? And if it be graunted that the scriptures be the most ancient of all bookes will it therefore follow, that they must needs be true, Will their Antiquitie prove them to be the Offspring of the Ancient of Dayes?

To this I answer, 1st with Tertullian 19.c. *Apol[ogiam]*,[177] that there is a natural propension in most men to ascribe much to that which is ancient, especially to Authors, Writers, Monuments; And therefore insisting upon this Argument (Antiquitie of the Script[ure]) to demonstrate the truth of it against the Heathen, he tells them that they themselves were greate admirers of things that were ancient. 'Tis little lesse then Religion with you (saith He) to give credit or beleef unto things according to their time. But

2ly, The more ancient any Religion or any writeings are, the longer they have been upon triall, the world hath had so much the more time, opportunitie and meanes to inquire into the state and condicion of it, and so to discover the Nakednes, falshood or vanitie of it, if it be unsound. Time is no lesse *Index* then *Edax rerum* as a confirmer, so a Trier of things. Any Doctrine or opinion, wheth-

---

174 He is the author of *Church History* and recorded such events as the martyrdom of SS. Peter and Paul. He was made bishop of Caesarea in 314, although until then he had only been a catechumen.

175 Grotius follows this line of argument in *True Religion*, pp. 44 - 57.

176 Tertullian says the same in the chapter below of *Apologiam* as quoted by Andrewes.

177 He was the first great Latin theologian in the very early Church. He is famous for such remarks as, "What has Athens to do with Jerusalem?" And, "What has the Academy to do with the Church?" His teachings thus broke from the strong Greek philosophical teaching of Christianity. He was particularly virulent in his writings against Marcion who rejected most of the Bible, and was excommunicated from Rome in 144 and then founded his own church. Yet in later life Tertullian joined the schismatic Montanists.

er it be sound or unsound, true or false, time will manifest. And therefore 't was Gamaliel's advice to the Jewes, that they should let the Apostles alone; for if that work and councell were of men, in time, it would come to nought, Act: 5.38. So such writeings, which containe sound and substantiall truthes, tho' they may for some Ages endure contradiction and censure, as erroneous and false, yet in processe of time, they will recover their native dignitie and honour, and those which are not true and sound, time will discover their error and vanitie.

3ly, to make this Argument drawn from the Antiquitie of the script[ures] little less than Demonstrative, I add in the next place; That when the Religion from generacion to generacion continued and professed in the world, hath withall prove first rise and profession of it, been still opposed and persecuted in the world, the Professors thereof, even for their profession made obnoxious to the malice, rage and fury of the world; if notwithstanding all this, those scriptures be still embraced, that Religion be loved, professed, live and prosper in the world. In such a case (I say) as this, the Antiquitie of a Religion is a great confirmacion of the truth and Revelacion of it from God. My reason is this, bec[ause] that Religion which doth expose the Professors of it to troubles, sorrowes and afflictions, doth alwayes lay a kind of prudential engagement upon men to enquire and search narrowly into the Quality and condicion of it, and so to satisfie themselves. Whether it be a Religion worth the suffering for, or no; it being a most irrationall and unworthy Act, for any man to sell his precious comforts, his peace and other accommodacions in the world, for such a thing which he knowes not, whether hereafter, 'twill any whitt benefit him, or no. All men are composed of flesh and spirit; and when men are to give sentence in matters which so nearly concern the flesh there is little fear they should be bribed by the spirit. So that doubtles, did not men see somewhat of divine Aut[h]oritie, somewhat that commands and overawes their consciences in such a Religion which so threatens the persecution of the flesh, they would never have to doe with it upon such terms of danger and ruine.

Lastly when a matter of so much concernment as the profession of Christian Religion grounded upon the h[oly] scriptures, hath passed thorow the hands, not of one, not of a few, but of many, very many generacions, 'tis not lightly possible, but that in case, one or two of those generacions had so little of men in men, as to look no better to themselves, and their Principles, then to goe on with the Profession of such a Religion, as threatned them with apparent ruine, as promised them nothing in compensacion therof upon any sure and certaine grounds; yet (I say), 'tis not easily possible, but some one or other of those generacions would have corrected the error of those that went before them and so have deserted and forsaken that Religion, which had so abused their forefathers, and occasioned so much sorrow and affliction upon themselves.[178]

The Result of all is this: Seeing the holy scriptures are so ancient that they were the first writeings extant in the world, and seeing they have waded thorow so many deep waters, so many Oceans of blood, and have passed throw so many fires, eaten up so many Professors, occasioned the martyrdome of so many abettors of them, and yet there are many who are ready to suffer for them, these Reasons are of no little force to prove the truth, soundnes and Aut[h]ority of them.

I will but add this, and then end this Argument, That the Doctrines contained in the bookes of the Old and N[ew] T[estament] are brought down and confirmed unto us by the unanimous consent of all Gods people, even of those which in other things are of infinite variance one with another. For amongst all those Sects of Jewes and Christians, questioning and quarrelling about other things, there were none that called in question the Aut[h]oritie of the scriptures, but the truth of them is conveyed unto us with the full stream of constant and universall Tradicion. And that not only of such as are within, but of those without the church; for not any Pagans, Infidells, not Porphyry,[179] Julian[180] but confesse

178 Cp. with Grotius "They that first taught the *Christian Religion* not onely wanted all civill power and authority, but were of meane condition, no better than poor Fishermen, weavers, and the like. Yet by such paines and industry that doctrine, within the space of thirty yeares or thereabouts, was published not onely thorowout all the parts of the *Roman Empire*, but also among the *Parthians* and remote *Indians*." True Religion, pp. 139 - 40.

179 His anti-Christian philosophical writings were directed in part against the great Christian philosophical writings of Origen in the third century.

180 Grotius wrote similarly "neither did *Julian* himself, nore any other adversaries of *Christianity* ever make doubt of it." And, "Neither did ever the Pagans or Jews make

those bookes to be the writeings of Mathew, Mark, Peter, Paul; which we term their Epistles and Gospells. Now if we beleeve Virgill's *Æneades* [*Aeneid*], Homer's *Iliades* and *Odysses* to be the workes and writeings of such men, bec[ause] of the Testimony of the Greekes and Latines concerning them; the Argument will follow *a fortiori*; you know the Rule *Testimonium plurimorum* - - - that which is [ap]proved by universall consent may not easily be denyed. And therefore (I say) if we beleeve such writeings to be the workes of such Authors because of the Testimony of a few, much more ought we to give credence to the Authors of those holy Bookes, because of that universall consent, the general Testimony of almost all Nations.

Dub[itatio]. But here many things may be demanded. As 1st it being graunted that there were such writers and that they were the Authors of these holy Scriptures, yet how we can know that they were faithfull witnesses and not such men, whose faithfullnes and knowledg we may justly suspect?

An[swer]: To this I answer, that if those writers doe fail us, they did it either 1. through ignorance, that they had not perfect knowledg of such things as they delivered, or 2. through Malice - that they did not faithfully deliver things according to their knowledge: there can be but these 2 wayes imagined they should fail us either in poynt of History or Doctrine.

For the 1st, It being graunted, that those very men are the Authors of those bookes which bear their Names and superscriptions; if we doe but consider when and where they lived, 'twill appear that they could not be ignorant of those things they did deliver. For the Writers of the N[ew] T[estament] to run over them particularly. 1. Matthew and John who wrote historically of our Saviour Christ, they were both of his Retinue, very inward with him, and one of them his bosome Disciple, and therefore being so privy to his Actions, words and miracles, being his constant followers, they could not be ignorant of the truth of those things they did historically relate. 2ly, For the other 2 Evangelists Mark and Luke, they lived in those times, and in those places, where our saviour

---

doubt therof, but *Julian* himselfe plainly confesseth that these were the writings of *Peter, Matthew, Mark* and *Luke* which Christians under those names have read and received." Likewise writings under *Homer* and *Virgil* are not doubted. True Religion, pp.78, 157.

Christ lived, while he was here upon earth; And both th' one and th' other were St. Paul's companions in travell, who was one chosen on purpose to publish the truth of [the] Christian Religion to the world, and from whom they learned the perfect knowl[edge] of those things which Jesus did from the beginning.[181] 3ly, For the Acts of the Apostles, St. Luke was an ear and an eye witnes of many of them. He is the largest in relacion of such things as St. Paul did act and suffer, where for the most part he was present. 4ly, For St. Paules Epistles which were written either to whole churches, or particular Persons as Philemon, Titus, Timothy; they contain 1.Things doctrinall, 2. Historicall, 3. Propheticall. 1. For the Doctrinall part of them, we have no reason to doubt, but that the Apostle knew very well what he wrote, seeing he was chosen by Christ, by a divine and miraculous call from heaven, to bear his name and preach his gospell to all nacions, 2ly, the Historicall part is so interwoven with the doctrinall, that they cannot well be severed. 3ly, concerning his prophesies, predictions of such things as should befall the church in after times, 'tis not probable that he who was in so high a degree of favour with our saviour, as 'twere one of Heavens darlings; (I say) 'tis not probable, that he should be ignorant of the truth of things to come, i.e. the truth of such things as he plainly professed to know. So of the Truth and Authoritie of those Epistles, no just cause of doubting. 5ly, The Catholique Epistles of James, Peter, John and Jude; these 4 were of the number of the 12 apostles, and so their presence, near relacion and attendance upon their Master may free them from being ignorant of those things they delivered concerning him in their writeings.

Lastly, for the book of Revelation, in which many things which concern the church of Christ are darkly shadowed out, and

---

181 Cp. with Luke 1.3. Grotius follows the same argument. "Thus it being plaine that the *bookes* of *new covenant* written by those *authors*, whose names they beare or by such as beare witnesse of themselves; if we adde further that they *knew* well the *matters* whereof they wrote to be *true*, and had no purpose to lye or dissemble, it will follow that the *things* which they comitted to writing were both *certaine* and *true*, because every untruth proceeds either from *ignorance*, or from a *wicked desire* to deceive. As touching *Matthew*, *John*, *Peter* and *Jude*, they were all of the *society* and *fellowship* of those *twelve* whom *Jesus* did chuse to bee *witnesses* of his *life* and *doctrine*, so they could not be *ignorant* of those things which they did relate." Ibid., pp. 161- 2.

obscurely foretold; the Truth of that Vision i.e. that it was such a vision, and what manner of Vision 'twas he knows best that wrote it, who affirmes that he wrote nothing but what he saw and what was revealed unto him.

So from this Induction of all the writers of the N[ew] T[estament] we may infer their knowledg of those things they did deliver. And we cannot distrust the Aut[h]oritie of the scriptures by reason that the Penmen of them were not sufficiently informed of the truth of those things they have delivered to posterity. Nor

2ly, may we imagine that to gull the world, they would purposely write those things for truth, which they knew to be false. For 1. we must grant them to be Christians and the Principles and Precepts of that religion forbid all lying, especially in such a busines as concernes the Eternall salvacion of mankind. 2ly, How do these scriptures labour and travail with the promoteing of pietie in the world? how unblameable the writers in their lives and conversacions? so that the worst of their enimies could not accuse them of any notorious crimes; all they layd to their charge was their rudenes and simplicitie, which is not apt to be the mother of falshood; I say these consideracions may move us to have a better opinion of them, then that they would deliberately and advisedly deliver untruthes. But

3ly, what glory, what profit what delight and content could they reap from being so unfaithfull, from useing their endeavours to deceive others, and leading them into such a path as leades to destruction? Did this tend to the preservacion of their Persons, to the safety or encrease of their Estates, to the gainning them any credit or reputacion in the world? No, by this they were accounted ὡς περιψημα, rubbish and offscouring of all things, by this profession they were exposed to all dangers and difficulties, divested of all livelihoods and other subsistances, they were forced to forsake all that was near or dear unto them. Now 'tis not to be conceived that any should be so base and lye *gratis*,[182] *si violandum est jus*,[183] if men do recede from their principles, and act or speak anything which is contrary to their knowledg, 'tis questionles for some

182 i.e. for nothing.

183 Translated it means "if the law is violated."

great gaine or conveniency, not for that which will endanger their present quietnes and future felicitie?

Now from what hath been said we may infer 1. that the Penmen of the h[oly] script[ures] were not ignorant of the truth of what they writt. And 2ly, That we have no just cause to suspect, that they writ that which they knew to be apparently false. Nay if they had been given to love and make a lye,[184] to be false witnesses, they would not have layd open, and proclaimed to the world their own faults and infirmities, as that they all forsook their saviour when going to his Passion, and how that Peter not only denyed but forsweare him. So for a man to come to this, that he will not conceal his own faults, that he will not forbear to speak against his own country and countrymen, yea against himself, this is against the nature of man, and cannot be wrought in him, but by a supernatural cause; for 'tis natural to every man, so far as he can, to cover his own faults, and the faults of his country and friends.[185] This we see holy men in scripture did not. Moses, when no necessity forced him to it, confessed that he came of a cursed stock; spared not his brother Aaron's fault, but committed it to writeing, spared not his sister Miriam in the cause of murmuring; no not his own fault in murmuring against the Lord at the waters of strife, Numb: 11.11; dispossessed his own children, and would not have them to succeed him in the Magistracy, but preferred Joshuah.[186]

---

184 Cp. with Rev. 22.15.

185 Grotius writers similarly. The writers "had no *will* or *desire* to tell an untruth. … For if any doe object and say that they spake for their owne advantage, upon enquiry it will appeare that they sought after no such by-end, having neither hope of getting *commodity*, or of eschewing any *danger*, but rather by their *profession* they were more likely to lose all their *commodities* and be liable to all sorts of *perils*. If they aimed any advantage, it was onely to gaine *honour* unto God, which doubtlesse cannot be compatible with *lying* and *dissembling*, specially in such a businesse as whereon depends the everlasting *salvation of mankind*: Farre be it then from any man to thinke they were guilty of so great *impiety*, their *doctrine* being full of *all sanctity*, and their *life* exemplary for *innocency* and *integrity*, free from the *accusation* of their greatest adversaries; who onely condemned them for lacke of *knowledge*, a fault unlikely to be the *mother* of falshood. No, if they had been guilty of never so little fraud or deceit in that kind, surely they would not have recorded to posterity their owne *trespasses*, as namely, their forsaking of Christ when he was in danger, and *Peters deniall* of him." *True Religion*, pp. 164-5.

186 Identical with M.L.E., p. 58. Cp. also with P.C.D. p. 51, and Preface to Genesis

And thus much breifly for the sacred Aut[h]ority of the h[oly] script[ures], confirmed by the Antiquity of them and universall tradicion, how they were the most ancient of all writeings, and how God was pleased to convey them to posterity by such persons as did deny themselves and all worldly concerns, that so they might the better propagate these sacred truthes to succeeding generacions; And now how thankfull ought we to be unto our most good and gracious God, that he hath not left us in the dark to worship sticks and stones, the sunne, moone and starrs and all the host of heaven, as many poore pagans doe to this day; but that he hath revealed himselfe and his blessed will unto us in the scriptures, which may serv as a lamp unto our feet, and a light unto our pathes, to guide and conduct us through all the dark mazes and meanders of this world, to that glorious and eternall kingdome of light in the world to come.

lecture, *Apos. Sacra*, p. 660. In *True Religion*, in regards to Moses, the translation of Grotius reads "forasmuch as himselfe reveals his owne fault and delinquencies, which hee might have concealed … By all which it appears, that there was no cause in him why hee should forge untruths." p. 43.

LECTURE THREE

OF THE AUT[H]ORITIE OF THE SCRIPTURES - PT. 2

Introduction

In this lecture Andrewes was concerned with the "antiquity" and "authenticity" of the Scriptures. As already intimated he held the Pentateuch to be older than the books attributed to Homer. Scriptures' antiquity was a crucial test of its authenticity as the older it was, the more reason to believe its contents. Another test for its authenticity was that Scripture has not perished; neither had it been corrupted nor altered as verified by writers shortly after the time of Our Lord, and even down to the time of Jerome and Augustine. It had also withstood the ridicule of atheists.[187]

Perhaps its authenticity, Andrewes posed, could be disputed on the grounds that not all the authors of the books of the Bible were known; such as the author of the letter to the Hebrews; or because there were discrepancies amongst the writers of the New Testament. Yet he felt that these discrepancies supported rather than detracted from its authenticity.

He also suggested that as the spiritual and moral precepts in the Bible were far superior to any of the ancient oracles, these too enhanced both its authenticity and authority. Another assurance of its authenticity was the conversion of so many people after Christ's ascension, of whom many signed "their belief with their own blood". Furthermore the precepts of the New Testament had become the foundation for civil order as they instructed men

---

187 Ms. 3707, pp. 32, 35.

in how to live in harmony and peace. He concluded that if we believe that the Scriptures contain God's word and precepts we should live by them as they lead to a life of holiness, purity, joy, peace and love, and of striving to overcome all the temptations of Satan. On the other hand to reject scriptural precepts sets one on the path to hell.[188]

> 2Tim 3.16-17.
> *All scripture is given by inspiracion of God and is profitable for doctrine, for reproof, [for correction, for instruction in righteousness: that the man of God be perfect, thoroughly furnished unto all good works].*

The course of Religion which we are to treat of, is compared to a Building, Math: 7.24 the teachers of it to Builders, 1Cor 3.10, the Principles of Religion to a foundacion, Heb. 6.1. Now the foundacion upon which we build the fabrick of Christian Religion and the Bookes which containe the truth of it, are the h[oly] scriptures. And therefore as in a building, that it may be firm and durable; so here that our knowledge may be well bottomed, we are to see in the first place, that the foundacion be layd deep that it is sure and firm.[189]

I have formerly observ'd to you out of this Text these 3 conclusions.

1. Concerning the Aut[h]ority of Scriptures, that all scripture [is given by inspiration of God].

2. Concerning the sufficiency of the scriptures, that they are able to make [the man of God perfect, thoroughly furnished unto all good workes].

3. Concerning the Usefulness of the Scriptures, that they are profitable for doctrine [for reproof, for correction, for instruction in righteousness].

For the 1st of these the Aut[h]ority. I put the Question thus; By what meanes are we taught the truth of this that all Scripture [is given by inspiration of God]? To which I answered, 1. Negatively, That no scripture can teach us divine Aut[h]oritie of the scrip-

---

188 Ibid., pp. 38-9.

189 Similar to P.C.D., p. 13 and M.L.E., p. 14.

tures, bec[ause] the Principles in every Science, are either taken as plain and evident in themselves; or as proved and graunted already, some former knoweledg haveing made them evident.

2ly, Affirmatively, that one meanes to know this truth is the Antiquitie of the scriptures; as namely that the Bookes of Moses[190] which comprise in them the summe and substance of Christian Religion, lye nearer the foundacion of the world, by many yeares, then any other writeings whatsoever. For that part of the heathen Religion which is <u>fabulous</u>, it began but with their Gods and their gods (as Orpheus and Homer that write upon them) began but the age before the Trojan war; for Hercules, Æenæas and the rest of their children lived at that war which war was 3030 years after the c[h]ronologie of the Bible. And bet[ween] Orpheus his write-ings, which was their ancientest Poet, and Moses[191] that man of God, are at least 800 yeares, if we beleeve Strabo[192]and Plutarch.[193] This for the Antiquitie of that parte of their Religion which was fabulous. Next for that parte which has any savour of truth in it, the ancientest Records of their Truth, come from the 7 wise men, of whom Solon is the cheif and ancientest; he lived in Croesus's time,[194] Croesus with Cyrus;[195] Cyrus and Esdras were contem-poraries; and Esdras is the last of the Canons of the Old Testa-ment, so that the whole old Testament was before any writer, any Recorder of the true parte of the Heathen stories. And by conse-quence, 'tis not the invention of man but the true word of God. For *quod primum verum* what is the 1st, the most ancient, is true; Bec[ause] as Truth is an affection of that which <u>is</u>: so falshood is an affection of that which <u>is</u> <u>not</u>: and therefore cannot consist in itself

---

190 Grotius argued similarly on "the undoubted *antiquity* of the books of *Moses*". *True Religion* p. 43.

191 The translation of Grotius' *True Religion* states, "Adde hereunto the undoubted *antiquity* of the books of *Moses* to which no other writers are therein comparable." He is "older than all other authors such as Homer, Orpheus." pp. 44, 45 - 47.

192 A Greek historian and geographer who lived 64 B.C – A.D. 19? He is the author of *Geographia*.

193 A Greek historian, philosopher and biographer. He lived A.D. 46 -126.

194 King of Lydia in the sixth century.

195 A great Persian king, founder of the Achaemenid dynasty and empire (599 -529 B.C.).

but in another; and so falshood must needs be after Truth.[196] And because 'tmay be objected, will the Antiquitie of the script[ures] prove their descent and originall from God? To this I answer'd.[197]

1. That the longer any scriptures have been in the world, the longer they have been upon triall; the world hath had more time and meanes to enquire into the truth or falshood of them. And 2ly, haveing passed through the hands of so many generacions and the Professors thereof haveing suffered so much sorrow and shame and miserie even for their Profession, 'tis not easily possible, but that some of those generacions, would thorowly have examined the truth of those scriptures and of that Religion they professed, to have known whether it were such a one as worth the suffering for, or no; and so have rejected it, if unsound.

2ly, It being granted that there were such writers as Moses and the Prophets, and that some of their writeings which contain the summe and substance of all the rest were the ancientest in the world, yet how shall we know, that they were faithfull witnesses and not such whose knowledg and faithfullnes we may justly suspect?

To this I answered, that if they did fail, 'twas either 1st through ignorance, that they had not perfect knowl[edge] of those things they delivered, or 2ly through Malice, that they did not faithfully deliver things according to their knowl[edge]. But that they failed us neither of these wayes. I then made manifest.

Dub[itatio]. I Proceed now to the 3rd demand which may be made concerning the Penmen of the h[oly] scriptures. As whether those very men whose names we read in the running Titles, and are mentioned in the Proemiums of the Bookes of the holy

---

196 This paragraph is an abridged copy of text in M.L.E., pp. 52 - 3. In this edition after "but with their Gods" is added "for further then their gods they cannot goe." After "Plutarch" is added "and Siculus. If their fabulous part commeth so short of our religion, then must the true part come farre short. Varro saith, that that truth which the Gentiles hold could not be much ancienter then 700 yeares before his time." After "the heathen stories" is added, "Their anceintest Histiographer is *Herodotus*; yet he presently after the beginning of his booke, entreth into the History of *Croesus*: By which we plainely see that the Christian religion is far more ancient than the Heathen." Refer also to P.C.D., pp. 47 - 8.

197 This paragraph is a repetition of the same argument in the previous lecture.

scriptures, were the very writers of them or no? For untill this be known, how can I firmly beleeve either the Doctrine or the History of the Scriptures?

Sol[utio]. I answer. This Argument supposeth 2 things as granted, both which are false and untrue. 1. That we have no certain knowl[edge] of the writers of the h[oly] Scriptures, who were the men. 2. That without such knowl[edge] we have nothing to ground our faith upon either in poynt of Doctrine or History. Both which are untrue. For

1. We may have as certain knowl[edge] who were the writers of the Bookes of the N[ew] T[estament] as who were the Authors of those Bookes we call Homer's *Iliad's*, and Virgill's *Ænæds* [*Aeneid*]. For if the Authors of Bookes of an ancienter standing may be known and beleeved in the world, why not those of a later date? There are scarce any who deny or doubt that Homer, his *Iliads* and Horace, his *Odes*, bec[ause] 'tis the voyce of the world, the generall consent of men will have it so; Now for the Authors of any writeings whatsoever, we have not such a crowd of witnesses, so many and larg testimonyes, and of such men, as in their Ages were reputed sober and prudent, as for the Penmen of the h[oly] scriptures, especeially of the N[ew] T[estament]. I add also, that those men were at odds and differed among themselves about many poynts of Religion, yet this Truth gained the universall consent of all, that the Bookes of the h[oly] scriptures were the writeings of those men whose names and superscriptions they bear. But

It may be replyed, what shall we say of such bookes, whose Authors are not yet known, not yet determined and agreed upon who were the Penmen of them; as the Epistle to the Heb[rews] and whether St. Paul, or Luke, or Barnabas, or Apollo[s] or any others were the Author of it?

To this I answer. That tho' the name of the Author of any writeing be not undoubtedly known, yet is not this of force to derogate from the Authoritie of the writeing, it ought not be accounted lesse worthy of our beleefe, either in matter of History or Doctrine, then if the Author were perfectly known, especially when 'tis manifest, that the same writeing is accounted true and orthodox, by those who best know whether it was true or false. And this is the case of the Epistle to the Hebrewes; in the primitive times when many were alive who had familiaritie with the

Apostles, that Epistle was generally approved of by all Christians; and that 'twas so anciently approved, amongst other Arguments this may be one, That the most ancient Syriack copie of the N[ew] T[estament] hath this Epistle in it. Eus[ebius] l.3. c.3, l.6. c.25.

And the same may be said of the Book of Revelacion. Some doubting and controversie there was about the Author of it, but not about the Truth and Aut[h]oritie; Justin Martyr, who lived almost about that time, 'twas writ, saith 'twas the work of John the Apostle and Evangelist; as Eus[ebius] 4. l.18c. and lib. 5.c.8. But suppose all this: 1. That the script[ures] are the ancientest of all writeings, 2ly, That the Penmen were the faithfullest of all writers. 3. That those very men whose names we read in the runing Titles, were the Authors of those writeings;[198]

Dub[itatio] 4. Yet 4ly, Those writeings passing through the hands of so many generacions, how can we know that they are pure and incorrupted, not falsified and depraved, either by the ignorance or malice of men? To which I answer

That there are but 3 wayes by which any writeings can be corrupted or perish.1. By an utter losse or perishing of the whole of every parte and parcell of the writeing, when no fragment, no broken piece is left remaining; and so our eyes and hands, and eares are witnesses, that they are not corrupted; they may be heard and seen and handled. 2. By the losse only of some parte, when some more considerable things, at first contained in them, are wholly lost or perished from the world. 3ly. Next way by which any writeings may be corrupted, is when the sense is altered, so that which was formerly clear is now obscured, if not quite altered, by falsificacions, substractions, addicions, and alteracions in one kind or another. Now that the scriptures are corrupted neither of these 2 later wayes, we say:

1. With some of the Ancients as Origen and Austin, and the greater parte of the learned modern writers; That no Book or peice of writing that was ever truly Canonicall, i.e. that did belong either to the old or new Testament is lost or perished, but the Bookes as well of the old as of the New and again, as well of the

198 Grotius's argument on authorship follows Andrewes' argument. *True Religion*, pp. 158 – 168.

new as of the old Testament are as whole and compleat as ever. The Reasons may be these.

1. if any Booke or parcell of the h[oly] scriptures, which was commended to the church of God, for a Rule of faith or manners be lost and wanting, it must argue the whole church guilty of such carelessnes and negligence as cannot easily be granted. Tis true, some particular churches and some single Persons have rejected some partes of the scriptures now generally acknowledged for Canonicall, but the whole church never did it.

2ly, for the Bookes of the old Testament against the entirenes whereof the Argument may seem to lye the strongest; as that the 3,000 Parables of Solomon, the 1000 and 500 hundred songs spoken of 1K: 4.32.[199] The Book of Nathan the Prophet and Gad the Seer, 1Chron. 29.29; and againe the visions of Iddo and Addo the seer, mentioned in 2Chron. 9.29, that these are wholly lost and past recovery. To which I answer That those writeings which are mentioned, and now wanting *spectabant ad ubertatem historiæ, non ad fundamentum fidei;* they concerned rather the compleating the History than perfecting the Doctrine or Canon of the Scriptures. For

1. If we consider the great zeal which the Jewish nacion always have had, and do still at this day bear to the writeings of Moses and their Prophets and other writeings which they counted sacred; there is very little ground to imagine, that they have suffered any of them to be lost. If we will beleeve Philo the Jew, they were so zealous in preserving the line of their scriptures, that they could tell precisely, not only how many letters were in their whole Bible, but how many in every Book of their Bible, and how often every letter in the Alphabet was used in every Book; and they would suffer any Death, rather than suffer that to be changed in the lest jot.[200]

2. They thought to have Eternall life in the scriptures. Joh. 5.39, Search [the scriptures; for in them ye think ye have eternal life: and they are they which testify of me]. And if they hoped to be

199 In the Authorized Version this is "a thousand and five".

200 Grotius also related how the Jews "have so religiously and exactly described and compared their Scriptures] that they know how often any one letter is found therein." *True Religion*, p. 199.

Eternally blessed and made happy by them, it is not probable, nor can reasonably be imagined, but that they should be exceedingly zealous and resolved, even unto Death to maintain that truth and puritie of them. Nor

3ly. Doe we read in the N[ew] T[estament] that either our Saviour Christ, or his Apostles who used frequently to reprove the Jewes, and to tell them soundly of the sinnes of their forefathers, yet when they had to do with the Scribes, Pharisees, Sadducies and expounders of the Law, we doe not read that they charged them with any such sinne, as either the defalcacion or dismembring of the scriptures, or the suffering any parte or parcell of them to perish; which (doubtlesse) had been such a sin as our saviour and his Apostles would not have kept silence at, but would have reproved them for it, had they been guilty of it. They were charged with transgressing the commandments of God by their Tradicion; and that they were the children of those who slew the Prophets, but not the children of those who slew the prophesies thems[elves], or with abolishing the letter or writeing of any jot, or tittle of the law.[201] So doubtlesse there is nothing of the scriptures of the old T[estament] that hath miscarried. Now

In the next place, that not any parte of the h[oly] scriptures was wanting in the Apostle St. Paules days, this Text doth witnesse. All Script[ure is given by inspiration by God] So that if we shall suppose, that any of the script[ures] were wanting, when the Apostle gave this Testimony of them; we must suppose withall, that those which were wanting, were little lesse then superfluous, at least in respect of those ends and purposes for which they were given, which to conceive of the Oracles of God, is little lesse then blasphemie. But more of this when we come to speak of the Sufficiency of the scriptures. Now

3ly, The next way by which any writeings may be corrupted is, when the sense is altered and perverted; whereby, the true genuine sense is impaired and cast out, and a sense that is spurious and unsound brought in: but by the good providence of God the Scriptures have been kept from this kind of perishing, from being thus corrupted and depraved.[202] For

---

201 Cp. with Math: 5. 17-8.

202 Tertullian, from whom Andrewes quoted earlier, stated that "It is as incredible to every man of sense that we should seem to have introduced any corrupt text into the Scriptures, existing, as we have been, from the very first, and being the first, as it is that

1. In our saviour's dayes (as I said before) we may conclude that no violence had been offered to the scriptures in falsifying the lettere of them; for if any thing in this kind had befallen them, doubtlesse our saviour who found so many corruptions amongst the Jewes, and so often remembred them of the sinnes of their forefathers, would not have gratifyed such a sin as this (forgery in the Records of Heaven) with silence, if they had been guilty of it.

2ly. Since the times of our saviour and his Apostles, there is little ground of fear, they should be corrupted.[203] For 1st for the space of 400 years after Christ, till the times of Jerom[e] and Austin, that the scriptures had not suffered in that kind, we may receive satisfaction from their Testimonies.[204] Hierom upon the 6th of Isaiah, taketh occasion to observ, how that many Testimonies alledged by our saviour and his Apostles, were found in the old Testament without any variacion or change. And Aug[ustine] 15 l. de Civ[itate] Dei. 13.c. Argues thus. 'Tis not to be beleeved that the Nacion of the Jewes, so far scattered and dispursed, should conspire together in the same designe of writeing a falshood: or that envying the Aut[h]oritie of the scriptures to thems[elves] and others, they should deprive themselves and their Posteritie, of the truth of them. And the same Reason holds good ag[ainst] those who object, either that the scriptures of the old T[estament] are falsifyed by the Jewes, or the script[ures] of the N[ew] T[estament] by the Grecians. For when the profession of Christianity was once scattered far and near, up and down the world, and the copies of the N[ew] T[estament] dispersed ac-

---

they have not in fact introduced it who are both later in date and opposed (to the Scriptures). Tertullian, *De Præscriptione Hæreticorum*.Ch. 38. The M.L.E. stated that "No Prophet that have beene since *Moses*, hath at any time gone about to correct *Moses*, or to correct any thing that he hath, *or* to put in; but hath yeilded to that as true, and sought more to confirme it." p. 56.

203 Grotius' argument is different. He suggested, "Now that all the *copies* of these *bookes* were corrupted by guilt or otherwise, either in points of doctrine or matter of *history* it will never be proved, there being no *evidence* or *testimonies* of former times ever to evince the same." True Religion, p. 188.

204 Cp. with Grotius, "We say then that those bookes which are not in question amongst *Christians*, but have certaine *titles*, are the very *workes* of those authors whose names they beare to wit because those *primitive* Fathers, Iustin, Iraneaus, Clemens *and others doe commend those* bookes under the same *Authors names, as also, because* Tertullian *witnesseth that there were Originall* copies of those *bookes* extant in his time." Ibid., p. 156.

cordingly, (I will not say altogether) but 'tis next to an impossibilitie that there should be an universall consent of all Christians that had copies of the scriptures, to agree together to have them all falsifyed, and that alike in the same places, and with the same falsifycacions. And except this be supposed, the conclusion holds good. That God, by a great and gracious hand of Providence, hath so protecteth the scriptures, that no jot or tittle of the native sense is perished, but in some transcript or other may be found. But

In the next place, what shall we say to the diverse readings of the script[ures], may we not thence infer, that in many places they are corrupted, the true and genuine sense perverted and depraved? To this I answer.

1. That from varietie and difference of readings which is found in some words between one copy and another, may follow, That the h[oly] God [i.e. Ghost] did not guide all the Pens of the Transcribers of the scriptures, with the same heavenly infallibleness, with which he guided the tongues and Pens of his immediat secretaries. Yet

2ly. The difference and variety of Readings doth not hinder, but that the true and clear sense of those places may be attained by the consulting with other expositors upon the places. For what by the help of other copies, where there is no such mistake; what by the series and carriage of the context, either before or after the place; and what by the diligent pondering, and compareing other scriptures with it; the dead may be raised to life, i.e. the sense of this script[ure] which was lost one way, may be restored and saved by another. And so

3ly, I say the varitie of readings doth rather argue the care of preserving the scriptures, then the study of corrupting them; for amongst the ancient writeings, that is least depraved, of which in many places are diverse readings; out of which diversitie a prudent Reader, by the use of reason and compareing of parallel places, many with little difficultie find out that which is true. But here again, 'tmay be demanded, when copies, or readings differ, how do I know which is the genuine and true, and which is the false?

1. If the difference be materiall and weighty, the truth between them is so much, the more easy to be found. The greater and more weighty any truth is, the more intelligiblenes it hath in it; and for

the same reason, the greater or broader our errour is, it is so much the more readily discovered.[205]

2. If the difference be light and less considerable, tho' it may be so much the greater difficultie, to know on which hand the truth lyeth; yet it is so much the more likely that there is no simple or direct errour asserted on either hand; but only that there is an uncertainty of the true sense and meaning of the holy Ghost in that particular place.

Now in case God preserv all and every particular truthes contained in the script[ures], that none of these be lost; tho' true exposicions and meanings of particular places should fail us not easily understood, yet God may be said to preserv the scriptures pure and uncorrupted.

Lastly, what shall we say of those repugnances and seeming contradictions in the scriptures; as that which in one place, they affirm, in another they were to deny; and this not only to be found amongst diverse Authors of the old and N[ew] T[estaments] but in the same. As St. Luke writeing the history of St. Paul's Conversion, saith Act 9.7 those that were with him, heard the voyce, but saw no man; and Act 22.9 the Text saith, they heard not the voyce of him that spake unto him. Now doth not one of these places seem to contradict the other? which cannot be incident to such writeings as are true and of divine Aut[h]oritie, for truth like the Author of it, is every where one and the same.

To this I answer, 1. in generall, that if with discretion and without prejudice we read and judge of those Bookes, we shall find, that in matters of moment either for Doctrine or Historie, there is such an harmonie and consent, as is not be found amongst the writers of any one sect whatsoever, whether Jewes or Grecians, Philosophers, Physicians, Lawyers, we may find these of the same sect, not only disagreeing one from another, but oftimes differing from thems[elves], denying what formerly they affirmed. But the

---

205 Cp. with "Withal, to reform our judgments in this point. For a false conceit is crept into the minds of men, to think points of religion that be manifest to be certain petty points scarce worth the hearing. Those - yea those be great, and none but those, that have great disputes about them. It is not so; Τὰ μεὺ ἀναγκαῖα &c. Those that are necessary He hath made plain: those that [are] not plain, not necessary." In 1607 Christmas Day Sermon. Andrewes, Vol. 1, p. 35.

Penmen of the h[oly] script[ures], injoyn the same things to be beleeved, the same dutyes to be practised; concerning the life and death and Resurrection of our saviour, they are all one and the same; or if they seem to differ, 'tis but about some circumstances of times and places, or the names of particular places, which by the help of reason and the knowledg of the customes and condicions of those times and places may be easily reconciled. I add that differences in matters of lesse moment do rather confirm then derogate from the Aut[h]oritie of the scriptures; for this frees the writers from all suspicion of fraud and deceipt, that they did not consent and combine together to write untruthes, as they use to do, who on purpose to gull the world, so compact their lyes, that there shall appear no shew of difference. But if for some small difference, which cannot easily be reconciled, we will not beleeve the scriptures, by the same reason, we should beleeve no historian whatsoever; for their same irreconcileable differences may be found, which notwithstanding do not destroy the Aut[h]ority of them.[206] But

2. To that place in particular, they did hear and they did not hear, the voyce of him that spake unto him; the difference may be solved with this distinction. To hear, is sometimes taken only to hear the sound of him that speaketh; and sometimes to understand the words of him that speaketh; as may be easily gathered by compareing those places together Gen. 42. 23, 2K: 18.26, 1Cor.

---

206 Grotius wrote similiarly. "Some doe further object that in these *bookes* there is some diversity *of senses* and interpretations. But for an anwser whosoever will but duly ponder this matter he shall finde the same to be another *argument* besides the formere to justifie the *authority* of the said *bookes*, namely because they doe most manifestly and apparently *agree* about such things as concerne any point of *doctrine* or *history*: Which *consent* and accord cannot else-where bee found among any other *writers* that are of one and same *sect* or *profession*, whether wee consider the *Jewes* or the *Greeke Philosophes*, the Physitians or the *Roman Lawyers*. All which doe not only differ much amongst themselves, yea even that are of the *same* sect as *Plato* and *Xenophon*; but oftentimes one shall find the same *writer* to affirme now one then another, as if he were *forgetful* of himself. ... But these ... holy *penmen*, of whom we speake, doe inculcate and expresse the same point of *faith; they deliver the same* commandments; *and* as for their *narration* of the life, and death and resurrection of Christ, the Summe and *substance* in them all is the very same. Therefore if were *unequall* that sacred *writers* should lose their *credit* for one or two semming slips." *True* Religion, pp. 182-4. Cp. with M.L.E., p. 56.

14.2. So the sense will be, St. Paules companions in travell did hear the sound, but did not hear the voyce, i.e. did not understand the words of him that spake unto them. So neither the variety of Readings nor the repugnances and seeming contradictions that are to be found in the script[ures] may any way prejudice or impair the Aut[h]ority of the script[ures].

But now further, to conspire the Aut[h]ority of the script[ures], and the truth of the Christian Religion grounded upon the Scriptures. Consider

1. The holy precepts therein contained 2. The Larg and gracious promises 3. The wayes by which both were delivered and confirmed, signes and miracles. 4. Persons, that were the first planters of it. 5. The Proceedings of this Religion in the world, and the strange successe that hath attended it. For the 1. The scriptures every where presse and perswade unto holinesse, bend themselves every way that lightly can be thought of, to commend the exercise of holinesse unto men; to interesse[207] their hearts and affections in the love, desire and study of it. Yea the scriptures are so impatient of being denied what they call for in this poynt of holinesse, that they threaten the losse of the sight and favour of God, and therein of all joy and peace and comfort forever, and consequently the vengeance of eternall fire to all those that are prophane and unholy. Hebrews 12.14 follow peace [with all men, and holiness without which no man shall see the Lord]. If we take a survey of all the precepts contained in these holy bookes, we shall find that not any Religion hath such holy Lawes, prescribes such Rules for innocency, uprightness, and intregitie of life and conversacion as the Christian; and therefore such holy Precepts must needs have their being from the holy God; for they are in no wise agreeable to flesh and blood. Reveng is forbidden; we must love our Enimies. And Lust, not look upon a woman to lust after her and Covetousnes, we must be ready to Parte with all; and for Truth, we must confesse and professe it, when we are called to give an account of our faith.[208]

---

207 Old spelling for *interest*.

208 This is expanded in M.L.E. "The Commandments and precepts in no wise agreeable to flesh and blood. For revenge: we must love them; *Love them that hate us, speake good of them that persecute us. Happy shall you be when men revile you and persecute you*: For

2. For the Promises, no higher, nor no more heavenly promises can be imagined than those God hath promised to such as fear and obey him. Godlinesse hath the promise both of - - - and in respect of the clearnes of those promises, the Christian Religion goes before that of the Jewes. And again those promises are not grosse and earthly but spirituall as here Redemption, Adoption, Sanctificacion and hereafter an heavenly Inheritance, unspeakable happinesse, which our leader Christ Jesus doth now fully enjoy; and which he hath promised to all his followers.

3ly, For the manner of giveing these precepts and makeing these Promises, 'twas extraordinary and from Heaven. For the Heavens opened, thence the h[oly] Spirit descended and out of the clouds a voyce was delivered to him that was the first Author of them, and all this to confirm their Originall from Heaven. And what can be imagined above this? For if all the wayes that God can use, be not able to give assurance that 'tis God that speakes, what are we better for knowing that God cannot lye, so long as there is supposed for us no way to know what at any time he speakes; Nay (as to this particular) to what use is his Omnipotency, if he cannot reveal hims[elf] to us in such a way, as may be reasonable for us to beleev, that 'tis he that speaketh, and not some Deceiver? But further, we may hear the Divells acknowledg him God, and proclaiming him their enimy. And tho' they may be thought to doe this for some greater advantage (as the Devill may suffer one charm to counterwork another) yet if Satan be divided [against himself; how shall then his kingdom stand? Math.12.26], and 'tis not probable they should use their endeavours to raise Christ to that power of destroying them. Indeed the whole Doctrine of our Saviour Christ was so directly contrary to that which had been maintained by the Oracles, that it cannot be imagined to proceed from that Principle. And the story is approved by Plutarch, who tells us of one Epitherses, in great credit with the Emperour, who sailing by Cyclades, heard a great bellowing and roaring as of infernall mourners, and a voyce was heard out of one of the Islands,

---

lust: we may not looke after a woman with our own eye, to lust after her. For covetousnesse: we must be ready to Parte with all. For truth: we must not onely confesse, and also professe it, when any one asketh of our faith: here is no plausiblenesse in the world. p. 63.

that great Pan was dead.[209] The Emperour hearing of this, called together all the wisemen and magitians, but none could tell what this great God Pan should mean. Nicephorus[210] saith that the Emperours from Augustus to Adrian, did not only enquire the cause of this defect, but also caused the wisemen to raise up the spirits thems[elves]. And one asking the Oracle at Delos, why 'twas put to silence, answer was made bec[ause] of *παῖς ἑβραῖος*.[211] From that time all Oracles ceased, i.e. the Divells speaking in them were put to silence.[212] And after this the gift of tongues, the power of miracles, and descents of the h[oly] Ghost did attend those who were the first Preachers and publishers of Christianity. This for the manners of it's delivery.

4ly, For the Persons who did deliver these truthes, they were *oculati testes*,[213] what they heard and saw and handled, that they delivered; they had the favour of seeing him after his Resurrection, and of using all meanes of screeneing themselves and the truth and realitie of it. Being thus assured they make it their whole businesse to communicate it to others. And in propagateing this Doctrine, as they used no strength nor force, (by which other Religions have been propagated) so they never endeavoured to disturb states or Governments, but contended only with their prayers to God, that they might live quietly and peaceably under

---

209 Plutarch related how Epitherses told of a voyage when the wind dropped and the ship drifted near the Echinades Islands, from the island of Paxi was heard this mysterious voice calling loudly to Thamus. Three times it called before a response. Then the voice announced, "when you come opposite to Palodes, announce that Great Pan is dead." Hence when Thamus came opposite the island he shouted, "that Great Pan is dead." After this great lamentations were made by all who heard it. Such a stir it caused that it reached the ears of Tiberius Caesar who made an investigation into it. This quote of Plutarch has sometimes been linked with the rise of Christianity when this mysterious voice announced the death of the "Great Pan". Plutarch, 'The Obsolescence of Oracles', Ch. 7, l. 419. Pan, half man and half goat whose original home was Arcadia, is the god of shepherds who offer kids goats or sheep in his honour.

210 Nicephorus Callistus, an early fourteenth century Byzantine historian, and author of *Church History*.

211 It means "a Hebrew Child", that is, Jesus Christ.

212 This same story appears in M.L.E., p. 62. It also listed those oracles that ceased. "Trophonius his cave, the Oracle there, the Oracle *Delos Jupiter*; and *Jupiter Dodonæus*.

213 It means "eye witnesses".

them. And which is a great Argument of the truth of the doctrine they delivered; they had no designe of any temporall advantages to themselves but suffered reproaches, torments, death it self, and so parted with the capacity of all temporall advantages. Now if these had not been reall Truthes, which they delivered, and if it had not been for the expectation of future blisse, they had been of all men the most miserable.

Lastly, the Proceedings of Religion in the world, and the strong successe that hath attended the Gospell, where ever it came, not withstanding the many and great disadvantages, which it was to encounter and overcome, are little lesse than a Demonstracion of the truth of it. The Instruments to propagate it were very unfit, men of no power, and of no learning, the matter to work upon, altogether unprepared, Jewes and Gentiles in deadly hatred against them.[214] For afflictions the 10 strongest and bloodiest persecutions against them, great and huge heapes of Christians, suffering everywhere, and every day for their faith. Now that from such small beginnings and mean instruments, without any kind of earthly Aut[h]oritie to back it, without any sword drawn in defence of it, that Christianitie should so soon obtain such a victorie over the hearts of men, in so great a parte of the world; it can be nothing but the truth that had this force to conquer and subdue the hearts and lives of men unto it; that such sholes,[215] such multitudes of men, and many of them the most knowing, learned men of all Nacions, should beleeve and signe their belief with their own blood.

What more shall we say for confirmacion of this poynt but that not to beleeve, that the scriptures were given by inspiracion of God, when by unsuspected witnesses, upon certain knowl[edge] they are sufficiently testifyed to be so, is very irrationall. To say, let God speak now from Heaven as he did, and work such miracles as He did, and then we will beleeve, this were for God to multi-

214 This sentence appears in a fuller form in M.L.E. "For the instruments, they cannot be devised more unfit, of nobility, of no power, of no learning, etc. but barbarous, rude, handicrafts men: for the matter to worke upon them, they had it alltogether unprepared; nay cleane against them. They had the Jewes in hatred against them; in as deadly hatred, as possibly could be. The heathen also at the first continued this hatred against them; after were converted by them; but afterwards returned to their former hatred." M.L.E., p. 62.

215 Old spelling of shoal, meaning a throng or crowd.

ply Prodigies improperly, unseasonably, unnecessarily, and to all that are not now present, these things would be as questionable as the former. For suppose at this present hour, we should hear a voyce from heaven, and see some such signes and wonders as have been done; what way is there to convince the Ages to come of the truth of these, but by the constant affirmacion of those who are now ear and eye witnesses of it? I say, beyond such testimony, there is no rationall evidence imaginable for those that lived not in this Age, but they might be forced to make use of their faith and beleeving. To conclude

Give me leave to make the same demand that St. Paul to Agrippa, Beleevest [thou the prophets? Acts. 26. 27], that they were given by [them], then read, hear and handle them as the word of the Eternall God. Have so many h[oly] men suffered so much shame and reproach and blood and death for bearing testimony to the truth of those scriptures? And shall any Christian set so lightly by them as to read a peice of Livy[216] or Sal[l]ust,[217] a play or Romance with more attention and delight then these h[oly] Bookes of God? how shall we escape, if we neglect and set at naught so great salvacion as is contained in them?

Againe, if we beleeve the scriptures, then we ought to practise the Dutyes and live according to the Rules and directions in the scriptures. For to acknowledg that the scriptures were given by inspiracion of God, and consequently that without sincere obedience to all the righteous precepts thereof, not only the infinite rewards of the Gospell are forteited, but the infinite torments of Hell are purchased; and yet to live lives of profanenes, luxury and debauchery, to pamper and cocker up our genuisses, to indulge to ourselves any sinne that suites with our humours, without fear or remorse, what is this but to act the specultative Christian, and the practicall Atheist? If we say we beleeve the scriptures, we are not in earnest, we do but say so. For if otherwise, men would hear and read and study them with more attention, care, and diligence. In brief, let us remember from whom they have their descent and

216 A Roman historian (59 B.C – A.D. 17) who wrote the history of Rome from its foundation to his own time.

217 A Roman historian of the first century B.C. (86 - 35B.C.) who was much concerned about the moral decline of Rome.

originall, G[od] All[mighty] and let us remember the h[oly] Precepts and holy promises, and let us labour to perfect holinesse in the feare of God, so live according to the Rules and directions of them here, that we may not fear to be judged by them hereafter.

This field of the h[oly] scriptures is so larg that I could not run it in these 2 lectures; what remaines concerning the Aut[h]oritie and the Sufficiency, I shall endeavour to comprise in the next.

LECTURE FOUR

Of the Aut[h]oritie or Sufficiency of Scripture - pt. 3

Introduction

This lecture reiterates much of Andrewes' teaching that Scripture has proved itself by its antiquity, acceptance and authority. Our faith, hope, and Christian duty depend on Scripture being authentic. Hence in this lecture Andrewes showed that despite some double meanings in the Old Testament, and differing accounts of the same events, the Bible gives an accurate account of the "remarkable history" of the Israelites, the chosen race. All this culminated in the coming of Christ, the teacher and saviour of the world.[218]

Andrewes maintained that one of the reasons that the Christian religion was based on written and not on oral tradition was because God desired that all should know "he would have none to perish". After all, redemption and salvation were too important to be left to peoples' memories.[219]

Of course parts of Scripture were originally oral until written, such as the accounts of the annunciation and nativity in Luke and Matthew's Gospels, and Paul's accounts in Corinthians on the institution of the Sacrament, Christ's passion, death and resurrection. These must be regarded as just as authentic as the inspired writings of the prophets but distinct from those oral traditions devised by the Church of Rome over the centuries such as indulgences and the supremacy of the Pope. Despite this Church's

---

218 Ms. 3707, pp. 41, 44.

219 Ibid., pp. 43 - 4.

claim that she is the true church, and therefore has the authority to introduce new dogma, her claim has never been acknowledged by "all the churches of Christ".[220]

Previously Andrewes explained why Scripture is termed holy, and in this lecture he conveyed why it is "perfect". Firstly, it comes from "a most perfect God" and points us to "perfection" through Christ, who makes "us wise unto salvation". Secondly, our "perfection" comes from continually working towards it, and so Scripture commands us "to walk, not stand still, not lay up our Talent, but to improve it."[221] As already stated, growing towards perfection was a favourite theme of Andrewes. He concluded with a brief discussion on the usefulness of Scripture to provide for the various needs and situations of all peoples. For example it speaks to sinners of varying degrees, all of whom are in need of repentance. Years later in a Court Sermon for Ash Wednesday, 1619 he reiterated that Scripture teaches that repentance consists "of renewing, as from a decay; of refining, as from a dross; of recovering, as from a malady; of cleansing, as from soil; of rising, as from a fall."[222]

Andrewes was concerned that his scholars would fall into one of the sins of the age by not listening attentively enough to the Scriptures in order to absorb its various teachings. Hence he warned them if they did not listen they would not be persuaded or "feared by the threatenings, that should deter us from sin". Moreover God will never bestow His graces "when men are not fit to receive them". How important then it was for them to hear with all reverence and then "apply them to our own use." He emphasised this by taking the every day example of doing "a great indignitie" to another person when "he is talking to us, we turn our backs, or looke another way. ... How much greater is the indignity, if when the Lord of Heaven speaketh to us, about the weighty affairs of our salvation, we turn from him, talk about other matters, sleight and neglect him." So "let us hear his word whether read or preached, not as the word of man, but as the word of God, able to save our soules." His final words to the students

---

220 Ibid., pp. 43, 45.

221 Ibid., pp. 42, 46.

222 Andrewes, Vol. 1, p. 360.

were thus ones of admonition: hear God's word as the means "to save our soules".[223]

2Tim 3. 16-7. *All scripture is given by inspiration of God and is profitable for [doctrine, for reproof, for correction for instruction in righteousness: that the man of God be perfect, thoroughly furnished unto all good works].*

'Tis the Apostles exhortacion, 1Pet: 3.15. That we should be alwayes ready to give an answer to every one that asketh us a reason of the hope that is in us. Now the truth of our hope and faith and other graces, depend upon the truth of the scriptures, if they be found false or fabulous then is our faith vaine, we are yet in our sinnes [1Cor:15.17].

I have therefore hitherto made it my businesse to prove the Aut[h]oritie of the h[oly] scriptures, that they were given by inspiracion of God. And in proof of this I insisted.

1. Upon the Antiquitie of the scriptures, that they were ancientest of all writeings; as likewise the generall consent of all sides, and to universall Tradicion for the Truth of them.

2. That the Penmen knew what they writ, and faithfully delivered things according to their knowledge.

3. That those very men were the Authors of the Bookes of the N[ew] T[estament] whose names we read in the runing Titles.

4. That tho' those Bookes have passed the hands of so many generacions of men, yet they remaine uncorrupted.

5. That neither the variety of readings nor the seeming contradictions in them do any whit prejudice the truth of them.

6. That the h[oly] Precepts and h[oly] Promises, and the confirmacion of them by signes and miracles, and the strong successe that hath attended the Gospell in the world, are Arguments to prove the divine Originall of it. That at that time when the meanes to propogate it were weake; the matter 'twas to work upon altogether unprepared, Jewes and Gentiles, both in deadly hatred against it;[224] and the most learned of them, writeing against the

223 Ms. 3707, p.47.

224 This argument also appeared in the previous lecture.

truth of it. Ulpian the greatest Lawyer,[225] Gallen the greatest physitian,[226]Lucian[227] the great[est] scoffer,[228] and Julian[229] useing all meanes that could be to suppresse it; by putting down of Catechiseing, by makeing Dialogues against our saviour, betw[een] him and Pilate, and causing those to be taught instead of Christian Catechismes, to alienate the minds of children from Christian Religion;[230] yet not withstanding all this that the Gospell should prevail and flourish; and then when the world was so full of eyes, that so many learned men, Pantænus, Clemens,[231] Origen,[232] Basil,[233] Austin,[234] Ambrose[235] should abandon the Religion in which

---

225 He was a Roman jurist under Caracalla, and his legal writings, based on earlier learning, were a chief source for the *Digest* of Justinian. He died in 223. M.L.E. tells us that he wrote 460 books against Christians. p. 62.

226 He was a Greek physician from Pergamum of the second century. His greatest contribution to medicine was that arteries carried blood, not air. He tried to systematise medicine, and much of his teaching was not accepted until mediæval times.

227 Before *Lucian* in M.L.E. there are also listed: *Plotinus*, the greatest *Platonist*: *Porphyry*, the greatest *Aristolean*: *Libanus*, a great writer in the Grecian tongue. p. 62.

228 He was a Greek writer who died c.190. His prose works included *Dialogues of the Gods, Dialogues of the Dead, The Sale of Lives.*

229 In M.L.E. he is referred to as "the greatest sorcerer". p. 62. Augustine in *De Civitate Dei*, stated,"Did he not persecute the Church, who forbade the Christians to teach or learn liberal letters, lib.xviii , cap 52. Socrates related in great detail the measure taken by Julian against Christians. Socrates, Bk. 3. So did Theoderet, Bk. 3.

230 This is almost identical to that in M.L.E., pp. 62 - 3.

231 i.e. Clement.

232 Origen has been brought up as a Christian. His father, Leonidas was martyred in 202 A.D. He only escaped the same fate through his mother's intervention who hid him.

233 This is not accurate. Basil was brought up in a Christian home and became the bishop of Caesarea (370-379). He defended orthodoxy against the Arian emperor, Valens, and was responsible for the monastic rule in the Eastern Church, still in use today.

234 The great Augustine of Hippo, who, although in youth dabbled in all kinds of religions, was brought up by a Christian mother, Monnica. He was baptised by Ambrose in Milan in 387. Returned to Africa where he was made a bishop against his will. As bishop in the early fifth century he devoted his energy against Manichees, Donatists, Pelagains and pagan philosophers. His famous *Confessions* unveiled his conversion and longing for God.

235 Bishop of Milan in the fourth century when elected bishop by popular demand

they were bred and brought up, and acknowl[edge] a crucified Redeemer, follow and embrace a persecuted Gospell,[236] and that that Gospell should prevail and come forth so glorious out of the fire of persecutions: these are Arguments for the truth and purity of it[237].

Now bec[ause] I would leave as few Rubbs, unremoved as may be; I proceed in the next place to answer some other Doubts that may be made against the truth of it. As

1. That many passages as of the Old Testament are cited in the New, which are not now to be found in the old; and therefore either the one or the other is imperfect and untrue.

2. That the Apostles and Penmen of the N[ew] T[estament] quote such passages of the Old as make nothing for their purposes.

3. That they do not keep themselves to the letter of the Text, but cite many places in the New Testament in expressions differing from what is to be found in the Old.

To the 1st I answer. That many Bookes h[oly] and usefull in their generacions are lost and perished. Yet with this Proviso, That not any parte of the scriptures, i.e. of the writeings which God intended for the perpetuall use and benefit of his church, or which were ever reckoned by the ch[urch] of God for the scriptures are lost. And therefore to the poynt, those testimonies and passages (as that of Enoch Jud.14 which are brought to light in the New Testament and not to be found in the Old), we may not say that they are untruthes, but that they might be read in those bookes that are wanting.

To the 2nd. That the Penmen of the N[ew] T[estament] make use of some such Passages of the old as, suit not to their purposes, the matters of which they treat, and therefore the truth of those

---

even though he was not baptised. He became a famous preacher and a champion of orthodoxy.

236 Cp. with Grotius. "*Sergius* governor of *Cyprus, Dionysius Aeropagite*. Polycarpus, Iustinus, Irenaeus, Athenagoras, Origen, Tertullian, Clemens Alexandrinus with divers others: who almost all being brought up in other religions, neither could have any hopes of wealth or preferment in Christianity, yet became worshippers of this *man* that died so ignominious a death." *True Religion*, p. 79.

237 Most of this is identical to M.L.E., pp. 62 – 3; Cp. also with P.C.D., pp. 79 – 80.

predictions and Promises may be called in Question. To this we say.

1. That many Passages of the Old Testament are made use of in the New, and applyed, not to those ends and purposes, to which they had Speciall reference at the 1st delivery of them, but by reason of some similitude and analogie. As that Math: 15.7-8. Well did Isayas prophesy of you, saying, this people draw nigh with their mouths [and honoureth me with their lips; but their heart is far from me], the which was spoken at first to the Jewes of the Prophet, Isay's dayes; but bec[ause] the scribes and Pharisees trod in their stepps, were as guilty of formalitie, and mere outside Religion,[238] therefore our saviour applyed it to the men of that present generation, and the like may be sayd of other places to the same purpose. And this is usuall with learned men in their writeings, to fetch diverse things out of Histories, and Poets and apply them to their purposes; tho' the first Authors of such sayings did never dream of those things, to which they are now applyed. But

2ly. Many Places of the old T[estament] may admit of a double sense 1. Literall and historicall. 2. Mysticall. And tho' some things taken in the literall and historicall sense be not so fit and suitable, yet in the mysticall sense, they may be very apposite to those purposes to which they are applyed. As that Math: 2.15, I have [called my son out of Egypt], the Evangelist applyes to the bringing of our saviour out of Ægypt after the death of Herod; tho' 'twas literally meant of the Israelites deliverance from Ægyptian thraldome. And so these premisees considered, the conclusion will be, that the Evangelists, Apostles and Penmen of the N[ew] T[estament] cite no such passages out of the old, but as in the one sense or the other are fit and suitable to those matters of which they treat.

To the 3rd. That many things are recited in different expressions. 1. 'Tis observed that the writers of the N[ew] T[estament] for the most part followed the edicion of the 70,[239] bec[ause] they writ in the same Dialect and bec[ause] that Translacion was accounted authentique with the Jewes. But 2ly, those h[oly] men

---

238 Cp. with part of one of Andrewes' Communion prayers, "I have beene more carefull of the outward ceremoniall part of thy worship, then of the inward and spiritual." Ms. 3708, p. 41, and in *A Manual for the Sick*, Andrewes, Vol. 11, p. 214.

239 i.e. The Septuagint.

of God willing to apply themselves, to the capacitie of those to whom they writ, and amongst whom they lived did not confine themselves strictly to syllables and words, but to the sense and meaning of the places, and so declared that whole counsell of God tho' in different expressions.

Now in the last place, (bec[ause] I would not be tedious in this point) That all those Predictions and Prophesies, which are contained in the scriptures, are exactly and punctually fullfilled, this may be one Argument to prove their Originall from God; that the h[oly] Author of them saw the occurrances, events, changings and turnings of things in the world, long before they had a being. Especially if we consider

1. That the Predictions of things in the scriptures (for the most part) are delivered in plaine, significant words, without ambiguities or doubtfullnes of sense in the expression. And 2ly, That they are of such events whose comeing to passe in respect of 2nd causes, depended upon those only, that were meerly contigent, as upon the wills and actions of men, and not upon such as act uniformly and with necessitie of causacion which (at a good distance of time) may be foreseen by an eye of reason, enlightened only with the knowl[edge] of the course and motions, and working of Nature, but these events were not of that nature. Now to insist particularly upon all the predictions of future Events, to compare them with the Events thems[elves] and to show how punctually they have been fullfilled, would take up more time, then we have at present to spare. I shall mention but one or two of them.

1. That famous Prophesie uttered by Jacob on his deathbed Gen: 49.10, the scepter [shall not depart from Judah, nor a lawgiver from between his feet, until Shiloh come; and unto him shall the gathering of the people be]. This Prophesie as touching the fullfilling of it, the compleat fullfilling of it, was suspended for well nigh 2000 years, yet when the fullnesse of time was come, the Prophesie itself was punctually fullfilled. And about this Prophesie there are many particulars of much weight and importance. As 1. when 'twas uttered by Jacob, the sonnes of Jacob were very low and very poor, and few in number and in a strang land; so there was no likelihood at all, that any of his posteritie should ever come to have any scepter, any kingly power amongst them in many of their Tribes.

2. In case such a thing should come to passe, there was very little likelihood this scepter, should ever come into Judah's hand, bec[ause] he had 3 elder brothers, Reuben, Simeon and Levi, who according to the law of Nature and custome of Nacions were likely to enjoy the dignity before him.

3. The Possession of the Government was put into the hands of Moses of the Tribe of Levi; and after him into the hands of Joshuah of the Tribe of Ephraim. And in the dayes of Samuel about 400 years after Moses, there was no appearance of any life in this Prophesie, the Government had not yet looked towards the Tribe of Judah. The first dawning of any such day was when little David was chosen out of the Tribe of Judah to be king over Israel. Yet

4ly. We know that 10 tribes of the 12 revolted from Judah, and never returned to their Obedience, but combined with the Gentiles to extirpate the Kingdome and Government of Judah. And

5ly. For the sinnes of David and his posteritie, the glory and power of that kingdome was given into the enimies hand; they were made tributary to other kingdomes for many yeares together, first to the C[h]aldeans, and afterwards to the Romans. Yet

Lastly, the Spirit of truth in this Prophesie made it's way and wrought through all these difficulties and improbabilities, and first brought the scepter into, and then maintained it in the hand of Judah untill Shiloh i.e. the Messiah Christ Jesus came; for Josephus and other such Historians of those times, tell us, that 'twas but a very little while before the birth of Christ, that Herod made that bloody massacre of the tribe of Judah, and slew Hircang the last king of David's race.

2ly, The next remarkable History recorded in the scriptures is concerning Cyrus, which was given out about 100 years before he was born;[240] as you may read Esay: 44.28 and 45 1-2.[241] Thus saith

240 This example is also in P.C.D., p. 28 and M.L.E., p. 31. Grotius also used this example. "So likewise the very name and chief acts of *Cyrus* foretold *by* Esaiah: the very event of Hierusalems siege by the Chaldeans, *Jeremiah*, so *Daniels prediction* touching the removing of the Empire the Asssyrians unto the *Medes* and the *Persians*." *True Religion*, pp. 57- 8.

241 Andrewes has taken Isaiah, the son of Amoz as the author of these verses. However it is now generally accepted that these verses were written by Deutero-Isaiah in the sixth century, B.C. who prophesied that the Jewes in exile would soon be liberated at the

the Lord of Cyrus, he is my shepherd, that shall perform all my pleasure, even saying to Jerusalem, thou shall be built, and to the Temple thy foundacion shall be layd, Now,

1. That a man should be called by his name above an 100 yeares before he was born. And

2. That at such a distance of time, it should be sayd, that such a man should conquer so great a Monarchy as Babylon.

3. That he should build again the Temple of Jerus[alem] which others of his own Religion had destroyed; these Predictions undoubtedly come from him, who with one view overlooketh the long tract and whole duracion of time, which extendeth itself from the beginning of the world, to the end thereof, with all the motions occurrences and events of things that rise up, and fall and come to passe, within the compasse thereof.

Nor can this Prophesie be any wayes suspected of forgery, for 'twas pronounced openly in the hearing of the People, and divulged into many hands before the captivitie; and after 'twas carried into Babylon, where 'twas dispersed, seen, read of many, many years before the accomplishment.

And for the Event, 1. That there was such a man as Cyrus, 2. That a man called by this name conquered Bablyon. 3. That the same man did restore the captivitie of the Jewes, and by contribucions of his own money, did further the building of the Temple of Jerusalem, heathen Authors thems[elves] do sufficiently witnes and confirm. So there is no reasonable doubt of the truth of this History, and of the Event of it.

To give instance in many more particulars of Script[ural] Predictions would be more burthensome to the hearer, than the undertaker. I will only add; that Predictions of Astrologers, and of all those who have made profession of that prophetique art, through the long experienced vanity in them, have long since exposed their Authors and professors, partly to the neglect, partly to the just censures of all knoweing and judicious men: but the true spirit of Prophesie, which hath now for some 1000 of years spoken out of the scriptures gaineth interest, Reverence and Aut[h]ority in the judgments of considering and understanding men. And thus

---

hands of Cyrus and would be allowed to return home when they would rebuild the Temple. Babylon was captured in 538 B. C. by Cyrus and indeed freed the Jews.

much of the Aut[h]oritie of the script[ures] that they derive their Originall from Heaven, they are given by inspiracion of God.

Now such is the fraud and malice of Satan, that when he cannot make us distrust or doubt of the divine Aut[h]oritie of the scriptures, he will endeavour to make us beleev the Insufficiency of them. And therefore our next conclusion was

2. Con[clusion] of the Perfection. That all things necessary required of a Christian to beleev and practise so that he may attaine everlasting salvacion, are contained in the Script[ures]. They are able to make the man of God [perfect, throughly furnished unto all good works. 2Tim: 3.17].

The Perfection of the Script[ure] is 2fold, 1. Absolute, which they have as comeing from a most perfect God, and therefore must needs be most perfect.[242]

2. Relative, in relacion to those ends to which they are ordained. And that the script[ures] are thus perfect, able to make us wise unto salvation. These Reasons may be given

I. Reason - that a man be eternally happy, is required that he be a new creature, Gal: 6.15. In Christ Jesus neither circumcision availeth [anything, nor uncircumcision but a new creature], and to make a man a new creature is required faith working with love, Gal: 5.6. for the one is a comment upon the other, And a 3rd place gives light to them both,1Cor:7.19. Circumcis[ion] is nothing and uncirum[cision is nothing,] but the keeping of the commandments of God. So that faith (under which is comprehended hope)[243] and charity, new obedience, this is the whole duty of a Christian. Now all this, the scripture sufficiently teach us, 1. upon what object we are to place our faith, in whom we are to put our confidence, Joh: 14.1. Yee beleev in God, beleev [also in me]. 2. what 'tis to beleev in him, the Apostle tells us He that cometh to God must beleev [that he is, and that he is a rewarder of them that diligently seek

---

242 Cp. with Hooker, E.P., 2. 8.5.

243 Andrewes always coupled faith with hope. In P.C.D. he stated, "Faith believeth the promise, hope looketh for it." p. 94. In an undated sermon delivered in St. Giles, he preached, "men hope to receive the end of faith" which "*is the salvation of [our] souls*, [1 Peter 1. 21]" Hope therefore is "the blood of faith." *Apos. Sacra*, p. 627. Easter 1607 he preached that Christ as the resurrected Lord is the hope of every Christian. Andrewes, Vol. 2, p. 209.

him. Heb: 11.6].[244] Next for Love and charitie, by which the Apostle understands all duties of piety: 1. Such as concern God, Love, reverence, invocation, thanksgiveing; 2. Such as concern our Neighbour, which are set down 1. in generall Rom. 13.8.[245] 2ly, in particular Math. 25. 36-7[246] and Rom.12.10,13.[247] 3ly. such as concern ourselves: sobriety, chastitie, puritie, patience, perseverance. All such precepts and directions as concern any of these are easy and clear to any acquainted with the scriptures. And therefore all things are therein contained, which are required to make all wiser to salvacion.

II. Reason. Whatsoever God required of the Israelites, as necessary to be performed by them, we may read at larg in the Law of Moses, Deut. 30.10[248] and 32.46-7.[249] Now the condicion of God's People under the Gospell, in this particular, is no whitt inferior to theirs under the Law; yea whatsoever besides those things set down in the Law of Moses, concernes the Duty of Christians, our saviour taught his Disciples, Joh: 15.15. All things that I have heard of the Father I have made known unto you, (i.e.) all things needfull to be known to make them eternally happy. And that Posteritie might reap the benefit of those things. 1. The Evangelists have delivered a perfect history of all that Jesus both did and taught, Acts: 1.1, Luc. 1.3.[250] 2ly, what further concerns the truth,

---

244 In P.C.D., the text is acknowledged. p. 14.

245 i.e. "Owe no man any thing, but to love one another: for he that loveth another hath fulfilled the law."

246 i.e. "For I was an hungred, and ye gave me meat: I was thirsty, and ye gave me drink: I was a stranger and ye took me in: Naked and ye clothed me: I was sick, and ye visited me: I was in prison, and ye came unto me."

247 i.e. "Be kindly afectionated one to another with brotherly love; in honour prefering one another; ... Distributing to the necessity of saints; given to hospitality."

248 i.e. "If thou shalt hearken unto the voice of the Lord thy God, to keep his commandments and his statutues which are written in this book of the law, and if thou turn unto the Lord thy God with all thine heart, and with all thy soul."

249 i.e. "And [Moses] said unto them, set your hearts unto all the words which I testify among you this day, which ye shall command your children to observe to do, all the words of this law. ... through this ye shall prolong your days in the land ... ."

250 Luke's declaration to Theophilus to set down "all that Jesus began both to do and teach."

the doctrine, or the difference of Christianity from the law of Moses, is prescribed and layd down in the Epistles of St. Paul, and the rest of the Apostles; so that (doubtles) all these bookes of the N[ew] T[estament] added to those of the Old cannot but be sufficient to make the man of G[od] Perfect, [thoroughly furnished unto all good works].

III. Reason. Many things are contained in the h[oly] script[ures] of which many may be ignorant without danger of Eternall damnacion; and if all things necessary to be known, be not set down, then either 1. the h[oly] Penman of the script[ures] were so busied in setting down things not necessary, that they omitted those that were; or 2. they were so carelesse of mens salvacion, that they purposely neglected to lay down rules necessarily conduceing to that end: neither of which can be affirmed of them so heavenly inspired.

IV. Reason. Seeing God hath been, and is so carefull of the salvacion of mankind, that he would have none to perish, but all to come to the knowl[edge] of the truth and live;[251] 'tis more agreeable to the wisdome and goodnesse of God, to commit all sacred Truthes (which he would have us to know) to writeings then to leav them to unwritten Tradicion; for Tradicions are grounded upon the memoryes of men, which are slippery and unfaithfull; and therefore that is no such sure way of propagateing any Truthes, but they will be changed, something added to them or taken from them. Whence is it, that we have so many fables of the heathen Gods, and that there are so many fabulous stories amongst the Jewes, but from diverse Tradicions? And therefore those things which God or Man would have carefully preserved to Posterity, they are commanded and desired to be written in bookes. Exod: 17.14, And the Lord said, write this for a memoriall in a book; and Job [said, ô that my words were written and printed in a book,] Job: 19.23 that men in after times might read them in legible characters. And when the People under the Law fell of[f] from the worship of the true God to Idolatrie, their errors were still corrected by that writeings of the Law, which by Gods providence were happily preserved. And therefore these things

251 Cp. with E.P., 5.21.3.

considered, we say, that the whole counsell of God is so committed to writeing, that no necessary part of it, is left to unwritten Tradicions.

Lastly. In that story or Parable (whether you will) Luc: 16.29 our Saviour brings in Abraham thus bespeakeing Dives. They have Moses and the Prophetts let them hear them. As if he should have said, the bookes of Moses and the Prophetts are sufficient for thy Brethren; thence they may learn such dutyes, which if they observ and perform, they may escape that place of torment. And if any object, that those concerned the times of the Old Testament, I answer, That any who is not ignorant of the Principles of Christian Religion, by dayly reading, study and meditacion upon those Truthes contained in the bookes of the old Testament, may attain unto such knowl[edge] as is necessary to salvacion; this appeares from the words before my Text, from a child thou hast known the h[oly] scriptures [2Tim: 3.15]; and then the bookes of the N[ew] T[estament] were unwritten and so no scripture. And he further confirmes what he had said in the words of the Text, All Scripture [is given by inspiration by God]. And thus much of the Aut[h]oritie and Sufficiency of the scriptures that they were given by inspiracion of God, and containe in them all such Truthes as are needful to be known, so that a Christian may be Eternally happy.

Now to speake a word or two of unwritten Tradicions. The Question is put thus: Whether besides the scriptures any Tradicion ought to be admitted, of the same Aut[h]ority with the script[ures], or whether besides this word of God written, there be some word of God not written, yet of necessity to be known and beleeved? For answer hereunto we are to observ that tradicion may be taken 2 wayes,

1. Absolutely, for that Doctrine or opinion, which was at first delivered by word of mouth, so propagated to posteritie, from one generacion of men to another, yet never comitted to writing.

2. Respectively, in regard of some men and some times, such Truthes as at first were delivered by word of mouth, but afterw[ards] for the better preservacion of them, and for the good and benefit of all that should see and read them, committed unto writeing: and in this sense, all the h[oly] scriptures were at first Tradicions (i.e) *vivâ voci literum*, delivered to particular men, or particular churches. Thus all St. Luke's Gospell, before he penned

it, was but Tradicions, Luc. 1.2. He sets forth a Declaracion of such things as were delivered to him by eye witnesses. So the Institucion of the sacrament 1Cor. 11.23. And the history of our saviours Passion and Resurrection, 1Cor 15.3 etc. these were but Tradicions in respect of the Apostle and the Corinthians, untill the time that he made them scriptures; after which time, even in respect of those men, they ceased to be Tradicions; And of this sort of Tradicion, is the Apostle to be understood. 2Thes: 2.15 hold the Tradicions which yee have been taught whether by word or our Epistle. Where he doth not oppose Tradicions to all the h[oly] script[ures], nay, not to all his own writeings, but only to that former Epistle writ to the Thessalonians: not denying also, but that those very Truthes which they had been taught by word, were written by him to others, or afterwards to the same Thessalonians. Againe, it cannot be denyed but that the Apostle was very sollicitous and carefull for the salvacion of his Thessalonians and therefore could not but by <u>word</u> teach them many things out of the writeings of other h[oly] men. So that place is of no force to prove, that some things are necessary to be known, which can neither be found in expresse termes, nor drawn from any place of the h[oly] scriptures. This is that kind of Tradicions, which we deny; the Reasons you have heard in proveing the sufficiency of the scriptures. But the Adversaries to this Truth, object

1. That of the Apostle, Joh: 21. 25 that all Christ's Actions are not registered in the scriptures; yea, if they should, that the world would not containe the bookes. And therefore there must needs be some unwritten Tradicions.

To this Answer, 1. That the Apostle speakes there of the Miracles our saviour wrought, not of the Doctrines of faith and obedience, which are the matters in Question. 2. The Apostle doth not say, that those Tradicions are so necessarily to be beleeved, as without that we cannot attaine salvacion; Nay, 3. He speaketh expressly, [Joh] c[h]ap. 20. v. ὦ.[252] that those things are written, that we might beleev that Jesus is the Christ, and that beleeving we might have eternall life.

252 i.e. the last verse, v. 31.

2. They[253]make use of those words of our Saviour, Joh.16.12. I have many things to say unto you, which you cannot now bear; but when the spirit of Truth shall come, he shall lead you [into all truth] which they miserably wrest, to prove that the Apostles have not written all things necessary to salvacion. Whereas, there is no show of any such consequences for 1. the Text saith by reason of the weaknes of their judgment they were not able to understand all mysteries of Religion; but 2. after they were inspired from above; and fitted for the work and office of Apostleshipp, they should be led unto all Truth (i.e.) all necessary truthes. But

3. Bec[ause] the men of Rome will needes have such Tradicions and 2. make themselves the only faithful keepers of those Tradicions we shall endeavour to show, that both the one and the other is false. For if any company of them (i.e.) any particular church assume to thems[elves] to be the only faithfull keepers of such Tradicions; they must suppose as graunted these 4 things. 1. That that ch[urch] is the only true ch[urch] and so acknowledged of all. 2. That the principall members of that ch[urch] do not any ways disagree amongst thems[elves]. 3. That they have kept those Tradicions from the Apostles times untill this present pure and incorrupt. 4. That those Tradicions do not contradict, or be contrary to the written word of God.[254] Now that not any of these can be truly affirmed of the Roman ch[urch] we say,

1. That shee hath had, and still hath many gayn-sayers, was never universally acknowledged of all the churches of Christ to be the only true church, and therefore cannot justly assume to herself that Title.

2. That there was not alw[ays] a perfect harmony and agreement amongst her members, is evident from that great dissention about keeping of Easter, mentioned by Socrates[255] l.5.c.22. which grew to that height, that victor Romanus excommunicated

253 Refers to "men of Rome" as in the next paragraph.

254 M.L.E. outlines how there were disagreement, disharmony and disunity within the Catholic Church. For example between Augustine and Jerome over the meaning of psalms, Paul's reproving of Peter, Pope Damasus subscribing to heresy, and the division between East and West. pp. 69. - 71.

255 A Greek Church historian who lived c.380 – 450.

the Asian churches, for which of Irenaeus[256] and others, he was sharply reprehended. I might here mention the varietie of judgments about other Tradicions, concerning meates and drinkes, giveing the Eucharist to Infants, about which there was no small contention.

3ly, If there were any such Apostolicall Tradicions, yet 'tis not probable, that the ch[urch] of Rome should have preserved them to this present age pure and uncorrupted. for 1. we see, they did not agree amongst themselves. 2. those Tradicions are grounded only upon the memories of men, that are frail and unfaithfull. 3. In all ages there hath been a great neglect of divine matters.

4. A g[rea]t distraction and perversenes of judgment; and all these considered, it cannot be but in a long tract of time, such things as are not, comitted to writeing, will perish and corrupt. And to say that by Gods powerfull Providence such Tradicions might be preserved, signifies nothing, unles they prove also, that as G[od] was able, so willing to preserv them.

4ly. That those Tradicions which the ch[urch] of Rome would impose upon us, are contrary to the written word of G[od] may be evidenced from the sacrifice of Masse, Indulgences, adoracion of the consecrated host, Purgatory, Pope's Supremacy, for which they do not so much alledge Scripture as Tradicions. Wherefore seeing they are destitute of these 4 Condicions required of those that are to be keepers of true Apostolicall Tradicions; it followes that they cannot justly glory in, or assume to themselves that Title.

And so I proceed from the Aut[h]oritie and sufficiency to the Usefullnes of the h[oly] Script[ure]. All Script[ure] is [given by inspiration of God] and is profitable for reproof [for correction, for instruction in righteousness], *πρὸς ἔγέγχον, πρός ἐπανόρθωσιν, πρὸς παιδειάν.*[257]

There are 3 sorts of men we have to deal with and here are 3 words befitting each of them

256 Bishop of Lyons in the second century. He is the first great Catholic theologian. He opposed Gnosticism and accordingly taught the necessity of God becoming man, so that man may become Godlike. Although he is usually venerated as a martyr, his martyrdom is uncertain.

257 Translated it means, "for enlightening of children".

1. *Inverecundi,* stubborn, refractory sinners, such as are past all shame, when they have done amisse cannot blush; were they ashamed when they had comitted such abominacions, nay [they were not all ashamed] neither could they blush Jer. 6.15. And for these here is ἔλεγχος, *ad monstrandum turpitudinem graviorum criminum* to show them the haynousnes of their sinnes that they are of deep dye.

2. *Teneri,* and *fragales,* more plyable and tender hearted sinners, such as may be more easily wrought upon, to sigh and mourn over their impieties: and for these here is ἐπανόρθωσιν, more gentle correction with their spirit of meeknes.

3. *Inceptores,* beginners in grace and goodnes and for these here is **παοδεία.** Instruction in the way of righteousness; the h[oly] Scriptures show them dayly more and more how they should hold on in the course of innocency and integritie; Thus such the words import and all these wayes are the Script[ures] usefull and profitable.

1 πρὸς ἔγέγχον.[258] Some sinne with an high hand, their sinnes are like those of Sodome, peirce the Heavens, and enter into the eares of the lord of Hosts. And for such as these, God hath Boanerges, sonnes of thunder, Mar: 3.17 and his word in their mouthes hath power to smite, wound, terrifie and shake all the powers of the soules and consciences of men; and sometimes like a storm and tempest of the wrath of the Alm[ighty] beares down all before it. Thus the word of God in the mouth of Paul a poor prisoner at Bar, made Felix a great Judg tremble upon the Bench, Act: 24.25. Will yee not fear mee, not tremble at my word, (saith the Lord) Jer: 5.22. Yes Lord, hills tremble at thy presence, a great Judg, in the midst of his greatest pomp, with his guard of strength about him, trembled at thy word. And the same word like a two edged sword, cutt it's way thorow into the consciences and made hard hearted Jewes to tremble Act. 2.37. If we be frozen upon our dreggs,[259] God's word is a fire, Jer: 5.14 yea, our hearts in script[ure] are

258 Translated it means "for trial/refutation".

259 Zephaniah 1.12. This is version from the Genevan Bible. The same quotation featured in Andrewes' First Temptation Sermon when he was preaching about Satan's temptations of desperation or preumption. Andrewes, Vol. 5, p. 483. His next lecture begins with a reference of living "in the dregs of Time."

called stony, and what good will fire doe upon them? if either iron or brasse, 'twould melt them; but being stone, there is no dealing with them, but by continuall battering to beat them to peices, and to that end God's word is a hammer, that breaketh the Rocks in peices. Her: 23.29 There is nothing too hard for it; it shakes such as are most confident, awakens such as are most secure, breakes such hearts as are most obdurate; as it fills up the valleyes, so it throwes down and levels the mountaines. Thus *πρὸς ἐγέγχον*. All Script[ure] is profitable for <u>reproof</u>.

2 *πρὸς ἐπανόρθωσιν*.[260] As it rendeth the mountaines that stand in opposicion and defiance of it, so it doth not break a bruised reed, but hath vertue in it, to heal the broken hearted, to restore such as are tender and plyable with the spirit of meeknes. Hear what comfortable and gracious expressions there are for all those who are cast down with the sense of their sinnes; the Lord is gracious, mercyfull, slow to anger and of great kindnes, and repenteth him of the evill; he hath motherly bowells, tender compassions; and let all that are weary and heavy laden come to him, and he will give them rest.[261] Thus *πρὸς ἐπανόρθωσιν*. All Script[ure] profitable for correction.

3 *πρὸς παιδειάν*.[262] It commands us to walk circumspectly, to <u>walk</u>, and not stand still; not to lay up our Talant in a Napkin, but to improve it, And (brethren) as you have received how yee ought to walk, to abound more and more, 1Thes: 4.1. you should every day, outdoe yourselves, strive to abound, like a river that overflowes the Bankes, that the streames of your goodnes may make glad your neighbours, your Nacion no lesse than yourselves. And again *εὖ μᾶλλον*, a word of comparison, like a goad in their sides, ever and anon pricking them on; abound more, and do more, and yet more, never leave; till yee become perfect men in Christ Jesus, Thus *πρὸς παιδειάν*. All script[ure] profitable for Instruction.

Lastly, bec[ause] all script[ure is profitable] Let us learn hence to hear them with attention, with Reverance, and apply them to

---

260 Translated it means "for improving".

261 Andrewes always stressed that mercy was God's prime attribute. Cp. with part of the section on *Penitence* in Brightman, pp. 150 – 5 and Andrewes, Vol. 11, pp. 219 - 200.

262 Translated it means "for education/discipline".

our own use. For 1. if we hear, and attend not, we do not learn by the Instructions that should teach us, we are not moved by the Exhortacions that should perswade us, nor are we feared by the threatenings, that should deter us from sin; that which should do us good, is but as water spilt upon the ground, which canot be taken up for any use. 'Tis attention that maketh G[od] willing to instruct us. Open thy mouth [wide, and I will fill it Ps: 81.10] but if we shut our mouthes when we should receive, God will shut his hand when he should give. As a wise housholder, bec[ause] he will not have his wine spilt, doth not pour it upon the vessel when the mouth is stopt, so God bec[ause] he would not have his graces lost, will not bestow them, when men are not fit to receive them. If our mind wander abroad and talk with the vanities of the world, while God speaketh to us out of his word, no marvell, if he take his word from us, and bestow it upon them who are better disposed for it. Is it not a great indignitie to a man, if while he is talking to us, we turn our backs, or looke another way; a man of place or fashion, would not take it well to be so neglected by us. Now how much greater is the indignity, if when the Lord of Host speaketh to us, about the weighty affairs of our salvacion, we turn from him, talk about other matters, sleight and neglect him. Let us consider this and let our behaviour in his presence be such as may be pleaseing to him, let us hear his word whether read or preached, not as the word of man, but as the word of God, able to save our soules.[263]

---

263 In P.C.D. it reads, "We must not talk during the time of God's service; it is a sign of reverence to be silent; as if one should turn from us to speak with another while we tell him a message, we would think he little regarded us." P.C.D., pp. 138 - 9. In the last Temptation Sermon Andrewes stated that it is Satan on whom we should turn our back. It is to him we should show "great disdain". Andrewes, Vol. 5, p. 551.

LECTURE FIVE

Of God; His Essence and Attributes

Introduction

A considerable part of this lecture, especially the first part, has common material with *The Morall Law Expounded* and *Pattern of Cathetical Doctrine*.

In this lecture, Andrewes informed his scholars that as they lived in a time when "the very grounds and principles of Christianity are questioned"[264] it was simply not sufficient to accept the existence of God. Atheism,[265] he suggested, was caused not from ignorance of the Christian faith, but from the doubt and disbelief that creep in. As theology is a science,[266] the first step is to learn the arguments for God's existence, and the second is to discover the kind of God in which Christians believe.

Firstly, on the existence of God, Andrewes followed the five traditional arguments. 1. The cosmological argument, that is, that everything has to have a beginning, and owes its existence to something greater and outside of itself. That something is what we call, God, the first mover. 2. The general consent argument,

---

264 Ms. 3707, p. 47.

265 Andrewes believed that "all have degrees of Atheisme" which are evident when 1. We embrace sin rather than the crosses in life. 2. We deceive, lie and perjure. 3. We ignore the promise of eternal life and stupidly continue in sin. 4. We refuse to humble ourselves in the presence of God, and try to make ourselves an equal with him. Ibid., p.52.

266 Hooker like Andrewes, in common with the great medieval theologians, also recognized theology as a science. E.P., 3.8.12.

that is, ever since man has lived on earth, there has been a "universal consent" from all different peoples in a belief of some kind of deity. 3. The teleological argument, that is, that nothing has been made by chance as there is an order, beauty, and purpose to all creation, which reflects the artificer who is perfect. As no created being is perfect it has to be God who is the cause for all creation. 4. The ontological argument, that is, that each soul has been endowed "with reason and understanding". This must come from "its own being" or "from some other". Of itself it cannot "for it knoweth not itself", and thus it "must be from some superiour reasonable cause, which is God." 5. The moral argument which teaches that every man has a conscience, which Solomon calls "the candle of the lord". This tells us that God exists, just as it exposes the sins we commit against Him. These arguments, Andrewes suggested, should "strengthen our faith" and make us more aware of God in our daily actions.[267]

Secondly the kind of God in whom we believe. Andrewes emphasised the Trinitarian nature, which he described through various analogies of sun, fire and water. He indicated that although not really explicit in Scripture, sufficient has been revealed for us to accept God as three persons in one, who collaborate in the creative, redemptive and sanctifying works in this cosmos. When teaching on the Trinity he especially stressed the work of the Holy Spirit who was neglected in medieval theology, and is quite distinct from angelic spirits. It is He who is the breath and spirit to all life; "He fills heaven and earth" and "every place". As God then is omnipotent, omniscient, and omnipresent, it should lead us to acknowledge His presence also in worship, and to imitate His holiness in our devotions and public prayers.

The emphasis that Andrewes gave to the Trinity in this and the next lecture was indicative of Andrewes' revival of the prominence that the early Fathers gave to the Trinity. This prominence is also found in his Penetecost sermons. "Our rule is, the works of the Trinity ... are never divided. What one doeth, all do." "The Father, the Fountain; the Son, the Cistern; the Holy Ghost the Conduit pipe." He believed that too often the various persons of the Trinity were restricted to a particular function as is obvious in the next lecture.[268]

267 Ms. 3707, pp.50-1.

268 Andrewes, Vol. 3, pp. 362, 381; *Apos. Sacra*, p. 38.

Regarding God's attributes, Andrewes stressed that as there is no variation in Him, God has only one attribute - perfection, but because of our variable natures and needs, Christians over the centuries have ascribed two kinds of attributes to God - primary and secondary. The former describe God, as He is, that is, perfection, whilst the latter depicts God as we behold Him according to our perception and needs. These are "life, power, will, mercy, justice, knowledge, holiness, happiness, love [and] truth."[269] Of these Andrewes always emphasised God's love and mercy because these form the golden chain in man's salvation. Without them man could not have been restored to his original glory, and are therefore more beneficial to us than His justice. Another reason for highlighting these two attributes, as already intimated, was to offset the Calvinistic teaching of double predestination which taught that most of mankind was condemned to eternal damnation.[270] This divine insisted that every Christian has the right to call on God's mercy and love for pardon and restoration.

Rev. 1.8. *I am Alpha and Omega, the begining and the ending, saith the Lord, which is, and which was, and which is to come, the Almighty.*

Because we live in the dreggs of Time, and are cast upon such unhappy dayes, in which the very grounds and principles of Christianity are questioned, and so not rightly understood; that we may not lose the Truth in the general and fatall rubbish of errors and heresies, I suppose 'twould not be amisse to lay again the foundacion of Religion, that we may know the better upon what grounds to build, so that after the dissolucion of these weak and earthly Tabernacles (which may be we know not how soone) we may not fail of that which we all aim at, eternall happinesse.

---

269 In his lecture on the first commandment at Pembroke he listed the ten attributes as: "majesty, truth, unchangeableness, will, justice, mercy, knowledge, power, ubiquity, and eternity." Of these "the two essentials are, His justice, [and] mercy", the former is linked with "knowledge", "fear and humility" and the latter with "love" and "hope". P. C.D., p. 84.

270 His Calvinist contemporary, William Perkins, had called his work on God's predestining the elect to heaven and the majority to hell *The Golden Chaine*.

I shall therefore at this time begin with him, who gave breath and being to all things, God Alm[ighty] as he here declares himself to St. John. I am the Alpha and Omega.

In these words God Alm[ighty] is pleased to be his own Herauld, to proclaime hims[elf] to the world, and to give us a short description of his infinite being. I am the Alpha and Omega, A and Ω i.e. what these 2 letters are in the alphabet, to the rest of the letters, that is He is to the creatures, the <u>first</u> and the <u>last</u>; of him and through him are all things, Rom. 11.36. In him all creatures live and move and have their Beeing Acts 17.28]. And if he should suffer the creatures to fall, then he should be the last, unto him, they would return. Thus he is A and Ω, the beginning [and the end] which <u>is</u> and which <u>was</u> and which <u>is to come</u>, [Rev: 1.8] i.e. He was from all eternity, and shall continue unto all Eternity. He hath no cause of his Beeing, but is from himself, by himself, of himself and for himself.

Now to speak of this great, and glorious, and incomprehensible Essence, *de quo periculosum est etiam vera dicere,*[271] whom we should never mention heedlessly but with fear and reverence. I shall lay down these 2 poynts. 1. <u>That</u> <u>he is</u>, for he that cometh to God must beleev that he is [Heb: 11. 6]. 2. <u>What he is</u>. i.e. so far forth as he may be known; and that 1. by his works 2. by his written word: And there 1. by his Names, 2. by his Attributes.

For the first of these. The very first foundacion of all Pietie and Religion, is to beleev there is a God. For how can there be any Religion, how can there be any godlinesse, where there is no God? if there be no beleef, no opinion of this Truth, there cannot be possibly any love of godlines, nor any effect of goodnesse. And therefore, the very Heathens, Plut[arch] and Seneca have observed, that the ignorance of this one poynt that there is a God, is the root of all impietie; which Abraham also confessed, when he thus thought in hims[elf], Gen: 20.11, surely the feare of God is not in this place, and therefore will they slay me. For where the fear of God is not, even there *homo, sacra res per ludum et jocum occiditur,* Sen[eca], 96 ep[istle], the shedding of innocent blood is but sport and pastime.

---

271 Literally, "About whom it is perilous to speak even the truth."

So to prove this poynt, is to lay in the hearts of men a ground and foundacion of Religion. And to demonstrate this truth, we may make use of these Arguments. 1. The consideracion of the Originall of all things. For it cannot be denyed, that many things are which had a beginning; and that those things which are, were not yet cause of their own beeing, (for nothing can act before it is) 'twill therefore follow, that they must have their Beeing from something else, and not from thems[elves] and so we shall come to a first cause, a first mover in all things, which is God.[272]

2. The next Argument may be drawn from the common and universall consent of all Nacions; for what at all times and in all places is professed, is truth; But so was and is the beleef of a Diety. Very few there were, who denyed this truth; and they were presently and sufficiently confuted by the Heathens thems[elves]. And the very small number of Atheists, is an argument that their opinion did not proceed from the use of right reason, (which is common to all men) but from the study of Novelty (as those who will affirm snow to be black) or from a peevish corrupt mind,[273] as a vitiated Palate will disrelish those things which are most savoury; or 3ly, out of a desire to have it so; as the theif would have

---

272 This is expounded in M.L.E. "There is a beginning of the World ... As a tree, though we finde no roote of it, yet we know a roote it hath; though we cannot finde the fountaine whence the river comes, yet we do know it hath one. So though we cannot come to know how the world had his beginning yet sure are wee it had a beginning. ... Where there are divers natures most discrepant, and therefore are brought into harmony and concord, it must necessarily be argued that there was one that accorded them, that tuned them; as in a Lute tuned: so the World being full of varities of natures; yet they agreeing in a wonderful sympathy, there must needs be a tuner of this so great a harmony." p. 29. Grotius on this subject wrote: "That there are *something* which had a beginning, is cleare to common sense, and by the confession of all: howbeit these things were not causes to themselves of their own being. For that which is not cannot produce anything, neither had power: to be before it was; therefore it followes, that the said things had their beginning from some other thing different from themselves." *True Religion*, p. 7

273 Cp. with this in lecture on Genesis 1.3. "There are some which will have a reason of Gods works, and would know how it could be that light should be first made, and four daies after the Sunne to be made, which was the cause of it: But to these, I answer, that their absurd doubt, doth argue small skill in Philosophy: for they speak, as if the light were an affection and quality only of the Sunne; for we see that the fire on earth, the meteors and lightnings in heaven, the scales of Fishes, and a dark wood, have also light in them. And what doth give light to these? I answer, not the Sunne; ... ." *Apos. Sacra*, p. 17.

the candle put out, that in the dark his treachery may not be seen and discovered, so some loose livers haveing a light in them that will not suffer them to walk in the darknes of their brutish pleasures, would have this light put out, that their consciences might not check them, and that they might not be tyed to that severe course of life, to those hard dutyes of Piety which Religion and the knowl[edge] of God layes upon them. And those that denyed this truth in their lives, their Deathes have proved it for them; God was pleased to confute the Atheists in the end of their dayes by remarkable judgments. Pherecides[274] the Syrian durst seldome come into any company; and having bragged at a Banquett, that he had lived a long time, and not offered upp, either prayers or sacrifice to any god, he was presently after consumed by lice. Julian the Apostate, being overcome in Battail, pull'd out his own bowells, cast his blood into the air, and so died with miserable yelling. And Lucian[275] leaving his hounds fast bound when he went out to supper; at that supper haveing spoken much against the truth of God, as he returned, his doggs ran madd, and breakeing loose, fell upon him, and tore him to peices.[276] I shall conclude this with that inscription upon Zenacharib's tomb, *εἰς ἐμὲ τίς ὁράων εὐσεβὴς*,[277] whosoever remembreth these, let him learn to be Godly, to acknowledg, there is a God, who ruleth unto the ends of the earth; and that he will one day inflict severe punishment upon all incorrigible workers of Iniquity.[278]

---

274 Lived in the 5th century, B.C. on the island of Levos. Pherecydes was one of the "logographi" who were the first to write history, mainly legendary, in prose rather than verse. He composed a genealogy of the gods which survives in fragments.

275 It was he and not Phercydes who was the Syrian as he lived in Samosata, 115 - 200 A.D. Lucian was a satirist who particularly mocked religion, mostly pagan. And his writings in Attic Greek inspired Rabelais and Swift.

276 Julian and Lucian have already been referred to as "destroyers" of the faith in the previous lecture. In P.C.D. and M.L.E besides Pherecydes, Julian and Lucian, there were also Diagoras who "for his damnable opinions was the cause of the destruction of the whole country of Melos, for revenge of his atheism" as recorded by Thucydides, Book 5; Apion who scoffed "at circumcision" was struck down with an ulcer as reported by Josephus Cont. Apion, Bk. ii, Ch..13. Vol. ii. p.1374); and Machiavel "rotted in the prison of Florence". P.C.D., p. 31, M.L.E., p. 34.

277 Literally, "he who is looking at me I proclaim holy."

278 Cp. with M.L.E., pp. 28, 33 and P.C.D., pp. 25, 31.

3. If we grant that all things had a beginning, then that must proceed, either from Chance or from Nature or from God.

1. Not from chance; for if a man come into a wildernes and see there a cottage erected, his conscience will give him, that it came not by chance, but was built there by some Artificer.[279] If Aristippus[280] see lines drawn on the shore, he will straight imagine (tho' he see no men) yet that there were some that drew them.

2. In things that come to passe by chance or fortune there is no order that can be observed, nothing but confusion and irregularitie; but in the world, there is a most excellent order in all things.

3ly. Neither can Nature, be the cheif cause of all things; for then seeing nothing can goe against the cheif cause, there should be nothing against nature: but we know the contrary: the sun stood at the commandment of Joshuah; and the same sun was Eclypsed in the full of the moon, against Nature at our saviours Passion. So all things can[n]ot have their beginning either from chance or Nature but from God.[281] And

4ly. God is so sensibly proved to us in his creatures, that we may as 'twere touch and handle him. The order of the creatures, the wonderfull frameing of them, the hidden power in them, and the generall Art in searching out the Nature and Qualities of them; those things which seem to be ordinary and contemptible, have wrought to the astonishment of all men. Pliny[282] marvelleth at the Gnat, at the trunk of it, wherewith shee maketh a noyse, and concludes, that without a power above Nature, that thing could not be created.[283] And Galen[284] *de usu partium,* having spoke blasphe-

---

279 Cp. with Hebrewes 3.4.

280 He was a fifth century philosopher and a friend of Socrates.

281 These last three paragraphs are almost identical to that in M.L.E., pp. 30 –1. Cp. also with P.C.D., pp. 28, 54, and lecture on Genesis 1.1, *Apos. Sacra*, pp. 4 – 5.

282 Known as Pliny the Elder (23-79) and the author of *The Natural History*. Completed in 77, it is divided into thirty-seven books, and covers a great variety of subjects, such as cosmosology, astronomy, geography, medicine, zoology, botany and agriculture. When Mt. Vesvius erupted, he was commanding a fleet in the Bay of Naples, and consequently went assure to ascertain the cause, but was overcome by the fumes and died on 24th August, 79.

283 M.L.E. adds here "as also the Butterflies and infinite others." p. 31.

284 He was a Greek physician from Pergamum (129-199) who became a court physi-

mously of the Parts of man; when he came to one of least account, he fell into admiracion of it, and was constrained to name God.[285] Thus may we learn from those things without us, that there is a God. And in the next Place, we may be taught the same truth, by things within us. We have a soul indued with reason and understanding; and then this must either be the cause of itself, of it's own beeing, or else have it from some other; of it selfe 'tis not, for it knoweth not it self; no not the house of clay in which it dwells, not the Body but by Anatomy. But every Cause knoweth his effect, not only after 'tis brought forth, but even before the Production, and as 'twere by what meanes 'tis produced; as he that makes a watch, or any ordinary work of Art, knowes all the junctures, all the wheeles and motions, or else 'tis impossible that he should make it. Now all inferiour causes, that have anything to doe in produceing of man, know not the makeing of him, neither the Father that begetts, nor the mother that conceives, know it. And after we be brought forth, we cannot command every parte of us; as the beating of the Arteries in the heart; therefore we proceed neither from ourselves, nor our Parents, but must necessarily have our beeing from some other cause; and there is no cause in the world partaker of man's understanding, but man; and seeing man is not from hims[elf], he must be from some superior reasonable cause, which is God. *ἀρχὴ τοῦ λόγου οὐκ ὁ λόγος ἀλλα κρεῖττον τι* Arist[otle] 9 Eth[ics]. Reason is not the cause of Reason, but it cometh from some more noble cause, some better thing then Reason; and what that is the poet Aratus[286] tells us, cited by St. Paul. Act: 17.28. *τοῦ γὰρ καὶ γένος ἐσμέν*,[287] our being is from God.[288]

Lastly, we may draw an argument from the Father of Lyes to

---

cian in Rome. He wrote various books on medicine.

285 Grotius also used this example from Galen. *True Religion*. p. 21.

286 He lived in the 4th century, B.C. and is the author of the poem *Phainomena* ("things brought to life") which described the stellar regions. The quotation cited by Paul comes from this poem.

287 Literally, "for we are also his offspring."

288 This long paragraph is identical to that in M.L.E., pp. 31- 2. Cp. also with P.C.D., pp. 28-9. Cp. also with Grotius, "It followes from that which hath bin spoken, that what things soever *subsist*, the same have their *originall and first being from God*: for we have

confirm this truth. If there be a Divell, a wicked spirit in the world, set on mischeif, seeking to endamage men in their goods, their Bodyes, their soules, and endeavouring as far may be to bring all mankind to destruction; then certainly there is a Superiour Power, a God to restrain this his fury and malice, and to set bounds to his tyranny; otherewise he would long ere this have brought to passe the utter ruine of mankind.[289]

To these arguments, I will add but one more, and that is drawn from man's conscience. There is a conscience in man, which upon all occasions will accuse, or excuse; Their conscience also bearing witnesse (Apostle) and their thoughts in the mean while accusing or else excuseing one another Rom: 2.15, tho' no man else be able to accuse a man, yet his conscience will do it.[290]

A notable example to this purpose, is that of Joseph's brethren, whose consciences a long time after accused them of selling their brother, when none besides themselves and Joseph (whom they then little imagined to be within heareing) knew of it, Gen: 42. 21-2. And therefore 'twas well said of Seneca *Quid refert neminem scire cum tu scias?* what matter is it, tho' no man else know what thou hast done, so long as thou thyself dost know it? So on the other side, tho' all the world bear witnesse against a man, yet if his conscience be cleare, it will testifie for him; and this is enough to comfort him. This is our rejoyceing, even the testimony of our Conscience (St. Paul) 2Cor: 1.12. And so the Heathens could say, that a good conscience is *murus aleneus*, a wall of brasse, a most sure defence against all calumny, and all opposicion. Now this conscience is the candle of the Lord, as Solomon calls it Prov. 20.27, it shewes plainly, that there is a God, from whom nothing is hid, and by whom all shall be rewarded.

Ob[jectio]. But, it may be objected, if there be a god who made the worlde, and governs the world, who is most great and most

---

proued that that which is necessary of it selfe, can bee but one whence we collect that all other things besides this had their originall from somewhat different from themselves.

Now such things as have there *beginning* from another, we have seene before how that either in themselves or in their causes, they proceeded from *him* which had no beginning, that is *from God*." *True Religion*, pp. 20-1.

289 Cp. with M.L.E., p. 29.

290 Cp. with P.C.D., pp. 30 – 1; M.L.E. p. 33.

good, most wise and most holy; how then comes it to passe, that there is so much evill, so much ataxie, and confusion in the world?

Sol[utio]. I answer God therefore sufferes evill, because he knowes how to bring good out of evill. A skilful Physician can so temper poyson, as to make a soveraigne medicine of it, and so God can cause sin it selfe to be subservient to his glory, and the good of his people: if there were no sin, the glory of God's grace in pardoning of sin would not appeare as it doth, Eph:1. 6,7,[291] Mic: 7.18.[292] Nor on the other side, the glory of God's justice in punishing sin Ps: 119.120. Aben-Ezra therefore a learned Rabbin saith well, It doth not belong to the supreme widsome bec[ause] of a little evill to hinder much good.[293]

But if any shall say with Thomas, except we may see him, we will not beleeve: To these we answer.

1. By the same reason they may deny that there is a soul in man; for neither doe any see it otherwise, then by the operacions and effects of it, and thus also they must needs see God, who are not all together blind and brutish.

2. And therefore 2ly we say that we may see him in his wondrous works; in the sweet consent and harmony amongst his creatures; in the fitnes and proportion of one unto another; in the reasonable actions of creatures in themselves unreasonable; in the impressions of skill and workmanshipp that is upon the creatures.[294] But

3ly. No man can see his Nature and essence. And the Argument is weak, thus to inferr, our shallow capacities canot comprehend the Nature of God, therefore there is no God; For 'tis the propertie of every inferiour creature not to apprehend that which is superiour, and more excellent then itself. The brute beasts know not, what man is; nor how he frames and governes commmon-

---

291 i.e. "In whom we have … the foregiveness of sin, according to the riches of his grace."

292 i.e. "Who is a God like unto thee, that pardoneth iniquity, and passeth by the transgression of the remnant of his heritage? He retainteth not his anger for ever, because he delighteth in mercy."

293 Cp. with M.L.E., p. 35 and P.C.D., p. 34.

294 Cp. with M.L.E., p. 31.

wealths, how he sailes over the Ocean, and measures the course of the starrs; all these are above their apprehension. And man, by the bounty of his Maker, being placed in an higher sphere above the condicion of the beasts that perish, must hence inferr, that he who placed him in that condicion, is as far above his apprehension, as he himself is above the apprehension of inferiour creatures.[295] And thus much of the first poynt that God is. Now to descend to some application.

1. When we hear such Arguments proveing this conclusion, that there is a God, the use we should make of it, is, to labour dayly to strengthen our faith in this Principle, and to have a speciall eye to God in all our Actions: for this is the reason given by the Apostle, why one man comes to God bec[ause] he beleeves that he is [Heb:11.6]: and another doth not, bec[ause] he beleeves it not fully, but by halves. What is the reason, that Moses broke thorow all impediments, overcame all temptacions, on the right hand and the left, passed thorow wealth and poverty, honour and dishonour, and went streight on, in the way to heaven? The reason is added in the Text. Heb.11.27, bec[ause] he saw him, that was invisible: Even so, if we did but see him, the God we now speak of, as we see a man that stands before us; our wayes would be more even, and we would walk with him more uprightly, than we doe. As the soul in the body, so God is in the world, in every place, and fills it with his presence; He is present with every creature, heareth all our words, seeth all our actions;[296] and if we could bring ourselves to a firm and settled perswasion of this, it would cause us to walk more evenly with God, then we doe, and to converse with him more frequently and more reverently.

Tho' I speak not now to Atheists,[297] but to such as beleeve there is a God, yet I may not think this labour lost. For tho' there be an assent to this truth in us, yet 'tis such a one as may receiv degrees; and tho' there are few perfect Atheists, yet there are some degrees of Atheisme in the best of God's servants. For Atheism is 2fold. 1.

---

295 Cp. with E.P., I. vi. 2-3. Grotius follows this argument completely. *True Religion*, p. 13.

296 Reminiscent of Psalm 139. 1-10.

297 In Andrewes' intercessions he prayed for the conversion of Atheists, Brightman, p. 59.

when a man thinks that there is no God, and knows he doth so. 2. when he doubts of the Diety and observes it not.

And this we may know from the effects it doth produce. As

1. When men shall avoyd crosses rather than sin, not considering, that the heavy wrath of an angry God goes along with it, which is the greatest evill that can befall us. And what is the reason, that when crosses and sin come into competicion, as two severall wayes of which we must necessarily chuse one; why will men turn aside from some little affliction, to sinne against an Eternall God; and rather violate the peace of their consciences then undergoe some losse, crosse or imprisonment? doth not this proceed from some secret Atheism?

2. Whence are all those deceits, lyes, perjuries, and shiftings in the world, to make things fair with men, when they know that God is offended, that seeth all things. And why are so many, more sensible of outwards shame, then of secret impieties, and care so much what men think of them, but make little Reckoning, what God sees or knowes? Are not these of the same mind with those Atheists Job speaks of, Job 22.14, they conceiv that God doth not descend beneath the Circle of the heavens to the earth, but that his eyes are barred by the curtaines of the night; that he doth not take notice of the wayes of men?[298]

3rdly, what is the reason of such stupiditie in men that threatnings will not move them, like brute beasts, they will be sensible of nothing but present strokes? Why will they not forbear sin, that they may receiv the promised rewards? Why doe they not look for those things which commend the soul to God and regard Eternitie, in which the soul must live? Is not this an Argument of secret Atheism in the hearts of men? And

Lastly, what is reason, that comeing into the presence of God, men demean thems[elves] so negligently, not careing what the behaviour of their spirits is before him, but speakeing of him and to him as to their Equall? doth not such fruit as this, proceed from the seeds of Atheism and infidelitie in the hearts of men, which bewitcheth them with desperate senslessnes against the vengeance of God, so that they will neither beleeve his words, nor tremble at

298 Cp. with M.L.E., p. 34 and P.C.D., pp. 31 –2.

his oathes, but commit sin with both hands, greedily [Eph: 4.19]; and so hasten to hell the sooner, to make tryall whether God be a lyar or no. Every man hath too much Atheism in his heart by nature, but such desperate stupiditie doth wonderfully improve it, and will bring men by degrees to the hellish presumption of those in the Prophet, the Lord will not doe good, neither will he doe evill; it is not the lord, neither shall evill come upon us; the Prophets shall become wind, and the word is not in them, Jer: 5.11-2. Now to those who sit in such grosse darknes, and have such mean and low thoughts of God, 'tis needfull to bring in more light, and to prove that God is and as holy in all his works, so righteous in all his wayes; what he hath said, shall undoubtedly come to passe; and therefore let them be warned to fly from the wrath to come, before the day of vengeance come, before fire come from the lord, to burn up as stubble, all the workes of iniquitie. And so we come to the second point, what God is. He is Alpha and Omega, [the beginning and end].

And here we say, 1. That the Nature of God, is not be comprehended by the understanding of man. And yet our defect of knowl[edge] in the Nature of God, is not so properly from the excellency of the Object, as from the deficiency of the faculty; our understanding being too narrow to comprehend the incomprehensible Essence of the Godhead; as whatsoever is finite, must needs be too short, either to reach, or to fathom that which is infinite. As the sun in itself is most visible, so is God in hims[elf], most intelligible; and therefore that the Sun dazleth the eye, and God the understanding, as it is from the abundance of glory in the one who is most glorious, and of light in the other which is most bright and shineing, so especially in respect of our weaknesse to see, and insufficiency to apprehend. Wherefore our God dwelling in that light of glorious excellency and inaccessible glory, which no eye of humane Reason can approach or enter; we not being able to comprehend him in a full knowledg, must content ours[elves] with some apprehensions of him by a divine faith, as he hath revealed himself to us in his Word.

In which word of truth God is described unto us.

1. By his Names
2. By his Attributes.

His Names especially, are Jehovah and Shaddai. His name Jehovah declares him to be a God absolute in his Essence. It denotes 3 things. 1. his Eternity, that he is Alpha and Omega. 2. that he giveth beeing to all things, Esa: 44.24. 3. that he doth fully accomplish and make good all his promises, Ex: 6.3.[299] His Name Shaddai, declares him a God all-sufficient in his fullnes, Omnipotent, the Allm[ighty], that hath scarcity of nothing, and who brings out of his storehouse sufficiency for all his creatures. And 3ly. The first expression, whereby God did ever shew hims[elf] in his Essence, was that, Exod: 3.14, I am [that I am] which implyes 2 things: 1. The incomprehensiblenes of Alm[ighty] God; as 'tis usually said by us, when we are asked a thing, that we will not reveal any further, or that we would not have another any further to pry into, we say it is what it is; so God to Moses, I am what I am. 2ly, such a kind of speech is used to shew the immutablilite of a thing, as Pilate said Joh: 19.22 what I have written, [I have written]. I will not chang it. So 'tis usuall with men to say, I have done what I have done to shew the constancy of a thing, that it shall not be altered; so when God would shew the constancy of his Nature, he adds I am, as if he should say, Moses, if they enquire of thee what my name is, tell them only this, ὀῶῦ He is hath sent thee unto them [Ex. 3.14]

So from the Names of God, we beleeve him to be an absolute and an infinite Spirit, so he is called, Joh: 4.24. God is a spirit. Now the Greek word *πνεῦμα* and so the Hebrew *ruach* which signifie spirit, are commonly used for breath, Ezek: 37.5. I will cause breath to enter into you: in the orginall the word is that, which in that language usually signifieth spirit, viz *ruach*, so Jam: 2.26 The body without the spirit is dead, i.e. the body without breath is dead. And Job 33.4. The spirit of the lord hath made me, and the breath of the Alm[ighty] hath given me life, saith Elihu: here, the spirit of the Lord, and the breath of the Alm[ighty] are *ἰσοδυναμοῦνται*,[300] terms that signifie one and the same thing. Indeed the word spirit in all the mother tongues signifies Breath, And Breath, tho' it be a Body; yet bec[ause] 'tis the most refined, subtle and

299 It should include the next few verses, i.e. 6. 3 – 8.

300 Translated it means, "powerful enough in themselves."

invisible Body, therefore immaterial substances, which we cannot otherwise conceive, are represented to us under the name of Spirits. And to tell you the nature of a spirit, these 4 things are to be considered.

1. 'Tis the property of a spirit to be invisible, not be discerned by any sense. And therefore our Saviour bad[e] his Disciples to feel and handle him, that therefore they might know, he was not a spirit as they thought him to be. Luc: 24.39. So a spirit is that which is withdrawn from the perceivance of any corporall sense whatsoever; and in this sense God is called a spirit because he is invisible.

2. Every spirit moves itself and other things besides itself: The body is but a peice of dull earth, not able to move at all, when the soul is gone out of it; 'tis the spirit that carryes the body where it listeth, and moves itself with all speed and agilitie, because it finds no resistance.

3. 'Tis the Propertie of every spirit, to move with exceeding great force and strength, with much vehemency; Esa: 31.3 The Prophet speakeing of the strength of the Æygptians, tells us they are flesh and not spirit; as if he should say all flesh is weak, but a spirit strong. And this we may see in such as are possessed by bad spiritts, they are able to breake the strongest bands.

4ly, 'Tis the property of a sp[irit] to insinuate and enter into any bodily substance, without penetracion of Dimensions i.e. 'tis not kept out of any place, by reason of any Body that is in it; but it may be in any place, tho' that place be otherwise full. Now to apply these Properties. 1. God is invisible, not seen by any eye, Joh:1.18. No man hath seen God at any time; and 1Tim: 6.16 whom no man hath seen, nor can see. It is said indeed of Moses, that he saw him that is invisible, Heb: 11.27 but that was by the eye of faith, (which is the evidence of things not seen Heb:11.1) he saw him, like as Abraham saw Christ's day many ages before Christ came into the world, Jon: 8.56. But properly Moses did not see God, neither could see him, God being (as in that very place is expressed) invisible. 2. He moves all things in the world according to his good pleasure. 3. Whatsoever he doth, 'tis with exceeding great strength, And 4ly, He fills Heaven and Earth, every place, what bodyes soever be there, yet he is there not withstanding.

And thus you see in what sense, this is to be understood, God is a spirit.

Now here, 3 things are to be added:

1. How God is said to be a sp[irit]; for Angells and the soules of men are called spirits? Answer. They are finite created spiritts, but God is infinite, increate, an incomphrensible spirit.

2. This blessed and infinite spirit may be taken 2 wayes, either 1. Essentially, and so all the three persons are spiritts, i.e. without composicion and merely incorporeall, or 2. Personally, and so 'tis attributed to the h[oly] Ghost only, who is called, *τὸ πυεῦμα ἅγιον*, the holy Spirit. Now God is called a spirit, as the word is taken Essentially, not personally. And

3ly. when in the scripture we read that God hath eyes and hands, and feet, as tho' he were a Body,[301] we must understand those expressions *θεοπρεπῶς*, the holy Ghost is pleased to lispe unto us in our language the scripture so speaketh of him, as we are able to conceiv;[302] and therefore in those and such like speeches humbleth itself to our capacity, and attributeth such members unto God, that we may the better apprehend his Actions, to shew that God doth see, the scripture attributes eyes; to shew that he doth hear, it attributed eares; to shew that he doth work it attributes hands unto him; but properly God doth see without eyes, hears without eares, and works without hands, haveing no bodily part or members whatsoever.

Thus much of the Names of God, and how he is said to be a spirit. Now in the next place, God is further described unto us by his

Attributes, which are of 2 sorts, 1. such as describe God in hims[elf]. 2. such as declare God as he is to us. Of the former sort are these, Perfection, unchangeablenes and infinitenes, which may be either, 1. in respect of Duracion, and so he is an eternall God, 2. in respect of Place, and so he is an omnipresent God; And these

301 Cp. with "These lights, though they have no tongue to speak unto us, yet by their beauty they poynt to our eyes, by their light they sing the glory and praise of God in our eares." In lecture on Genesis 1.14. *Apos. Sacra*, p. 73.

302 Cp. with "But when they are ascribed, it is for no other end but even *humanum dicere*, for our 'infirmity,' to speak to us our own language, and in our terms, so to work with us the better." Sermon for Whitsunday, 1613. Andrewes, Vol. 3, p. 214.

Attributes are so proper, unto him, that they are incommunicable to the creatures; they declare unto us what God is in himselfe.

2ly, Other Attributes there are, which are secundary, such as declare, what God is to us, as Life, Power, Will, Mercy, Justice, Knowl[edge], Holines, Happines, Love, Truth. In all which God is infinite; and these are Attributes communicable to the creatures, not in Essence but by Analogie, according to that impresse of Divinitie which God hath stamped upon Angells and men, either by nature or by Grace or Glory. Concerning these Attributes, we are to observ these two things,

1. That all these Attributes are equally communicated to the whole Trinitie: Father, Sonne and h[oly] Ghost; As the Father is Perfect, unchang[eable], infinite, [omnipresent].

2. That all the Essentiall Attributes of the Godhead, are not so many severall Qualities and Accompaniments in God, but the one very entire Essence of God. His omnipotence, omniscience, mercy - - - and other his sacred Attributes, not being distinguished one from another really in God's Nature; but only formally in our conceptions; for tho' as they are conceived by us, they seem diverse and different Attributes, yet in God, they are but one most single and pure Act; which single act in God, is diversely expressed to us in different Names, as the divine Essence is called Mercy, when it freeth the miserable, and justice when he judgeth the guilty: and this is bec[ause] of our weaknes, who cannot in any measure conceiv of it, but in different Notions. And if it be objected, that oftentimes those Attributes are unequally proposed, as God is said to be slow to wrath, of great Goodnes, and that his mercy hath the preeminence over all his works.

Answer. Gods Attrib[utes] are not unequall in themselves, but in regard of their effects tow[ards] us; as God's mercy is said to be more then his justice; not in respect of God, but in respect of us, with whom he dealeth more in Mercy, then justice, to the great comfort of his servants.[303]

Lastly, the Essence and being of our God is without mixture or composicion; and therefore in him there are not diverse qualities, virtues and Passions, as there be in us: when we read of love, and

---

303 In M.L.E. of the ten attributes listed, Justice and Mercy are described as the principall ones as the other eight "fall into these two alike". p. 126.

anger and hatred ascribed to him, they are spoken ἀνθρωπειῶς for our capacity and understanding; that so we may the better perceive what manner of God he is.

I might now descend to speake more largely of the Attributes of God in particular, but they will be the Subject of severall lectures upon another Text; so it shall suffice at this time, to have spoken thus much in generall.

I proceed now from the Nature of God considered absolutely in it self, in the unity of the Godhead, to his manner of subsistence, in the Trinitie of Persons where we are to observ.

That the same God which is one in Nature or Beeing is also 3 in Persons or manner of subsisting, Father, Sonne and h[oly] Ghost: which three persons do not divide the Unitie into severall Natures, or severall Partes, but distinguish the Trinity by their Properties. And the resemblances, which are commonly brought by Divines to shadow out unto us the mystery of the blessed Trinitie, are these.

1. The sunne begetteth his own Beames and from thence proceedeth light, and yet is none of them before another, otherwise then in consideracion of Order and relacion. i.e. the Beames are begotten of the body of the sunne, and the light proceedeth from both.

2. From one Flame of fire proceed both light and heat, and yet but one fire.

3. In waters, there is the well head, the spring boyling out of it, and the stream flowing from them both; and all these are but one water: And so there are 3 persons in one Godhead, and yet but one God.

These are shadowes and representacions of the Trinity; but 'tis impossible, that a finite understanding should comprehend that infinite Mystery. And yet tho' Reason cannot instruct us to know what is hid, it doth direct us to beleev what is revealed concerning this mystery. And so what we cannot attain by a naturall knowl[edge], we may receive by a divine faith, when revealed unto us by God in his word.

Which word teacheth us, that the 3 Persons in the Godhead are not 3 partes of God, but one only God, Joh: 10.30. The Father God, Eph: 1.3; The Sonne God, Joh: 1.1; And the h[oly] Ghost, God. Act: 5. 32. And yet not 3 Gods but one, Esa: 6.3. All the 3 persons being coesentiall and coequall Joh: 5.18, Phil: 2.6.

And not to trouble you with many, there are 2 places in the N[ew] T[estament] which more clearly prove this doctrine of the Trinitie. The first is, Math: 3. 16-7 at our Saviour's Baptisme; the Father from Heaven witnessed of the Sonne; the h[oly] Ghost appeared in the likenesse of a Dove. Joh[n] Bapt[ist] saw the sonne in his assumed Nature goeing out of the water; there is one Person. He saw the h[oly] Ghost descending like a Dove upon him, there's another Person, And he heard a voyce from Heaven saying, this is my beloved sonne, there is a 3rd Person, St. Aug[ustine in *De Trinitas*, Bk. 2. Ch. 18.].[304]

The 2nd place is 1Joh: 5.7 where the Apostle speaketh expressly, There are three that bear record in Heaven, the Father, the Word, and the h[oly] Ghost and these 3 are one. Whence we may learn, That tho' the word Trinity, be not found literally expressed in scripture, yet 'tis plainly implyed; there is a certaine ground from whence it may be drawn a Trinity of Testimonies which doth plainly intimate a Trinitie of subsistances. *Sed credenda est Trinitas, non discutienda,* this great and glorious mystery is fitter for our belief than enquiry. And seeing this is a wonderfull mystery which the Angells adore, we should not dare to speak any thing in it farther than we have warrant out of God's word": yea, we must tye our selves in a manner to the expressions of the scripture, least we soar too high, in searching exceed our bounds, goe too far, and so be dazled and overwhelmed with the glory. I will therefore conclude this poynt with that ancient doxologie, Glory be to the Father [and to the Son and to the Holy Ghost] composed (as is conceived) by the 1st Council of Nicaea, and appoynted to be used in the ch[urch] as a Lesser Creed or confession of the Trinitie, of the **ὁμούσια**, consubstantialitie of the Sonne and the h[oly] Ghost with the Father against the Arrians who denyed that Truth.[305]

And thus much of the Divine Nature considered absolutely in it self, and of it's subsistence in three Persons. I shall add a word or 2 of Application and so conclude.

You have heard, how God is described unto us out of his word

---

304 This is repeated in Pentecost Sermon for 1612. Andrewes, Vol. 3, p. 188.

305 Cp. with E.P.,5.42.11.

by his Names and Attributes; that he is an eternall, omnipotent, all-sufficient God; And this should strengthen our faith, and encourage us in all our wants and afflictions, it should raise our spirits, and stir up our hope in us, in all distresses that we fall into upon any occasion. This was the very scope and drift of God's revealing his Name to Moses, goe tell the People, I am, hath sent thee unto them, a very happy message, and in a very seasonable time; for then a man would have thought it impossible, that they should have been delivered from Ægyptian thraldome, Pharaoh beeing so mighty a Prince, and so bent against it: yet God bids Moses goe, and tell them that he that IS hath sent him unto them. He that is. He that can makes things to be, when they have no rudiments of beeing, he hath sent him. Let us consider that He who is the Lord of being; He that is full of Beeing, as the sunne is of light, and the Ocean of waters, he alone is able to give Beeing to every grace, to supply all our wants, and make up every defect; to give what we have not, and to make those things good and usefull that we have; and therefore let us goe to him and give him the praise and glory of this his Name.

2. God is a spirit; whence we may gather.

1. That his eye is cheifly upon the spirits of men; He is called the Father of sp[irit]. Heb. 12.9 not but that he is the Father of the Body also; but he is *κατεζόνην*, most peculiarly the Father of spiritts, he cheifly respects them, being most like to hims[elf]. Now, if his eye be especially upon the spirit: we should labour also to be like him, have a speciall eye to our spiritts; let out eyes be upon our soules, to keep them clean, that they may be fit for communion with him who is an h[oly] and a pure spirit. We should labour to cleanse our selves from all filthines of flesh and spirit, and perfect holines in the fear of God.[306]

2. God is a spirit and the use which the Scripture makes of it is this, worship him in spirit and Truth the meaning of which place,[307] is this, we must not doe it for by-ends, not in appearance and show, in the sight of men, but in sp[irit] i.e. plainly, heart-

306 Cp. with "I have touchinge thee O Lord been full of rovinge imaginations and evill thoughts." In Ms. 3708, p. 41 and Andrewes, Vol. 11, p. 213.

307 Cp. with "I have not worshipped Thee in spirit and in truth" in Ms. 3708, p. 41, Andrewes, Vol. 11, p. 214, Brightman, *Manual*, p. 38.

ily, syncerely, not customarily, not formally; but when we pray unto him; when we come into his house to hear his word read or preached, we must be sure that our soules, our spiritts join with the outward performance.[308] In our Devotions and Addresses to him, we must have an eye to these 3 things, 1. That our spiritts be as near him, as our lipps are; 2. That we worship God with all the might and strength and endeavour of our mind, and faculties of our soules, this is to worship God in spirit. 3. That we have an eye upon him, when we come to worship him. For if we have an eye to men, to the praise or dispraise, that shall follow the performance or neglect of the Duty, so far we worship not God but men; but when our hearts are left naked and stript of all other respects in the world, and so overawed with the presence of God, that all other things doe vanish, then we serv God, and worship Him in spirit and in Truth.

3ly and lastly, when we think of this great and glorious God, as we must abandon all vaine, leud and licenious [living], so we must season our minds with holy thoughts, so we must raise our thought to Godwards by meditateing on his word and workes, by thinking on our duty and the work we are about, by considering Gods greatnesse in whose presence we are, and by pouring out our soules to God in our prayers, that he will direct our actions, and blesse his own ordinance and honour himself, in our voluntary service.

This Rule Solomon prescribeth us, Ecc.5.1 keep thy foot when thou goest into the house of God or (as another translacion hath it) take heed to thy foot *considera etiam atque etiam quò tendas et quem adeas* (Beza). Think upon it again and again whither thou art a goeing, and into whose presence thou comest. Thus he commandeth and so should we doe; when we are to appeare before God at the solemn times of his service; we should think whither it is that we goe, who it is that we deal with, even with him who is A and Ω, Alpha and Omega.

---

308 Cp. with "I have been carefull of the outward ceremoniall part of thy worship, then of the inward and spirituall/ I have drawn neare to thee with my lips, but my heart hath beene farre from thee." Ms. 3708, p. 41 and Andrewes, Vol. 11, p. 214.

LECTURE SIX

Of The Creation

Introduction

As already mentioned Andrewes believed that not only was Moses the author of Genesis, but also that his account of creation was literal, and so God made the world in six days and on the seventh day rested. As creation was a mirror of God, all was perfect from the tiniest to the largest and from the lowest to the highest forms of creation. Any imperfections in creation came from "the sin of man", Andrewes taught.

This lecture is comparable with lectures that Andrewes gave on the first chapter of Genesis at St. Paul's Cathedral in the academic year of 1590/1. All these lectures emphasised that creation is a joint effort of the three persons of the Trinity, despite our desire to divide them. For instance we mostly refer to the second person as the mediator in terms of redemption only, but "the Word of God is also the generall mediator." Therefore He is the mediator between "God and his works in this Creation". It was through the Word that "all things had their being ... and were set joynt and in order by him." Then when all was set out of joint "by Adam's sin", He "together with that powerfull working of the sanctifying Spirit," set all things "in right order and joynt again."[309] Indeed Andrewes suggested that God wants us "to discover the mysterie of the Trinity, in the three properties of the three persons, which appear in the Creation". "Power which is the property of God the

309 *Apos. Sacra,* p. 38.

Father; ...Wisdome, which is the property of God the Sonne, ... and ... the riches of his Goodness, which is the property of the holy Ghost, by which all things were adorned and made perfect." In summary the Father is the originator, the Son gives the reason for it, and the Spirit makes it all possible.[310]

Andrewes maintained that creation not only reveals the glory of the Trinity but it also manifests many of God's attributes: orderliness, perfection, power, goodness, wisdom and eternity.[311] For example God's orderliness was manifested in how the night and morning, winter and summer, sowing and harvesting all follow one another, whilst His perfection was revealed in the "variety of Partes" and "the strangenes of shape" in plants and creatures.[312]

In the process of creation God firstly created the inaminate such as light, secondly the animate such as flowers, herbs and brute creatures, and thirdly man. Andrewes also highlighted the distinction between the "immediate" and the "mediate" in creation, that is between the angels and man. Regarding the angels Andrewes drew attention to the theory that these must have existed before God's act of creation, as they were not mentioned in Moses' account of it. Such an opinion, he suggested, denied that when God created the heavens, He made not only the visible, such as the stars, but also the invisible, including the angels as set out in Colossians. Indeed in this lecture he gave one of his few comprehensive teachings on angelogy.[313] They are spiritual beings but of "reall substances", in a hierarchical order.[314]He suggested that there could be other angels outside this hierarchy but it is a matter too great and incomprehensible for man to fathom. Neither did he encourage belief in the medieval teaching that each person has his/her guardian angel, nor of praying to or adoring angels. They

---

310 Ibid., p. 10.

311 In his previous lecture Andrewes does not list wisdom, goodness and eternity as amongst the attributes of God.

312 *Apos. Sacra,* pp. 66, 70.

313 Other sermons given on angelogy were preached at Michaelmas, 1599 in his parish church of St. Giles, Cripplegate and Christmas 1605 at Court.

314 The "celestial hierarchie is constituted in a most holy order: archangels, angels, virtues, thrones, dominions, principalities, powers, cherubim and seraphim." Andrewes, Vol. 11, p. 265.

must not be regarded as mediators, as he also indicated in Lecture Eleven. Yet he had no doubt that they do pray for us, shed tears for penitents, and as God's servants wish us well. Indeed one of their main functions is to protect and support us in our daily warfare against the devil's temptations, as God's "swift winged Messengers". But their main task is undoubtedly "to sing Halleluiahs in heaven ... to the Lord their God."[315]

God made man His crowning glory, the masterpiece of His artistry and handiwork and the lord of all creation. He is thus the "microcosm, the compendium of the whole creation". Andrewes suggested that he was made last "so that he might be the world's High Priest to offer up the sacrifice of praise to God for all the creatures." Like all creation he too is an expression of God's beauty. Within his "exquisite frame" there is no "place, use, form, [which] doth not admit wonder and exceed it. No vein, no sinew, no artery is idle or may be wanting; how carefully and wonderfully is he made."[316] In his Genesis lectures Andrewes declared that God made the world as an expression of His "great love to Mankinde" and therefore He provided everything man might possibly need: "grain, seed, corn, pulse, spice, the grape, and other fruitfull trees." Furthermore he was made "monarch of the earth, all in *Paradise* were at his command until he disobeyed God" who "sent him out of paradise." By his disobedience "Gods image in man was defaced", but not erased; he is potentially good for "we are the clay, ... [and] the work of thy hand."[317]

Unlike his Calvinist contemporary, Perkins, Andrewes never depicted man as a depraved and despicable being. The former had taught that "every man is by nature dead in sinne as a loathsome carrion, or as a dead corps lieth rotting and stinking in the grave having in him the seed of all sinnes."[318] To see man as this, Andrewes believed, was to insult Christ who wedded Himself to us when He took our "earthly bodies of clay". This he made

---

315 *Apos. Sacra*, p. 587.

316 Ms. 3707, pp. 66-7

317 *Apos. Sacra*, pp. 107, 118, 179; Andrewes, Vol. 11, p. 281.

318 Perkins, Vol. 1, pp. 3-4. Cp. this also with the Ninth Article in the Prayer Book that "man is of his own nature inclined to evil."

clear in his first Nativity Sermon before James 1 in 1605 when he preached that God united the Word with our flesh, so that our nature might be restored in the person of Christ. Henceforth His manhood "ennobled" every person born into the world, and raised him to "a little lower than the angels". Indeed God in becoming man "bestowed upon us a dignity which upon the angels He bestowed not." Thus "he hath given us a preeminence above the angels themselves, granted us that that He hath not granted the angels - that is a comparison at the very highest, and farther we cannot go." God also gave man another privilege, not given to the angels. After he fell "from his first estate" He opened "to him a door of repentance." Thus man alone is privileged to "crave God's favour."[319]

Andrewes also believed that creation, as the handiwork of God, is one of the best teachers of the Christian faith. As he taught in the Second Lecture, "every grasse pile we tread upon, may serv as a little Catechism to teach us a Diety." It should primarily give us a desire "to love, worship, invocate and praise God"; yet "this naturall know[ledge] is not sufficient to salvacion, to make us eternally happy." Nevertheless it teaches us various Christian virtues. For instance we learn obedience from the greater light, the sun, which graciously gives way to the lesser light, the moon, and humility from our own insignificant beginning from dust in the overall greatness of the cosmos. And when we ponder on our fall, it should further abase us. Many, many times during his ministry Andrewes stressed the need for humility as he viewed it as the main virtue for Christians to possess. Without it was nigh impossible to be a disciple of Christ.[320]

Psalm 140.5. *Let them praise the name of the Lord: for he spake the word, and they were made, he commanded and they were created.*

And who he was I told you in my last [lecture] A and Ω which is [Alpha and Omega, the beginning and the ending, which is, and which was, and which is to come, the Almighty.] He spake the word [and they were made]. He who was without a begin-

---

319 Andrewes, Vol. 1, pp. 1-2, 9; *Apos. Sacra*, p. 287.

320 Andrewes, Vol. 1, p. 67.

ning, gave a beginning to time, and in time, Beeing, Form and Perfection to the world.[321]

He 1. gave a beeing to the matter without form, then a form to that matter, and lastly beauty and glory to that form. And all this he did without any help, labour or trouble, by the breath of his mouth, He commanded and they were created.

Haveing hitherto spoken of his Nature and Attributes, of the unitie of his essence, and Trinitie of Persons, I come now to speak of his workes, in which are manifested his Wisdome and Power and Goodnesse; his Wisdome in the varietie, distinction and excellency of his severall creatures; his Power in fetching all things out of nothing; and his Goodnesse in that haveing all sufficiency within himselfe, having no need of any externall Beeing, he was pleased to create all creatures, that he might communicate and manifest his goodnes.[322]

His workes may be reduced to these 2 heads (Creacion
(Providence.

And being to speak 1st of his workes of creacion, we shall observ 1st the various acceptions of the word; 2ly speak of the workes themselves.

1. The word create in Scripture hath a 3fold significacion, Tis taken 1st for the change of some Qualities in the mind, so Ps. 51.10 Create in me a clean heart (ô God) and renew [a right spirit within me], where creacion is the same with Regeneracion. So Esa: 65.18,19.[323] Behold I create new Heavens and a new earth, [...] I create Jerusalem a rejoycing and her People a joy, where *creare* is the same with *instaurare, reficere,* to restore and repaire. 2ly, the word is taken for bringing back from the dead, rematureing of that which is perished, Ps. 104.30 thou sendest forth thy spirit, they are created and thou renewest the face of the earth. 3ly, 'Tis

---

321 Cp. with "First, to create the beginning, both of all times and all things, as the matter and beginning of all superior bodies, and the beginning of all inferior bodies, of nothing. After the work of creation, followeth the work of distinction .... And lastly, ensueth the work of perfection, with beauty to adorn all his works ... ." from Andrewes' lecture on Genesis 1.2. *Apos. Sacra*, p. 10. Refer also to M.L.E., p. 100.

322 This also is very similar to text on the Trinitie in the above lecture from Genesis. Ibid. Cp. also with MS. 3708, p. 20 and Brightman, p. 101.

323 In the Authorized Version this is 65:17-8.

taken for the produceing of a thing out of nothing; which proceeds only from the infinite power of an infinite creatour. And so the word is to be taken in the Text, He commanded [and they were created].

Now before we come to speak of the workes of Creacion, obs[erve]. 1. The Causes. 2. the Adjuncts of it. In handling the causes we say, 1st The Author, or efficient cause is God; who as a most free Agent, without any necessitie compelling, or any externall cause moveing him, to manifest his glory and communicate his goodnes, of his own good pleasure and of his own most powerfull will, he made the world. And 2ly, bec[ause] *Opera Trinitatis ad extra* [*sunt indivisa*][324] therefore we say in the next place, That the creacion of the world was the proper work of God alone, not from any one Person, but all the whole Trinitie; as being a work of infinite power, wisdome and love; as of infinite power, so from the Father; as of infinite Wisdome, so from the Sonne; as of infinite love, so from the holy Ghost; and yet from all the 3 Persons, as 'tis from one entire cause, one single essence, God's. Mal. 2.10 hath not one God created us? And that as a free Agent, Eph. 1.11 as a God all sufficient [almighty in A.V.] in hims[elf], Gen. 17.1 And the reason of this is clear.

For if the world were made of God by a necessitie of his Nature, and not according to the libertie of his Will; or if the world <u>made</u>, did add any thing to the fullnes and perfection of the maker, it must needes have been, as hims[elf] is, from eternitie, and should not cease to be in the end of Time: but Reason and experience teacheth us the contrary, that all things which are must have a first cause from whence they proceed, and must ow[e] their Beeing and perfection to some supreme Beeing of infinite wisedome, of when all things are made and ordered to such good purposes as they are.

But here it may be demaunded, cannot men or Angells, is it not in the Power of any creature to create?

---

324 i.e. "The externally directed works of the Trinity are undivided." What follows in this paragraph is in M.L.E., p. 99. The material reappears in Genesis lecture on Genesis 1.2, *Apos. Sacra*, p. 10; and in the last sermon that Andrewes prepared for Whitsunday in 1622, Andrewes, Vol. 3, p. 381.

No, *creaturæ cum sint, creatores esse non possunt,*[325] Damasc[us].[326] The work of Creation is properly and peculiarly God's. And therefore whatsoever the Devill, any Jugler or sorcerer seemes to doe, 'tis nothing but a delusion of the senses. 1. The witch that is said to raise up Samuel [for Saul], 1Sam. 28.11 did but raise up a Devil in Samuel's mantle. And Jannes and Jambras the sorcerers of Ægypt [2Tim: 3.8] if the Froggs and serpents were reall, [Ex: 7.12, 8.5-13] yet not created by their own Power for 1st, God to shew that his Miracle was of Power, th' other of permission, made Moses his serpent devour them. 2. those that could bring froggs and serpents, could neither make, nor kill lice; to shew them that those froggs and serpents were not their own workmanshipp. 3ly. they that had permission to bring Plagues upon Ægypt, had not power to remove one, and it is as easy to annihilate, as to create. So to begin that which never was, whereof there was no example, whereto there was no inclinacion, wherein there was no possibilitie of that which it should be, is proper only to such a power as is infinite, Alm[ighty], Omnip[otent], And thus of the Author or Efficient cause of creacion. Only God [can make].

Next for the materiall cause, which was nothing. But here we are to distinguish of a 2fold creacion. 1. Immediate 2. Mediate. 1st some workes, by an immediate creacion were made out of simply nothing, Heb: 11.3 by the will of God made subject to no essential chang, or utter dissolucion; Such were the Angells, and the highest Heavens created together (as supposed on the first day of the creation), Gen: 1.1 [In the beginning God created the heavens and the earth,] Job: 38.7 [When the morning stars sang together, and all the sons of God shouted for joy]. 2ly, others of the creatures were formed by a mediate creacion, of matter pre-existent; as man was made of the Dust of the ground, whose first originall was nothing, and which matter was of itself so indisposed, and so incapeable of vertue and power to produce man, that it was to be accounted as nothing. This for the Material cause.

3ly, For the formall cause, or manner of createing; God used no meanes, no instruments (for he had no need of any) but his

---

325 Literally it means "as they are together creatures, they cannot be creators."

326 John of Damascus. *An Exact Exposition of the Orthodox Faith*, Bk. 2, Ch. 3.

own powerfull word, his own holy will, by the word of the Lord were the Heavens made, and all the host of them, by the breath of his mouth Ps. 33.6. He did but speake the word, said, let it be, and the whole world arose out of nothing; where we may observ the ineffable power of alm[ighty] God who could speake such a Masse of things, such a world of wonders out of simply nothing.

4ly, Finall cause, his own glory. 1. In workes of creacion he manifested his eternall power and godhead, Rom: 1.20, the invisible things of him from the creacion of the world are clearly seen, even his eternall power and Godhead, being understood by things that are made. 2ly, His infinite Wisdome; how fitly, how wisely, are all the parts disposed? every little creature would be a greater wonder to us, if we had but eyes to see, and hearts to weigh and consider it. He hath made the world by wisdome, and stretched out the Heavens by his understanding, Jer: 10.12, and he repeats the same words c.51.15, as if he should have said, ô what a glorious heaven is this which he hath spread over our heades? with how beautifull and spacious[327] a vault hath he walled in this our inferiour world? what a world of light hath he set above us? those things which we see are wondrous, how such more those which we beleeve and see not? 3ly, His infinite Aut[h]oritie doth appeare in the workes of the creation; what a perfect concord and harmony, what ready and constant obedience is performed by all his creatures to his primitive commands? How doe the jarring Elements keep the same places that were first assigned them? how doth day dye into night and rise again into the morning? how doth winter and summer, seedtime and harvest continue and succeed one another in their seasons?[328] How doth he call those things which are not, and how doth he command those which are; Heaven and earth, sea and Air, and they obey him? And thus much of the finall cause of Creacion. I proceed now from the causes to the Adjuncts, the Goodnes of the creatures; at the dayes end, God looked upon the work he had made, and he saw that it was good. Gen: 1.4,10,12. And at the end of the week,

---

327 Spelt "specious" in manuscript.

328 Clement of Rome had already expressed this point in his letter to the church in Corinth. Clement, Ch. 20. Cp. also with lecture on Genesis 1.1, *Apos. Sacra*, p. 7.

takeing a view of all his works together, he saw every thing he had made, and behold it was very good. Gen: 1.31.

Now the Goodnes of the creatures consists 1. in the perfection of their Natures; 2ly, in their Properties and qualities, whereby they are made serviceable to those ends for which they were created.

1. God created everything perfect in it's kind: in it's kind, I say, for tho' there be severall kinds of creatures, and some more beautifull and excellent then others, yet is every creature perfect in it's kind tho' there be a greater birth, yet not more natural perfection in the Elephant than in the Ant, the one as perfect and compleat in his kind, as th' other.[329]

So whatever deformitie, imperfection or disorder there is in the creatures, this came not by the Nature of their creacion, but the sin of man. And that some of them are not serviceable, but hurtfull to us, we have none to blame but ourselves; For God made all things very good, and for the use and benefit of man.[330]

Hitherto of the creation in generall, of the causes and adjuncts of it. Next for the particular creatures, which may be reduced to 2 Heades 1. Superior 2. Inferiour creatures. By superior, I understand the highest Heavens, the Place where God's honour dwelleth, where his throne of Majesty is placed. Ps. 11.4. And the Angells, those glorious creatures, that wait about the throne, Rev. 4.4. These are called things invisible.

2ly, By Inferior creatures we understand 1. The visible Heavens which may be distinguished into 2 Regions. 1st The Air wherein we breath, and wherein snow and hail and thunder etc are begotten; next the skye, where the sun and moon, and starrs are placed. 2. By Inferior creatures, the earth and all creatures that move thereupon.[331]

To begin with the highest, the Angells. Some are of opinion, that they were created before God made the world;[332] bec[ause]

---

329 Refer also to lectures on Genesis 1. 24 – 5. Ibid., pp. 669 – 70.

330 Cp. with "Thus doth our sinne and ungratefulness overthrow and prevent, and stain the whole course and order of Nature." Ibid., p. 9.

331 Cp. with Commemoration in Prayers for Monday, Brightman, p. 56 and the Sermon on *In Earth as it is in Heaven*, Andrewes, Vol. 5, pp. 406 - 7.

332 John of Damascus stated that Gregory the Theologian was of the opinion they

Moses setting down the history of the creacion, makes no mention of their creacion and it is not probable he would have omitted the story of such glorious creatures. To the 1st of these we Answer 1. with the Apostle, Col: 1.16 By him were all things created that are in Heaven, and that are in earth, visible and invisible, whether they be Thrones or Dom[inions], Princip[alities], or Powers; all things were created by him and for him, where mention made of creac[ion] of those glorious creatures, with their wonderful Degrees and Dignities. 2ly, Moses doth not expressly mention them, bec[ause] he setts forth the History of the creacion of things only visible; and therefore the story of mineralls, and things hid and inclosed in the bowells of the earth [are omitted]. Thus that they were created.[333]

2ly, For the Nature of Angells, they are substances wholly spirituall, and therefore in respect of their simple essence in scripture they are called spirits, Ps. 104.4. He maketh his Angells spirits - and again, are not all ministring spirits sent out [to minister for them who shall be heirs of salvation?] Heb:1.14. When we say that they are spirits, we mean, 1. That they are not shadowes, or Phantasmes but reall substances. 2. That they have spir[ituall], incorporeall matter such as the soul of man hath. 3. That they are invisible. 4. immortall, incorruptible; yet not so immortall but that God may destroy them. He that hath power to create, hath the same power to annihilate them. And in respect of their subtle, incorporeall, immortall essence, they are called the sonnes of God, Heb: 2.6, Luc: 20.36.[334]

Thus much of their materiall cause. Lastly their Finall cause; to what end they were created, their very name declares it to us; Angells are the same with Messengers; swift winged Messengers: such as God is pleased to use upon any occasion when he manifests his justice in the destruction of his enemies, or his mercy in the preservation of his servants. Examples of this are very frequent in the scriptures, as in the Destruction of Sodome and preserva-

---

were before the creation of other things, others after the first heaven was made. John of Damascus, Bk. 2, Ch. 3. Refer also to Oration No. 2, ch. 7 of Gregory of Nanzianus.

333 In his lecture on Genesis 1.7 Andrewes stated, "the Angells and celestial spirits were created when God said *fiat lux*." *Apos. Sacra*, p. 46.

334 Similar with text in Nativity Sermon for 1605, Andrewes, Vol. 1, p. 4.

cion of Lot, Gen: ch. 19, in the smiteings of Herod and delivering of Peter, Acts. 12.6, 23.

And here to speak a word or two of the ministerie and function of Angells. We are not to doubt of the protection of God's Angells, that he is pleased to make use of their minisiterie to keep us in all our wayes, Ps. 91.11. Yet that every one hath a proper and particular Angell appointed for his protection from his Nativitie, for this we have no ground in Scripture. For

1. Sometimes one Angell hath the charge of a multitude as the Angell that smote the first born of Ægypt, but preserved the Israelites, Exod: 12. 20, 23, 29.

2. Sometimes many Angells are ready for the defence of one man, as an Host of Angells met Jacob, Gen: 32.1.

3. The soul of poor Lazarous is said to be carried into Abraham's bosome, not by one Angell but by Angells, Luc: 16.22. But if he had had one Angell only appoynted to be the president of his life from his Nativitie; then it had been part of that Angell's charge to have conveyed his soul into Heaven.

4. Seeing that not one evill spirit, but many doe assault us; as Mary Magdalene had 7 Devills cast out of her Luc: 8.2, and another professed with a Legion of Devills Mar: 5.9 we are to think that God hath set as strong a guard of good Angells to defend, as there is of bad Angells to offend; and therefore 'tis probable that more than one Angell are appoynted for the custody of the faithfull. Thus much of the ministery of Angells about our custody and Protection. Next for their Ministry about our prayers.

1. They pray for us in generall, wishing well unto all God's chosen upon earth, as their fellow servants; as in their Heavenly Anthem, they wish peace in the earth [and good will towards men], Luc: 2.14. And there is joy in Heaven for one sinner [that repenteth], Luc. 15.7. *Aqua poenitentiae* ... our penitent teares are such wine as the blessed Angells drinke. But

2ly, That they offer up our Prayers to God as Mediators, that we are to pray unto them, or perform any worship to them, for this we have no ground, no warrant in the scripture. Yea we read of an Angell forbidding it, Rev: 19.10, See thou doe it not, For [I am thy fellow servant]. Ps. 65.2, Thou that hearest Prayer, unto thee [unto thee shall all flesh come]. So in our Devotions we are to make our addresses to God only, through J[esus] Ch[rist] our Lord.[335]

Lastly, for the Hierarchie or Degrees of Angells. As the starres in the firmament differ in place and light; one star differeth from [another star in glory], the like difference may be among the Angells: for there is no doubt, but that the celestiall hierarchie is constituted in a most holy order; And as there shall be difference among the Saints even in diversitie of mansions, Joh: 14.2, so the like may be affirmed of the Angells. Jud: v.9, and Dan: 10.13. We read of Michael the Archangell, and Eph: 1.21 of Principalities and Powers and Mights and Dominions. And the like may be affirmed of bad Angells, there is order even amongst the spirits of Darknes; For we read of Belzeebub, the prince of Devills, Math: 12.24. And of Principalities and Powers and Rulers of the Darknes of this world, Eph: 6.12. By these places it appeareth, that there are severall Names and distinct Orders of Angells; But to know the Number of them and how they are distinguished into their distinct orders and places, 'tis a poynt of needles curiositie to enquire and we shall only then know when we shall be *ἰσάγγελοι* like unto the Angells.

To conclude this point. In the Angells 4 things are to be considered 1. Their Nature and Substance, which is incorporeall, incorruptible, invisible. 2. Their Properties, wisedome, power, swiftnes, industrie, in all which they excell. 3. Their office and ministery, which is to sing Halleluiah's in Heaven; Salvacion and glory and honour and Power to the Lord their God, Rev: 19.1 and in obedience to their makers will, to goe about his busines to all men, in all places of the world. 4. Their Hierarchie and Dignitie, whereby there is *sub* and *supra*, one order superiour to another. And thus much in breif of the creacion of those glorious Creatures the Angells.

In the next place we descend to the creation of things inferiour and visible, where we shall observ.

1. The order in which God did create them; the dwelling places were first framed, then the creatures to dwell in them; Provision was made for the Inhabitants of the earth, before he made the

335 Refer to Andrewes' reply to Cardinal Perron on this subject. Andrewes, Vol. 11, p. 74.

Inhabitants thems[elves], as grasse for the Beasts, and light for the benefit of all liv[ing] and moving Creatures and all for the use of man.

2. In the works of the creacion, God proceeded from things more imperfect to those that are perfecter as from things inaminate to those that have but one life, herbs and Trees, and all vegitables; then to sensitive creatures, fowles of the Air, Fishes of the sea, and Beasts of the Earth. And from them to reasonable creatures, Men. To begin with the 1st of these.

1. Things inaminate. The first creature that God created, was light, Gen: 1.3, which for 3 dayes was dispersed thorow the whole heavens, till on the 4th day God was pleased to gather and unite it in one body of the Sun;[336] which one star God made the Treasury of light to the Heavens and the earth Gen: 1.4. And the benefits which all inferiour creatures receiv from this one star, is very great.[337]

1. It affordeth light, to know and discern the variety of things, to see and perform such Dutyes as are required of us: the Sun ariseth - and man goeth forth to his work and to his labour untill the evening Ps: 104.23.[338] And this makes our lives comfortable to us, this sweetens all our labours, truly the light is sweet, and a pleasant thing it is for the eyes to behold, the sun Eccl: 11.7. How miserable would our condicion be, if we should live in continuall darknes, be debarred the light and comfort of the day?

2. By it's heat and influence, it produceth liveing creatures, nourisheth them when they are produced, and so brings them to maturity and perfection.

3. That all partes of the earth might the better enjoy the comfort and benefit of the sun; God hath given it a 2fold motion 1. Diurnall 2. Annuall. 1st. Diurnall, so in the space of 24 houres, it compasseth about, viewes and enlightens the whole world.

And 2ly, by it's Annuall motion, it makes summer and winter, seedtime and Harvest in diverse Partes of the earth. By which mo-

---

336 Cp. with similarity in lecture on Genesis 1.3, *Apos. Sacra*, p. 17.

337 Refer also to Brightman, p. 211.

338 Cp. with "The Sunne is the protector of man, and when he ruleth, it is the time of labour: but when the Moon ruleth, the night commeth and restoreth strength." *Appos. Sacra*, p. 82.

tions it comes to passe 1. That one sunne is sufficient for the whole earth, 2. That 'tis beneficiall to all Partes of the earth. And that the light of this Body is interchanged with darknes, not perpetuall but by successions, as there is pleasure in this vicissitude, so profitablenes; for if the beams of the sunne should beat continually upon the same place, that part of the earth would perish with heat, and the rest for want of heat; but the most wise God hath so ordered, that as the presence, so the absence of it is beneficiall; as the day is made for man and other creatures to labour, so the night to take their rest in.

And as the sun, so God made the moon usefull and beneficiall to his creatures. 1. with her borrowed weak light to qualifie the darknes of the night, yet not so, as to make it unfit for rest. And again with her heat to moderate the vehemency of the cold. And besides, God hath placed the sun and the moon and starrs for signes and seasons, without which what a confusion would there be in the world? what order in the Actions and busines of men, without distinction of times; and therefore (saith God) let there be lights in the Firmament, and let them be for signes and for seasons and for dayes and for yeares Gen: 1.14.[339]

To descend yet lower, God hath made the Space between the Heavens and the earth, full of Air, not a solid but liquid body, that it may not hinder the light and the influences of the Heavens from makeing their way thorow to comfort and refresh the Earth. Thus saith the Lord, I will hear the Heavens and the earth, and the earth [shall answer the] corn, wine, [and the] oyl Hos: 2.22.[340] All these have recourse to the Heavens, and God hath made the Passage clear bet[ween] them and the earth. The time would fail me to goe down to the great deep, the womb of moysture, the well of fountaines, the great and wide sea; how doth it roar and foam and swell, as if it would swallow up the earth; and yet how the rage of it is stayed by an insensible violence, and his waves confined as by a naturall Miracle? Why this boyling element moved and why it stayes, to us equally wonderfull. They that goe down to the sea

339 Refer also to lectures on Genesis 1. 14 –9, Ibid., pp. 72 – 84; and Commemoration in Prayers for Wednesday, Brightman, p. 71.

340 Similar to that in Sermon on *Give us our daily bread,* Andrewes, Vol. 5. p. 417.

in shipps, see the workes of the lord and wonders in the deep. Ps. 107. 23-4.[341]

To proceed now from inaminate creatures, to those which are animate; and to begin at the lowest, Herbes, Flowers, Trees, Leaves, Seeds, Fruites, vegetative creatures; wherein we may read infinitenes of power and of skill, and see the footstepps of a dietie. Our hearts are too strait, our capacities too shallow sufficiently to admire, even those things which we tread upon; how necessary are they for the preservacion of life in other creatures, and how usefull both for our food and physick? [342]

Next to the Plants, are brute creatures; which if we duly view and consider, we shall be brought to confesse, that he who made the Angells and starrs of Heaven, made not only the Lyion and Leviathan, but the least vermine on earth. How are they beautified with variety of Partes, strangenes of shapes; how are they furnished with instruments of motion, feet and wings and scales, and with weapons to preserv their beeing; and how industrious are they to provide Dens, and Nests and cells and to lay up provision of food and nourishment; so that man is sent to the school to them to learn diligence of them Prov: 6.6 - 8.[343] What shall we say to the maker of all these? O lord how wonderful are thy workes in all the world, in widsome hast thou made them all. Thus much of the workes of the fifth dayes creacion Ps 104. [24].[344]

Lastly, the last of all the creatures that was made, was Man, a Microcosm, the compendium of the whole creacion; who is very fitly called the lesser world, bec[ause] he hath something of affinitie with and participation of the severall parts of the greater world. He hath affinitie with the Angells in his soul, as being sp[iritual], invisible, intelligent, immortal, with the h[oly] bodyes in the excellency of his constitucion, and harmony of his partes, with the 4 elements in the substance of his body, naturall partes

341 Cp. with similiarity in lecture on Genesis 1. 6, *Apos Sacra*, p. 42.

342 This is similar to what Isaacson wrote in his *Life and Death of Andrewes*, Andrewes, Vol. 11, p.vi.

343 Cp. with that in Sermon on *Give us this day our daily bread*, Ibid., Vol. 5, pp. 422 – 3.

344 Refer also to lecture on Genesis 1.21. *Apos. Sacra*, pp. 84 – 9.

of his composicion, the superior Elements being predominant, the inferior more abounding in their matters, whereby man is said to be framed of the Dust of the earth.[345]

Now man was made the last of all the creatures.

1. bec[ause] he was the most excellent of all the workes of God in this inferior world. 2. bec[ause] he was the end of all unreasonable creatures; and therefore that he might be the world's High Priest, to offer up the sacrifice of praise to God for all the creatures that he saw the world was furnished with for his sake. 3ly, bec[ause] God would have him first provided for, ere he brought him into the world, and he being to be Prince and Lord over it, he would have his Palace furnished with all things convenient. This for the time of his creacion.

Againe, Man, cheif of the visible creatures, consisting of Body and Soul, was made in the Image and after likenes of God, Gen. 1.26, where we are not to understand any bodily shape but 1. the inward dignitie and excellency of his soul, that holinesse, righteousness, and uprightnesse of desires and actions, which were imprinted in the soul of Man at his creacion.

2ly, Outward gifts and endownments as 1st God set such a grace and Majesty in the Person of Man, as all the creatures could not look upon him without fear and trembling. 2. God gave him dominion and rule over them all [Gen: 1.26], to be his sole vicegerent upon earth. 3. God gave him a Body answerable to his soul, endued with beauty, strength, immortality. 1. Beauty, there is no peice in this exquisite frame whereof the place, use, form, doth not admit wonder and exceed it. No vein, no sinew, no artery is idle or may be wanting; how fearfully and wonderfully is he made. 2. Immortalitie, yet not absolute, but by sp[ecial] priviledge and dispensacion. For the body of man, even before his fall, by reason of those contrary elements, contrary humours, members of contrary temper, whereof it was composed, was in it self dissoluble and mortall. Again, if man had been in this respect simply immortall before his fall, he should have continued so after his fall, as the Apostate Angells did.[346]

---

345 Cp. with similarity in Christmas Sermon for 1623. Andrewes, Vol. 1, p. 275.

346 Refer also to lectures on Genesis 1. pp. 26 – 7, *Apos. Sacra*, pp. 93 – 100.

And thus much of man, made after God's own Image as 'tis taken in a larger sense, for that dignity and excellency, given unto man in his creacion, which was partly inward in the soul, and partly outward in the Body.

To apply this

1. In the works of creacion is manifested, the glory of the creator (*mundus ut speculum Dietatis*), the world is a mirrour or glasse, wherein we behold the excellency of it's maker: his eternall power and Godhead, are clearly seen from the creacion of the world, being understood by things that are made, Rom: 1.20. The Heavens declare the glory of God, Ps. 19.1. (i.e) as much of it as can be expressed by them, or apprehended by us, but the glory of God in itself exceeds all expression and conception, His glory is above the earth and heaven, Ps. 148.13. All that we can doe is this, to return the glory of all, to him who made all, and to say with the Levites, Neh. 9.5, 6 Blessed be thy glorious name, which is exalted above all blessings and above all praise: thou even thou art lord alone, thou hast made heaven, the heaven of heavens with all their host, the earth and all things that are therein, the seas and all that is therein, and thou preservest them all and the host of heaven worshippeth thee; and Rev. 4.11 the four and twenty elders cast down their crownes before the throne of God saying: Thou art worthy O Lord to receive glory and honour and power: for thou hast created all things, and for thy pleasure they are and were created.

More particularly, by the creacion we may see the excellency of God's Power, goodnes, wisdome and Eternity.

1. His Power is gloriously manifested in his createing all things out of nothing: Philosphy tells us *ex nihilo nihil fit*, that nothing is made of nothing.[347] It is true indeed in respect of natural Agents, they must have some matters to work upon, otherwise their work will come to nothing. But Divinity tells us, that all things were made of nothing; that those things which are seen were not made of things which doe appear Heb: 11.3. This is most true in respect of God; by this God shewes himself to be God, doeing that which none can doe but he.[348] Whereupon one saith excellently, if any

347 This is also in M.L.E., p.30.

348 Cp. with similarity in lectures on Genesis 1.1 and 2, *Apos. Sacra*, pp. 8, 11- 2.

besides, the true God, shall say I am God, he must shew us such a world as this is, and say, this is mine, of my makeing.[349] The lord (saith David) is great, and greatly to be praised; he is to be feared above all God's: for all the Gods of the Nations are Idolls Ps. 96.4,5. And the Gods (saith Jeremie) that have not made the Heavens and the earth, even they shall perish from under the Heavens; He hath made the earth by his power, Jer. 10.11,12.

2. The excellency of God's goodnes is manifested in his communicateing a proportion of life and blessednes unto his creatures; Thou art good and dost good (saith David) unto God Ps. 119.68. This was that which moved him to make the world, not that he had any need of the creatures (for from all eternitie he was most blessed and happy in hims[elf]) but that he might communicate his goodnes to the creatures; the earth is full of the goodnes of the lord, Ps. 33.5. And Aug[ustine] de Civ[itate] dei. L.11. c.23 *Rerum creatarum causa non est nisi bonitas creatoris,* there was no other cause moveing God to make the world, but that he being good, might make things that are good.

3. His wisdome in that admirable harmony of order and of use; that excellent beauty of proportion, and of Partes which is in the creatures, that he could make, such an infinite variety of creatures, and not the least or meanest of them, but to have it's use and office in the universe: He hath established the world by his wisdome, and hath stretched out the heavens by his discretion, Jer: 10.12 and 51.15. And Ps. 104.24 O l[ord], how manifest are thy workes! in wisdome hast thou made made them all. And

Lastly, his Eternitie is gloriously manifested in his being the Author and efficient Cause of all things who therefore must needs have his being, before they could have their beginning; and haveing his being before time he must be Eternall. Before the mountaines were brought forth, or even thou hadst formed the earth and the world, even from everlasting to everlasting thou art God, Ps. 90.2.

Now seeing God hath manifested hims[elf] in his creatures to be a creator, in Power, Goodnes, and Wisdome, infinite and eternall; even the light of Nature doth direct us to love, worship, invocate and praise him. O that men would praise [the Lord],

349 In P.C.D. the author of this quotation is given in the text, Pythagoras. p. 66. Refer also to M.L.E., p. 78.

and tell of all his wondrous workes; and of this amongst the rest, that he should make such a little creature man, lord over the great world. The least graine of sand is not so small to the whole earth as man is to the Heaven. So from the Doctrine of the worldes creacion,[350] every man must learn in the 1st Place to be humbled, for nothing can be more properly applyed to abate the swelling of our proud conceptions then a due consideracion of the other works of God with a sober reflexion upon our own originall. When I consider the Heavens the work of thy fingers, the moon, and the starrs which thou hast ordained [Ps.8.3]; when I view those glorious apparent bodyes with my eye, and contemplate those far more glorious spirits, beyond the power of my sight, the Inhabitants of the heavens and Attendants on thy throne; I cannot but break forth in that admiracion of the prophet, What is man that thou art mindfull of him? What is that offspring of the earth, that dust and ashes? What is that son of man that thou visited him? [Ps. 8. 4][351] What is there in the progeny of an ejected and condemned Father, that thou should first look down from Heaven the place of thy dwelling, and take care or notice of him? But if our orginall ought so far to humble us, how should our fall abase us? That of all the creatures which God made, we should comply with him, who first opposed his maker. How can we looke without confusion of face upon that monument if our infamy, recorded by Moses, who first penned the originall of humanity. Gen: 6.6 It repented the Lord that he had made man on the earth and it grieved him at his heart. And can we grieve our God, and not be grieved ourselves; oh, how should we bewail our own corruption and be humbled in the sight of our creator whom we alone of all creatures by our unrepented sins drew unto repentance?[352]

---

350 The text of the rest of this lecture was taken by John Pearson and incorporated as the first article of the Creed, Chapter 5, *Maker of Heaven and* Earth, Pearson pp. 103 - 6.

351 In M.L.E this quotation has the following comment: "*David* considereth the great glory of the Heavens; then the eternity of them: and he wondreth how God could passe by them a most glorious body; and put the soule of man, a most excellent creature, into a vile lump of clay and earth." p. 39. The text is also similar to text in Nativity Sermon for 1605, Andrewes, Vol. 1, p. 14.

352 Refer also to Pentecost Sermon 1613. The theme of this sermon is how we grieve

2. This doctrine of the Creacion, should teach us chearfull and universall obedience. The most loyall and obedient servants which stand continually before the most illustrious prince, are not so ready to receive and execute the commands of their Sovereign lord, as all the host of Heaven and earth attend upon the will of their Creator, Esa: 40.26, lift up your eyes on high and behold who hath created these things that bringeth out their hosts by number: he calleth them all by names, by the greatnesse of his might for that he is strong in power; not one faileth but every one maketh his appearance, ready prest to observ the designes of their commander in cheife. Thus the lord commanded and they fought from heaven, the starrs in their courses fought against Sisera. Jud: 5.20. And 1K: 17.4,6 He commanded the ravens to feed Elias, and they brought him bread and flesh in the morning, and bread and flesh in the evening; and so our prophet lived merely upon the obedience of the foules of the air. He spake to the devouring Whale, Jon: 2.10 and it vomited out Jonah upon dry land; and so another Prophet was delivered from the Jawes of death, by obedience of the fishes of the sea. Nay do we not read of fire and haile, snow and vapour, stormy wind fullfilling his word? Ps. 148. 8. Now shall there be a greater coldnesse in man then in the snow? more vanity and disobedience in us, then in a vapour? more inconstancy, blustring and rebellion then in the wind? If the universall obedience of the creature to the will of the Creator cannot move us to the same affection and desire to serv and please him, they will all conspire to testify against us and condemn us, when God shall call unto them, saying Hear ô Heavens, and give ear ô earth for the Lord hath spoken: I have nourished and brought up children and they have rebelled against me Esa:1.2.[353]

Lastly, from this Doctrine of the creacion, the true servants of God, may reap comfort and consolacion in all the variety of their condicions. Ps. 146. 5,6 Happy is he whose hope is in the lord his God, who made Heaven and Earth, the sea and all that therein is. This happines consisteth partly in a full assurance of

---

God by our unrepentened sins. Andrewes, Vol. 3, pp. 214 – 8.

353 Refer also to Sermon on *On earth as it is in heaven*, Andrewes, Vol 5, pp. 407 – 8.

his power to secure us, his abilitie to satisfie us. Ps. 24.1,2 The earth is the Lords, and the fullnese thereof, the world, and they that dwell therein. By vertue of the first production, he hath a perpetuall right unto, and power to dispose of all things; and he which can order and dispose of all must necessarily be esteemed able to secure and satisfy any creature; Esa: 40.25,[354] Hast thou not known? hast thou not heard that the everlasting God, the Lord, the Creator of the ends of the earth, fainteth not, neither is weary? There is no externall resistance or opposicion, where omnipotency worketh; no internall weaknesse or defection of power, where the Almighty is the Agent; and consequently there remaineth a full and firm persuasion of his abilitie in all conditions to preserv us.[355] Again, this happinesse consists partly in a comfortable assurance, ariseing from this meditacion,[356] of the will of God to protect and succour us, of his desire to preserv and blesse us. Ps. 121.2, 3 My help cometh from the Lord who made heaven and earth, he will not suffer they foot to be moved, saith the prophet David, at once expressing the foundacion of his own expectancy, and our security. God will not despise the work of his hands, neither will he suffer the rest of his creatures, to doe the least injury to his own Image. Behold (saith He Esa: 54.16) I have created the smith that bloweth the coales in the fire, and that bringeth forth an instrument for his work; No weapon that is formed against thee shall prosper. This is the heritage of the servants of the Lord; he will protect and defend them by his grace and power here and bring them to glory hereafter.

---

354 In the Authorised Version this is 40. 28.

355 Cp. with M.L.E., p. 38.

356 Commending meditation upon a lecture or sermon was characteristic of Andrewes. There are many examples in his teaching and preaching when he commends to his auditors thoughtfulness on what they have heard. Examples are found in Andrewes, Vol. 1, pp. 14, 361, Vol.3, p. 199, Vol. 5, p.202.

LECTURE SEVEN

Of Gods Providence

In Romans 11.36. [For of him, and through him, and to him, are all things: to whom be glory for ever, Amen].

Jer.12.2. [Thou hast planted them, yea, they have taken root: they grow, yea, they bring forth fruit; thou art near in their mouth, and far from their reins].

To apply this.

1.

(This was never completed).

LECTURE EIGHT

Of the Two Covenants

Introduction

A covenant, as stated in an earlier lecture has similarities with a testament. Andrewes defined it as a "solemn Act done by two Parties, whereby they mutually bind themselves to doe, give or receive something, some outward signes used to ratifie and confirm it that the promise may be inviolable." On the surface, this definition was not dissimiliar to that of the Puritans. On closer inspection it will be discovered that for Puritans this covenant between God and man is limited to the elect only. Andrewes tried to balance this Puritan teaching by emphasising that all could enter into a covenantal relationship with God. He offers His "mercyes and gracious promises" to man who in return renders "obedience" and "repentance".[357]

God made two covenants with man, "the covenant of works" and "the covenant of grace", both of which were compacted in the Garden of Eden. The first was voluntary when Adam lived in a state of innocence and perfection. This covenant was "imprinted in the heart of man, whereby he knew what was good, ... and had abilitie to perform it." God through His mercy had provided man with everything he needed, and all that was required of him was "obedience" to God's one command. Yet Adam chose not to obey

357 Ms. 3707, pp. 72 - 3.

this command, and thus he forfeited "his crown", and was "condemned to death".[358]

However before casting Adam out of paradise, God through His mercy announced his second covenant, the covenant of grace. Through the seed of the woman He would restore mankind "into his favour, and to that state of happinesse they had lost by the meanes of a mediatour Christ Jesus (Gal. 3:22)." This covenant was renewed through Abraham, the prophets and most clearly in Christ when He took "our nature upon him, and in that nature of ours" rendered complete obedience to God. By Christ's blood the covenant was sealed.[359]

The covenant of grace is "a covenant of better promises" as it firstly, assures men of "eternal life", and secondly, "it requires of no man an exact and absolute obedience in all points." Thus "perfect obedience is [not] required of us" as this is unattainable on earth. Instead God in His mercy "is content with true repentance and with such an amendment of life," from man who undertakes not "to offend God any more; and endeavour[s] to walk in the wayes of piety and goodnes." God on His part gives us "such a measure of grace, as may enable us to love, not forever without sinning ... but such as is sufficient to perform such dutyes, as are necessary under ... the second covenant." Indeed the more we use our talents, the more grace we receive, so that in the end "there is promised a crown of glory". Nevertheless God requires obedience in surrendering our "whole heart unto Christ" which safeguards us against surrendering too much to the temptations of body and soul. Thus Andrewes expressed the covenant of grace in more merciful terms than Perkins who had defined the covenant of Grace as "that whereby God freely promising Christ and his benefits, exacteth againe of man, that he would by faith receive Christ, and repent of his sinnes." Hence for Puritans, once the elect had bound himself to God by contract in the covenant of grace, it could not be broken.[360]

---

358 Ibid., pp. 75 - 6; Perkins, Vol. 1, pp. 32.

359 Ms. 3707, pp. 77-8.

360 Perkins, p. 71.

There is a remarkable similarity between this lecture and the one in *The Morall Law Expounded* on the Covenant.[361]

Galatians 4. 22 - 24 *Tis written, that Abraham had two sons: th' one by a bond-maid, th' other by a free-woman: But he which was of the bond-woman was born after the flesh, but he of the freewoman*

---

361 "Covenants: as in a Will or Testament, there are two partes: So much in each covenant, there were two parties: in the first God and *Adam*. The Covenant on God's side, eternall felicity, both in this life, and in the life to come: on *Adams* perfect obedience, man received strength to performe; but abusing his strength, and setting it against God, justly incurred the forfeiture, i.e. of his felicity: and the penalty, i.e. eternal death, and hell, opposite to Paradise, to which his strength should have kept him si morte morieris, namely that thou shalt die the death, by this meanes the first Covenant being broken and made voyd, yet not in regard of the forfeiture, but of the penalty, it pleased God to make a new covenant, in whichF are two bonds. 1. Betweene God and Christ. 2. Betweene Christ and us. On God's side, felicity; or the conveyance of his eternall right to Christs. On Christs satisfaction to God: to us, to restore all to us that we had lost. On our side, faith unfained. As man fell, and by his fall, lost all he had; so if he would recover that he lost, he was, to make satisfaction and beside, if he could fulfill the Law he had promise of eternall felicity. Christ undertook this perfect satisfaction of man: suffered all that man should have suffered; and so tooke away the penalty: satisfied lost: and so came to two rights; one of inheritance, another of purchasement. The right of inheritance, which he had by nature, in that he was the Sonne of God, he reteineth himselfe: the other of purchasement, he giveth to all them that lay hold of him, *Fide non ficta*, with faith unfained, and that not of our owne strength, but in Christ: and therefore is called the covenant of faith, and that with no losse; for if a thing be taken away; and a recompense be made by a better thing, there is no taking away, the reason of this second covenant is, that if the first covenant had stood, and Adam had remained in his own strength, he must needs have had some part of the honour for using it well; and not abusing it when he might: Therefore that God might have the glory, he suffered the first to be broken; for God in creating required only one honour, Therefore man fell for his fall he was to make satisfaction this was not to be performd but in Gods strength; the grace of God preventing us, and making us of unwilling, willing; and of unable, able: in that measure that God will require at their hands: we have all our strength from God. So that the first covenant i.e. Moses his Law, being weake and unperfect, standing on a promise in figure, and curse without figure: in truth the figure was performed in Christ: the curse taken away by his death: then when perfecta; things perfect came, imperfecta abiere things imperfect were done away; one Covenant of God maketh not any bond but onely in part: that is, the curse taken away by grace: the ceremony by the truth of Christs: and that which is fulfilled shall be taken in the Court of Grace, not pleaded in the Court of Moses: that is, in the sincerity of faith, not in the perfection of the Law." M.L.E., pp. 71-2.

was by promise, which things are an allegory, for these are the two covenants.

'Tis written. And what we read written here, is taken out of Gen. 16.15 and 21.3. Where we may read the history of Abraham's two wives, Sarah and Hagar, and of his two sons, Isaac, and Ishmael and of their twofold Originall, th' one was born after the flesh, th' other was by promise, i.e. considering the deadnes of Sarah's womb, then 90 yeares old, th' one not by the ordinary course of nature, but by God's meer grace and mercy, who is able to give life where there is none; th' other was born after the flesh, when Hagar was young and fit for childbeareing. Lastly, their twofold condicion, Sarah to liberty, Hagar to bondage, for as the mothers were, so the Offsprings.

And the Apostle proceeds to interpritt this history allegorically; which things (saith He) are an Allegory, indeed a true story of things past, but yet doe signifie somewhat besides, as being types of things spirituall: The 2 mothers are the 2 covenants, the old and the new; of the Law wherein the promise is made, that those who perfectly keep it, shall thereby obtain salvacion; and of the Gospell where in life Eternall is promised to sinners that repent and beleev in Christ Jesus. Of which two covenants I come now to speak.

1. The law or the covenant of workes.

2. The free Promise or covenant of Grace.

And before we descend to Particulars, 'twill not be amisse to set down the generall Definicion, and show the Nature of a Covenant what 'tis. And this we may gather from the meaning of the word and the solemnity that was formerly used at the making and confirming of a covenant. 1. Some would have the word *foedus* to come *a Fide,* from that mutuall faith which the 2 Parties that entred into covenant gave each to other, whereby they so mutually bound their faith, that 'twas not lawfull for either Party to rescind or revoke the league. 2. *Foedus a feriendo* (Isodor)[362] whence *ferire et percutere foedus* is commonly used to strike and make a covenant. And this

362 Isidore became bishop of Seville in 600, and presided over the second council of Seville in 1619 and the council of Toledo in 633. He influenced both the theology and culture of western medieval Europe.

is drawn from the solemnity used at the confirmacion of a league or covenant which was anciently by blood. So the Poet [Vergil].

Armati Iovis ante aras paterasaque tenentes
stabant et causâ jungebant foedera porcâ[363]

And we read of the blood of the covenant, Exod: 24.8 and the Apostle tells us, that the first covenant was not dedicated without blood, Heb: 9.18[364] and we read of the blood of the Everlasting covenant, Heb:13.20 and *Servius* will have *Sanctio* the establishing of a covenant to come a sanguine from Blood; so that in generall a covenant may be thus defined: 'Tis some solemn Act done by two Parties, whereby they mutually bind themselves to doe, give or receive something, some outward signes used to ratifie and confirm it that the promise may be inviolable.

And hence we may gather the difference between a Testament and a Covenant, which tho' promiscuously used yet differ as *genus* and *species* for every Testament is a covenant but not à *contra;* And tho' the heir do not covenant with the Testator at the makeing of the Testament (bec[ause] that may be done without his knowledge) which is necessarily required in him that covenanteth: yet he covenants at the validity of the Testament, when it takes effect by his acceptance of the condicions specified in it, and by his entrance upon the inheritance; then (tho' before he was free) he binds hims[elf] to perform the will of the Testator. So that every Testament when 'tis consummate and valid is a kind of covenant, not before.[365]

And to give you the Definicion of a Covenant as we are now to speak of it, betw[een] heaven and earth, God and us; 'Tis a mutuall compact betwixt God and man, consisting of Mercyes and gracious promises on God's parte, made over to man; and of condicions of obedience on man's parte required by God. And this Covenant is 2 fold, 1. *Foedus naturae*, or the covenant of workes 2. *Foedus gratiae* or the covenant of Grace.

1. Covenant of workes concerning which we are to observ 1st

363 Translated it means: 'Armed men stood before the altars of Jupiter and holding libation bowls and they joined in a treaty with (the sacrifice of) a pig.'

364 A similar text appears in Andrewes' Paschal Sermon for 1624. Andrewes, Vol. 3, p. 91.

365 This text is also in the above sermon. Ibid., pp. 90 - 1.

what 'twas. 2. when, with, whom and upon what grounds 'twas made. 3. What were the promises and condicions required in it.

For the 1st 'twas that voluntary, free and perfect obedience, which God required of man, and thereupon his promise of reward, i.e. the confirming man in his created condicion of life, holines and happines to which was added upon his disobedience a threatening of punishment. Gen: 2.17 in the day [that thou eatest thereof thou shalt surely die] to manifest God's power over man and lest the Covenant should seem to be altogether between Equalls. Now

2ly, This covenant was made with Adam in his Innocency as soon as he was created, and in him with all mankind. In his Innocency I say, before his fall and that for these Reasons;

1. Bec[ause] 'twould not stand with the justice of God, to require perfect, exact obedience from man, if he had not had perfect strength and abilitie to perform all that was required of him. And therefore when Adam had perfect knowledge of God's revealed will; when he had power and abilitie to perform all that God commanded, then God entered into this Covenant with him and required this obedience from him.

2. If this covenant was not made with Adam in his Integritie then the 2nd covenant had been before the first; for that was immediately after the fall, Gen: 3. 15. [I will put enmity between thee and the woman, and between thy seed and her seed]. And

Lastly, the Ground of the Covenant of works was the law of nature, the same in substance with the law morall, which, in the beginning was imprinted in the heart of man, whereby he knew, what was good, was inclined thereunto, and had abilitie to perform it.

Ob[jectio]. But how shall we know that man had such abilities, such a law given him, and that the substance of the law morall was engraven upon the Table of his heart?

Sol[utio]. 1. By the effects of it in our first Parents who immediately after their transgression, were forced by the guilt of their own consciences to hide thems[elves] from the presence of God, Gen: 3.11 who told thee [that thou wast naked? Hast thou eaten of the tree, whereof I commanded thee that thou shouldst not eat?] Adam might have answered, mine own conscience, the light of nature showed me my trangression.

2. There are some *vestigia*, some remainders of this Law in all mankind, who (as the Apostle saith) even without the law, by the light of Nature are a law unto thems[elves], Rom. 2.14.[366]

But why then doe we read that the law was not before Moses, and why is it so often in Scripture called the law of Moses?

It is not so called, *ratione originis*, but *solemnionis patefactionis*; bec[ause] 'twas solemnly published by Moses; engraven in Tables of stone by the finger of God; but the same law was at first written in the fleshie tables of the heart [2Cor: 3.3]. So 'tis called Moses law, bec[ause] by him fully published, delivered and committed to the church for direction of our obedience to God.

Thus much of the 1st; what the first covenant was, 2. when, with, whom, and upon what grounds it was made. Now

3ly, what were the condicions required on man's Parte, you have heard, perfect unsinning obedience, proportioned to the measure of that strength, God had given him. Next, for the mercyes on God's parte. 1. some were actually bestowed upon him. 2. some promised upon condicion. The former sort, those mercyes, that happines which man did actually enjoy, were partly inward and partly outward. As 1st that holy and heavenly Image of God, wherewith his soul was blessed and beautified, shining in him without any blemish. 2. that holy law teaching him his whole duty and that wonderfull knowledge, whereby he was able to know, and to make use of all the creatures of God, above the greatest Philosopher, that ever was. 3ly, that power he had to perform all God commanded, and that possibility to have lived for ever without sinning.

2. For outward mercyes, as 1st the Place where he was created, Paradise, which all the Principall creatures of God did beautify and adorn; and therefore tho' God made all the world, yet more extraordinarily that place is said to be planted by God, Gen: 2.8. And Moses is large in describing the precious stones, pure metalls, wood's and other creatures, that it seemes to have been a shopp furnished for man, to see in, and learn by it, God's wisdome, power and majesty.

2ly, For the Perfection of his Body, 'twas a comely and glori-

366 Cp. with that in First Sermon on *Preparation for Prayer*. Andrewes, Vol. 5, p. 307.

ous Body, free from all infirmity pain and shame. And 3ly, He had given him a comfortable use, not only of Paradise, but of all the world round about him; to receive nothing but comfort and content from every creature. And lastly, God had promised him continuance of light and knowledge to direct him; and strength and abilitie to assist him in a continuall performance of perfect obedience; and a glorious crown of such endeavours, assumption to eternall happines.

For 'tis probable, that if our first Parents had continued in their Integritie, and performed perfect obedience to God's righteous Precepts, after they had lived a sett time upon earth, by the interveening chang of a natural, mortall, corrupt Body, into a spirituall, immortal, incorrupt, they should have been translated to have lived an eternall and happy life in heaven.

And thus much of the 1st covenant made with Adam in his state of Innocency, when his knowledge and holines and righteousnes, were like the 1st copy from whence they were drawn; as soon as he could see, he saw hims[elf] happy; he saw heaven above him, earth under him, the creatures about him, God before him, and he knew what all these things meant, as if he had been long acquainted with them all; nay he saw the inside of all the creatures at first; and by his knowledge fitted their Names to their disposicions; He had fullnes of all knowledge, content and happines.[367] But man being in this honour, continued not [Ps: 49.12]; this Cedar of Paradise had his fall; this glorious creature was dethroned, his crown forfeited, hims[elf] cast out of Paradise, condemned to death, and so deprived both of Eternitie and felicitie; and from that hour to this, not any of his posteritie are justifiable by that first covenant of works; for the Apostle tells us, that all have sinned and comed short of the glory of God, promised in that covenant, Rom. 3.23. And by works of law shall no fleshe be justified, Gal: 2.16.[368]

But here it may be demaunded; why should God inflict so severe a punishment upon all mankind for the sin of one man; why should all his posterity suffer for his miscarriage?

---

367 Refer for similar text in lectures on Genesis 2.19 & 20, *Apos. Sacra*, pp. 204 – 16.

368 This text on man and his relationship with the rest of creation and his Fall is an expansion of *Creation, Providence and Redemption* in *Preces Privatæ*. Brightman, p. 211.

1.Bec[ause] God entred covenant with Adam not as one single person, but as he represented all mankind, of which he was the root and the Head; and therefore as by Adam's obedience, all his posteritie should have received the reward of life promised; so upon his disobedience all should undergoe the curse of death threatned; And thus as the blessing of the covenant, had not rested in Adam's Person, so nor doth the Curse; and as not the Curse, so nor doth the sinne: but both sinne and Curse being seated in humane nature, as well as Adam's Person, he propogateing his nature doth propagate also his sinne and with his sinne the curse of death; so that as many as by naturall generation descend from Adam, are shapen in iniquitie Ps: 51.5; they are children of disobedience[369] Eph.2.3.[370]

2. Bec[ause] God intended to make a 2nd covenant with man, which should tend as much, if not more then the first could have done, to the Eternall happines of mankind, therefore he tooke the forfeiture of the first covenant, and so our Saviour is called the meditatour of [a better covenant, which was established upon better promises], Heb: 8.6. But again, God haveing given Adam free will, and left him to hims[elf], to stand or fall, was he no wayes the cause of his fall?

No, no wayes at all. In that fall, God was neither compelling, nor commanding, nor perswadeing, but permitting and disposeing. And to stop the mouth of all irrationall reasoning, we may make this instance by way of illustracion. In the building of an house, 'tis necessary, that for use, conveniency and beeing, it have a door, which is made of sufficient strength to keep out the theif, so the Inhabitant have sufficient care to keep it shutt. Now if the theif by fair words, not violent force, get entrance and spoil the goods, whose is the fault? the workman's, that built the house, or the Inhabitants that set open the doores?[371] Thus God Allm[ighty] created man holy, gave him sufficient strength to withstand the subtle suggestions, and plausible perswasions of Satan; but he

369 Cp. with *Another Act of Penitence* in *Preces Privatæ*. Brightman, p. 143.

370 In the Authorised Version this 2.2.

371 Cp. with Sermon Four of *The Temptation of Christ in the Wilderness*, Andrewes, Vol. 5, pp. 520–1, and also Cosin's undated sermon on Christ's Temptation, Cosin, Vol. 1, p. 67ff. In this sermon Cosin has simply lifted text from Andrewes.

makeing ill use of that light and strength, and power God gave, was overcomed and spoiled and hath none to blame but hims[elf]. With the applicacion of this, we may stop and curb the curiosity of men, that it run not into blasphemy, and where they cannot satisfie their reason, they are taught to exercise their faith, and to take a parte in that heavenly Anthem, Rev:15.3 Great and marvelous are thy works, ô Lord God Alm[ighty]: just and true thy wayes ô thou king of saints.

Thus much of the 1st covenant which is called *Foedus naturae* or the covenant of workes. We proceed now to th' other.

11. Covenant of Grace, or the New covenant bec[ause] by it we are renewed in the inner man. And here we shall observ 1st what 'tis; 2. when, and with whom 'tis made; 3. the Tenor and condicions of it, and so show how this covenant of grace differs from that of workes.

1. Covenant of grace is God's 2nd contract with Adam after his fall, and in him with all mankind, for the restoreing of them into his favour, and to that state of happinesse they had lost, by the meanes of a mediatour Christ Jesus, Gal: 3.22. And

2. This covenant was made with Adam in Paradise, immediately after his fall, in these words, the seed [shall bruise thy head], Gen: 3.15. Where we may observ God's unspeakable mercy, in propounding the remedy before he pronounced the sentence; before he drove Adam out of Paradise, or told him of his doom, he told him of the promised seed - the seed of the woman [shall bruise his heel].

And afterwards this covenant was [in] sundry wayes declared to Abraham by God hims[elf], Gen: 22.18. In thy seed, i.e. in Christ (Gal: 3.16.) shall all the Nacions of [the earth be blessed] and partly by ordinary meanes, partly by the Prophets, extra[ordinary] sent by God; to him (Apostle) give all the Prophets [witness, that through his name whosoever believeth in him shall receive remission of sins], Act: 10.43, i.e. they were all to declare and publish this covenant; but it was never fully and clearly declared, untill our saviours comeing in the flesh; In these last days i.e. time of the Gospell, God hath spoken to us by his sonne, Heb: 1.2 who was sanctified by God and sent into the world to publish and confirm the New Covenant; and therefore he is called the Mediatour of the New Covenant, Heb: 8.6. Now what is it to be a Mediatour? It is nothing else, but to be the Interpretor of God, or the Intercessor passing between God and men, with mutuall messages, to make and finish up the covenant on both parties: by which Intermessenger God declares and testifies his will to men; and they again informed in the knowledge of God's will, do comply and contract with him; are reconciled to him; and afterwards enjoy their Peace, the end of their faith and obedience, the salvacion of [their soules, 1Pet: 1.9].

3. For the Tenor and conditions of this covenant we are to consider 1. Mercyes made over to us; 2. condicion required of us in this covenant. The first thing promised is the seed of [the woman] i.e. Christ Jesus, John: 3.16, God so love [the world] that he gave [his only Son] to take our nature upon him and in that nature of ours, 1st to perform perfect exact obedience, and to so to be perfect and just; and yet 2ly, being perfect and faultlesse, to undergoe a painfull and shamefull death for the sinnes of all mankind; as (the Apostle) to tast death for every man, Heb: 2.9. Thus the 2nd covenant was made in Christ Jesus, sealed in his blood, (according to the custom of the Eastern nacions) and so confirmed by him, which is the importance of those words, 2Cor: 1.20. All the promises of God in him, are yea and Amen, i.e. verified and confirmed.[372]

2ly, Mercyes made over unto us <u>in</u> and <u>by</u> Christ are 1. A full revelacion of his will, Heb: 8.10 I will put my lawes in their minds, and write them in their hearts: i.e. As if he should have said thus: In the old covenant I wrote some of my lawes in tables of stone, and Moses wrote other some in a Booke and put them into the Ark to be kept there. But my New Covenant shall not be so; by it, I will write my lawes, put them in their hearts, to be kept there; my lawes shall be such, as that their minds may easily conceive them, their memories retain them, and their own consciences acknowledge them to be convenient, just, right, and good. And besides, they shall not have a bare understanding of my lawes, to know them, but an hearty affection to doe them.

This is the 1st mercy, revelacion of his will, called the law of

372 Cp. similarity with the Paschal Sermon for 1624, Andrewes, Vol. 3, pp. 91- 2. Christ as the "yea and Amen" also feature in Andrewes' Nativity Sermons for 1605 and 1616. Ibid., Vol. 1, pp. 10, 185.

faith, according to which we Christians ought to live. 2ly, Next mercy, is Promise of Pardon to all our sinnes and iniquities. Heb: 8.12. I will be mercyfull to their unrighteousness, and their sinnes will I remember no more; Here God opens and unfolds the Nature of this covenant, that he will be mercyfull to all the sins of his people; he will give plenary and perfect remission, not only forgive, but forgett; whereby such as are truly and seriously penitent, and afterw[ards] live holily, are released from the guilt, or bond of all their former sinnes; not only in respect of temporall punishment, but also of eternall. 3ly, Next mercy promised is such a measure of grace, as may enable us to live, not forever without sinning, (for) but such as is sufficient to perform such dutyes, as are necessary under in the 2nd covenant. In which respect St. Paul saith that hee can doe all things through [Christ which strengtheneth me]. Phil: 4.13.

4ly, there is promised also a greater measure and supply of grace to them that make good use of it; he that improves well his 5 talents shall have 10, Luc 19.13 to him that hath shall be given, and he shall have more abundance.

<u>Lastly</u>; after our making a right use of God's Mercyes here, there is promised a crown of glory, 2Tim: 4.8. Eternall life, Joh: 17.3; such joyes as neither eye hath [not seen, nor ear heard, neither hath entered into the heart of man] 1Cor: 2.9. These are the Promises of Mercyes made over unto us in this covenant on God's parte. Next, let us see what condicions are required on our Part; And to this we shall answer.

1. Negatively; That not such a perfect obedience is required of us, as never to sin in any poynt for this is not the priviledge of any saint of God upon earth, but only of such as are at home, in their country; 'twas an Apostle that said it, in many things we offend all, Jam: 3.2 and another seconds him: 1Joh. 1.20, If any man saith he hath no sin he is a liar. Nor

2ly, is it required of us never to have committed any deliberate sin, for David did so sin in the matter of Uriah; nor to have gone on, in any habituall customary sin, for so many servants of God have done. But

3ly, There is required of us universall obedience, 1st, *experti hominis*, in giveing up the whole heart unto Christ, Math: 22.37. 2ly *Ex parte legis*, in obedience to the whole law of God: for hee that offends in one poynt is guilty of all, Jam: 2.10. He that said do not commit Adultery, said also, do not kill; and he that abhors Idolls, must not commit sacriledge. And then 3ly, this must be honest, syncere, faithfull obedience, free from hypocrisie, the rust and canker of all grace and goodnes; God loves integretie, truth in the inward partes, Ps: 51.6. And lastly we must often bewail our sins and infirmities, both past and present; labour to mortify every lust and corruption; and from every fall rise again by repentance and reformacion.

I might here add Faith, hope, charity, self denyall and all the rest of the Gospells graces, which ought to be rooted in every Christian heart under the 2nd covenant, Luc 1.74. But I proceed in the

Last place to show the difference betw[een] these two Covenants of workes and grace.

1. They differ in respect of time, for that was made with Adam, in his Innocency, this with the same Adam after his Fall.

2ly, In respect of their Grounds, for the former was grounded upon man's own righteousnes, requireing perfect obedience of every man in his own Person; the latter is grounded upon the righteousnes of Christ, admitting payment and performance by another in behalfe of so many as shall receive it, Gal: 3.14.

3ly, In respect of the Promises, for the covenant of grace is called a covenant of better promises, Heb: 8.6. And that 1st bec[ause] eternall life was not openly promised in the old covenant, and 2dly 'twas promised to them who exactly kept all the precepts of it; But the new covenant containes a most open and clear promise of eternall life;[373] and then 2ly requires of no man an exact and absolute obedience in all poynts; but is content with true repentance, and with such an amendment of life, as caryes along with it a will never to offend God any more; and an endeavour to walk in the wayes of piety and goodnes. Now to apply this, and so to conclude.

This Doctrine should have a speciall influence upon our lives and conversacions. For you have heard that in the covenant of grace, as mercyes are promised on God's part, so condicions are

373 Refer again to Paschal Sermon for 1624, Ibid., Vol. 3, p. 92.

required on ours, without which those mercy's doe not belong to us. He became the Author of Eternall salvacion, Heb: 5.19 but it followes, unto all them that obey him; there those persons are specified, namely the obdedient; whence it appeares that all who will have their sinnes expiated and obtain salvacion by him, must obey him. And againe, Heb: 9. 14 the blood of Christ shall purg our consciences from dead workes, to serve the liveing God; Here is the effect of expiacion wrought in us by the blood and offering of Christ; and the effect and complement of our expiacion depends reciprocally upon our duty, and our duty and will to serv God ought to flow immediately from it; for what one man among a 1000d would serv God, upon the expiacion of his sinnes, if he knew that without this service, he could be released from the guilt of all his sins, and enjoy a full right to eternall life? And therefore Zachary joynes them together in his Benedictus Luc: 1.74.[374] And the Apostle bids us follow after holines, Heb: 12.14.[375] So this necessity, indispensable necessity of syncere obedience, shutts the door against all Temptacions to carnall securitie, sloth, presumption, hypocrisie, partiall obedience, or customary continuance in any sin. To speake of the mercyes in this covenant and not of the condicions required of us, is to speak but of half the covenant; we cannot assure our soules of any of those mercyes promised, without the performance of our dutyes. The grace of God which bringeth salvacion hath appeared, teaching us, Tit: 2. 11,12 and if we will not so be taught by it, we shall never be saved by it. To be holy here, is to be happy hereafter; He that truly maketh a conscience of his wayes; that is a faithfull servant of God in this kingdome of grace, shall be a true sub[ject], and raign triumphantly in that kingdome of glory. He shall receiv the end of his faith, the fruit of his obedience, the fruicion of his Hope, theg salvacion of his soul.

So let us all strive to make our calling and election sure [2Pet: 1.10], to strengthen our interest in this covenant, by constant dutyes of piety and new obedience, by a good husbanding

374 i.e. "That he would grant unto us, that we being delivered out of the hand of our enemies might serve him without fear."

375 i.e. "Follow peace with all men, and holiness, without which no man shall see the Lord."

of that grace we have, by frequent and fervent prayer for increase in grace, and by diligent attending to the meanes of grace before they be hid from our eyes. Now, whiles as yet God speakes to us by his messengers, wooes us by his mercyes, patience and long-suffering, and threatens us with severe judgments, now in this our day, let us know the things that belong to our Eternall peace. Which [is in Christ Jesus].

LECTURE NINE

Of Sin, Originall and Actuall

Introduction

This lecture is significant in Andrewes' ministry as it is the only time he clearly defined his view on original sin. He explained how the term, *original sin*, was first coined by Augustine in his writings against Pelagius, and ever afterwards was adopted by the Church. He then outlined this Augustinian doctrine that from Adam's sin every human being has an "inbred [de]pravity and corruption of Nature". Thus sin is propagated to all through Adam and all are tainted with *ab origine* from conception. "It is *origo*, the source and fountain of all other sins." However it is clear that Andrewes does not wholly accept Augustine's teaching. For him it is not so much a "collective guilt" but "a contagion".[376] He also differed from the Augustinian hard line that in Adam "all have sinned" when he taught that "we all have sinned". It is our sins which crucified Christ, not the Jews, not Herod, not Pilate; it is we who drove that sword into His side. As Lossky stated, "each one, then, by his sin is held responsible for the Passion of Christ. That implies that the sin of each one is in the image of the sin of Adam and Eve and consequently committed freely and not simply in virtue of the fallen state of nature that acts blindly." Indeed in his 1602 Ash Wednesday Sermon Andrewes declared in the words of John Chrysostom, "'it is far worse to be matched with a beast than to be born a beast'. ... But to be born a man and to become match-

376 Ms. 3707, p 81.

able with beasts, that is our fault, our great fault, and therefore, the worse certainly."[377] Thus Andrewes was more Eastern than Augustinian in his teaching on sin, as he implies that man has a certain freedom in which he either binds himself to the slavery of sin or chooses to live in Christ. However he never subscribes to the hard anti-Augustinian line as Jeremy Taylor later did in his *Unum Necessarium*.[378] After setting out Augustine's teaching, Andrewes, unlike most Reformers, preferred to lecture on original sin according to Anselm who defined it as "the privacion of originall Righteousnes" (which is how Augustine defined evil).

The second half of the lecture was devoted to actual sin, which he described as "every action, outw[ard] or inward disagreeing with the law of God" which springs "from our naturall corruption". These are committed both internally and externally. In short we sin by either omission or commission, and mostly these are connected. There were some actual sins that could be called "minor" ones as they were caused by weakness or infirmity, but nevertheless they were still sins. He was therefore critical of the Roman Church's classification of sins as either mortal or venial, as sin is sin in Andrewes' mind, and Scripture teaches that all sin, unles repented, brings death to the soul. Of all sins the worst one is that committed against the Holy Spirit as this is a wilful act to deny God's redeeming grace and leads to eternal death.[379]

As Andrewes was indeed a lover of souls, he concluded with this reminder that our souls are "precious" and that "the joyes of Heaven" outweigh any gain or pleasure from sinning. To be deprived of "the gracious presence" of God was the worst punishment that could be inflicted upon any soul. If that was not a sufficient deterrent, then the image of the "fire of Hell" where our souls will be eternally punished should be. In this lecture he informed the boys that they were privileged in attending this school where they were given opportunities others were not given. "We

377 Andrewes, Vol. 2, pp. 125-7, 166,349; Lossky, p. 173. Cp. this with Augustine: "For God ordained that infants should begin this world as the young of the beasts begin it, since their parents had fallen to the level of beasts in the fashion of their life and death." *De Civitate*, Vol. 2, p. 246 (Bk,13, Ch. 3).

378 Taylor, Vol. 7, pp. 17-8, 252-7, 303-40, 541 – 585.

379 Ms. 3707, p. 84.

of this place, that have more opportunities of serving God, that know our maisters will, if we doe it not, we shall be beaten with many stripes."[380]

Roman. 5.12. *As by one man sin entred in the world, and death by sin: and so death passed upon all men for that all have sinned.*

In these words, the Apostle proceedes to sett forth more fully the exceeding riches of the love of Christ toward sinners. As by one man sin entred into the world, and death by sin: - here wants the other part of the similitude; which may be thus supplyed; even so by one man, the man Christ Jesus, righteousnes entred in the world, and by righteousnes, life, and so life passed upon all, in that all, who are renewed by grace, are justified by him.[381] But not to trouble you either with the coherence of the words, or a comment upon the Text; our Task at this time is to speak of sin in generall, and of the severall species and sorts of sin, and somewhat of the punishment that attends them.

1. Definicion of Sin what 'tis. The Apostle tells us it in one word, 1Joh: 3.4 ἄνομια [sin is the trangression of the law], sin is that which is disagreeing and repugnant to God's revealed will. And answerable hereunto the names of sin in three languages are very significant. In Hebrew 'tis *hhatah* from the root *hhata, a viâ vel scopo deflectere vel aberrare,* so Judg.20 speaks of the Benjamities, that 700 men could sling a stone at an haires breadth, and not misse, the Hebrew is not sin. 2ly, in Greek, to the same purpose, ἁματία, which the Etymologists deduce παρὰ τοῦ μάρπτειν which is as much as καλαλαμβάνω, *assequor* so then prefixing the privative particle ἁμαρτία, or ἁμαρπτία, which in Latin we call, *Error, lapsus, peccatum.* Now *errare* or *peccare* is (as Tully) *lineas transilire,* to trangress the Bounds. So that to sin, is to misse the mark, to wander out of the way, hence Repentance is called conversion;

---

380 Ibid., p. 87. This is identical to what he told the Lord Mayor and the affluent of London in his Spital Sermon on Easter Wednesday, 1588. "The world now 'knoweth his Masters will and doeth it not; it must therefore certainly be beaten with many stripes,' with many more than the ignorant world was." Andrewes, Vol. 5, p. 24.

381 This is a paraphrase by Andrewes on Romans 5.17 & 19.

the mark we should hitt is G[od]'s law; and therefore the Apostle well defined it ἄνομια (trangression of the law).

Now for the causes of sin, it hath no efficient, but a deficient cause, and so it hath no positive, but a privative Beeing, 'tis not nothing, and yet 'tis not any thing. It may be considered 2 wayes

1. Materially, for that Action wherein it inheres and so 'tis good, as proceeding from the Author of goodnesse, God. 2ly, Formally or properly, for the obliquitie, disorder, and error of the Action and that is properly sin; 'tis not the work, but the evill of the work; a deviacion from the rule of righteousnes, the law of God which is the sin. As the jarring of a Musicall Instrument is not the string, nor the sound, but only the disharmony and discord of the sound.[382] The desire of the heart is good, and so is the motion of the hand: but to desire the goods of another, to move the hand to murther, here is the sin.

Againe; sin I called a Privacion, but Privacions are 2fold. 1. Pure, as rest is the privacion of motion, and sleep of wakeing. 2. Mixt, such as badly affects the subject, as in sicknes, there is both a want of health, and a painfull indisposicion of the whole body; and sin may be called such a privacion as this. And thus much of the Definicion of Sin.

Ob[jectio]. But 't may be here demanded; If sin be a transgression of the law, and if where no law is, there can be no trangression [Rom: 5.13]; what shall we say then of the murther of Cain, and of other sins of that first age of the world; surely they were properly sins, and yet we read, the law was not before Moses?

Sol[utio]. To this answer, 1st Lawes given by Moses were either ceremoniall, Judiciall or morall; the two former were not before Moses, the last was. 2ly, Morall law may be considered 1st as engraven upon tables of stone, and so not before Moses; 2ly, as written upon the fleshly Tables of the heart, and so 'twas before Moses, from the beginning: This law considered as a Rule, was, is, and will be in force; it can no more be abrogated, then the nature

382 Cp. with M.L.E. "Every action, and every motion is from God, but the obliquity or imperfection of the action is not from God, but from the pervesenesse or weakness of the instrument ... the action whatsoever it is from God; but if it halt, the deformity is of the crookednesse of the instrument." p.35.

of good and evil can be changed. I proceed now to the 2nd thing, severall sorts of Sinne.

2ly. All sin, is either Originall or Actuall; such as doe either defile our nature or our Actions.

For the 1st of these, Originall sin; St. Aug[ustine] having to doe with the Pelagians (who deny any such thing as propagacion of sin from our first Parents) was the first that gave the Name of Originall sin to the corruption of our Natures; To intimate these 3 thing[s]: 1. that this sin is propagated to all mankind from Adam who was *humani generis origo*. 2. that we are tainted with it *ab origine*, from our nativitie and conception Ps.51.5. 3ly, that 'tis *origo* the source and fountain of all other sins. And ever since, it hath through all Ages of the ch[urch] retained this Name of Originall sin, as the fittest and most significant.

This sin supposeth 1. The actuall trangression of Adam, in whom we all sinned. 2. the inbred [de]pravity and coruption of human Nature. 3. the guilt, or binding over to punishment: the first is cause of the 2nd; the first and 2nd are cause of the 3rd. So that we may thus define Originall sin, according to Anselm, 'Tis *Carentia originalis justitiae debitae inesse*. Originall sin in Adam's Posteritie, doth consist formally in the privacion of Originall Righteousnes; as 'tis an evill defect through Adam's default, we not haveing through the demerit of his sin, what we ought to have by the law of creacion, and the bond of the 1st covenant made with our God: by the breach of which law and covenant in Adam, 'tis, that whosoever descends from him by natural generacion, is therefore a child of wrath, bec[ause] a child of Adam communicateing in his sinne by partaking of his Nature.

I shall show 1. that Originall sin is the privacion and want of Orig[inal] Righteousnes, 2. that the contagion of orig[inal] sin extends to the Persons of all mankind and 3ly to every parte of the whole man.

1. If orig[inal] sin formally and precisely considered be any thing besides the want of orig[inal] Right[eousness], then 'tis either the soul of man or the Faculty of the soul, or an habitt or an Act, or some other quality. But 1st it cannot be the soul, bec[ause] the soul is that which sinneth, that which is punished for sin, and therefore cannot be sin for which it is punished. 2ly, It cannot be any Power of the Soul bec[ause] all the Powers of the soul, for

substance are the same in man after his fall, that were in him, in his state of innocency. 3ly, It cannot be any habitt, for then it should be either an infused habit, and so God should be the Author (which to affirm is blasphemy) or an acquired habit, but so it cannot be, bec[ause] 'tis orig[inal] sin, and in us by Nature; and by the same reason, it cannot be any Act for then it should be not originall but actuall sin. Nor lastly, can it be any reall quality, for then it should have a reall positive cause, and so God should be the Author of it. It remaines therefore, that (as Anselm hath defined it) Orig[inal] Sin be the privacion of originall righteousnes. As for the bad disposicion of the faculties and powers both of soul and body, whereby we are naturally prone to evill, only, and wholly to evill, this is a consequent of that first originall sin, of which afterwards.

2ly, That the contagion of Originall sin extends to the Persons of all mankind; for proof of this, we need goe no further than this present text, Rom. 5.12. By one man sin entred in to the world, [where by world (Grotius) we are to understand all mankind;] and death by sin; i.e. not only dissolucion of the frame of the body; but all those sorrowes and diseases, and afflictions that accompany, and are the forerunners of death; and this passed upon all, for that all have sinned, or *σὺν ᾧ per quem,* by whom all sinned. So that a child of a dayes old is not innocent; not the children of faithfull beleeving Parents; for men beget not children, as they are regenerate, but as they are men; as clean seed-corn cometh up with straw and chaffe, and other wrecks; so men, tho' they have obtained grace, are parents of children which are born in sin.

Again, if all by Nature, be not children of disobedience and wrath, then why should children conceived in the womb, dye there? and why should new born children be baptized into the remission of sinns? For as sin doth inseparably bring forth death Rom. 6.23, so doth death infallibly presuppose sin; which in the quickened Embryo, and new born Infant can be none other than this of orig[inal] sin. Lastly, we read, how that the heart of man is evill from his youth Gen: 8.21; that he is a Transgressor from the womb, Esa: 48.8, that he is conceived in sin Ps: 51.5, that there is none that doth good, Ps: 14.3. and that from this evill of his Nature proceed evill thoughts, murthers, adulteries, fornicacions, thefts, blasphemies Math: 15.19. So that since Adam fell, there was never any such thing in the world, as good Nature, all being tainted with originall corruption; if there be any good thing in any man, 'tis all from Grace. Nature is all naught, even that which seemeth to have that preeminence in Nature, τὸ φρόνημα τῆς σαρκὸς, Rom: 8.7 [the carnal mind] is enmity against God. This inbred sin, wherein every[one] is conceived, hath equally polluted all men; so if some be of better disposicion, better natured then others, yet that thing in them which we use to call good nature, is indeed but a subordinate meanes whereby God restraineth some men more then others from sundry outrageous exorbitances, which they would run into, if left to the wildnes of their own nature. 'Tis the last, and 'tis the fearfullest of all other judgements, for a man to be given over to hims[elf], left to follow the counsells of his corrupt nature, Ps: 81.11,12 My people would not hear my voyce, Israel would none of me. So [I gave them up unto their own hearts' lust: and they walked in their own counsels]. But

3ly, As our naturall corruption is generall in respect of the Persons, overspreading the whole lump of our nature, not a child of Adam free from the common infection, so 'tis generall in respect of the subject overrunning the whole man, soul and body, with all the partes and powers of either. 1. There is an universall darknes and blindnes in the minds of men, Eph: 4.18,19, the Apostle observing the customary demeanour of the Gentiles before their conversion, he saith, they walked in the vanity of their minds, [having the understanding darkened, being alienated from the life of God through the ignorance that is in them, because of the blindness of their heart] so that by reason of this vanity and blindnes there is in the heart of men naturally, without a teacher, the originall and seedes of all errours and heresies. 2ly, there is an universall weaknes and disabilitie in the will of every man, to any thing that is good. Rom: 7.21. I find a law, that when I would doe good evill is present with me. 3ly, there is dulnes in the memory, forgetfullnes of all good things we should remember; how easily, and with what readines do we remember that we should not, retain errors, toyes and vanities, much more then matters of piety and religion. 4ly, there is corruption, disorder and rebellion in the affections, all the imaginacions[383] [of the thoughts of his heart was

383 Cp. also to a sermon that Andrewes gave on imaginations at St. Giles, Cripplegate, 1592/3. Andrewes, Vol. 5, p. 54ff.

only evil continually], Gen: 6.5. love, joy, hatred, fear, hope, sorrow, anger, either these are set upon wrong objects, or if upon right, then there is disorder and excesse in them, when we are more angry and sorrowfull for our own injuryes, then God's dishonour. Lastly the conscience is defiled, Tit: 1.15 the judgment of what is right and wrong is perverted; whence followes a stupidity and senslessnes in the soul; and the sinners are ἀπηλγηκότες without sense of sin, or the danger ensuring, damnacion; And so they give thems[elves] over to wantonnes, Eph: 4.19, τῃ ἀσέλγειᾳ, to an itching, unbridled desire of sin, to work uncleanes, or to trade in uncleannes. Thus the originall corruption of man's nature, doth extend to all men's Persons, and the whole man is corrupted and polluted by it; it spreads it's contagion in to the understanding by ignorance, into the memory by forgetfullnes, into the will by perversnes, into the conscience by confusion; into the affections by disorder; and into the very members of the body, as the instruments of sin, Rom: 6.19. So as from the sole of the foot unto the crown of the head, there is no whole parte. Esa: 1.6.

Ob[jectio]. But if our naturall corruption be generall, overspreading the Persons of all men, why then doth the Apostle say, that the children of beleeving Parents are holy 1Cor: 7.14.

Sol[utio]. Answer, Holy, i.e. in a capacitie of holines bec[ause] God doth help the beleeving Parent in the educacion of their children; An example whereof we have in Timothy, Act. 16.1 and 2Tim 3.15 [(see Grotius)]. And *sanctos procreari ait* (Tertull[ian]) *tam ex seminis prerogativa quam ex institutionis disciplinâ.* When the children of Beleevers are said to be holy, 'tis to be understood of such a federall holines as consists in a capacitie of right and priviledge of claim, unto the promises of life and glory, not of saveing sanctified holines. As in the Roman state, a Consul did begett a sonne, in a politicall right to the citties privileges, which sonne was not born a Consull, tho' politically free: thus in the Christian church a saint doth begett a child in a federall right to the ch[urch's] promises; which child is not born a saint, tho' federally holy.

Ob[jectio]. But 2ly, if the sin of Adam our first Parent be propagated to all his children, why is it said then, that the son shall not bear the iniquity of the Father, Ezek. 18.20?

Sol[utio]. Answer. That place is meant of those sinnes, which are meerly personall; not of that disobedience, which Adam committing as our representative, doth become ours by imputacion nor of that corruption, which being seated in human nature doth therefore become common to Adam with his Posteritie as his naturall branches.

Ob[jectio]. But 3ly, if that sin of our first Parents do so taint and infect all their Posterity: why then should not the sinnes of after Parents doe the like to their children? And why should we read of the good son of a bad father?

Sol[utio]. Answer. The reason is this: Bec[ause] the 1st man Adam received originall righteousnes not only for hims[elf], but his whole Posteritie; the which originall Righteousnes, if he had continued in his primitive integritie, he should have propagated with his nature to his posterie: they should all have been holy and just and good; but if he should loose that originall Justice, then with his Nature he should propagate his sin to all his posteritie. Now bec[ause] no Parents but only the first are in the like condicion, therefore their sinnes can be no more derived unto their children, then their righteousness; but all are singular or personall sinnes.

Now for the manner of propagateing orig[inal] sin, 'tmay be thus illustrated. As poor, ignoble and obscure Parents derive the Poverty and ignoblenes of their stock to their posterity, negatively, rather than positively; for therefore are the children poor and obscure, because the Parents are so, who cannot give that which they have not: so every new born Infant wants orig[inal] Righteous[ness], bec[ause] the Parents want it, who cannot propagate that happines and righteous[ness] to their children, which they want themselves.

And thus much briefly of Orig[inal] sin, of the Definicion of it; what 'tis; of the extension of it to the Persons of all Mankind; and to the contagion of the whole man; and how 'tis propagated. I proceed now to the 2nd member of the Division.

II. <u>Actuall Sinne.</u>

As the Body which hath lost it's health must needs be sick; the member which hath lost its strength must needs be weak and lame: so man haveing lost his integritie, must needs be crooked and wicked; having lost his puritie must needs be corrupt. Which orig[inal] corruption doth break forth into inordinate desires, and actuall lustings, and irregular workings, contrary to the rule of life, the law of God; so that orig[inal] Corruption is to actuall sin as fuel to the fire, as the fountaine to the stream, as the tree to the fruit, as the body to the members or as the habitt to the Act.

We shall 1. show what 'tis. 2. the severall sorts or Divisions of it. 3. the guilt, 4. the punishment of it.

1. Actuall Sin, is every action outw[ard] or inward disagreeing with the law of God. Or 'tis a particular breach and violacion of God's commandments in the course of our life, called in the text, (v. 14) sin after [the similitude of Adam's trangression].

Now 1st the immediate internall causes of this sin are the Understanding and Will; as defective in their proper offices, the former to guide, the latter to observ, the rule and direction of right Reason.

2ly, Remote internall causes are the imaginacion and sensitive appetite, moveing and inclineing the understanding and will to what is evill, prompted on by the inordinate propension of orig[inal] concupisence.

3. For evill spirits, evill men, and outw[ard] sensible objects they may perswade, but they cannot sufficiently induce to any sin, without a conspiracy in the inward man, even of the judgment and the will. So that every[one] is tempted when he is drawn away of his own lust and entised. Jam: 1.14.[384]

4. One sin may be and often is the cause of another. As when man by his sin doth run the round or maze of sin, Ps: 12.8, his sinfull Acts begetting evill disposicions; those evil disposicions customary habitts; those customary habitts bringing forth sinfull Acts; yea when one sin prepares the way, and brings fuel to another; as when covetousnes and Ambition make work for strife, debate and murther, ariseing about wealth and honour who shall possesse and command most of this molehill, the Earth. Lastly, actuall sin proceedeth as an evill fruit from our naturall corruption. And thus of the definicion of Actuall sin and the causes of it.

2ly, All actuall sin whatsoever, is either, a sin of Omission, in not doeing what God's law doth command; or of commission, in

384 Cp. with a similar comment in Sermon on *Lead us not into temptation*, Andrewes, Vol. 5, p. 445.

doeing what God's law doth forbid: and this either in thought, in word, or work, all in one verse, Mat: 15.19.[385]

Now the sin of Omission, tho' it be a meer Negative in itself, yet considered in the causes and concomitants of it, it never goes without a sin of commision, joyned with it, so Esa: 65.12[386] and Jer: 25.7.[387] Thus when a man wills the not attending God's worship at the time he is required, besides the omission of his duty, he committs a sin in his will, because he wills that omission; for he that wills the occasion of any sin, doth by consequence will the sin itself, yea if through some intemperance or carelessnes he becomes indisposed for the performance of God's worship, and thereby neglects it: tho' he wills not the omission directly in itself, yet he willed it antecedently in it's cause, and so becomes guilty of a double sin, that of omission ushered in by that of commission.

The Division of sin into that of Thought [word and deed] is not a distinguishing sin according to it's compleat species or kinds, but parts and degrees. For the same sin, which takes conception in the heart, may have it's birth in the mouth, and full growth in the outward work. As when reveng in the heart, breaks forth into contumelious words, and injurious Actions, 'tis one and the same sin perfected by severall Degrees.

Yet the evill thoughts of the heart, the first inordinate motions of lust and concupiscence are properly sin, Math: 15.19, Rom: 7.7, 21;[388] and therefore ought to be suppressed and kept down by the watchfulnes of the soul: we should not suffer our minds to be a thorowfare for vain, lewd, licencious thoughts to passe thorow.[389] Which if well thought of, would make men more humble before God, more carefull of their houres, day and night, to marke how their mind is occupied and imployed. Yea further, sinnes in

---

385 Cp. with part of a prayer of penitence in *Preces Privatae*, Ms. 37 08, p. 1, Brightman, pp. 134-5.

386 i.e "Therefore will I number you to the sword, and ye shall all bow down to the slaughter: because when I called, ye did not answer; when I spake, ye did not hear; but did evil before mine eyes, and did choose that wherein I delighteth not."

387 i.e. "Yet ye have not hearkened unto me, saith the Lord; that ye might provoke me to anger with the works of your hands to your own hurt."

388 It should be 7.7-8.

389 Cp. with part of Litany of Deprecation in Ms. 3708, p. 3, Brightman, p. 247.

thoughts are more spir[itual] sinnes such as immediately affect and defile the soul, and therefore ought not to be lightly thought of.

Next Division of sin, is into sins of weaknes and infirmity; or of willfullnes and set purpose, raigning sins.

1. Sins of Infirmity are such as proceed from a bare want of knowl[edge] in the understanding, as sinnes of Ignorance; or from some present prevailing Temptacion which we cannot overcome, tho' we use all meanes we can; or from some advantage taken by Satan assaulting us on the suddain; or from the frequency and often repeticion of the Temptacion; or from the lightnes of the matter; or from any other principle, which by that measure of grace God affords us, we are not able to resist.[390] Provided allwayes that this disabilitie proceed not from some former willfull sin of ours, that God by way of punishment withdrawes this grace necessary for the resisting of it; for if so, then tho' 'tmay be truly said, that we cannot now resist that sin for want of grace; yet when we come to make up our reckonings, will not that sinne passe for a sin of infirmity?

2. By this Description of sins of weaknes, we may gather the Definicion of sinnes of Willfullnes as such as are against clear knowl[edge], proceed not from any prevailing temptacion; in breif all such as are not included under some of those heads of sinnes of Infirmity. But to show in particular, what sorts of sins are sins of Infirmity, and what not, 'tis a business of great difficulty, bec[ause] some have more knowl[edge], more grace, more strength, then others have. And therefore every one after the commission of a sin, ought to examine whether he made use of that knowl[edge], that grace, that strength and so accordingly pronounce his sin either of weaknes or wilfullnes.

3ly. This ch[urch] of Rome distinguisheth sinnes into 1. Mortall 2. Veniall. Such as bring death to the soul and are worthy of eternall punishment, and such as neither bring such death, nor deserv such Torment. But this hath no sure ground upon the word

390 Cp. with, "though the messenger of Satan buffet us never so much yet God's grace shall make us to have the victory, without which we are not able to resist the first temptations." Andrewes Vol. 5, p. 445, and also the above mentioned passage of penitence from Ms. 3708, p. 1.

of God. For there we read that the soul which [sinneth, it shall die] Ezek: 18.4 and the Wages of sin is death Rom: 6.23 and he that offends in one is [guilty of all] Jam: 2.10. Sin may be considered two wayes. 1. In its own Nature and so there is no sin but 'tis mortall. 2. In respect of Christ who hath satisfied, and so there is veniall sin, i.e. such as obtaines pardon, tho' it deserv punishment, in which sense no condemnacion [to them which are in Christ Jesus], Rom. 8.1.

Lastly, sin against the h[oly] Ghost. 1. 'Tis a wifull sin, against clear light, and true knowl[edge] of the truth; and so Infidells not guilty of it. 2. 'tis a malicious sin of set malice. 3. 'tis accompanied with finall impenitency; and therefore 'tis said, this sin shall not be forgiven, not bec[ause] it exceeds God's grace or outvyes Christs meritts, but bec[ause] it excludes the work of Repentance, in despitefully opposeing the spirit, rejecting the sacrifice of Christ, and wilfully denying his Truth.[391]

And thus much of Actuall sin, what 'tis, the severall sorts and Divisions of it. Now those things which accompany sin are 3: Guilt, and stain, and punishment.

1. Guilt of sin is the merit and desert of sin, whereby we become subject to God's curse, Gal: 3.10: to eternal condemnacion Rom: 2. 15. 'Tis compared in scripture to the stroak given upon the heart and soul of man, the effect of this a wounded conscience, which maketh a man flee, when none pursueth, Prov: 28.1: to be afraid at the fall of a leaf, Lev: 26.36.

2. Besides the guilt, there is the stain of sin.[392] Hence 'tis that we read of sin and pollucion, Zach:11.1;[393] of filthines of flesh and spirit, 2Cor: 7.1; and of purging the conscience, Heb: 9.14; of cleansing and washing, Jer: 2.22, now these supposed filthines and pollucion.

3. Punishment of sin, and that either here or hereafter, temporall or spirituall. As all disorder in the world, Calamities, extremities, hunger, thirst, nakednes, wearines, outw[ard] shame and infamy; losse of the limbs, use of the senses, deformity in the

391 Based on Hebrewes 10.29.

392 Refer also to Pentecost Sermon for 1620, Andrewes, Vol. 3, p. 352.

393 A better reference is 13.2.

body, want of rest and ease, paines of the Body, aches, sores, sicknesses, diseases of all sorts, are the punishment of sin. 2ly, Sorrow and anguish of soul, frenzy, blindnes and distemper of mind, terrour and vexacion of spirit, the fury of a despairing soul, beginning even in this life to feel the torment of another. Lastly Death, corporall and spirit[ual], separacion of the soul from the Body, and of the whole man from the gracious presence, and comfortable fellowshipp of God's most glorious presence, and the perpetuall imprisonment, in the company of the Divell and his Angells, to endure the heavy wrath of God, unspeakable torments in Hell fire for ever more. So considering the guilt, the stain, the punishment of sin, I hope I need not say much more to deter any from the commission of it.

1. Let us remember what God did to the Angells that sinned; He cast them down to Hell, delivered them to chaines of etern[al] darknes [Math. 25.41, 2Pet. 2.4, Rev. 12.9] what to the old world, He drowned them all but 8 persons (Gen. 7.23); what to Sodom, consumed them with fire from Heaven [Gen. 19.24]; what to Corah and his accomplices; made the earth open her mouth and [swallowed them up, Num. 16.32]. (*Cautior exemplo tu;*) St. Peter, makes up the applicacion, 2Pet: 2.4, 5 etc. And if God spared not the Angells that sinned [but cast them down to hell, and delivered them into the chains of darkness, to be reserved unto judgment].

2. Let us remember the busines upon which we are sent into the world. Eccl: 12.13, this the whole Duty of man, conclusion of the whole matter, fear God [and keep his commandments]. And we of this place, that have more opportunities of serving God, that know our maisters will, if we doe it not, we shall be beaten with many stripes.[394]

Lastly, if we would avoyd sin, let us avoyd all occasions of sinning, let us not tempt the Tempter, which we doe by Idlenes which is the very tidetime of Temptacion. The Idle man is the Devills Cushion, where he takes his repose and delight; whom he carryes with much ease, and without any contradiction to any cursed sin; so if we desire not to be overcome by the temptacions

394 An adaption of Luke, 12.47.

of Satan, let us avoyd that sin, by which we entice him to tempt us.[395]

To conclude; Consider your souls are precious, the joyes of Heaven unconceivable, the tortures of Hell just punishment for sin, not expressible, and therefore as you tender that life of your soules, as you desire to avoyd the guilt and stain and punishment of sin; the worm and fire of Hell, take heed not only of open profanenes, professed impiety, but even of secret small sinnes (as accompted). Know that even the least wickednes, allowed and approved, is enough to work your eternall woe. If you hope and expect to be Inhabitants of the new Jerusalem; then looke that here below, you become new men; shake of[f] your old sinnes and corruptions, and cloth yourselves with holines and innocency that you may wait upon the Lamb in his bl[essed] Kingdome.

395 Cp. with his lecture on Genesis 2.15. "As the idle mans Garden is full of weeds, so his soul is full of sinne, and when our soul is become such an evill and idle mans Garden, *Esay* 5.1,2 &c. then God made our Garden on earth like unto it, namely, full of weeds, thorns and thistles," *Apos. Sacra*. p. 180.

LECTURE TEN

Of Christ as Mediatour

Introduction

This lecture, the first of five lectures on the heavenly offices of Christ as mediator, priest, king and prophet, covers Christ as mediator. The lecture follows on logically from the previous one as it depicts the consequence of original and actual sins – death. There are three kinds of death. The first is "spiritual" or "the death of the soul", whereby man is totally deprived of "originall righteousness"; the second is bodily when man is laid in his grave; and the third is eternal when man is separated forever "from the gracious presence of God". To experience the last death means living in hell, a place of eternal torment and pain, which Andrewes described in vivid medieval imagery.[396] Similar imagery features in Sermon Three.

However there is a remedy for man's "sin and misery" in Christ our mediator through "the Person" and "the Office." In this lecture Andrewes concentrated on "the Person". Christ is both God and man, that is, He has two natures in the one person. Both these natures are needed for Christ to be the Saviour of souls, and as it was important for scholars to think aright about Christ in the process of salvation, he explained both natures to them. This Person is the Word, the Son of God, co-worker of creation, who became incarnate by being born of Mary by the overshadowing of the Holy Spirit. This meant that His divinity never left Him,

396 Ms. 3707, pp. 88-9.

and thus He always had the same power as His Father in whose authority He forgave sins and raised the dead. Only God could perform such actions.[397]

As God He alone could "satisfie for sin", and as man He appeased God's wrath for man's rebellion. Hence God put "aside the robes of His glory and majesty to be covered with the raggs of our nature". Thus as man, Christ lived as us, except without sin. He therefore experienced all our infirmities, pain and temptations. Both these two natures were always present in Christ, on the cross, and now in heaven.[398]

In explaining how Christ is our Saviour Andrewes followed Anselm's teaching as set out in *Cur Deus Homo*. The latter had argued from the Pauline epistles that God became incarnate in order to pay the debt of man's sin through the disobedience of the first Adam. Any reconciliation between sinful man and God could only be achieved by a sinless person whose self-sacrificing offering would appease the wrath of God, satisfy Justice and restore the image of God in man. So God the Son offered to His Father the "raggs of our nature" to do what man could not do for his own salvation. Hence by the mercy and goodness of God in the Son's offering, the Incarnation was "the very height of his goodnes". Such emphasis on the two natures in Christ, what is theologically described as the hypostatical union, was to forearm the scholars against some of the old heresies in modern guise that denied either the divinity or humanity of Christ.[399] In his sermon for Christmas day in 1611 he preached explicitly on these heresies:

> Why then, *factum est caro*, 'the Word is made flesh;' this makes up all. For, *factum est, ergo est*; 'He is made flesh, therefore is flesh.' *Fieri terminatur ad esse*, 'the end of making is being.' And *per modum naturæ* (so is ἐγένετο the Greek word:) 'this being is natural;' *et nativitas est via ad naturam*, 'and nativity is the way to nature.' So, to be born; as this day He was. *Venit per carnem, santat per verbum*, 'that all flesh may see the salvation of God.' 'Made'

397 Ibid., pp.87, 90.

398 Ibid., p. 92.

399 Ibid., pp. 87, 93.

> it was; against Manicheus holding that He had no true body; as if *factum* had been *fictum*, or making were mocking. Made it was, but how made? Not *convertendo*, 'the Word converted into flesh,' as Cerinthus; or 'flesh converted into the Word,' *Verbum caro facta est*, as Valentinus; for the Deity cannot be changed into any thing, not any thing into it. Nor made *conciliando*, as friends are made, so as they continue two several persons still; and while the flesh suffered the Word stood by and looked on, as Nestorius, that is *cum carne*, not *caro*; 'made with flesh,' not 'flesh;' and never was one person said to be made another. Nor made by compounding; and so a third thing produced of both, as Eutyches. For so, He should be neither of both, Word nor flesh, neither God nor man.

Andrewes continued by indicating that there was a similarity between the soul and body of human beings with the hypostacial union.

But 'made' He was; St. Paul tells us how; *assumendo*, 'by taking the seed of Abraham.' His generation eternal, as *Verbum Deus*, is as the inditing the word within the heart. His generation in time, *Verbum caro*, is as the uttering it forth with the voice. The inward motion of the mind taketh unto it a natural body of air, and so becometh vocal: it is not changed into it, the word remaineth still as it was, yet they two become one voice. Take a similitude from ourselves. Our soul is not turned into nor compounded with the body, yet they two though distinct in natures grow into one man. So, into the Godhead was the manhood taken; the natures preserved without confusion, the person entire without division. Take the definition of the fourth General Council: *Sic factum est caro ut maneret Verbum, non immutando quod erat, sed suscipiendo quod non erat, nostra auxit, sua non miniut; nec Sacramentum pietatis detrimentum Deitatis*; 'He was so made flesh that He ceased not to be the Word, never changing that He was, but taking that He was not; we were the better, He was never the worse; the mystery of godliness was no detriment to the Godhead, nor the honour of the creature wrong to the Creator.'[400]

Andrewes also used this hypostatical union to illustrate that

---

400 Andrewes, Vol. 1, pp. 90 – 1.

there was no longer a partition between God and us when we are truly penitent for our sins and try to obey God's law.

Similar Anselmian and hypostatical teachings also featured in the remaining lectures and various sermons, two of which are One and Five in this manuscript, and some of his Jacobean Court Sermons. Besides the Nativity Sermon for 1611, these are the 1604 Passion Sermon, 1606 Paschal Sermon and the 1614 Nativity Sermon.[401]

> 1Tim 2.5-6. *There is one God and one Mediator betw*[een] *God and men, the man Christ Jesus, who gave him[self] a ransome for all, to be testified in due time.*

God made man upright (Solomon) but he found [sought in A.V.] out many inventions. And man never yet found out more inventions to undo hims[elf], then God hath done to save him; nor was he ever varied into more shapes of sin and misery, then God hath been of goodnes and mercy. But above all, the very height of his goodnes, the originall and foundacion of all his mercyes to mankind was the Incarnacion of his sonne, whom he appoynted to be a reconciler and Meditaour betw[een] God and man, and to give hims[elf] a ransome for all, even the man Christ Jesus.

Now haveing formerly shown you the Nature of sin, the severall sorts and divisions of sin; as also those things that accompany sin; Guilt and stain, and Punishment, I shall add a little of the last of these; and then proceed to the remedy or meanes of freedome from the Guilt and curse of sin by a mediatour the man Christ Jesus.

The Punishment of sin is Death, Rom: 5.15.[402] And this death may be considered 2 wayes; 1. Formally, and so it doth consist in a beeing separated from the blessed communion, and banished from the gracious presence of God. 2ly, Materially; and so it doth consist in a miserable privacion of that life and happines which man did either actually possess by Creation or might assuredly have obtained in a more eminent manner and a more abundant measure upon condicion of his obedience.

---

401 Ibid., Vol. 1, pp. 21-2, 90-3, 57-8, 140, 183-5, Vol. 2, pp. 150, 196-7.

402 A better reference would have been Romans 6.23 (A.V).

Again This Death is either 1. Spirituall, or 2. Corporall, or 3ly swallowed up in that Death which is eternall.

1. Spirir[itual] Death is the death of the soul; whence men are said to be dead while alive, dead in trespasses and sins, Eph: 2.1. And shee that liveth in pleasure is dead, while shee liveth, 1Tim: 5.6 and Math: 8.22 let the dead bury their dead. All which places are meant of the death of the soul. And this death is a totall deprivacion of primitive integrity, and originall righteousness; whereby man is despoyled of all those sanctifying and saveing graces, wherewith he was endured in his creacion. So that 1st the Understanding, tho' it have some glimpses of morall righteousnes, as the Gentiles did by nature the things contained in the law, Rom: 2.14; yet it hath not the least light of evangelicall truth; for the natural man receiveth not the things of the spirit of God, 1Cor: 2.14. And therefore all the wisdome of the meer naturall man is rendred in the very abstract, foolishnes 1Cor: 3.19.

2ly, As the understanding is full of ignorance, so the will of perversnes; indeed as free faculty it retaineth it's liberty which it exerciseth in naturall and morall actions; but through the servitude of sin, 'tis wholly disabled, (as of it's self) for supernaturall and divine actions, Rom: 8.7. It hath lost it's freedome, in respect of its voluntary servitude and slavery unto sin, whereby it becomes necessitated, so as to will nothing (in spir[itual] things) but what is evill; yet in respect of the naturall liberty of it's acting, it hath not lost it's freedome, so as to be compelled to will this or that evill; for man so to loose his liberty, were to lose his will, to loose his liberty in the exercise of its act, were to loose his will in the faculty of it's beeing. 3ly, For the conscience, tho' sometimes awakened, yet 'tis polluted, Tit: 1.15. And 4ly, Affections, tho' restrained from some evills, 1Cor: 5.1 yet are they inordinately carried into other impieties, Rom: 1.29. So that this is the condicion of the soul of every naturall man. 1. The rationall faculties of the soul remaine whole, in regard of the naturall essence of the soul. But 2ly, the soul is spoyled of all spir[itual] habitts; whereby the Understanding, Will, Conscience, affections, become averse, undisposed, and altogether insufficient for what is divine and spirituall. This is the 1st Death, which we call Spirituall.

2. Corporall Death, which surpriseth the Body. And this is first begun in this life in sicknesses and sorrowes, Gen: 3.17; in ser-

vitude and slavery, Deut: 28.36; in toyl and wearines, Eccl: 2.22, calamities and wants, Deut: 28.39; the very creatures intended for man's use, being cursed for man's sake Gen: 3.17. 2ly, This Death is consummate, when at last it doth put a period to man's dayes, and adds a complement of his temporall miseries, and then begins the anguish of eternall torments. The body being layd in a grave of corruption, the soul is hurried to an hell of perdicion, where they remain till Death spirituall and corporall be swallowed up in Death eternall. And this the absolute, the full punishment of sin, which is Death Eternall.

So 3ly, The last Death mentioned is Eternall Death, which is the separacion both of body and soul at the last day (by an irrevocable sentence of the last judgment) from the presence of God, into Hell, the place, the prison of the damned, where they shall suffer an insufferable and eternall punishment. And this 2fold: 1. of Losse 2. of Sense.

1. Punishment of losse doth consist, in a totall and finall separacion from the gracious presence of God, and from all the joy and blisse, and glory which doth accompany that beatificall vision and full fruicion of him, expressed, Math: 25.41[403] Depart from me yee cursed into everlasting fire, prepared for the Devill and his Angells.[404]

2. Punishment of sense, doth consist especially in that worm of an evill conscience, which ever gnaweth with unspeak[able] tortures, and in that fire of hellish flames, which ever scorcheth with uncessant torments, which cause endles, easeles and remediles weepings and wailing, and gnashings of teeth.

And this Punishment is eternall. The time of their continuance in those flammes, in this darknes adds the greatest weight unto their torments; for tho' their punishment were never so great, and the place never so bad; th' one so great and th' other bad; as the

---

403 Cp. with "the damned sinner is not ... utterly and irrecoverably banished from the comfortable presence of God, the beautificall vision and fruition of the 1st and chief good; the unspeakable joy and happinesse of that heavenly Jerusalem, the sweet society of glorious saints and Angells" in Sermon Three. Ms. 3707,p. 155.

404 In his lecture on Genesis 1.8 Andrewes stated that on the second day of creation, there is lacking that qualification, *And God saw it was good*, and so it has been suggested that the fall of Angels was on this day. *Apos. Sacra*, p. 664.

greatnes of God's power could any wayes make it; yet if they might hope for any end, they might conceiv, some of comfort: But when they shall consider that if there were so many worlds, as there be starrs in the heavens, and in every world so many trees as there be dropps of water in the ocean; and on every tree so many boughes, as there be piles of grasse upon the earth; and upon every bough so many leaves as there be graines of sand upon the sea shore, and every single grain of sand should passe for a mill[ion] of yeares, and that after all these multitudes of years and unlimited times, beyond all the rules of Arithmetique, they are anew to begin their endles paines, and as far from their end, as when they first began: so the highest link in all this chain of intollerable sorrowes and miseries, is the miserable perpetuity of torments, the thought of which cannot but be dreadfull and terrible.[405] And this is the estate and condicion of man fallen, the portion of every naturall man without the interveening meritts and satisfaction of Christ; he is a wretched, lost undone creature, a captive to the Prince of darknes, sold under the power of sin, involved in the curse of Death and liable to the condemnacion of Hell, that eternall punishment which is intollerable and unconceiveable; so that unlesse God in the unsearchable riches of his wisdome and unconceiv[able] tendernes of his mercy, had found out a meanes for recovery and redemption by a mediatour, Adam and all his posteritie must inevitably have perished in their sin. But thanks be to God, who hath given us a Redeemeer,[406] a Mediatour, the man Christ Jesus who gave hims[elf] a ransome for all to be [testified in due time, 1Tim: 2.5-6].

And so after the disease and misery, sin and punishment we come to the cure and Remedy, our Mediatour and Redeemer, Christ Jesus: He is the good Samaritane, that is only able and willing to heal all our maladies.

Now touching our Mediatour, the scriptures teach us two things, 1. His Person, 2. his office. In his Person we are to consider 1. The Distinction of the 2 natures, 2ly, the Personall Union of both Natures into one, Immanuel, God and man. 1. Our Mediatour is

---

405 There is a similar description of hell in Sermon Three. Ms. 3707, p. 156.

406 This is the text for Sermon Two in this manuscript. 1Cor. 1.57.

the 2nd Person in the bl[essed] Trinitie, the sonne of God, so the Apostle tells us, Gal. 4.4. God sent his sonne made of [a woman, made under the law]. There we have both his divine and humane Nature. And

1. That he was God of God, light of light, very God of very God, we have 1. Apparent script[ure]. 2. Reasons drawn from script[ure] to make it plain and clear unto us. 1. Script[ures] call him God Esa. 9.6 unto us [a child is born, unto a son is given ... and his name shall be] called Wonderfull Counsellour, the mighty God. So the Apostle calls him, my lord and my [God] Joh. 20.28. And the blood whereby the ch[urch] is purchased is called God's own blood Acts. 20.28. And the word was made flesh (St. John) and that word was God, Joh 1.1. And in many other places of script[ure] which we may obviously meet with and would be tedious here to relate.

2. This truth may be manifested by reasons drawn from Scripture; as 1. from the Incommunicable properties of the Dietie, which are properly ascribed unto him. 2ly, from the Relations that he hath with God. 3. from those Epithetes which are given to him and are only agreeable to the Divine Nature.

1. From Incommunicable properties of the Diety; as 1. Omnipotency, Phil. 3.21 he is able to subdue all things to hims[elf]. 2. Power to remit sins not instrumentally, but absolutely, by his own proper power and authority Math. 9.6, Mar. 2.5,9. 3ly, To have the same power with the Father Joh. 5.17, [19] My Father worketh hither to, and I work and what work the Father doth, that doth the Son. 4ly, To raise hims[elf] from the grave he was declared to be the Son of God with power, by the resurrection from the dead [Rom. 1.4].

2. From those relacions that he hath with God as to be *μονογενής*, the only [begotten Son, which is in the bosom of the Father] Joh: 1.18. To be the brightnes of his glory, the expresse Image of his person, Heb: 1.3. To be the very form of God, Col: 1.15. He being in the form of God, thought it no robbery to be equall with God, Phil: 2.6. And therefore he must needs be true God. 1. Bec[ause] the form of God is most simple and essentiall, for that in God there is no composicion, no accidents *quicquid in Deo est ipse Deus*. 2ly, because the word *ὑπάρχων*, once existing and being in the form of God, doth signifie the very Nature of God; For as his

being in the form of man proveth that he was a very man; so his beeing in the form of God, and that he thought it just and lawfull, no wrong, no robbery to be equall with God [Phil: 2.6], doth prove unto us that he a very God by nature, before he was incarnate and made man; for who can be in the form of God who can be equall with God, but God?[407]

3ly, this truth may be further evidenced from those epithets, which in scripture are ascribed unto him, and are only agreeable to the divine nature. As 1. to know the secretts of our hearts, Mat: 9.4,5 and Luc. 5.22. 2ly to illuminate us Joh: 1.9 he the true light, which enlighteneth every man that cometh into the world. 3ly, to hear the prayers of all them that call upon him. 4ly, to judge the quick and the dead Joh: 5.22 for the Father judgeth no man, but hath comitted all judgment unto the sonne. 5ly, to give to all his servants everlasting life, Joh: 5.24. To these we may add the universall effects and proper works of God, which are as well ascribed to the son as to the Father. As 1. the works of Creacion by him all things were made, Col: 1.16.[408] 2ly, works of preservacion, he beareth up all things, by his mighty power, Heb: 1.3. And also miracles which are works, either above or against the order of Nature, peculiar to God, were done by him; as his commanding the wind and the storm, Mar: 4.39, cureing diseases by the word of his mouth, Math: 8.3, and raiseing men from the dead, Luc: 7.14. The star at his birth, the Eclipse at his death; the glorious transfiguracion of the mount; and above all, his glorious ascension and receiving up into heaven; all which considered, well might the Apostle say, we saw his glory, as the glory as the only [begotten] of the Father Joh: 1.13.[409]

Lastly, to stop the mouthes of all gainsayers, and to satisfy all wavering and doubting minds, I shall add one reason further. The Gospell of St. John was cheifly penned for this end, to prove the Diety of our Saviour; and among other Arguments alleadged, this is one, that Christ gave a resolute and constant testimony of hims[elf] that he was the Sonne of God, and very God. Now if any

---

407 This text is repeated in Sermon One.

408 Cp. with his prayer on creation in Brightman, p. 198 and Ms. 3708, p. 1.

409 In the Authorized Version this is 1.14.

shall say, that sundry Persons, since the beginning of the world, have taken upon them, and that falsly, to be Gods. I answer, That never any creature took this title and honour to him, but sooner or later, the fearfull judgments of God were upon him for it. And so if Christ had been but a meer man, and not very God; undoubtedly the hand of God would have been upon him: but when he suffered for us, when he bare the punishment due for our sinnes; he then most of all triumphed; And the judgments of God were upon Herod, Pilate, Caiaphas, and upon all those that were enimies to him, and his church, partly in life, and partly in death. Wherefore considering God cannot endure that his glory, should be given to any creature, and seeing for that cause he takes reveng on all those that exalt thems[elves] to be Gods; it remains that the Testimony which Christ gave of hims[elf], that he was God, is true, and without all question to be beleeved of us.[410] And to conclude; how could it come to passe, that Christ by publishing the Doctrine of the Gospell, that is as contrary to man's reason, will, and affections, as water to fire, should get such a conquest, win almost the whole world to become his Disciples, and to give their lives for him, unles he were God indeed, as he professed himself to be?[411] Thus much for the confirmacion of that poynt, that he was God.

Now there be sundry reasons, why 'twas requisite that Christ should be God; as

1. Bec[ause] there is none which can satisfie for sin, and be a saviour of soules, but God alone, Ps: 49.7. I, even I, am the lord, and besides me there is no saviour, Esa. 43.11.

2. No finite creature was able to abide and overcome the infinite wrath of God, the sufferings due unto us from our sins; and therefore must our saviour be God, that he might abide the burthen of God's wrath in his flesh, sustaining and upholding the manhood by his divine power; and so might restore to us, the righteousnes of life which we have lost.

3. He that is a saviour, must be able 1. to deliver men from the bondage of their spirit[uall] enemies, sin and satan; to defend

---

410 Cp. with "the faithful are taught to return all glory to God" etc. in Sermon *For Thine is the Kingdom* , Andrewes, Vol. 5, p. 465.

411 Similar to theme of Sermon Six.

them from Hell, death and damnacion. 2. to restore the Image of God and to conferr righteousnes and life everlasting 3. to give them full Redemption from all their miseries both of Body and soul, and to place them in Eternall happines; all which none can doe but he who is very God. And thus much that our meditaour was God and why he is God.

Now follow the Dutyes required of us, which are these two 1. sorrow and contrition. 2. thankfulnes.

1. We beleev that Jesus Christ, who was to be the Saviour of mankind, must needs be God because no creature, no, not all the creatures, in Heaven and earth were able to save one man; so vile, wretched and miserable is our condicion by Adam's fall. And therefore the sonne of God hims[elf], pittied us; was content to lay aside the robes of his glory and majesty to be covered with the raggs of our Nature;[412] and tho' he was lord of all, yet he became a servant, and suffered death for our sinnes, which otherwise every one of us should have suffered both in body and soul for all eternity. To evidence this yet further; Suppose a man to have committed an offence against a Prince; and suppose this trespasse so hainous, that no man can appease the Kings wrath, but the King's only sonne; and which is more, the Kings sonne cannot do it, unles he suffer the punishment in his own person, which is due unto the offendour: is not this man's case miserable, is not his trespasse notorious? And so 'tis with every one of us by nature. No man could save our soules, no, not all the Angells in Heaven, unles the sonne of God had comed down from heaven, and suffered for us. Now the consideracion of this should humble us for our sinnes and make us pray that the Lord would send some Moses or other which might smite the rockes of our hearts, that some teares of sorrow and repentance might flow thence for our sinne and misery.[413]

2. God the Father was pleased to give his sonne to be our saviour, and therefore as we must be thankfull to him for all his mercyes, so especially for this great and unspeakable benefitt.

---

412 This text reappears in the opening of Sermon One and in Nativity Sermon for 1611, Andrewes, Vol. 1, p. 93.

413 This consideration also appears in Brightman, pp. 161 –2.

Common blessings of God, as meat, drink, health, wealth, liberty, must at all times move us to be thankfull; but this, that Christ Jesus redeemed us beeing utterly lost; this should be the main point of our thankfullnes.

Thus much of the Divinitie of our Redeemer. In the next place let us seek out his

Humanitie. And for this we have expresse Texts of script[ure] Joh: 1.14 Word [became flesh], i.e. he assumed 1. All our humane Nature, a true humane body, and a reasonable humane soul. 2. All our naturall properties and infirmities, sin only excepted.

1. This was long agoe foretold that the *Messias*[414] should come of the seed of David, of the stock of Jesse, Ps: 132.11, and long before that, that he should be the seed of the woman Gen: 3.15; and answerable thereunto, the Apostle tells us that he was made of a woman, Gal: 4.4. that as before all worlds he was from the bosome of his Father; so in the world from the womb of his mother; he was made man, made of a woman, did not abhor the Virgin's womb.

2. He had all the proper Qualities of man, and was subject to all the infirmities of man without sin, Heb: 4.15. He was an hungry, Math: 4.2. He was weary, Joh: 4.6; He was asleep, Math: 8.24. He dyed, Joh: 19.33.[415] Now all these are not incident to the Nature of God, but of man. So he was made flesh, took our Nature upon him and was subject to sorrow and suffering, and death, as we are. And that our Redeemer should be God. And that he should be made flesh was necessary for these reasons.

1. Bec[ause] th' one had been in vain without th' other, this work he was to doe, was to deliver the seed of Abraham Gal: 3.16. And them he could not deliver, except he destroyed Death, and the Lord of Death, the Divell; and them he could not destroy except he died, (for such was Gods love to justice, and hatred to sin, that he should not have his justice swallowed

414 Greek spelling for messiah.

415 This text is also in Brightman, p. 212, Ms. 3708, p. 14, and Nativity Sermon for 1605, Andrewes, Vol. 1, p. 10.

up with mercy, nor sin pardoned without such a propitiacion) so then dye he must, and dye he could not except he were mortall, and mortall he could not be except he took our Nature upon him; so 't was necessary, that beeing God, he should become man, that he might become mortall, dye, destroy death and deliver us.

2. It beeing the proper office of our Redeemer to be a mediatour betw[een] God and man, 'twas meet, that he should partake with both. And beeing before all Eternitie consubstantiall with his Father, at the appointed time he should be consubstantiall with his children, such a Redeemer, such a Mediatour became us, Heb. 2.17.[416]

In the next place, we are to consider 1. Distinction of the two natures. 2. Union of the 2 Natures, the word and the flesh i.e. Diety and humanitie of our Saviour Christ.

1. Distinction of these 2 Natures is set down by the Apostle Rom: 1.3,4 where he saith that Christ was made man according to the flesh and declared to be the sonne of God according to the spirit of sanctificacion; for that according to his humane Nature, he was made of the seed of David, who according to his divine nature was still declared to be the sonne of God. So St. Paul shewes here two Natures to be in our Saviour Christ, humane and divine, remaining entire after his incarnacion; bec[ause] as he was made only of the seed of David in respect of his manhood, so was he declared only to be the son of God in respect of his Godhead.

2. Tho' the two Natures be still distinguished in substance, properties and actions; yet we must not imagine that our saviour is therefore two sonnes or two Persons, but one only Person, consisting of both these Natures Hag: 2.7 I will shake all nations *vehiashtiy et kol hagoyim* [and the desire of all nations shall come] *desiderium venient,* Again the script[ure] saith that we have one Mediatour 1Tim: 2.5 and one Lord Eph: 4.5 but if in Christ there were two persons then we should have two Mediatours, and two Lords. 3ly, whom do men say that I the sonne of man am? Math: 16.13. Peter answered, thou art Christ,

416 Similarly in Sermon One.

the sonne of God, therefore he is but one Person, bec[ause] Peter confesseth the sonne of man to be the same with the sonne of the liveing God. And further this hypostaticall Union of two Natures in one Person is inseparable, tho' one can never be separated from th' other. And therefore that ejaculation of our Saviour's, My God [my God, why hast thou forsaken me] is not to be understood, as if he has lost his Divinity, no, *non adfuit ad defensionem, sed intus non defuit ad unionem*; the Divinity was ever a companion to the manhood, but not alwayes an helper; it never ceased to be with our saviour, tho' it did not then aid him; as the Sun may be present, tho' not shine: so the divine nature may be personally united, and yet no effects seen of so great a majesty; 'tis true God had then so far forsaken him, as to suffer his body to be torn from his soul, yet not his manhood from his Divinitie.[417] But without controversy, great is this mystery of Godlines, God thus [manifest in the flesh 1Tim:3.16] and tho' the Fathers endeavoured by many similitudes to illustrate and make it plain, as by the Union of the Body and the soul, of a branch ingraffed into a tree, of a fiery iron and the like; yet, all come too short for the full expressing of this inexplicable mystery. God's wayes are in the seas, his pathes in the great waters and his footsteps not known [Ps: 77.19].

And thus much of the Person of our Redeemer, of his two natures, humane and divine, of the distinction of them both, and the union of them both, into one Immanuel, Christ Jesus.

Now to apply this

The Benefitts of the union of these 2 Natures in respect of us, are our spirituall union with God and the enriching of us with all those graces that doe prepare us, and bring us to everlasting happines; for our sinnes had separated us from God, made us aliens [from the commonwealth of Israel, and strangers from the covenants of promise, having no hope, and without God in the world, Eph:2.12] and were like a partition wall betw[een] God and us [Eph:2.14]: but now, as God made the Personall union of soul and body, for the constitucion and continuacion of the common Nature of Mankind: so he united the

417 Cp. with similar text in Passion Sermon for 1604, Andrewes, Vol. 2, pp. 146 – 7.

Word with our flesh, that our Nature might be restored in the Person of Christ; and by reason of this union of our nature unto the sonne of God, and thereby our communion with God, we receiv all those gracious motions and gifts, that are necessary for sustaining of our spirituall life, and this spirit[ual] life shall be consummate in glory; when we shall fully attain the blessed fruicion of God for ever.

LECTURE ELEVEN

Of Christ's Kingly Office

Introduction

The first part of this lecture continued the meditatory role of Christ, which is to reconcile two previously irreconcilable parties, in this case, God and man. For God this reconciliation could only be achieved in the person of Christ Jesus whose sinless life enabled Him to offer a perfect offering upon the cross for the sin of man and to satisfy God's justice. On man's behalf God is pleased to accept his sacrifice through Christ's. Only Christ could accomplish this, not even the Holy Spirit or the angels or saints could perform Christ's role which is to "advocate for his church and doth in his own Person in heaven apply his meritts and with his Father further the cause of our Salvacion."[418] Andrewes made it clear that the Reformed English Church rejected the medieval practice of praying to the saints as a mediator. There was a difference between the saints having our welfare at heart and pleading to God on our behalf, he declared.[419]

In the second part Andrewes introduced the three offices of the Mediator: King, Priest and Prophet. Beginning with Kingship he discussed this under four headings, of which the first three are discussed in this lecture.

1. Ordination and qualification of Christ for his Kingdome.

---

418 Ms. 3707, p. 98.

419 Andrewes elsewhere expressed that the saints do pray for us. Andrewes, Vol. 5, p. 370.

2. Quality or nature of his Kingly Power.

3. Administration of his Kingdome.

4. Continuance or duration of this Kingdome

1. Christ's appointment and ordination are derived from God who has "crowned him", and entrusted to Him the administration of the Church. The qualification for this office is that God the Son became man who was given power from His Father to make laws for the Church and to remit or retain sins.[420]

2. The nature of Christ's kingdom is essentially spiritual, and therefore is quite distinct from secular ones. The Father has given Him the authority and power to rule in "the hearts of men" and their "soules and consciences". Membership of Christ's kingdom is voluntary, as He does not force anyone into it. Nevertheless "by the secret, ineffable and sweet operation of the spirit of grace" He converts many hearts from their sinful ways, and these are given "all things which pertain to life and Godlines".[421]

3. Christ's administration is based on His teaching of faith, repentance, love and charity, which means Christ has superseded the Jewish "ceremoniall and judiciall law". To love God and one's neighbour take on a new meaning as Christ taught in John 15. Those who respond to Christ's teaching undergo a change *(metanoia)* and henceforth live according to His precepts. The aim of Christ's administration is to bring all His subjects who are part of the royal priesthood "to the obedience of His laws". For this He employs varying methods according to the type of sinner. Unlike earthly kings, Christ always shows compassion and fulfils His promises to all His subjects by protecting, upholding and succouring them. However with His enemies, Christ "doth confound ... all their projects" by ruling His kingdom "in the midst of their malice" as "his Truth" shines even "brighter, for the shakeing". Finally on Judgment day His enemies will have to face "the justice of his wrath."[422]

1Tim 2.5-6.There is one God, and one Mediatour between God and

---

420 Ms. 3707, p. 99.

421 Ibid., p. 101.

422 Ibid., p. 105.

men, the man Christ Jesus who gave hims[elf] a ransome for all to be testified in due time.

Haveing spoken heretofore of the Humanitie and Divinity of our Saviour, that he is true God and perfect man; of the distinction of his natures, and of the union of his Natures in one person, Christ Jesus; we proceed now from the person to the Office of our Redeemer, his Mediatourshipp betwixt God and man, whereby he was appoynted to discharg all that was requisite for the reconcileing of us to God, and the perfecting the work of our salvacion. And here we shall show

1. What 'tis to be a Mediatour.
2. That we have only one Mediatour.
3. That Christ is this Mediatour in both natures.
4. Offices of our Mediat[our]: King, Pr[iest] and Prophet.

1. To be a Mediatour is for one to interpose himself, to reconcile two parties at odds and variance. And to Reconcile is 1. To intercede for the Partie offending, to the Partie offended. 2. To satisfie for the injury done. 3. To be a Sponsor and to promise that the partie offending, shall not doe like againe. Now the Partie offended was the eternall, immortall God, the Partie offending mortall man; for sin, guilty of eternall death; and the Mediatour, the Reconciler of these two thus at variance, Christ Jesus who made intercession for us by vertue of his own blood, gave hims[elf] a propitiacion for our sinnes, 1Joh: 2.2, so satisfied the Justice, appeased the wrath of an angry God, and made a firm peace between Heaven and earth, God and mankind. All this he did with the Partie offended; Now to us Parties offending; 1. He comes an Interpretor of God and messenger from Heaven to declare and testifie the will of God, and to inform us, how God is pleased to accept his satisfaction for us. 2. To apply this satisfaction to us. 3. By the grace of his spirit, to begett faith and willingnes in us, to beleeve and to be ready to embrace this satisfaction made for us; for unles both parties consent, there can be no Reconciliacion. 4. By the same spirit, to renew us, to keep us in faith and obedience; Untill lastly, this corruptible put[s] on incorruption [1Cor: 15.53], he raise[s] us up and glorifie[s] us with hims[elf] in Heaven. All these Blesings are contained in Christs Mediatourshipp.

2. That we have only one mediatour. 1. This Text tells us so;

there is one God and one [Mediatour], and 2ly, this was shadowed forth under the Law. For the Jewish High Priest is acknowledged by all to the Figure and type of Christ; but that Priest was but one; and when he went into the holy of holyes, he went in alone to make expiacion as we may see it ordained, Lev:16.17. By which is intimated thus much; that Christ is our alone and only Mediatour before the throne of God.

3ly, The Apostle makes this evident by a comparison 1Cor: 15.21. By man came Death; and by man (not by more then one) came alsoe the resurrection of the dead: so Rom: 5.15. Through the offence of one many be dead, much more the grace of God, and the gift by grace, which is by one man Christ Jesus, hath abounded unto many. So there is but one Mediatour, and Christ only hath this prerogative; neither any saint nor Angell but only the man Christ Jesus is our Mediatour.

Ob[jectio]. But it may be here demanded; Have we not also another Mediatour and Advocate, the holy Spirit; and doth not he intercede for us? Rom: 8.26. The spirit maketh intercession for us with groanings which cannot be uttered.

Sol[utio]. To satisfie this demand, and to note the difference betw[een] Christ and the h[oly] spirit in this particular; we are to obs[erve] that there may be a Mediatour and Advocate. 1. by office 2. by operacion, instruction and assistance. First by office, when one Person takes upon himself the cause of another, and in his name pleades it. Thus Christ by the office of his mediacion and Intercession is an Advocate for his church and doth in his own Person in Heaven apply his meritts, and with his Father further the cause of our Salvacion. 2ly, advocate, by operacion, by instruction and assistance; which is not where a work is done by one person [o]n the behalf of another; but when one by his counsell, inspiracion and assistance enableth another to manage his own busines and to plead his own cause. And such an Advocate the spirit is, who doth not intercede, nor appeare before God in Person for us, as Christ doth, but maketh intercession for men, in and by themselves giving them an access unto the Father, Eph: 2.18, emboldening them in their feares. Heb: 10.19.

Ob[jectio]. But 2ly, may not saints or Angells be our Mediatours? Aquin[as] would have it so, and he gives this reason for it. If they pray for us when they are on earth, and carefull for themselves: then much more after they have obtained the crown and victory; for then they are in the promised glory, and more full of charitie then before.

Sol[utio]. Answer: 1st That the Saints in Heaven do Magnifie and praise the God of Heaven; we deny not, 2ly, that they have a generall desire and longing both for us and for thems[elves] and all the chosen of God, that the time of refreshing were come [Act: 3.19]; and that all the people of God were joyned in one, this also we learn out of Scripture. But 3ly, that they should offer up our prayers, and so make particular request to god for us, as Mediatours, we have no ground in scripture; and that only ought to be our Rule of faith and obedience. Lastly, the saints in Heaven know not our wants, nor what is done on earth (for the dead know nothing at all, Eccl: 9.5), and therefore they cannot be Mediatours, not intercede for us. Thus much of the 2nd Particular, that we have only one Mediatour.

3ly, That Christ is this our one Mediatour, according to both his Natures, as God and man. For 1st the Work of mediacion was wrought in the Humanity, as far as concerneth sorrowing, suffering and dying, of which the Godhead was not capeable; 2ly, 'twas wrought by the Godhead, as concerning makeing the sacrifice efficacious and of infinite price; for unlesse he were God, he could not be the cheif Doctor of the church, the eternall high Priest; neither could he exercise kingly Power in heaven and earth; overcome the Divell and death, send the h[oly] spirit, renew the hearts of men, and confer eternall life. So being God from all eternity, in the fullnes of time it behooved him in all things to be made like unto his brethren, that he might be mercyfull and faithfull high Priest in things pertaining to God, to make reconciliacion for the sinnes of the People Heb: 2.17. Thus either Nature doth work with the other, that which is proper to be wrought. The Word worketh that which belongeth to the word, maketh his death and passion satisfactory, of infinite worth and value; and the flesh performeth that which pertaineth to the flesh, suffered misery and shame and Death; the Manhood being as the instrument to the Godhead, that he might suffer; and the Godhead as the principall mover or worker of the Manhood, that he might overcome in suffering.

Thus we have a mediatour and only <u>one</u> Mediatour, and this one mediatour is Immanuel, God with us, God in our Nature, Christ Jesus.

4. We come now to speak of the species of his Mediatourshipp, or his 3 Offices, that he is K[ing], and Preist and Prophet. And these concern the good of his ch[urch], all mankind; for to no other end was he named Christ, sealed of his Father, sent into the world and incarnate, but to repair what was decayed and restore what was lost. Luc: 19.10. To begin with the

1. Kingly Office. And here let us consider

1. Ordinacion and qualificacion of Christ for his kingdome.

2. Quality or nature of his kingly power.

3. Administracion of his kingdome.

4. Continuance or duracion of this kingdome.

1. His Unction, appoyntment and ordinacion unto his kingdome was from God hims[elf], Heb. 9.27[423] him hath God the Father sealed; and God himself proclaimes it. Ps: 2.6. I have set my K[ing] upon my [holy hill of Sion], so that Christ's Kingdome belongs to him, not by usurpacion, intrusion or violence; but legally, by order and obsignacion from his Father.

All Kings raign by God's Providence, but not always by his approbacion; for God declares against some, Amos 1.4,5[424] and 8.4.[425] But Christ is a king both by the providence, and by the good will and consecracion of his Father; he loved him and hath given all things into his hand, Joh: 3.35. He hath entrusted him with the actuall administracion of that power in the church, which originally belonged unto hims[elf]; he hath made him to be lord and Christ Act: 2.36. He ordained him judge of [the] Quick and dead, Act: 10.42. He hath crowned him with glory and honour; set him over the works of his hands; and hath put all things in subjection under his feet, Heb: 2.7,8. But

Here we are to distinguish betw[een] Christ's naturall Kingdome which belongeth unto him as he is God, coessentiall and coeternall with his Father, and 2. His dispensatory Kingdome, as

423 A better reference would have been Heb. 1. 2 or Joh. 6.27.

424 i.e. "The house of Hazael, the palace of Ben-hadad, the ruler of Beth-eden, the inhabitants of the Aven valley and the people of Aram."

425 i.e. "Hear this, O ye that swallow up the needy, even to make the poor of the land to fail."

He is Christ the Mediatour, which was his not by nature, but by Donacion and unction from his Father, that He might be the head of his church, a Prince of Peace; and a King of righteousnes unto his People. And thus much of his ordinacion unto his Kingly Office.

Next for his Qualificacion. 1. God prepared him an humane Body, Heb: 10.5, and by the grace of personall and hyperstaticall Union caused the Godhead to dwell bodyly in him, Col: 2.9.

2. He anoynted him with fullness of his spir[it]: not such a fullnes as his saints and servants had; for they had a fullnes too, Act: 7.55, but 'twas the fullnes of a measure; a fullness for themselves only, Eph: 4.7. But Christ had a fullness of the spirit without measure, like the fullnes of light in the Sun, the fullnes of water in the Ocean, an unsearchable, inexhaustible sufficiency and redundancy for the whole church,[426] Joh: 3.34 [and] Eph. 3.8. So that as he was furnished with all spirituall endownment of wisedome, power, love, holines, Esa: 61.1. So from his fullnes did there run over a share and portion of all his graces to his church, Joh: 1.16.

3ly. God did solemnly proclaime his Kingdome unto the church Mat: 3.17 a voyce from heaven was heard, saying, this is my beloved sonne in whom I am well pleased. 4ly, He hath given him a scepter of Righteousnes, Ps: 45.6 which very place of the Psalmist we find quoted by the Apostle Heb. 1.8. But unto the sonne he saith, thy throne O God is for ever and ever, a scepter of righteousnes is the sceptre of thy Kingdome. 5ly, He hath honoured him with many Ambassadors and servants to negotiate the affaires of his Kingdome, some Apostles, some prophets, some [evangelists; and some, pastors and teachers], Eph. 4: 11,12. 6ly. He hath given him the soules and consciences of men, even to the uttermost parts of the earth for his possession, Ps: 2.8. 7ly. He hath given him a power concerning the lawes of his church; a power to make lawes, the law of faith, Rom: 3.27. A power to expound lawes, Math: 5.23, a power to abrogate lawes, Col: 2.14. Lastly he hath given him a power of remitting sinnes and sealing pardons which is a prerogative royall, Math: 9.6. And thus much of the qualificacion of his Person for his Kingdome.

---

426 Cp. with "And it was given to Him without measure, ..." in Pentecost Sermon for 1618. Andrewes, Vol. 3, pp. 307-8.

2ly, Next thing proposed was the quality and nature of his kingly power. 1. Negatively, 'tis no temporall, no secular power over the naturall lives or civill negotiacions of men; this he disclaimed, when by force they would have made him such a King, he withdrew hims[elf] from the people Joh: 6.15. And he hath told us that his Kingdome was not of this world, Joh. 18.36; that he came not to be ministred unto, but to minister, Math: 20.28. And that in this poynt he might not give offence he hims[elf] paid tribute unto Caesar[427] Math. 17.26.[428] So we see that his Kingdome is no temporall, no secular Kingdome.

2ly, His kingdome is spir[itual] and heavenly, not so much over the estates and fortunes, as over the soules of men; to bind and loose the conscience, to remit and retain sinns, to awe and overrule the hearts, to captivate the affections, to bring into obedience every thought, 2Cor: 10.5, to subdue and pull down strong holds 2Cor. 10.4; to break in peices his enimies with a rod of iron, to slay them with the words of his mouth, and to give peace, security, protection and assurance to his People; this is the nature and quality of Christ's Kingdome, to rule in the hearts and consciences of men; God hath given to him, the soules, the hearts, the very thoughts of men, to be made obedient unto his scepter; and these he enters upon by way of conquest; for the old man within us [Rom: 6.6], will not yeild to be crucified upon termes of peace. And yet Christ doth not compell men against their wills to become his subjects, but brings them in by a way of voluntary obedience, by the secret, ineffable and sweet operacion of the spirit of grace, opening the eyes, convinceing the judgment, perswadeing the affections, enclineing the heart, enlighteneing the understanding, quickeneing the conscience; a man shall be swayed unto the obedience of Christ, and shall come unto him so certainly, as if he were drawn and yet so freely, as if he were left unto himself. And this brings in the 3rd thing I proposed.

3ly, Manner or Actuall administracion of Christ's Kingdome. And this implies severall particulars. As 1. Publicacion and Abrogacion of some lawes, for that is a prerogative royall belonging to a King. 2. Conquering and subdueing of subjects bringing them to

---

427 This appears also in Sermons Two and Four.

428 Verse 27 in the Authorized Version.

the obedience of his lawes. 3. Ruleing and leading those whom he hath brought into obedience. 4. Protecting and upholding his subjects against all temptacions and discouragements. 5. [Rewarding the good. Lastly,][429] vanquishing and confounding all his enemies; these are the properties of a powerfull and absolute Prince.

1. Publicacion of some fitt lawes, by which his church and kingdome shall be governed; and this he did after he was raised from the dead, he commanded that in his Name Repentance and remission of sinnes should be preached to all [nations], Luk: 24.47. And Heb: 12.2 He is called the Captain, the Author and finisher of our Faith; 'tis in the originall *τῆς πίστεως*, not of faith simply, but of <u>the faith</u>, to specify unto us, some particular and singular <u>faith</u>, which is denominated from him, and called the Christian faith, because Christ was the Author and captain of it, the first that ever taught it; And again the finisher of our faith, to bring it to an issue, and put an end to it, for then a thing is finished, when it hath attained it's proper end; so our faith shall be finished, when it is comed to the issue of it, whereby we attain the salvacion of our soules which is the end of our faith, 1Pet: 1.9. And this end is attained by Christ.

2. How often is Repentance injoyned, both by hims[elf] and his followers; the first time he preached the first word of his sermon was Repent [for the Kingdom of heaven is at hand], Mat: 4.17. And againe he tells us the necessity of Repentance, that without it we all perish, Luc: 13.3. And the former ignorance God winked at (St. Paul) but now [commandeth all men everywhere to repent.] Act: 17.30. So this is one of his precepts he gave unto his ch[urch]: And this Repent[ance] is not only sorrow and contricion, a confession and hope of pardon, but 'tis *μετάνοια*, an universall change of the whole course of our Life, and an wholly applying our[selves] to dutyes of Piety and holines; for this end the grace of God appeared, teaching us [salvation hath appeared to all men], Tit: 2.12.[430] And how often are Regeneracion, renovacion of mind, self-deniall, awakeing from sleep, purgeing our selves from all filthines of flesh and spirit, laying aside all guile and malice and hypocrisie,

429 This is crossed through in the manuscript.

430 In the Authorized Version this is 2.11.

pressed home in scripture, all which do but explain and declare the nature of Repentance.

3ly. He tells us of a new commandment, Joh: 13.34 a new commandment give I unto you [that ye love one another] which he calls a new commandment (Grotius) bec[ause] he speakes not of common love and charitie towards all; nor of love between Brethren and Kinsfolke, nor between Beneficiaries and Benefactors; but of that speciall love that ought to be amongst thems[elves], Christians to bear one with the infirmities of another, to construe all things in the best parte. And this law he presseth thrice in one chapter, Joh: 15. This is my commandment that yee love one [another] v. 12, and these things I command you, that yee love one [another] v.17, and a third time, by this shall men know that you are my Disciples, if yee love [one another].[431]

4ly. He hath given a law against scandall and denounced a woe to them by whom offences do come, Math: 18.7 and how carefull his subjects are to observ this law, you have the example of St. Paul in his own person 1Cor: 8.13, and he injoynes it to others, Rom: 14.21 we should neither by command nor perswasion, nor example nor any other way occasion another to sinne.

And thus much of our Saviour's Kingly Power in makeing and establishing lawes; you have heard of some of them; the law of faith and Repentance, love and charity. And as he had power to make lawes, so also to abrogate lawes, such as he saw not fitt for his kingdome. And such were the ceremoniall lawes of the Jewes, such as consisted in rites and ceremonies, types and shadowes, as also their judiciall lawes, concerning offences and severall sorts of punishments.

Ob[jectio]. But it may be demanded, how could Christ chang those lawes when God commanded that they should be observed for ever. Exod: 12.14 and 2Ch: 17.21.[432]

Sol[utio]. For ever i.e. as long as that common-wealth endured; it should not be lawfull for any of them to change them when and how they pleased, but when that common-wealth ceased, when

431 John Chrysostom on whom Andrewes draws frequently also remarked on our Lord's quick repetitions of this command to love. Chrysostom, p. 275.

432 Preferably 2Chron. 7.17.

the fullnes of time was come, that the Messias came, then such as were not agreeing to Christian Religion he abrogated, as the ceremoniall and judiciall law, which were but the shadowes of things to come; such as concerned not the inner man, and therefore not agreeable to the nature of Christian Religion, which is spirituall.

In brief, 3 reasons may be given for the abrogation of these lawes.

1. They were shadowes of things to come and the Body, the truth of those shadowes being come there was no more need of those shadowes; we under the gospell having clearer Promises, 'twas requisite also, that we should have clearer precepts.[433]

2. God having determined to gather the Jewes and Gentiles together, and of them both to make one People; this could not be done unles the ceremon[ial] law[s] were taken away, which was as a partition wall to sever the one from the other, so that those two might become one, twas fitt this wall should be pulled down.[434]

3ly. God by abrogating this law, would have the Jewes to understand, that Jesus Christ was their King, who had power, so to null and abrogate their lawes.

2ly, Next act in the Adminstracion of his kingdome, consists in the conquering and subdueing of his subjects bringing them to the obdience of his lawes. And this is done by converting the hearts, by bringing their very thoughts into the obedience of his Kingdome. And is done 1. Ministerially, by the word of reconciliacion, which is powerfull over the consciences of obstinate sinners; 'tis more cutting then any two edged sword, peircing to the divideing assunder of the soul and spirit, Heb: 4.12. Is not my word like fire (Lord), and like a hammer that breaketh the rock in peices? Jer: 23.29. Like a soft fire, to dissolv and melt the hearts of relenting sinners; but like a strong hammer, to batter and break in peices the rockie and flinty consciences of obstinate and hardened sinners; Examples hereof are frequent in scriptures, in the stories of Saul mourning when Samuel reproved him, 1Sam: 15.24; the

433 Cp. with "He, of Whom all the promises made mention ... of Whom all the types under the law were shadows, ..." in Nativity Sermon for 1610, Andrewes, Vol. 1, pp. 75 -6.

434 This is based on Ephesians 2.14.

Ninevites drooping, when Jonah threatned them Jon: 3.5. Felix trembling when Paul discoursed before him, Act: 24.25. Now these effects might seem strang, if the causes were not apparent; the cheif principall cause working effectually, is the spirit of God, working in this ordinance of his. For in His hands are the hearts and tongues and eares both of Kings and Prophets; and he can easily when he pleaseth, put the spirit of zeal and of power, into the heart of the poorest prophet, and as easily, the spirit of fear and of terror into the heart of the greatest King; we commonly say, words are but wind, and we say truly, the words of the best of Gods Messengers are no better, as they are uttered by sinfull mortall man, whose breath is in his nostrills: but yet this word, as it is inspired, by the powerfull and eternall spirit of God is strong enough, not only to shake the top branches, but to rend up the very root of the tallest Cedar in Lebanon, Ps: 29.4,5 the voice of the Lord is powerfull and mighty in operacion; the voice of the lord is full of majesty; the voice of the lord breaketh the Cedars, yea, the lord breaketh the Cedars of Lebanon. When it rowseth up the dull and drowsy sinner from the bed of security; then sackcloth and ashes, and fasting and weeping and mourning and rending the garments, and outcryes to heaven and all those other things which he could not endure to heare of in the time of his former securitie, are now in all hast and greedily entertained.

This is Christ's Kingly power in conquering and subdueing subjects to himself, Ministerially by his word, and effectively by the power of his spirit.

3ly, Christ as a King doth rule and lead those whom he hath converted in his way, continuing unto their hearts his gracious and heavenly voice, not depriveing them of the exciteing, assisting, cooperating grace of his holy Spirit, but giveing them all things which pertain to life and Godlines 2Pet: 1.3 and 1Pet: 2.9 he makes them a chosen generation, a royall Priesthood, an holy nacion, a peculiar people, that they should shew forth the praises of him, who hath called them out of darknes into his marvellous light.

4ly, As a King, he doth protect, uphold and succour his subjects against all temptacions and discouragments. By his compassion pittying them, Heb: 2.17; by his power and promises helping them, Joh: 16.33; by his care and wisdome, proportioning their strength to their trialls, 1Cor: 10.13; by patience and experience establishing their hearts in the hope of deliverance, Rom. 15.4. And Rev. 3.10 he thus bespeakes the church, bec[ause] thou hast kept the word of my patience, I also will keep thee from the hour of temptacion, which shall come upon all the worldlie to try them that dwell upon the earth.

5ly, Christ as a King doth confound all his enemies. 1. all their Projects, maintaining his Kingdome in the midst of their malice, and makeing his Truth like a Tree settle the faster and like a Torch, shine the brighter, for the shakeing. 2. he doth confound the Persons of all his enimies whom he doth here torment by the scepter of his word, forceing them to subscribe to the justice of his wrath; and whom he doth reserv for the day of his appearing, when they shall be put all under his feet.

And thus much of Christ's ordinacion and qualification for his Kingdome; of the Nature and quality of his kingly Power and of the Administracion of his Kingdome; of his Power in makeing and abrogateing Lawes, of subdueing, ruleing, protecting his subjects and confounding his enimies. I should now proceed to the continuacion of Christ's Kingdome, or the limitacion of it when it shall have an end, as also how tis besett with crosses and afflictions and is generally disliked and hated in the world etc.

LECTURE TWELVE

OF THERE IS ONE GOD AND ONE MEDIATOR

Introduction

Andrewes first summarised his previous lectures on Christ as Mediator and King before commencing his teaching on how Christ administers His kingdom. He firstly takes care that His laws will be kept by having them taught by His ministers ever since the Apostles to the present day in a way similar to His, that is, by teaching a little at a time in language and imagery understood by the people. Secondly, just as He feeds the birds, Christ looks after those who are faithful to Him by providing both their bodily and spiritual needs. Thirdly, Christ punishes His enemies and the ungodly, and will show no mercy upon them as they will be eternally punished by the torments of Gehenna. However he maintained that there was no excuse for any to perish as Christ has made clear that the keeping of His laws will lead to eternal life, and those who strive to keep them will always have His assistance. Accordingly Andrewes presented Christ the King as "the good Shepherd" who "shall gather" His flock and "carry [His lambs] in his bosome" rather than as a tyrant.[435]

He then proceeded to the fourth aspect of the kingdom, its continuation and limitation. Here a distinction has to be made between Christ's kingdom of Glory and of Grace. The former is eternal when Christ will rule over all, even His enemies, whilst the latter is eternal in substance but temporal in form. It is eternal in that Christ will always be the Head, but temporal as it will only last until "the consum-

435 Ms. 3707, p. 109.

macion of all things" when Christ has subdued all His enemies, that is, those who oppose Christ, either through power or disobedience. Then Christ will deliver up His kingdom to His Father as His role of mediator will have finished.[436]

And what of the Church, which was brought by Christ's blood? Will it survive until the end of this world? Andrewes assured that it would whilst ever Christ "sitteth at the right hand of God". Although there will be times, as indeed there have been in the past, that local churches will fail, there will always be a visible church on earth as Christ had promised His continual help. This divine took the opportunity here to teach on the nature of the Church, another of the contentious doctrines at the Reformation. Most Reformers spoke of the true church as being invisible; that "true body of Christ", the elect, who are known only to God.[437] Andrewes accepted that the Church in some sense is "invisible" in the way that "those graces and qualities which make a man a true member of [the] Body of Christ, be things invisible." However as he loved souls he was always more concerned with the visible church, that is, "a company of men" who profess "the true Doctrine of Christ". Even though there may be enemies within, Christ's Church "doth never totally fail" as there will be always the faithful.[438] It will therefore always be visible.

His lecture finished with another admonition to the scholars to be attentive to what Christ demands of them, and to give His laws the precedence over all earthly things. How essential it is that "we acquaint ourselves with his lawes", and realise that we all have to "render an account" of all our actions. Therefore we should allow God to speak to us each day to unveil our sins as he is always waiting to hear the sigh of contrition and the cry of penitence. So in true Andrewes' fashion he tempers God's sternness with the longing He has for sinners to repent. He also reminded the scholars that when they hear about God's laws in church they must be mindful where they are and pay due respect to God's house.[439]

---

436 Ibid., p. 111.

437 McGrath, pp.199 – 200.

438 Ms. 3707, p.113.

439 Ibid., p. 115.

Tim 2.5-6 *There is one God, and one Mediatour betw[een] God and [one Mediatour between God and men, the man Christ Jesus Who gave himself a ransom for all to be testified in due time].*

Out of these words we formerly observed 1. what tis to be a Mediatour; 2. that we have but only one Mediatour; 3. that Christ Jesus is this Mediatour where we considered 1. The Person of our Mediatour and there 1. both his Natures, his Godhead and his Manhood. 2. Distinction of those two Natures; 3. union of them both in one Christ. Next from the word Christ anoynted, we inferred the 3 offices of our Redeemer, of King, and Priest and Prophet. Concerning his kingly Office we observed 1st his ordinacion unto, and qualificacion for his Kingdome; that 'twas not by usurpacion, intrusion, violence, but by order, obsignacion, and appoyntment from his Father, Joh: 6.27.[440] 2ly, Quality or nature of his kingly Power, that 'tis spirituall and heavenly over the soules of men; to bind and loose the conscience, to awe and overule the heart, to captivate the affections, and to bring into obedience every thought, 2Cor.10.5. 3. Actuall Administracion of his Kingdome. And this implyes severall Particulars as 1. Abrogacion and Publicacion of Lawes. 2. Conquering and subdueing of subjects, bringing them to the obedience of his lawes; and that 1st ministerially, by the word of his Kingdome. 2ly, Principally and effectually by the power of his spirit.

I proceed now to show the manner how Christ doth administer his lawes; And that

1. By taking care that they be observed.

2. By proposeing rewards to such as do observ them and punishments to those that do not.

3. By aiding and assisting those that endeavour to please him, and observ his lawe[s].

In the last place, we shall speake of the continuance of Christ's Kingdome, the limitacion of it, when it shall have an end; as also, how 'tis beset with crosses and afflictions, and is generally disliked and hated in the world, and show the reasons why 'tis so.

1. Christ takes care that those lawes which he hath given be duly observed. And that 1. by provideing that they be often inculcated and repeated and expounded by his Messengers, that none pretend

440 preferably 6.37.

ignorance of them. Esa: 28.10. Precept hath been upon precept, precept upon precept; line upon line, [line upon line] here a little [and there a little], i.e. they have had the same things often told them, they have been taught as little children, time after time, line after line, with half words, lisping language or as in the 11v with stammering lipps; which God did for this very end, that they might attend unto his word, understand it and be saved. So Ezek. 2.7 son of man, whether they will hear or whether they will forbear, be not afraid of them, but speak my words unto them; cease not thou to doe thy Duty, tho' people be never so obstinate, never so rebellious. And 'twas our Saviour's last charg to his Disciples when he took his leav of them. Math. 28. ῶ[441] Goe teach all Nations, teach them to observ all things whatsoever I have commanded you. And before this, what paines did he take to teach the people in country Rhetorique, in Parables of merchants, and husbandmen, and vine-dressers as they were able to hear it, Mar: 4.33.[442] And St. Paul to the men of Ephesus, Act: 20.27,31 I have not shunned to declare unto the whole counsell of God; and remember that by the space of three yeares, I ceased not to warn every one day and night, with teares. And 'twas his principall and chief charg to Timothy 2Ep: 4.1,2. I charg thee before God and the Lord Jesus Christ; this deep kind of charging, in so vehement and patheticall a manner, sheweth how urgent and important the matter is, preach the word, be instant, in season, out of season, upon all occasions, with an holy importunity. And St. Peter 2ep: 1.12-13, I will not be negligent to put you in mind of these things; bec[ause] through the multitude of worldly busines they were apt to forgett them, at the best they were dull and drowsy in spirituall matters; and therefore I will endeavour (Apostle) that you may have these things always in remembrance [2Tim 2.14]. Thus Christ takes care that the lawes he hath given be duly observed, by provideing, that they be often inculcated, repeated, expounded both by hims[elf] and his messengers.

2ly, Not only so, but by proposeing rewards to such as do observ them. And those partly temporall and partly Eternall, such as concern the body and the soul, Math: 6.33 Seek ye first [the kingdom of God, and his righteousness; and all these things will be added unto

441 i.e. the last verse of ch. 28, verse 20.

442 This is a repeat of text in the opening lecture.

you.] what things? Food and Rayment and Preservacion. And this he proves by an Argument drawn, *a minore ad maius*; he cloathes the lillies, the lillies of the field; and feedes not your domestick birds, but the fowles of the air, such as are not indebted to man's Providence, and therefore he will much more feed and cloath his own servants. Next for our preservacion, all the hairs of our heads are numbered, Math: 10.30, and not one of those hairs shall perish without, [Luc: 21.18]. *Non te deseram, neque derelinquam,*[443] Heb. 13.5. So we may confidently say, the Lord is with us, we will not fear, what flesh [can do unto me], Ps: 118.6. And here we are to observ, that God promiseth these temporall blessings, not absolutely but so far forth, as may make for his glory, and our own Eternall good; So Ps: 34.10 they that feare the Lord, shall not want anything that is good, i.e. what he sees fitting and convenient for them.

Now for spirituall blessings. 1. He bids us cast the whole weight of our guilty spirits and empty all the feares and cares and requests of our distracted and sinking soules into his bosome, Math:11.28. Come unto me [all ye that labour and are heavy laden, and I will give you rest] 2ly, not any one that hath adventured fortunes, or life, or liberty, forsaken anything for his names sake, but shall receiv an 100fold, and [shall inherit] everlasting life, Mat:19.29, which made St. Paul say, that the sufferings of this life, are not worthy to be compared with the glory that shall be [revealed in us], Rom: 8.18.

3ly, As he proposeth rewards to such as observ his Lawes: so he threatenth[444] and will inflict severe punishment upon such as disobey him, such as contumaciously stand out against him, such as sett up lawes of their own, follow the devices of their own hearts, and will not have him to raign over them. The Lord will shew his wrath and make his power known in the vessels fitted for destruction, Rom: 9.22; yea, Christ hims[elf] tells us this in that Parable, Luc: 19.14, 27, those mine enimies, which would not that I should reign over them, bring hither and slay them before me. Reveng is his royalty and peculiar prerogative; whence the Apostle inferrs, that 'tis a fearfull thing to fall into [into the hands of the living God], Heb:10.31. And there are these Arguments for the fearfullnes in it. 1. I shall be

443 Translated it means "I will never leave thee, nor forsake thee."

444 Cp. with that in Brightman, p. 127.

in judgment without mercy, Jam: 2.13; there shall be no mixture of any sweetnes in the cupp of Gods displeasure, but all poyson and bitternes; there shall not be afforded a dropp of water to a lake of fire, a minute of ease to an eternitie of torment. 2ly, It shall be in fury without compassion; In humane judgements where the law of a state, will not suffer a Judge to acquitt or shew mercy, yet the law of Nature will force him to be compassionate, not to be so senseles of anothers misery, so destitute of all bowells of compassion, as to pronounce a sentence of condemnacion with laughter; But the lord will condemn his enimies in vengeance without pitty. Prov: 1.26, I will laugh at your calamity and mock when your fear cometh. So that unto them that are contentious, and do not obey the Truth, but obey their own lusts and unrighteousnes, indignavion and wrath; Tribulacion and anguish upon every soul of man that doth evill, Rom: 2.8,9.

And what we read here threatned, we may read elsewhere performed; upon Ananias and Saphira, Act: 5.9.[445] Upon Elimas the sorcerer Act: 13.11 and upon the whole Jewish commonwealth.

And God useth often to fitt punishments to the quality and measure of the sinnes committed. Dives that on earth denyed a crum[b] of bread, in Hell was denyed a dropp of water;[446] Man who being in honour, would needs be as God, was thereby debased to become like the Beasts that perish. Nadab and Abihu offered strang fire, and were consumed by strang fire from the lord [Lev. 10.1-2]. Sodome and Gomorrah burnt in unnatural lusts, and they were drowned in an unaturall tempest of fire [Gen. 19.24]. That Apostate in Cyprian, who opened his mouth against Christ in blasphemy, was immediatly smitten with dum[b]nes, that he could not open his mouth unto Christ for mercy.[447]

Now these things are our examples, they are written for our admonicion, 1Cor: 10.11 to the intent that we should not fall after the same example of disobedience. There is but a *bivium* in the

445 In the Authorized Version this is 5.10.

446 Andrewes preached similarly in the Spital Sermon of 1588, Andrewes, Vol. 5, pp. 38, 43 especially.

447 In full this reads, "One of those who of his own will ascended the Capitol to make denial, after he had denied Christ, became dumb. The punishment began from that point whence the crime began;- so that now he could not ask, since he had no words for entreating mercy." Cyprian, p. 443 (*The Treatises of Cyprian, no. 3* 'On the Lapsed', ch. 24).

world, a way of life, and a way of death; and Christ in the ministry of the word, gives us our choice, I have set before [you life and death, blessing and curseing; therefore choose life, that both thou and thy seed may live: Deut: 30. 19]. And he that beleeveth shall be saved, but he that beleeveth not shall be damned, Joh: 3.36. To the former he invited, beseecheth, enticeth us, with promises, with oathes, with engagements, with prevention of any just objection that can be made; we beseech you in Christ's stead (Apostle) that you be reconciled unto God, Eph: 4.2.[448] From the other he deterrs us, by forewarning us of the wrath to come, and of the Period which either some temporall afflictions, or death will put to all our lusts and sinns with our lives. Now as Tertull[ian] once of the Oath of God, so may we of his entreaties, and threatenings, ô happy, whom the lord is pleased to sollicite and entice unto happines, but miserable are they who will not beleev, nor accept of Gods own entreaties; And yet thus miserable are we all by nature; There is in us so much Atheisme, infidelity, and distrust of God's word, so close an adherency of sin unto the soul, that we chuse rather to run the hazard, and to goe to hell entire, then to goe half or maimed unto heaven, yea, to make God a lyar, to blesse ourselves in our sinns, when he curseth; and to judge of him by ourselves, as if he tooke no notice of our wayes.[449] 'Tis not therefore without good cause, that God so often threatneth to remember all the sinns of wicked men, and to proceed against them as he hath threatned.

And thus much of the 1st things I proposed, that Christ as a King takes care that those lawes he hath given be duly observed; and that first by providing that his ministers do often repeat and inculcate them. 2ndly, by proposeing rewards to such as do observ them; and 3ly, threatening and inflicting punishment upon such as will not obey them.

2ly, He doth aid and assist all those who use their best endeavour to keep them, to perform willing obedience tho' imperfect.[450]

---

448 More appropriately 2Cor. 5.20.

449 Based on Math. 18.8.

450 A similar reference to God's help appears in Sermon Four on Prayer, Andrewes, Vol. 5. p.333.

Christ is a King, no rigid Tyrant and he knoweth we are but flesh, yea, he remembreth wee are but Dust, Ps:103.14;[451] and therefore he will not overburthen this flesh, he will not scatter this dust; if we be but willing and obedient, we shall eat the good of the land, Esa. 1.19, Then when we settle and compose ourselves to our prayers; bec[ause] those prayers are weak and sinfull; therefore 1. his spirit doth help our infirmities, Rom. 8.26 *συναντιαμβάνεται*, the word doth properly imply such an help as when one carrying a peice of timber, which he is not well able to bear, another stepps in, setts his shoulder under, and helps to bear up and sustain the burthen: so his spirit helps and coperates with ours.[452]

2. Bec[ause] our prayers are sinfull, he therefore punisheth them and offereth them up to his Father mixed with the sweet smelling odour of his own meritts, Eph: 5.2. Againe we may build upon his word, he hath promised not to break the bruised reed, nor quench the smoaking flaxe, Math: 12.20.[453] Not to cast down those that are weak, but rather support and strengthen them. He shall feed his flock like a shepherd, Esa: 40.11. Like the good sheph[erd] he shall gather the lambs with his armes, carry them in his bosome, and gently lead those that are with young, such as be feeble and weake, such as have any dawnings of grace in them; yet act and walk according to the measure of their strength, of those he will be exceeding carefull. Lastly, He is our Mediatour and Advocate, 1Joh: 2.2,[454] the openly Practiser in the Court of heaven, 'tis his office to dispatch the affaires of all those that come unto him; and he is both faithfull and mercifull in his Place,[455] Heb: 3.2; and whosoever cometh to him for his counsell and intercession, he will in no wise cast out, Joh: 6.37.[456] And this is one greate assurance we may take comfort in,

451 This reference is in Brightman, p. 147 and Sermon Four on Prayer, Andrewes, Vol. 5, p. 333.

452 This is the theme of Sermon Four on Prayer, that "the Spirit helpeth our infirmity." Ibid., pp. 99, 332 - 41.

453 This is also in Brightman, p. 141.

454 In the Authorized Version this is 2.1.

455 Cp. with "We are not acquainted with with the phrases of court, … ." in Sermon Five on Prayer, Andrewes, Vol. 5, pp. 349 –50.

456 Cp. with "Let prayer come up …" in Brightman, p. 131; Ms. 3708, p. 6.

that be our matters never so foul, and inexcuseable, cases of sorest extremity, of most hideous guilt, of most black and uncomfortable darknes of soul, which pose not only the presumptions, but the hope, faith, conjectures, the thoughts and contrivances of the hearts of men, yet the very entertaining him of our counsell, and the leaning upon his wisdome and power and fidelity, and mercy to expedite our businesses, to compassionate our Estate, to free us from our own demeritts, doth as 'twere alter the property of our cause, and produce an issue, clean contrary to that which the evidence of the matter in triall would of itself have produced. So altho' we be as the vine, of all other Trees the weakest; as sheep of all other beasts the simplest; yet we have for our Vine a Gardiner, and for our sheepheard Christ Jesus, who watcheth over us, who searcheth and seeketh us out, in our straglings, and feedeth us. In a word; God in his servants will reward not the dignity of the worke, but the willingnes, the obedient disposition of the heart, passeing over our failings, and weaknesses; he will commend our endeavours, and pardon our miscarriages. And thus much of the 2nd Particular, that God will aid and assist those that endeavour to please him and observ his lawes.

IIIly, We proceed now to speake of the continuance and limitacion of Christ's Kingdome, when it shall have an end. And here we are to distinguish of Christs 2fold Kingdome.

1. His Kingdome of Glory, when he shall rule over his enimies; and of this there shall be no end.

2. His Kingdome of Grace, whereby he ruleth amongst his enimies by the scepter of his word; and this is the Kingdome we now speake of.

Again even of this Kingdome, the scriptures affirm, that 'tis eternall, Dan: 2.44. in Mount Sion, where God hath sett him he shall raigne from henceforth for ever, Mic: 4. 7. Of the increase of his Government and Peace, there shall be no end, Esa: 9.6,7. [457]

So here, we must distinguish 1. between the substance of Christ's kingdome, and 2ly, Form or manner of administring and dispenseing it. In the former respect, 'tis absolutely eternall; Christ shall be an Head, a Rewarder of his Members an everlast-

457 The quotation is only 9.7.

ing Father, a Prince of peace unto them for ever. In the latter respect 'tis not so, but shall remain only untill the consummacion of all things; i.e. as long as there is a church of God upon earth, there shall be no new way of spirituall and effectuall Government prescribed unto it, no other Vicar, Successor, Monarch, but Christ only by his spirit, in the dispensation of his ordinances, shall order and overrule the consciences of his People and subdue their enimies. The Apostle saith, he must raigne untill he hath put all enimies under his feet, 1 Cor: 15.25.

And here we will show 1. who those enimies are, that must be subdued and put under. 2. why, when these are subdued, he must cease thus to raigne; and deliver up the Kingdome to his Father?

Concerning the former, the enemies of Christ may be reduced to three Heads.

1. Generally, all men who would not be obedient to him, submit thems[elves] to the scepter of his word: these shall be punished with everlasting destruction [from the presence of the Lord, and from the glory of his power], 2Thes. 1.9. And that we may know what manner of Punishment 'tis, in Scripture 'tis sett forth, by diverse Names, as 1st tis called the last Judgment, that we may know this punishment is not inflicted upon the ungodly rashly, through error, or in inadvertancy, but a strict accompt taken and judgment given upon all their words and thoughts [and] Actions. 2ly, Fire of Hell, Mat: 5.22. *ignis Gehennæ,* a periphrasis taken from that valley of Hinnom, or valley of Tophet[h], 2Kings 23.10 where the Israelites burnt their children, offered their sonnes and daughters to Divells. 3. Eternall Destruction bec[ause] there shall be no end of it, from Hell no Redemption. 4. Outer darknes, Math: 8.12 bec[ause] 'tis a place removed from all heavenlly light and comfort; where weeping, and [gnashing of teeth]; poor damned soules giveing thems[elves] over to teares and sorrow, feeling the extremitie, and knowing the eternitie of their Torment. These the first sort of Christ's enimies.

2. Next sort are all Aut[h]oritie and power 1Cor: 15.24: i.e. all secular Power opposed to his Kingdome, and the Divell and his Angells, not as tho' these were not now subject to him, in as much as he refraines their feircenes, curbes and keepes in their malice, but the Apostle speakes of full, perfect, finall subjection when it

shall be that they [are] cast into that fire which is prepared for [the devil and his angels].

3ly. Last enemy shal be destroyed is Death, 1Cor:15.26. And as this the last, so the worst of his enemies; which as yet not brought unto Christ's subjection. For we see not only those who wallow in all filth and uncleannes, but those who are given to the study of Holines, who wholly devote thems[elves] to God's service, Dy[e] and perish, as well as the ignorant and foolish. And these enemies, Death and the grave Christ shall fully vanquish, when he shall cast them into the lake of fire, Rev: 20.14. And thus much of the 1st thing I proposed, who and what those enemies are that must be [put under his feet].

2. Why then, when all these are subdued must Christ cease thus to raigne, and deliver up the Kingdome to his Father?

The reason of this is, bec[ause] then, he shall cease to exercise the office of a Mediatour, in compassionateing, defending, interceeding for his church. For the scope and end of Christ's Kingdome, was to begett and increase in us, Faith and Hope, and charitie and at length to bring all his subjects to a Kingdome of Peace and everlasting happines; and in order to this end to remove and destroy all letts and impediments, as the Malice and machinacions of ungodly men, the stratagems of Satan, the infirmities of our bodyes and the violence of Death; and then it followes that when all these are removed and subdued, Christ should resigne up that Power and commission, deliver up the Kingdome to his Father, when he put down all Rule and Aut[h]oritie and Power *acqisito Fine*.

And here we may answer these two Questions.

1. Whether the church of Christ may *deficere*, fail upon the earth or no?

2. Whether that church which remaineth be alwayes visible?

To the 1st we answer, That the church may be taken either mystically, spir[itually] and universally; And in that sense it can never fail; but there must be upon the earth a true church of Christ, a People gathered unto him by the preaching of the Gospell, maugre[458] all the malice and power and policy of all his enemies. Nev-

458 This means "in spite of".

er was Heresy and darknes so thick, never Satan so loose, never persecution so prevalent, never tail of the Dragon so long, as to sweep away all the starres of Heaven, to devour all the remnant of that seed of the woman. The Gates of Hell, all the policy and power and machinacions of the Kingdome of Darknes, shall never root out the vine, which God the Father hath planted.

And the grounds of this continuance of Christ's evangelicall Kingdome, is not the nature of the church in itself considered, But first the ordinacion and appoyntment of God, Ps: 2.7, and what ever men project, the Counsell of the Lord must stand. 2. Christ's own purchase and price which he paid for his church. He died not in vain (saith the apostle), but as his blood was shed from the beginning of the world, so doth it continue to the end in regard of it's merit and efficacy; so long as he sitteth at the right hand of God, which must be till the time of the restitution of all thing[s], the merit of his blood shall work amongst men. 3. Christ's own promise to be with the preaching of his Gospell, to give it assistance and success unto the end of the world, Math: 28.20.

But 2ly, If the church be considered particularly in the severall parts and places of the world, where the Gospell is planted, denoting a company of men professing the same faith of Christ, and reduced unto a quiet, peaceable and composed Government, and so there is no church in the world so safe, but it may fail and be removed out of it's Place. The light of the Gospell arose and shone gloriously upon primitive Christians in the East: but now what is become of those churches St. Paul wrote to, Corinth and Ephesus, and Philippi; is not the sun gone down over their Prophets, and darknes unto them instead of Divinacion? And as those, so this torn and divided ch[urch] of ours, so any particular ch[urch] may fail and loose the true light. We may say to any church in her greatest splendour and glory, what the Apostle saith to the Roman ch[urch]; Rom: 11.21, If God spared not the naturall branches, take heed also lest he spare not thee.

2ly, Seeing [the] church of Christ doth never totally fail whether is that which remaineth always visible?

To this we answer, 1st That if we take the church for the true spirituall body of Christ; so 'tis in a sort still invisible; bec[ause] those graces and qualities which make a man a true member of the Body of Christ, be things invisible; seen indeed they may be by an eye of charity in their fruites, but not by an eye of certainty, in their own infallible Beeing.[459]

2ly. If we take the church for a company of men professing the true Doctrine of Christ, then we say, that those men in thems[elves] are visible, i.e. in the worst Ages of the church, some there were who witnessed the truth against a deluge of ignorance, error and heresie, which invaded the world. But then if we speak of these men, as concurring to make up a distinct externall Body or church, then we say, Professors of the truth may be so few, and they so persecuted, traduced, suppressed, cryed down, as that in this sense we may justly deny the ch[urch] of Christ to have been always visible i.e. the very few true Professors of Christ to have had a free open, and distinct Ecclesiasticall Body of their own. For tho' Christ rule in the midst of his enimies, yet his enimies may be so many and his subjects so few, that there may be no shape nor face of a ch[urch]; the good wheat may be invisible for the Abundance of tares, tho' in it[self] very apt to be seen. And thus much of Continuance of Christ's church unto the end of the world, and how it may be said to be visible[460]. Now to make some Applicacion and so to conclude.

You have heard how carefull Christ our King is, that his lawes be observed, what rewards he hath promised, and what punishments he hath threatned, and how he hath provided Ministers as his embassadors, often to inculcate, and put his subjects in remembrance of these things. And hence we may inferr, that what ever men think of the Ministry and dispensacion of the word, yet the neglect and scorn which is shewed unto it, is done unto Christ hims[elf]: he that receiveth not his word, rejecteth his person; for tho' he be in heaven (which is now the court of his royall presence) yet he hath to do upon earth, as one of the cheif territories of his Dominion, and in the Ministry of his word, he speaketh unto us from Heaven still. And long may he speak! But long he will not speak, unles we be attentive to hear and carefull to remember, and conscionably to practise what we hear, and what he speakes unto

459 Cp. with E.P. 3.1.2.

460 Hooker expresses a similar view on the visibility of the Church, E.P., 3.1.3-4,7-10.

us. For would not an Earthly Prince take it haynously out, to have his embassadors and his embassies scorned or sleighted? And can the King of Heaven take it well, when we give such sleight audience to his messengers, that we scarce take notice what they say? When our hearts remain dull and cold, without any feeling of what is spoken; nay, when we are more attentive to a frivolous tale, when we preferr our own vain lusts and thoughts before his holy lawes. Is it his care that his lawes be often repeated, that they may be known and observed? and is it our care, either not to frequent the Place, where they may be heard, or to thwart his lawes by lawes of our own, our own Inventions? The lord is in his holy Temple (prophet) let all the earth be silent before him, Hab: 2.20. And dare any tongue speak when he who made the tongue commands silence? God standeth in the congregacion, (David) Ps: 82.1. 'Tis true of this congregacion; and me thinks his standing, his being there should make us more devout, more carefull and use more reverence as in his more immediate presence. Let us take heed, lest by our contempt, neglect, not takeing any notice of his dreadfull and glorious presence we turn his standing with tenders of Mercy, into walking against us in fury. If we have precept upon precept, line [upon line], and be never the better but still unfruitfull, tho' watered with the sacred dew of Heaven we may fear that God will either plague us, or forsake us; either send his judgments, or curse his Blessings. And therefore [let us take heed].

Lastly, when we tread the courts of the kingdom of heaven, to have his lawes published to us, let us demean ourselves, as in the presence of so holy and high a Majesty, make it our businesse to acquaint our selves with his lawes; haveing such and so many opportunities of hearing and reading, 'tis a shame, nay, 'tis a sin which must be answered for, to be ignorant of them. And bec[ause] every proud and careles hearer will be an unprofitable Liver, let every soul therefore come with this conclusion: 'tmay be this day, God will speak home to my soul; I am an usuall prophanor of his holy Name; he will peradventure, lay close to my conscience that guilt which hims[elf] hath declared to be in this great sin, and tell me that whatsoever is sin, is Hell to my soul. I am a companion of vain, loose and riotous Persons, it may be God will urge the charge of his own word, to have no fellowshipp with the unfruitfull works of darknes. I am unprofitable wanton and rotten in my discourse; 'tmay be that he will convince me out of his word, that for every idle word I must render an account. In these or any the like cases, if a man come with first Paul's temper of heart, not to consult with -- but lord what wilt thou have me to do [Acts 9.6]; or with the answer of Samuel, Speak Lord for thy servant heareth [1Sam. 3.4]. If we come with such a fram[e] and temper of heart, not hold out any disloyall Fort, any rebellious lust, any sin against him; if we come so resolved to hear what the lord will say unto us, then he will speak Peace unto us, Peace amidst distractions, or if not peace externall, yet internall in our bosomes, and at length Eternall, when he shall deliver up the Kingdome to his Father which God grant unto us all. Amen.

I might add something here concerning the opinion of the Millenaryes[461] about Christ's temporall Kingdome upon earth. But

1. Scriptures tell us but of one Kingdome of Christ upon earth.

2. They joyn Christ's 2nd comeing and last judgment as the one immediately following the other.

3. Sole aim of Christ and of the doctrine of the Gospell, to take our affectiones from the earth. And therefore 'tis not probable, that Christ shall have any temporall Kingdome upon earth.

---

461 Based mainly on Revelation 20, millenaries believed that Christ would overthrow all His enemies and usher in a thousand years of peace. Amongst those who held millenarian beliefs in Andrewes' time were the Anabaptists whose teachings Andrewes frequently attacked.

LECTURE THIRTEEN

Of Christ's Priestly Office

Introduction

This lecture introduced Christ as the High Priest who sits "on the right hand of the throne" in all "dignitie and majesty" to be co-regnant. Indeed Andrewes' teaching is basically a paraphrase of chapters nine and ten of Hebrews. On Christ's priestly office, Andrewes intended to teach it under five headings. I say *intended* as the series of lectures comes to an abrupt end after the third of the following headings.

1. what necessity we have of such an h[igh] Priest.
2. what kind of Qualifications are requisite in him who must be unto us such an h[igh] Priest.
3. what are the Parts of his Priestly Office; or wherein the Acts and Offices of such an h[igh] P[riest] do principally consist.
4. what is the efficacy, the fruites and ends of such a Priesthood.
5. what Dutyes are required of us, or what uses we should make of it.

In this lecture, Andrewes answered the question, why did man need a High Priest? He needed a High Priest as he had transgressed the law that every creature is subject to the laws of his creator. By his wilful act of disobedience he became "justly subject unto [God's] wrath". Nevertheless God wanted man to be restored to his original state as He "delighteth to see things reduced to their first primitive beauty". Moreover God needed to have a church upon earth. But as He no longer received the obedience due unto Him from man, He could not let sin go unpunished. However man was incapable of repairing himself, nor could he "undergoe the punishment" as God demanded a sinless offering as reparation. Andrewes once again resorted to Anselm's teaching based on Psalm Eighty-five, verses ten and eleven, that Truth, Mercy, Righteousness and Peace all meet. Whilst Mercy cried "loud for pitty and compassion" Justice demanded retribution, but God the Son (Love) intervened, and offered Himself as a Priest.[462] This teaching also appears in Sermons Three and Five in this manuscript, and also in the 1616 Nativity Sermon.

Next Andrewes outlined the functions of a priest who "offer sacrifice for the obtaining of righteousnes and remission of sinnes". From Scripture there are two types of priesthood, firstly, of Aaron and the ritual of the priests under the Law who offered both the sacrifices of expiation and thanksgiving; and secondly, of Melchizedek who bestowed blessing and peace. Christ embraced both; the latter Christ fulfils now in heaven where He blesses his people after His offering of His sinless sacrifice to God on the cross terminated His Aaron's priesthood. In making this sacrifice Christ fulfilled all the qualifications of a priestly sacrifice. Firstly, by being a mediator between two parties (God and man); secondly by paying the debt (obedience to God and surety of man's soul); thirdly by offering a sacrifice (man's sin); and fourthly by offering that sacrifice on an altar (the cross).[463]

As our High Priest "offered himself without spot unto God" for our sins, Andrewes returned to his one of his persistent pastoral themes, sin and man's reluctance to hate it. Why should "we be so careles of our soules ... as to sin with security?" Why should sin "seeme light to thee, which was so heavy to the soul of thy saviour?" Why should we not be "thankfull and obedient" to Him "who was so compassionate unto us?" Why do we allow sin to "destroy the soul" when we know that one day we must stand

462 Ms. 3707, p. 118.

463 Ibid., p. 120.

before our Lord as Judge? These were some of the questions Andrewes posed for the scholars' reflection.[464]

Yet it is because of our many sins that we need our High Priest to mediate for us, and to "cleanse [our] nature with his spirit". Thus Andrewes concluded with yet another of his admonitions, that we must "work out our salvation with fear and trembling" so as to be ready to meet our Lord on Judgment day. Otherwise just as surely God will punish us as He will punish all unrepentant sinners.[465]

> Hebrews 8. 1 - 2 *Now of the things which we have spoken, this is the summe; we have such an high-Priest, who is set on the right hand of the throne of the Majesty in the heavens: A Minister of the sanctuary, and of the true tabernacle, which the Lord pitched, and not man.*

The author of this Epistle had before spoken many things concerning Christ our high Priest, both for his Qualities, what manner of Person he is, and for his Dignitie, how he exceedeth the Priests under the Law. Now beeing partly to add something further, and partly to repeat something formerly spoken, he calls this repeticion the summe of what he had spoken. And the summe here may signifie, either the Breviat and compendium, or that main head and Principall poynt of what he had spoken. q.d. of all those things which have been, or may be spoken concerning our h[igh] Priest, Christ Jesus, the cheif and principall point is this, that we have such an h[igh] Pr[iest] who is set on the right [hand of the throne of the majesty in the heavens].

By sitting on the right hand of the throne of the Majesty is signified unto us, so great a Dignitie and Majesty in Christ, as of which there was scarce any shadow extant in the Priests under the law. The h[igh] Priest when he went into the Oracle, where God was said to dwell, did not sit down with God between the Cherubims, but stood as a Minister or waiter with great reverence of the divine majesty, offering and sprinkling that blood wherewith he entered. But Christ entering into Heaven, did not stand before the throne of God, as a Messenger or supplicant, but sate

464 Ibid., p. 124.

465 Ibid., p. 125.

down at the right hand of God's majesty yet not by way of assistant, as Nobles and Councellors doe to earthly Princes: but by way of Co-regnant, to reign with him, haveing absolute power over the People of God, and for their sake over all things. Againe he is called a Minister of the true Sanctuary and Tabernacle, which are called true, not in reference to false and faigned sanctuaries, but in respect of earthly sanctuaries, which did but represent and signifie, the true, perfect, solid and heavenly Sanctuary, wherein God himself doth really and truely dwell. Thus much for the meaning of the words. Now beeing to speak of Christ's Priestly Office we shall show,

1. what necessity we have of such an h[igh] Priest.

2. what kind of Qualificacions are requisite in him who must be unto us such an h[igh] Priest.

3. what are the Parts of his Priestly Office; or wherein the Acts and Offices of such an h[igh] Pr[iest] do principally consist.

4. what is the Efficacy, the fruites and ends of such a Priesthood.

5. what Dutyes are required of us, or what uses we should make of it.

In answer to the first, we shall 1. Premise a generall Rule to be granted. 2. Proceed by some gradacions to find out the necessities of Christ's Priesthood.

1. Sacrifices, which every high Pr[iest] was to offer, are of 2 sorts: 1. Sacrifices of Thanksgiveing, as testimonies of homage, subjection, duty and service, as Dedicacion of the first fruites, the offering of Abell, meat and drink offering under the Law. 2. Sacrifices expiatory for the washing away of sinnes, for giving Satisfaction to the Justice of God which by sinne had been violated. Now we say, there can be no necessity of a Priest in this sense, to offer propitiatory sacrifices, but between a guilty Creature and a righteous God. For if man were free from sin and innocent, he would stand in no need of Expiacion; and if God were unrighteous, there would be due unto him, no just Debt of satisfaction.

This Rule being premised, I shall proceed by some graduacions to find out the necessity of Christ's Priesthood.

And here 5 things are to be considered.

1. That every Creature, is of necessitie to be subject unto the will and lawes of the Creator. For he made all things for himself,

Prov: 16.4, and all things are to return that honour and glory to him, for which he made them. *Omne Esse* (Philosopher [Aristotle] *est propter operari*; the Beeing of every Creature is for some work and operacions; so 'tis contrary to the Quality of a creature, not to be subject to some law and indebted in some obedience to him that made it.

2. Man being made a reasonable Creature, he was made to serv God after a reasonable manner, whence our service is called a reasonable service, Rom: 12.1; out of judgment, discretion, and election: as holines in scripture phrase is called judgment, Joh: 16.11, he shall convince the world of judgment; and he shall bring forth judgment into victory, Math: 12.20, i.e. the spirit of holines ruleth in the children of obedience by way of reason and conviction.

3. No Creature and so no man in those Dutyes and services which he owes to God, is of hims[elf] immutable; 'tis God's own peculiar Honour to be without variablenes or shadow of chang, Jam: 1.17. Man was made in such a condicion, as he might stand or fall, chuse life or death; God did not set any overruleing law, or determinating power over his Actions, bec[ause] he would be obeyed by judgment and free choice, not by any fatall stoicall necessity.

4. Man being created in this condicion did swerv from that Rule, that righteous Law God had given him, he did deviate from that reasonable service, that true active obedience, which he should have performed, and by that willing and chosen transgression of the Law, he became liable to the curse and malediction of the Law which he had transgressed; haveing incurred God's displeasure, he became justly subject unto his wrath.

5. By this fall and sin of man, God's Justice and truth and power, in his most righteous threatnings, were despised, his glorious image in man utterly defaced; and by that meanes, man was become altogether unprofitable, abominable, and unfit for the Master's use, and for those holy ends to which he was ordained. So that man could not return to his primitive perfection, nor God receive that obedience which was due to him untill 1. Gods justice were satisfied and 2. Man's nature repaired; which two man of hims[elf] was utterly unable to perform; God's justice, which was wronged, is infinite, and God's glory of which man had attempt-

ed to spoyl him is infinite; and man is both finite in hims[elf] and very impotent by reason of sin; and between finite and infinite, there can be no proportion,[466] and so from the one to the other no satisfaction.

Now here we see the necessity of an h[igh] Priest of such a middle Person, as hath both Zeal tow[ards] God, that he may be satisfied, and compassion tow[ards] man, that he may be repaired. And this is the Person here spoken of, we have such [an high Priest].

Dub[itatio]. But what should be the reason, that God should find out such an h[igh] Pr[iest] for us? Might he not have left us to have perished in our sinnes, condemned up to chaines of darknes, with the bad Angells that fell? Or if not so, might he not have passed by our sinnes without such reveng and punishments?

Sol[utio]. No, neither of these. In answer to this demand we say. 1. That God did not purpose utterly to destroy his Creature. 2. Neither did he purpose to let his sin passe utterly unavenged. And 3ly, man was utterly unable to endue the burthen of God's wrath due unto sin; and therefore 4ly, God's infinite wisdome found out such a way to effect all this, as the Angells of Heavens gaze on with admiracion and astonishment.

1. God did not purpose utterly to destroy his creature Man; and the Reasons of this purpose we may gather out of his revealed word, which are these two. 1. His free and everlasting Love, that infinite delight which he taketh in shewing mercy, Exod: 34.6, 7 the Lord, the lord God (merciful and gracious, long suffering, and abundant in goodness and truth, Keeping mercy for thousands, forgiving iniquity and transgression and sin, and that will by no means clear <u>the guilty</u>; visiting the iniquity of the fathers upon the children, and upon the children's children, upon the third and fourth <u>generation</u>). And this Nature disposeth him abundantly to pardon and to shew loving kindnes in the earth. Mic. 7.18, Who is a God like unto thee that pardoneth [iniquity].

2. The delight he taketh to be glorifyed by the subjection and voluntary obedience of his creatures; herein is my Father glorifyed, that yee bear much fruit, Joh: 15.8. And he hath no pleasure

466 This text reappears in his sermon on Justification in 1610 in Latin *Finiti ad infinitum nulla est proportion*. Andrewes, Vol. 5, p. 121.

in the death of the wicked, but that [the wicked turn from his way and live], Ezek: 33.11. God delighteth to see things reduced to their first primitive beauty, and therefore esteemeth hims[elf] more glorified in the services, then in the sufferings of men. The Lord loveth the Gates of Sion, more than the dwellings of Jacob, Ps: 87.2. And we read in Script[ure] of many prayers made for Sion; to do good unto Sion; arise and have mercy upon Sion [Ps: 102.13]. And why is Sion so often mentioned and not Jerusalem? bec[ause] upon Mount Sion stood the Temple and there God was more solemnly worshipped and served.[467] And therefore he purposed not utterly to destroy all men, lest he should not have a church, not a generacion of men, no Religion upon the earth. When the Angells fell from their obedience, their fall was not universall, many were left to glorife him; but when Adam fell, all mankind, all his posterie fell in him; so that there was no tree, no branch left, to bring forth any fruit unto God, and bec[ause] God is a God of mercy, and had rather his Trees should be for fruit then fuell, therefore for this reason he was pleased to restore mankind againe.[468]

Dub[itatio]. But if so, yet what necessity of an h[igh] Priest, to offer up such a sacrifice as his own blood?

Sol[utio]. Bec[ause] God did purpose not to let sin passe unpunished, unrevenged. And that for these reasons. 1st, Because of his great hatred unto and detestacion of sin. Hab: 1.13. He is of purer eyes then to behold evill, he cannot look upon iniquitye; it causeth a nauseousnes, loathing, and abhorrency in him. Ps: 5.6 The Lord doth abhor the bloodthirsty and deceitfull man; And he will spue the lukewarm Christian out of his mouth, Rev: 3.16. And I will not hear, I will not regard nay (saith God) I hate your solemn Assemblyes, Amos 5. 21. Now these expressions are used to show God's great hatred unto and detestacion of sin. 2ly, God would not let sin passe unpunished, bec[ause] of his Truth, and the law which he hath established against sin, which he will in

---

467 Cp. with that in Andrewes' sermon to commemorate the delivery from the Gunpowder Plot in 1617. Vol. 4, p. 226.

468 There are shades of this teaching of Andrewes in Baro's University Sermon at Cambridge in 1597. Porter, p. 381. Cp. also with Ash Wednesday Sermon for 1624/5 when Andrewes stated that if our repentance is superficial, even if there is any fruit, it is worthless, and so is the tree. Andrewes, Vol. 1, p. 447.

no wise abolish. Math: 5.18 one jot or tittle, shall in no wise passe from the law, till all be fulfilled; 'Tis not agreeable to the wisdome and righteousnes of God, that sin which deserveth and provoketh the execution should procure the abrogacion of his Law, that that should supplant and undermine the law, for the preventing whereof the law was established.

Againe, *omnis peccati impunitas, per se hoc efficit, ut peccata minoris aestimentur;*[469] if the law be not executed, if impieitie passe unpunished, the sinner will be encouraged in his wayes, hopeing that he may sin at a cheaper rate. Bec[ause] sentence against an evill work[470] is not executed speedily, therefore the heart of the sonnes of men, is fully set in them to do evill, Eccl: 8.11. And therefore 3ly, God will not let sin passe unpunished, bec[ause] of his dreadfull majesty, that he would have men alwayes to tremble before him, and by his terrour to be affrighted from sinning, 2Cor: 5.11. He hath reserved to hims[elf] entire the punishment of sin, and therefore (saith our Saviour) fear him who is able to destroy both body and soul in hell - - - fear him, Math: 10.28. 'Tis a fearfull thing to fall [into the hands of the living God] bec[ause] he is a consuming [fire], Heb: 10.31. and 12.29.

Dub[itatio]. But 3ly tho' God had resolved not to let sin passe unpunished; yet why should another, and not man be punished for his own sin; the soul that sinneth shall dye, Ezek: 18.4.

Sol[utio]. Bec[ause] of man's disability, either to satisfy God, or repair hims[elf]: if he has been put to bear the punishment due unto his sinnes, he had for ever sunke under the burthen of them.[471] Of hims[elf] he was utterly unable to perform any of God's will, beeing altogether Carnall, Rom: 8.7 and utterly unable either to suffer or to break thorow the wrath of God, haveing neither strength to endure, nor obedience to submitt unto it.

Now lay all these consideracions together, and we may easily gather the absolute necessitie we had of such an h[igh] Priest. 1st

469 "The impunity of every trangression brings it about that sins are valued less", that is, esteemed of less of importance.

470 In the manuscript 'matter', the word used in Genevan bible is crossed out and replaced by 'work' the word in the Authorized Version.

471 Cp. with "their religion sunk and gone, a meer delusion without a Resurrection" in Sermon Six.

God would not suffer his whole displeasure to arise; he would not execute the severitie of his law, bec[ause] by that his creature man should for ever loose the happy fruition of him, and he should lose the service and obedience of his creature. 2ly, God would not destroy and abolish his law, lest his Justice should be abused, his hatred against sin not sufficiently declared, his truth questioned, and his dreadfull Majesty slighted and neglected.[472]

3ly, man was not able to undergoe the punishment, not to suffer or endure the vengeance due unto sin; and therefore 4ly some course must be found out to translate this man's sinnes on another's person who may be able to bear them; and to interest this man's person in anothers righteousnes, which may be able to cover him.

And here Divines frame an holy reasoning, or[473] (as twere) an earnest conflict in God's Attributes. 1. Man is sinfull, and therefore an accursed creature, fitt jewell for Hell and Destruction, and therefore God's Justice calls for condemnacion; and his Truth demands of him to make good that threatning. Gen. 2.17 In that Day [that thou eatest thereof thou shalt surely die].

2. On the other side, Mercy cryes as loud for pitty and compassion, tow[ards] miserable man, wofully seduced and overthrown by Satan; this is for peace and reconcilement betw[een] an angry Judge and an undone creature; Hereupon the Infinite Widsome of God, to make his Mercy and Truth; Righteousnes and Peace meete together, and kisse each other, found out a way how to reconcile them. A priest is resolved upon, the 2nd Person of the blessed Trinity, who by his Father's ordinacion, his own voluntary undertakeing, the spirit's sanctificacion, should be fitted for this great busines. This is He, the h[igh] Priest, who is set on the right hand of the Throne of Majesty.

And thus much of the 1st Particular, what necessity we have of such an h[igh] Priest etc.

I proceed now to the 2nd, what Qualificacions are requisite in him who must be unto us such an h[igh] Priest.

---

472 This Anselmian teaching reappears in Sermons Three and Five.

473 This argument reappears in the Nativity Sermon for 1616 where Andrewes mentions the Divine as Bernard. This sermon has as its text Ps. 85.10-11. Andrewes, Vol. 1, p. 180.

2nd part. And here we shall first show, what manner of Priest Christ was to be. 1. How qualified, or what he was to perform in order to that Priesthood.

1. Every priest (Apostle) is ordained for men in things pertaining to God, to offer sacrifice for the obtaining of righteousnes and remission of sinnes, [Heb: 5.1]. And in Scripture, we read of 2 Orders of Priesthood, one after the order of Aaron; another after the order of Melchizedek [Heb: 7.11]. The office of a Priest after the order of Aaron was to offer sacrifice, to make an atonement and to blesse the People. And bec[ause] we read nothing in the Scriptures of Melch[isedek's] Priesthood, but only his meeting Abraham and blessing of him, therefore 'tis supposed that the office of his Priesthood did consist only in Blessing, as may be gathered out of Gen: 14.18,19. And tho' Christ be often stiled in the epistle to the Hebr[ews, Chs. 5 -7] a Priest for ever after the order of [Melchisedek, Heb. 7.21][474] yet he was also a Priest after the order of Aaron; for as he hath and doth now blesse his People; so he did offer sacrifices for them. For he was appoynted first to offer up sacrifice for the sinnes of the world; which he performed once for all, when he offered hims[elf] upon the crosse, Heb. 7.27, and therein exercised the office, or rather put a period to the office of Aaron's Priesthood, to all the rites and ceremonies, and sacrifices under the law. And this being finished he entered into the heavens, and there continually from that time to the end of the world, doth exercise the office of an h[igh] Priest in interceding for, and blessing his People, and is therefore called a priest for ever after the order of M[elchisedek].

And bec[ause] we often meet with this phrase in this Epistle, we shall therefore give a reason, why Christ is said to be made a Priest for ever after the order of Melch[isedek] bec[ause] between them there is a great conveniency and likenes. And for applicacion of this figure we may safely tread in those stepps, which the h[oly] Ghost hath marked out to us. 1. Melchiz[edek] had a name most agreeable to that of Christ, <u>Melch[isedek]:</u> <u>King</u> of <u>Righteousnes</u> and Christ is not only righteous hims[elf], but called the Lord our Righteousnes, Her: 23.6. 2ly, he had a kingdome

474 The previous twenty verses of this chapter also relate to Melchisedek's priesthood.

most agreeable to that of Christ's. He was king of Salem; which Salem was a Kingdome so called wherein Melchizedek reigned; for if this had been only an appellacion of him, then the Author would have said, Melchisalem; as he said not, King of Sedeck but Melchizedeck; so Salem notes the place where he did raign. And this Salem is conceived to be the same with Jerusalem, which at first was called only Salem, afterw[ards] by adjection of the word *Jeru*, called Jerusalem, as a man would say, Sight of Peace. And this is agreable to the Kingdome of Christ, who is a King of Peace, Esa: 9.6; the procurer and maintainer of our Peace; at his Birth he proclaimed Peace, Luc: 2.14 at his death he bequeathed peace, Joh: 14.27. 3ly, As Melch[isedek] met Abraham and blessed him: so Christ blesseth us with all spirituall blessings in [heavenly places in Christ], Eph: 1.3. 4ly Melch[isedek] is said to be without Father and Mother, not that he had no Father or Mother, but bec[ause] neither his Father nor Mother are declared in the Annalls of the scripture. For he is suddainly brought in Genesis 14.18 as a Priest of the most high God; the scripture neither before, nor after makeing any mention of him; as if he has been a man suddainly comed down from heaven, and as suddenly returned thither again, not to be accounted amongst the Genealogy of the Fathers. Haveing neither beginning of Dayes, nor end of life, i.e. both the beginning and end of his life are concealed; he is mentioned with no respect had either of his Predecessour, or successor. And in this respect, he was a Type of Christ who abideth a Priest continually; i.e. so long as there is any use of a Priesthood, or so long as the state of things shall so continue, that there is no further use of any Priesthood.

For a thing is said to abide for ever which both lasteth a long time, and also so long as the nature of the things will bear. So in this sense David saith, that he will praise God for ever [Ps: 52.9]; so the Law is said to be eternall and the Gospell Eternall, and many other things Eternall; and Christ is said to abide a Priest continually, i.e. so long as there shall be need of any Priesthood; untill the People of God be translated into heaven, and need no further expiacion of their sinnes. In breif, the likenes betw[een] Melch[isedek] and Christ in this place, consisteth in these 3 things. 1. As in the Priesthood of Melch[isedek] there was no respect had of his Parentage or Family; for he is said to be without Father,

Mother, or descent; so neither in the Priesthood of Christ, who according to the flesh descended from that Tribe (Judah) which had no title to the Priesthood. 2. That both were perpetuall Priests, Melchz[edek] in a figurative way, but Christ solidly and really. 3ly, as Melchiz[edek] in his Priesthood had no Predecessor nor successor; so neither had our saviour Christ in his. And thus much of the comparison, betw[een] Melchisedek's Priesthood and our Saviour Christs, and what manner of Priest Christ was, both after the order of Aaron to offer sacrifice, and also of Melchisedek, for ever to blesse his people.

11ly what Qualificacions are requisite in him who must be unto us such as h[igh] Priest?

1. Christ being a Priest, must also be a Mediatour and surety between two Parties, that he might have one unto whom, and others for whom to offer a sacrifice.

2. He was to be a Mediatour, not only by entreaty and request but satisfaction.

3. Beeing a Priest, he must also offer a sacrifice for every Priest was ordained to offer sacrifice.

4. He must also have an Altar upon which to offer the sacrifice.

5. Inasmuch as he was to offer himself a sacrifice and this sacrifice to be of infinite worth and value; 'twas necessary that God and man, one Christ should be that sacrifice. All these Qualificacions are to be found in Christ our h[igh] Priest.

1. He was appoynted by God to be our surety, Hebr: 7.22. He was made surety of a better covenant, the word is *ἔγγμος*, the plighter of his troth, the promiser, the undertaker, it comes from the verb *ἐγγυάω*, *promittere*, and that from *ἐγγύων*[475] (*in manibus*) strikeing hands, or giving ones hand, as a signe of a covenant; so Prov: 22.26. Be not thou one of them, that strike hands. (70)[476] Give not thyselfe *εἰς ἐννγύνι*, to suretishipp. And unto this suretishipp there must concurr the consent of the parties between whom 'tis negotiated. Now God giveth his consent, by laying on him our

475 This is now thought to be incorrect, the verb derives from *ἐγγόη* (*έυ γυῖον*, a putting a pledge in one's hand).

476 i.e. The Septuagint.

iniquities and makeing his soul an offering for sinne, Esa: 53.10. And man giveth his consent, when by faith he receiveth Christ and so becometh not only the friend but sonne of God, Joh: 1.12.

2ly, He was to be a Mediatour, not by entreaty and request but satisfaction. He undertook unto God for us both to pay the Debt by undergoing Death in our stead, and so to satisfie God; and to work in us all that God required should be done by us in the covenant of Grace. Yea Christ became such a surety for us in this covenant, as is not to be found among men. For on earth, sureties are wont to enter into one and the same Bond with the Debtors, so as the Creditour may seize on which of the two he will, whether on the Debtor or on the Surety; and usually on the Debtour first, for him we call the Principall: But in this Covenant God would have Christ's single Bond and hence 'tis that he is not called only surety of the Covenant but the Covenant, Esa: 49.8, and therefore he trod the wine-presse alone, Esa: 63.3. So he was the debtor, he alone the Covenant; all our Debt, our Punishment was layd upon him, and he was to loose it.

3ly. Beeing a Priest he must have a sacrifice answerable to the Debt, which was due to his Father. The Debt we were owing was the forfeiture of our soules and Bodyes to the Wrath of God and curse of the Law. God is able to destroy both soul and [body in hell], Math: 10.28. 'tis to be understood, not only of his absolute power; but of that power which as a just Judge he hath over us, as we are his prisoners and so obnoxious to the curses of his Law. And therefore our Priest was to have a soul and Body to pay as a surety for our soules and Bodyes, 1st (saith the Prophet) thou shall make his soul an [offering for sin], Esa: 53.10 and his soul was made an offering - - - Math. 26.38 My soul is exceeding sorrowfull [even unto death]. Again a Body thou hast prepared mee [Heb: 10.5]; and in this Body, his own self bare our sinnes on the Tree. 1Pet: 2.24.

4. He must have an Altar upon which to offer this Sacrifice; and the Altar on which it was offered, was the Divine Nature Heb: 9.14. through the Eternall spirit he offered hims[elf] without spott unto God, and so by his blood purgeth our consciences from dead works. He was to be God as well as man, that so he might undergoe and break thorow the weight of sin and the law; and haveing so done, might have merit and efficacy enough in his sac-

rifice, to satisfie the justice of God, and swallow up the sins of the world. So that

5. This sacrifice of Christ being of infinite worth and value, sufficient for the satisfaction of God, and reparacion of man, it was necessary, That God and man should make but one Christ, in the unity of the same infinite Person, whose Natures they both were, that which suffered, and that which sanctified. The humane Nature was not to be left alone, lest it should have sunk under the burthen; but to have dependence upon aid and assistance from the Person of the Sonne.

Hence ariseth a Communicacion of Properties betw[een] the 2 Natures, when by reason of the Unity of the Person, we attribute that to one Nature which is common to th' other. As the lord of life was slain, Act: 3.15. They crucified the Lord of glory, 1Cor: 2.8. And the sonne of man came down from Heaven, Joh: 3.13. And these expressions are used by reason of the communion of 2 Natures in one end, and one Person. And thus much breifly of the Qualificacions of our h[igh] Priest, what requisite in him who is unto us such an high Preist. To make some appl[ication] and to conclude.

Appl[ication]. You have heard the necessity, we have of an high Priest to make satisfaction to the justice of God, and to reconcile the world, lost mankind without him utterly ruined and undone. And hence we may learn, how much we ought to loath and hate and abhorr sinne, which hath done, doth, and will arm the law and justice, and power of God against us. And as sin is perfectly hated of God, so is it most odious and hatefull in itself; for he judgeth uprightly without passion, prejudice, or partiality. And as it is abominable and hatefull in itself, so should it be unto us, as the only ground of all our misery, of the creatures Vanity; of all that trouble, sorrow and affliction, which we meet with in the world. God certainly will punish it; if he spare thee, yet he will not spare thy sin, tho' he punish his own sonne for it. And shall we make a mock of sinne? shall we be so careles of our soules and their eternall saf[e]ty, as to sin with security? why should that seeme light to thee, which was so heavy to the soul of thy saviour? why should that be thy pleasure which was his Passion? why that hon[e]y to thee, which to him was gall and vinegar? why shouldst thou cherish or allow that in thee, which God so severely punished in his own sonne? Wee had been lost, and undone creatures, if Christ had not carried in his body, as well the guilt of our idle words, vaine thoughts, loose impertinent actions, as of our Oathes, execrations and blasphemies. If great crying, scandalous sinnes were as the spear and nailes that wounded his side his hands and his feet; then certainly smaller sinnes were the thornes, that peirced his head. And therefore we should learn with David to hate every evill way.[477]

2ly. Wee see by this necessity of an high Priest, how deeply we are engaged to the Mercy and goodnes of God, who was pleased to look upon us, and help us in our greatest extremity. How thankfull and obedient should we be unto him, who was so compassionate unto us? How should we admire and adore the unsearchable riches of his Wisdome and goodnes, who when we were desperately gone, found out a way of escape and deliverance for us? Where could man have found out, in heaven or earth, amongst men or Angells, a Priest that durst accompany such a sacrifice, into the presence of so consumeing a fire? No the misery of man was too deep and inextricable, for all the created counsell in the world to indent a deliverance. Now then, if God hims[elf] did so study to save us, how great reason is there, that we should study to serv him? Certainly we doe not thorowly apprehend the horrour of sin, the heavinesse of Gods wrath, the curse of the law, the end, the purpose, the merit of Christ's death; if we will not crucify a vanity, a lust, a pleasure, an earthly member for his sake.[478]

And therefore lastly, we should labour to be touched with our own wants, to know and feel the necessity we have of such a Priest. For 'tis not the bare apprehension will serv the turn,[479] but the inward sense and feeling is required. If a man did seriously consider, and lay together such thoughts as these: I am very busy for the affaires of this present life, which will quickly passe away like a weavers shuttle [Job 7.6], or a tale that is told [Ps: 90.9], I

---

477 Cp. with similarity in Good Friday Sermon for 1597. Andrewes, Vol. 2, p. 126.

478 This theme is also in Sermon Three.

479 This expression appears in both Sermons One and Two and also in a Sermon on Righteousness in Andrewes, Vol. 5, p. 109.

have another, an abideing life to live after this is over. All that I care and toyl for here, is but for the back, or the belly, or the bagg, meat, drink, pleasure, riches. And am I not nearer to myself, then to my wealth? Am I not nearer to my soul than I am to my carcasse?[480] Why am I so carefull of this, and careles of that? why do I let that parte which is brutish in me, command that which is rationall? ease and feed the body, to starv and destroy the soul? Do I not know that I must one day stand before him who is a consumeing fire? that I must one day be weighed in the ballance, and woe, eternall woe and misery will befall me, if I am found too light.

Appear before him I must, and appear before him I dare not alone, without a Priest to mediate for me; my Person wants a Priest, 'tis clogg'd with infinite guilt; my Nature wants a Priest, 'tis overspread with universall corruption; my sinnes want a Priest, they are in number and quality above measure sinfull; my best services want a Priest, they are blemished with many failings, pollucions, and imperfections; and therefore unles my h[igh] Priest, Christ Jesus cloth my Person with his righteousnes, cleanse my nature with his spirit, wash away my sinnes with his blood, sanctify my prayers and devotions with his Incense and intercession; all of them must passe thorow the triall of such a fire as will comsume them. We should labour to possese our selves with such serious thoughts as these, and they would make us more thankfull and obedient to God, more carefull and serious, and conscionable in our wayes, and to work out our salvacion with fear and trembling [Phil: 2.12]. Let us all consider what hath been said, and the Lord give us understanding in all these things. Amen.

480 There is a similar theme in the Good Friday Sermon for 1604. Andrewes, Vol.2, p. 154.

LECTURE FOURTEEN

Christ as Intercessor

Introduction

This lecture discussed the third heading, "Christ's Priestly Office", and His acts of oblation and of intercession. The former focused on His sacrifice for the sin of man, much of which is a repetition of the Anselmian teaching, and the latter concentrated on His mediation on man's behalf in heaven. Andrewes compared the similarities between Christ's oblatory sacrifice with those made under the Law: 1. The shedding of blood. 2. The sacrifice offered by a priest on behalf of the people to God as a peace offering. 3. The people partaking in the offering. There were also differences: 1. Under the Law it was an offering for sin, whereas Christ's sacrifice was for the "expiation for sin". 2. The priests offered many sacrifices whilst Christ's was once and once only. 3. The priests' ordinations were temporary and perishable whilst Christ's is endless. 4. The priests offered the blood of goats and calves, but Christ offered His own. 5. The priests only offered an animal, which did not struggle, but Christ offered Himself willingly. 6. The priests' sacrifices were temporal but Christ's sacrifice was forever. All these legal sacrifices had certain deficiencies because they could not purge sin as illustrated by the countless repetition and the variety of sacrifices. Hence they were all ineffective until they were absorbed into the sacrifice of the true Lamb, Christ.[481] Christians

481 Ms. 3707, pp.127- 8.

partake in that sacrifice each time the Eucharist is celebrated in the breaking of bread and receive the Body of Christ.

Christ's entry into heaven to sit at the right hand of the Father showed that His sacrifice has been accepted, Justice was satisfied and our sins expiated. Andrewes indicated that the importance of Christ's priestly work is reflected in its inclusion as one of the articles of the creed. Accordingly the scholars were "to adore this great mistery" and to hate sin for what it did and does to Christ. Although Christ has appeased God's anger for sin, it does not mean we can do what we like, "live and wallow in all sinful pleasures" and hope that God will be merciful. No, the scholars must dedicate their "souls and bodyes" to God by living "soberly, righteously, and godly in this world."[482]

It is obvious other lectures were to follow this one as Andrewes did not conclude Christ's priestly office under headings four and five: "What is the efficacy, the fruites and ends of such a Priesthood?" and "What Dutyes are required of us, or what uses we should make of it?"[483] Furthermore he did not lecture on Christ's office as Prophet. There is no way of telling whether these were ever given. One would like to think so!

Romans 8.34 Who is he that condemneth? It is Christ that died, yea rather that is risen again, who is ever at the right hand of God, who also maketh intercession for us.

The Apostle after a larg discourse of Justificacion by Christ's Righteousnes in the former parte of this Epistle in this chapter he sitts down as a man convinced, yea overconvinced, and all his reasons for ever silenced [Rom. 8] v.31. What then shall we say to these things? He speakes as one satisified, and even astonished with abundance of evidence, haveing nothing to say, but only to admire God's goodnes in Christ; and therefore presently throwes down the Gauntlett and challengeth a Dispute in this poynt with all commers: Let Conscience and Carnall Reason, and the law and sin, and Hell bring in all their strength; who is he that condemneth? He dares to answer them all, and carry it with these few

482 Ibid., p. 175.

483 Ibid., p. 125.

words (it is Christ that died yea rather [that is risen again who is at the right hand of God]). Here is the foundacion or ground of his bold challeng.

Now haveing proposed to you 5 things, to be observed concerning our saviours Priestly office: 1. what necessity we have of such as h[igh] Priest. 2. what Qualificacions are required in him, that is to be unto us such a h[igh] Priest. 3. what be the Parts of his Priestly Office. 4. what is the Efficacy fruites, and ends of such a Priesthood. 5. what dutyes are required of us, or what uses we should make of it. I have dispatched the 2 first of these, and proceed now to that 3rd to show the Partes of our saviours Priestly office, wherein the Acts and offices of our h[igh] Priest do principally consist. And this verse tells us what they are, the Death of Christ, his Resurr[ection], Ascention and Intercession; or bec[ause] his Resurr[ection] and Ascension are but the complement of his Passion, or his publ[ic] triumph after death, therefore we shall reduce the Partes of his Priesthood to these 2 heades.

1. His Act of Oblacion, when he gave hims[elf] a sacrifice for sin.

2. His Act of Intercession, his appearing and mediateing in Heaven for us.

1. Our h[igh] Priest offered up his Flesh, as one common sacrifice upon the Crosse, at once to be both expiatory to God and Pacificatory betw[een] man and man, Jew and Gentile. And here we are to obs[erve]: 1. Analogy betw[een] this sacrifice of Christ, and other sacrifices of old, wherein they agree. 2. Differences between this sacrifice of Christ and those under the Law, wherein they disagree.

1. To that yearly sacrifice under the Law, this of Christ's is answerable, in that as the high Priest then was not to enter into the earthly Tabernacle without blood, Heb: 9.7. So that Christ was not to enter into the heavenly Tabernacle without blood neither, after many sorrowes and sufferings, after a shamefull and painfull death. Luc: 24.26. Ought not Christ [to have suffered these things, and to enter into his glory]?

2. This sacrifice of Christ was agreeable to sacrifices of old in

this, that it was to settle and establish peace betw[een] man and man, and betw[een] God and man. For sacrifices were offered, not only by way of Expiacion, but some were by way of Pacificacion, and solemn covenant. The rites of that sacrifice were these: They cutt a calf in twain and passed between the Parts of the Calf, even the Princes and all People, Jer: 34.18,19. And this was in use among the Heathen; Livy 39, Dec.[484] tells us, how they cutt a Beast in two; the midst and the head with the bowells were placed at the right hand of the way: and the hinder parts on the left hand, and both the Armies passed betw[een] this divided sacrifice. And Tacitus An[nals] 12 gives us an account of the Imprecacion they used to make; *Si prius defexit Tu illum Jupiter sic, ut ego hunc porcum hodie feriam;* let God strike him that breakes it, as I strike this swine (said the sacrificer). And the h[oly] Ghost speakes in the like language. Ps: 50.5. Gather my People together unto me, those that have have made a covenant with me by sacrifice. So agreements and pacificacions had their confirmacion by sacrifice. Now a correspondency unto the rites used in those sacrifices of peace, holds good also in this sacrifice of our saviour's. In those the Beast was divided and cutt into two, for both Parties to passe thorow and so peace to be made between them. And in this, Christ to make both one, was divided, and cutt (as 'twere) in twaine: the God-head for a time forsaking the manhood. Ps. 22.1 My God [my God, why hast thou forsaken me][485] His soul also being by Death departed from his Body, his joynts loosened, the vail of his Flesh rent and He cut in twain as one common sacrifice between both.

Again, tho' the Priest only offered up the sacrifice for the people, yet to shew 'twas their act, they used after to eat of it, or of that which was offered up with it, and by that eateing of it, that they did partake of it, the Apostle tells us 1Cor: 10.18, they that did eate of the sacrifice were partakers of the Altar, (i.e.) they declared the sacrifice to be theirs, the offering of it up to be their Act, that they had an hand in it. In like manner to show that we were consenting to, and partakers in this sacrifice of our h[igh]

484 The writing is *ab urbe condita*, or *The History of Rome*. It was divided into 'decads', that is, of ten books.

485 Cp. with Sixth Sermon on *Prayer*, Andrewes, Vol. 5, p. 359, and Passion Sermon for 1604. Andrewes, Vol. 2, p. 139.

Priest, we partake of that sacrifice by eateing of it. 1 Cor. 10.16 the bread which we break, is it not the communion of the Body of Christ? considered as sacrifice upon the Altar of the crosse; and so by eateing thereof, we are all partakers of that one bread as the thing signifying, and of that one Body as the thing signified.[486] So Grot[ius] upon Math: 26.26. They are in Christ's intent so partakers of this his sacrifice, as if yourself had offered it up. Thus much of the Analogie of this sacrifice of Christ with other sacrifices of old, wherein they agree.

2. Let us see the Differences, wherein they disagree. And that 1. in respect of the Priests themselves; 2. in respect of their sacrifices.

1. Priests were sinfull, they thems[elves] wanted an expiacion, Heb: 5.3 but our h[igh] Priest was holy, harmles, undefiled, separate from sinners, Heb: 7.26.

2. Ordinacion of those Priests was Carnall, they were made after the Law of a Carnall commandment, Heb: 7.16. i.e. of a temporary, perishable and externall ordinance: which is therefore called carnall bec[ause] it had respect only to the flesh, to the linage, birth and death of the Priest, binding the Priest to a certain Tribe, and to a certain Family in that Tribe, and provideing for the mortalitie of the Priest, by determining the rights of succession; all which consideracions are carnall, respecting only the flesh. But our h[igh] Priest is after the power of an endles life, i.e. he is not a carnall, frail and mortall Priest, that after a little time should need a succcessour: but a most potent Priest that hath an absolute power, an Eternall Priest that hath an endles life.

3. They differ in the manner of their ministering; the services of those Priests under the Law never came to a Period or perfection, in which the Priest might give over and sit down; they stood dayly ministring, Heb: 10.11. whereas Christ after he had offered one sacrifice for sin, sate down [on the right hand of God], Heb: 10.12.

4. The old h[igh] Priest entered the most holy Place, not without blood, but 'twas the blood of goates and calves: but our h[igh]

---

486 Cp. with "the breaking of bread" in Sermon on *Imaginations*, Andrewes, Vol. 5, p. 67.

Priest entered not by such blood, but by his own most precious blood, Heb. 9.12. So he was both the Sacrifice and the Priest.

5. H[igh] Priest under the Law might enter upon his office before the slaughter of those Beasts he was to offer: but our h[igh] Priest was not inaugurated to his Priesthood, till after his sacrifice, after his Resurrection Heb: 5.5. Christ glorified not hims[elf], to be made an h[igh] Priest, but he that said unto him, thou art my son [to day have I begotten thee. Ps: 2.7], which words may seem to belong to his birth, but if compared with Act: 13.33 'twill appear they belong to the Resurrection of Christ; so that he did not perfectly perform his Priestly office before his Resurrection.[487] And his Priesthood shall last for ever in his Person without haveing any successor; and his Office shall last as long as there needs any expiacon for sinnes, even to the end of the world. Thus much for the differences betw[een] the h[igh] Priest under the Law, and our high Priest Christ Jesus. Now in the next place, see the differences betw[een] the sacrifices and the Deficiency of the Legall Sacrifices.

1. They would not serv to purg away sin, bec[ause] they were not expiacions, but only Remembrances and commemoracions of sinnes. Heb:10.3. In those sacrifices there is a Remembrance made of sinnes every year; so necessary twas that heavenly things should be purged with better sacrifices, Heb: 9. 23, where by h[eavenly] things is meant the h[oly] sanctuary; and by purifying the dedicateing of it for our use, makeing an accesse open for us to enter into it.

2. Sacrifices under the Law were not available of thems[elves]; without that typicall relacion they had to Christ they were utterly weak and unprofitable, Heb: 7.18, as the shadow hath neither beeing of itself, nor can give refreshment to another, but by dependance on the Body to which it belongeth. And this their insufficiency appeares in two things, 1. Their Reiteracion for the repeating of the sacrifice shewes that that Person for whose sake 'tis repeated, is in the same condicion now, as he was in, at the time of the former oblacion. 2. their variety, there were both gifts and sacrifices for sinnes; Bulls and Goates, calves and lambs, Heb:

487 Cp. with similar text in Paschal Sermon for 1622. Andrewes, Vol. 3, p. 57.

9. 9, 12, 13, and those shew unto us, that no one thing was fit to typify the full expiacion wrought by Christ; whereas He offered but one sacrifice, and by that perfected for ever them that are sanctified Heb: 10.14.

And thus we see the Deficiencies of Legall sacrifices, 1st they were not expiacions but commemoracions of sin; 2ly they were of themselves not available.

We proceed now to show 1. what made this Death of Christ a complete Sacrifice; his <u>own willingnes</u> to suffer. 2. that this one sacrifice was sufficient and satisfactory.

1. And his willingnes was seen in this, in that he offered up hims[elf], Heb: 9.14 and gave hims[elf] for us, an offering and a sacrifice to God for a sweet smelling savour, Eph: 5.2. And therefore he is called the Lamb of God, that [taketh away the sin of the world, Joh: 1.29] bec[ause] as a meek lamb he was dumb and opened not [his mouth, Is. 53.10] but was obdedient unto death, Phil: 2.8. I lay down my life (saith He) no man taketh it from mee, but I lay it down of myself, Joh: 10.17. His death did not proceed out of the condicion of his Nature, neither was it inflicted on him by reason of an excesse of strength in those that executed it,[488] (for he was the lord of glory) but only out of mercy tow[ards] men, out of obedience tow[ards] God, and out of power in hims[elf]: 'Tis a good Maxime of the schooles, *Omnis Christi infirmitas fuit ex potestate*; Christ by his own power assumed those infirmities, which the dispensacion of his Priesthood on earth required, and by the same power he layd them aside againe, when that service was ended. And this oblacion, this laying down his life, this willing obedience, this offering hims[elf] to God for us, is that which gives beeing to a sacrifice. For *hostia si ad aras luctabat, invito numine offerri putabant*, (Macrob[ius])[489] the very Heathens, if they were to sacrifice a Beast, and if that Beast did struggle at the Altar with the sacrificer, they thought the Gods were not pleased with it. Nay, *non nisi volentem et amoenentem mactabant* (Plut[arch]). They would not kill any sacrifice, but that which was gentle, willing and obedient. And therefore that voluntary Act of our saviour's, that he

488 What follows is a summary of Sermon One.

489 A 16th century classicist and theologian.

gave himself willingly for us, was that which made his death a sacrifice; as when men freely lay down their lives for the profession of the truth is that which makes their death Martyrdome, which otherwise would be but a Butchery; or as (Hierocles)[490] πυρός τροφὴ, fuell rather than sacrifice.

Dub[itatio]. But here, it may be demanded. How did Christ offer up hims[elf]? And how was his death voluntary, when the scriptures tell us that God the Father had before determined it, and so 'twas a necessary Death, Act: 4.28.[491] Againe he was slain with wicked hands, Act: 2.23 and so 'twas a violent death?

Sol[utio]. Answer. Tho' the malice of the Jewes, the falsenes of Judas, the fearfullnes of Pilate, and the iniquity of the times he fell into, conspired to take away his life, yet in respect of none of those was his Death a Sacrifice. But in answer to those Places.

1. He was delivered by God, Act: 2.23 and in regard of God, it was Justice and Mercy. God so loved [the world that he gave his only begotten Son] Joh: 3.16.

2ly. He was delivered by Judas and the Jewes Math: [26. 47, 57], 27.2, and so 'twas murder and cruelty, Act: 7.52.

3ly. He was yeelded and given up by hims[elf], Gal: 2.20,[492] and so 'twas obedience and humilite Phil: 2.8. And in this sense Christs death was a sacrifice. But

Dub[itatio]. Againe it may be replied; Christ's death was against his own will, for he exceedingly feared it, Heb: 5.7 and he earnestly prayed against it, O my Father if it be possible [let this cup pass from me], Math: 26.39, and therefore in this sense his death was not a sacrifice because not voluntary, but against his will?

Sol[utio]. This we answer; that Christ may be considered

1. As a private person, liable to, and endued with the same natural Passions, desires and abhorrences with other men; and the cup he was to drinke may be considered as it was *calix amaritudinis*, a cup of gall and vinegar; and so Christ justly feared and

490 Hierocles of Alexandria is best known for his commentary on Phytagoras' *Golden Verse*.

491 This is a wrong reference. What is referred to here, is covered in the next reference Acts 2. 23.

492 A better reference is John 18.8.

declined it, knowing that it would be a wofull, heavy, and bloody combat which he was to enter.

2. He may be considered in a publ[ic] capacity, as a Mediatour, a Surety, a mercyfull and faithfull h[igh] Priest; and the cup he was to drinke, as *Calix salutis*, a cup of salvacion, and so, he willingly and obediently submitted unto it. And here observ that his willingnes was much the greater, bec[ause] his will could not but shrink from it. 'Tis easy to be willing in such a service, as is suitable to our natures and affections; but when Nature shall shrinke, and sweat, and startle, and stand amazed at a service, then not to repent, decline and throw off the burthen, but with willingnes and submission of heart to lye down under it; this is of all other the greatest obedience, when a bloody conflict with wrath and death and hell is welcome. In breif, consider Death in it self, and so nature teacheth Christ to shun and avoyd it: consider death as a meanes to procure the salvacion of the world; and mercy worketh in Christ a willingnes of mind[493] to undergoe it.[494] 'Twas the Voyce of Nature, the implanted desires of the Flesh, that said, *Transeat Calix ---;* Father save me from this hour; 'Twas the retractacion of mercy, to say, For this very cause, came I into the world; Father glorifie thy self, Joh: 12. 27, 28. Whatever my nature declines, whatever my will desires, whatever becomes of mee, yet still glorify thy self, save thy ch[urch]; If it cannot be but by drinking this cup, thy will be done. And this may serve for answer to a 3rd objection that may be made;

Dub[itatio]. How could God in justice inflict so severe a punishment upon Christ for the sinnes of others? Doth not he say, the soul that sinneth, it shall dye? Ezek: 18.4.

Sol[utio]. Answer that Christ as God hath power over his own life; and he being willing to lay down his life for the salvacion of mankind, no wrong was done to him, *volenti non [fit injuria],* to a willing man no injury can be done. And herein we are to admire and magnifie the great Mercy of God to us, that tho' he would not spare sinne, yet he would not punish sinners. For if he should

493 Up to this point this sentence is exactly the same in E.P. and this whole page is very similarly expressed by Hooker, E.P., 5. 48. 10.

494 Cp. with similarity in Brightman, p. 214, and Sermon Three.

have resolved to have judged sinners, we must have perished in our own persons; but being pleased to deal with sin only in the abstract, and to spare the sinner, he was contented to accept of a sacrifice, which stood in his sight as the body of sin alone by itself; in which respect Christ is said to be made a curse for us, Gal: 3.13. And he who knew no sin, was made sin for us, 2Cor: 5.21. And thus much of the 1st Particular what made Christ's death a complete sacrifice, his own willingnes to suffer.

2ly, that this sacrifice of Christ was sufficient and satisfactory. And this we may confirme by 2 articles of our Creed, 1. Christ's Ascention, his entring into Heaven; 2. His sitting at God's right hand.

1. See him entring into heaven, and observ how God looked upon him at his first comeing to court there. He let him enter; he came confidently and boldly thither; and God letts him stay there; therefore we may be convinced that hee hath given God full satisfacion, yea our Saviour Christ useth this argument as the strongest that could be brought to convince the world, that his Righteousnes was the only Righteousnes by which men were to be saved, and upon this very ground, Joh: 16.10, bec[ause] I goe [to my Father] i.e. By this Argument 'tis, and shall be evinced that I who undertook to satisfie for sinne and to procure a perfect righteousnes, have perfectly performed it; and that 'tis such a righteousnes which God's justice doth accept of, to save sinners by; hence it shall appear that after my Death, after my finishing this work, I will ascend up to my Father into heaven and keep my standing there, and you shall see me no more. Yea but we should have seen him, Heaven could no more have contained him, then Paradise did Adam, if the handwriting had not been cancelled, if the debt had not been payd;[495] we may be sure there would have been no goeing into heaven, no remaining there, but he should have been sent back againe to perform the rest; but being there, and so maintaining his station there, God's justice is fully satisfied because we see him no more.

2. Consider Christ sitting at God's right hand, and thence inferr, that by his sacrifice God's justice is satisfied. As soon as he

495 Cp. with Passion Sermon for 1604, Andrewes, Vol. 2, p. 150.

was carried into Heaven as all the Angells in heaven fell down and worshipped him so his Father welcomed him with sitt thou [on my right hand, until I make thine enemies, thy footstool] Ps. 110.1 which words import two things. 1st that Christ hath perfectly done his worke, and that there is no more left for him to doe by way of satisfaction: this the word sitting implies.[496] 2ly, It argues that God is as fully satisfied on his parte: this his sitting on God's right hand implies.

1. The phrase of sitting doth betoken rest, when the work is fullfilled and finished, so in those words, God gives him a *quietus est*; rest here, return no more, the work is accomplished. The Apostle Heb: 10.11,12 compareing the force and excellency of Christ's sacrifice, with those of the Priests under the Law, tells us, that they stood dayly offering of sacrifices, which could never take away sinnes; but Christ after he had offered one sacrifice sate down; observ, how he opposeth their dayly to his once; their standing to his sitting down; he that is entered into his rest hath ceased from his work, Heb. 4.10.

2. Sitting on the right hand of God, notes unto us the consummacion of all those offices, which he was to perform on earth for our Redemption; and so the satisfaction of Gods justice; for if God had not been infinitely well pleased with him, he would never have let him come so near him, to take the highest place in the court of Heaven, to sitt on God's right hand. And this is the Argument our Saviour useth when he prayeth to be glorifyed, Joh. 17.4-5. I have finished the worke thou gavest me to doe and now (ô Fr) glorify me with thine own self. So that untill he had made such a complete expiacion, as should never need to be repeated, untill he had finished the worke, he was not able to perfect those that are sanctified, nor fitt to sitt on God's right hand. But now being there placed, he hath evidently manifested to us, that he hath offered up such a sacrifice, as hath pleased God for ever. And thus much of the first parte of our Saviours Priestly office his Act of Oblation, whence he offered hims[elf]; once a perfect and complete Sacrifice for the sinns of the world, as also of the Analogy and differences between this sacrifice of Christ, and those under the Law.

---

496 Cp. this and next two paragraphs with text in Brightman, p. 253, and Ms. 3708, pp. 66 - 7.

To Apply this

1. Let us learn to adore this great mystery, God manifested in the flesh, and the unsearchablenes of that Love, which appoynted this, God to be man, the Creator of the world to be dispised as a worm, for the salvacion of such Rebells, as might justly have been left under chaines of darknes and reserved to the same inevitable Destruction with the Divells, that fell before them.

2. Have always an eye to the haynousnes of sin, to the stain and guilt and pollucion, which no sacrifices under the law could expiate; not the blood of Bulls and Goates, nor ramms upon a 1000 hills, the severitie of God's justice was so inexorable, that no satisfaction could pacifie it; no obedience, but humiliacion sorrowes and sufferings of God himself. And if he who had strength of a Diety to suport him, the fullnes of the spirit to sanctify and prepare him, the Message of an Angell to comfort him, the relacion of a beloved son to refresh him, the assurance of ensueing glory and victory to encourage him; yet that, even the son of God, notwithstanding all these abasements, should pray with strong cryes and bloody dropps and wofull conflicts of soul against the cup of his Father's wrath, and seemed to shrinke and decline that very work, for which only he came into the world. O! what a condicion will that sinner be in, who must stand or rather everlastingly sink and be crusht' down under the weight of that wrath, which amazed and made heavy unto death the soul of Christ himself! And now tho' this one sacrifice of Christ be sufficient and satisfactory; yet there are some *ὑστερήματα*, Col: 1.24, We must fill up that which is behind not by way of satisfaction, but exercise and triall of our Graces. We may not think that now we may run as far on score as we please, every day, every hour build a new sconce[497] on Gods mercy, live and wallow in all sinfull pleasures according to the bent and inclinacion of our corrupt natures; No, that of the Apostle deserves our attention and meditacion. Tit: 2.11,12 The grace of God which bringeth salvacion hath appeared to all men, teaching us that [denying ungodliness and worldly lusts, we should live soberly, righteously, and godly in this world.] One good turn deserved another, and one sacrifice requires another.

497 It means a small fort to defend.

Rom: 12.1 I beseech [you therefore, brethren, by the mercies of God, that you present your bodies as a living sacrifice]; by these suffering sacrificeing Mercyes; as you hope to have a share, and to reap any benefit by those Mercyes, that you present your Bodyes and soules, a liveing sacrifice, holy, acceptable unto God, which is your reasonable service; yea, all the reason in the world that if Christ died for you, to redeem your soules and bodyes from eternall death; that you should present them both alive unto him, And this you cannot doe better and more acceptably then in your young and tender [years], but such as have passed those yeares must take the present time; you must neglect no meanes, balk no opportunities of dedicateing your soules and bodyes to God; Now God calls for them, and now he will be pleased with them, so pleased as to crown your riper age, the close of your life with comfort and happines and your bodyes and soules with glory that fadeth not away.

PART II

The Sermons

SERMON ONE

At Christmas

Introduction

Andrewes as always has a very scriptural approach as the first part of the sermon embellishes not only the verse of his text but also those preceding it and following in the second chapter of Philippians. There are similarities of text, (some of it is identical) in this sermon with others Andrewes preached such as the Christmas Sermons for 1605, 1607, 1611, 1615, and 1618 at the Jacobean Court, and Sermon Five in this manuscript.

In presenting this sermon Andrewes addressed those early heresies that were counteracted by the Chalcedonian formula, which he defined in his 1611 Nativity Sermon as "'He was so made flesh that He ceased not to be the Word, never changing that He was, but taking that He was not.'" He was too ever conscious that the heresies of his day were based on the old ones, and he always felt it a pastoral duty to expose these heresies to his auditors. Therefore he taught that Christ must be believed as one person but with two natures, human and divine. Of Christ's two natures, in this sermon, he stressed His humanity to defend the orthodox teaching against those heresies such as Manicheeism and the modern day Anabaptists who denied the humanity of Christ. So we find Andrewes preaching that Christ "really took our nature upon him, was made like unto us, sensible of cold, hunger, thirst, wearinesse, sorrow, Death." So strongly did Andrewes feel about this heresy that it reappeared in Sermon Five in this manuscript in which he emphasised that Christ's "body was no airy meteor, an empty phantasm, a meer shape or shadow but a true humane Body." [498]

He too upheld Mary as *theotokos*, the name given to her at the Council of Ephesus in 431, and venerated her as she is in the Orthodox Church. "Here was a new thing under the Sun, that God should be born of a woman; that the Bl[essed] virgin should be both the Mother of her Father, and the Daughter of her son." In his *Preces*, one of the intercessory prayers is taken from the liturgy of St. Chrysostom that commemorates the blessed Mother of God: "Commemorating the all holy, immaculate, more than blessed mother of God and ever virgin Mary, with all the saints, let us commend ourselves and one another and all our life unto Christ our God."[499]

Of course many of the Fathers had similar writings against these early heresies on the natures of Christ. In counteracting these heresies often their works focused on the great mystery of the Incarnation, evident in these words of St. Basil quoted by Andrewes. St. Basil's, "Behold I tell a wonder above all wonders, the great God was made a little child."[500]

Much of this sermon was devoted to another favourite teaching of the Fathers - the *kenosis* and the humility of Christ. Like them Andrewes never ceased to be amazed "That heaven" should come "down to earth", and that God emptied Himself of all His splendour.[501] It is one the great mysteries of the Faith, and therefore in this sermon as elsewhere he maintained that we should marvel at, rather than trying to fathom out why the Word forsook His glory and took "upon Him the nature of this flesh, a body of clay", a body subject to "Death and corruption" and "weaknesses and Infirmities" as we are. He also emphasised the significance of God taking our "human nature" instead of becoming a human person. He informed his auditors that if they reflected on why the Word Who had made "the sun, moon and starrs" and all created things took our flesh they would discover it was for our salvation.

498 Andrewes, Vol. 1, p. 91; Ms. 3707, p.172.

499 Ibid., p. 137; Brightman, p. 85.

500 Ms. 3707, p. 134; Andrewes, Vol. 1, pp. 90 - 1.

501 Ibid., pp. 5 – 6.

It was only He who could reinstate man in his proper relation to God by His perfect obedience to the will of His Father. Andrewes indicated that the Fathers including Irenaeus, Athanasius and Cyril all commented on man's difference before and after the Incarnation. "This honour is to us by the dishonour of Him; this the good by Christ an embryo." Henceforth man with all his frailty is now the brother of his blessed Saviour, and is made righteous through Christ's righteousness.[502]

This mystery of the Incarnation was also emphasised in his 1607 Nativity Sermon as obvious with its text from 1Timothy 3:16, "And without controversy great is the mystery of godliness: God was manifest in the flesh, ... and received up in glory." Although many "invisible things of God" had formerly been made manifest such as His eternal power, wisdom and providence in and since the creation, they are no mysteries - only this, God taking flesh. "Today, in the flesh of a poor babe crying in the cratch, *in medio animalium*; after in the rent and torn flesh of a condemned person hanging on the cross, *in medio latronum*, in the midst of [criminals]."[503]

God's humility was further illustrated in "the person of whom he was made, a poore virgin" She "was so poore ... she had not swadling cloathes to wrap him in. ... But the Savour of the world passed by all the great Potentates and sent his angell to an handmaid of low degree to tell her that the Holy Ghost should overshadow her and he would be born of her." His humility is even more amazing when, as the Psalmist tells us, man is but "a vapour that appeares for a little while and then vanisheth"; and of "extreme vanity". Even the village where Christ was born was a lowly place. Bethlehem Ephratah, was an insignificant place compared to the kingly cities of Jerusalem and Tiberias. So was the place - a stable, not even an inn. But yet Bethlehem, meaning "the house of Bread", was most fitting for Him who is "the bread of life."[504]

In his 1615 Nativity Sermon Andrewes reiterated the signifi-

---

502 Ms. 3707, p.137; Andrewes, Vol. 1, p. 141.

503 Ibid., p. 38.

504 Ms. 3707, p. 137; Andrewes, Vol. 1, p. 169.

cance of Christ being born in "a sorry poor village". Yet this Bethlehem leads us to "the Tree of Life, even the Bread of life" where the star shines perpetually above as Christ is always present in the Sacrament.[505]

Christ's humility was a central theme in the sermons for Christmas days of 1618 and 1620 where he used similar language. It is "His sign" at Christmas; "humility is His place - humility, as I may call it, the Bethlehem of virtues." His crib was a pulpit from where Christ preached, "learn of me, for I am humble - humble in my birth you all see." Hence the crib is a sign for all to follow if they wish to enter the kingdom of heaven. "If the sign of Christ's birth be the proper-sign of a Christian's new birth, 'wherein Christ is fashioned in us anew;' *hoc erit signum*, that they who to faith have not joined humility, are not yet come so far as to be babes in Christ; not yet, as St. Basil speaketh, come to their 'swaddling clouts in the state of salvation.'"[506]

But Christ's humility stooped even lower when He took the form of a servant. All through His life He was servile to His Father, parents, and even to the disciples but never more so than in His passion and death when He was stripped of all decency and finally life. Andrewes therefore presented Christ's life as the example to follow, that is, to be "humble, meek, patient," and self-denying rather than swelling with pride and murmuring and bearing grudges against others.[507]

> Text Philippians. 2. 7. *But he made himself of no reputacion, tooke upon him the form of a servant and was made in the likenesse of men.*

The first words of the Text but he tells us of their dependance upon, and their relacion unto somewhat goeing before. We must therefore look higher to know who 'twas that made himself of no reputacion. And that we may gather from the two former verses immediately preceding the Text, Let this mind be in you, which was also in Christ Jesus, who being in the form of God thought it not robbery to be Equall with God. So then 'twas the Lord Jesus,

---

505 Ibid., pp. 157, 173.

506 Ibid., pp. 197, 205-6, 238.

507 Ms. 3707, p. 133.

God's Equall, who for us men and for our salvation was made of no Reputacion.

He was the house and Lineage of David, Luc: 2.4. And that Lineage had neither any Eternity stampt upon it nor any Majesty shineing in it. David at the best was no better then his Fathers. And what the best of them was, even Abraham the Father of the Faith-full, you may hear from his own mouth, Gen: 18.27, I have taken upon me to speak unto the Lord, which am but Dust and ashes, or if you will not beleeve Abraham, hear what the Apostle saith Gal: 6.8, Seed of Abraham is Flesh. And what is the very harvest of this seed of flesh, but corruption, wormes and rottennes, Job: 17.14? This is the Originall of flesh, and to this it shall return.[508]

And yet the Lord Jesus took upon him the nature of this flesh; a Body of clay, such a Body as was capable of Death and corruption, a Body subject to the same Passions, weaknesses and Infirmities that ours are [based on Math: 8.17], sin only excepted. And here we may see the height and depth of his goodnes [Eph: 3.18], the infinite riches of his mercy to lost mankind.

That Heaven should thus come down to Earth, that God should become Man; that the Father of Eternity should be born in time. Well might the Apostle stand amazed at it, 1Tim: 3.16. Without controversy, great is the mystery of Godlynesse, God manifest in the flesh. Yet so 'twas, He in whom all fullnes dwelt [Col:1.19] ἐκένωσε he was pleased to empty, to lay aside the Robes of his Majesty, and to vail the lustre of his glory with the Mantle of our flesh. He who is Lord over all, God blessed for ever, Rom 9:5. He whose dwelling is not with flesh Dan: 2.11. He came, pitcht his Tabernacle, and dwelt in our flesh, Joh: 1.14.[509] He that was before Abraham [Joh: 8.58], had his birth almost 2000d yeares after Abraham. He who hath neither beginning of Dayes, nor end of life, was born, and cut off out of the land of the living, Esa: 53.8. This is He, the very same who made hims[elf] of no Reputacion, took upon him the form of a servant, and was made in the likenesse of men [Phil: 2.7].

---

508 This text reappears exactly in the 1605 Nativity Sermon. Andrewes, Vol. 1, p. 4.

509 Cp. with Nativity Sermon for 1611. Andrewes, Vol. 1, p. 93.

The occasion of which words was this: the Apostle being Prisoner at Rome and heareing of severall Disorders amongst his converts, both in Doctrine and manners, out of his fatherly care had over those churches he had planted, he writ divers Epistles, as to others, so to these Philippians; wherein he endeavours to rectify what was formerly amisse, and to put them in a right way for the future. Matter of his Exhortacion is touching diverse faults he wisheth them to be free from, and diverse graces they should follow; and the manner of his Exhortacion is very patheticall, - If there be any consolation, any comfort of Love, any fellowship of the Spirit, any bowells of mercies [Phil: 2.1]: as if he should say - my request is for all the Love under Heaven; that you would doe nothing through contention, vain-glory, self-conceit; but above all to put on Humility, meeknes of mind, brotherly love, and to yeeld and submit thems[elves] to their Inferiors [Phil:2.3]. And that he might the better prevail with them in this poynt, he presseth the example of their Saviour, v. 5. Let the same mind be in you that was in Christ Jesus [Phil: 2.5]. Learn of him, whose Disciples, whose servants, members of whose Body you are. And what must they learn of him? To be humble, meek, patient, to deny thems[elves], their own worth and excellency for the good of their Brethren. For he who was in the form of God [Phil: 2. 6] and without any injury to the God-head, equall in glory - honour, Majesty to the Father, yet made hims[elf] of [no reputacion, took upon him the form of a servant, and was made in the likness of men, Phil: 2.7] was like to man in desires, infirmities, sorrowes, in all things, sin only excepted; Yea being man, he so far humbled hims[elf] that he was obedient unto death [Phil: 2.8]; and therefore let the same mind be in you [which was also in Christ Jesus Phil: 2.5] who tho' he was able to raise the Dead to life, to still the rageing of the sea, to command the Divells, to cure Diseases by the word of his mouth; yet not withstanding all this Power Mar:7.[37]. Worth, Excellency, He made hims[elf] of no reputacion, took upon [him the form of a servant and was made in the likness of men].

Text[510] is a full and compendious History of our Saviour's Incarnacion, Birth and Humility. Where you have 3 gradacions of it.

---

510 This introduces the *division*, which was a feature of the famous *Ninety-six* Sermons.

1. He humbled hims[elf] so low as to take our nature upon him, He was made in the likenesse of men. And his very Humanity had been humility enough. But 2. yet lower, he became the meanest of the sonnes of men, He took upon him the form of a servant. 3. Lower yet, He who did this was lord over all, God blessed [for ever Rom: 9.5], and therefore ἐκενωσε, made himself lower than the meanest of servants, became of no Reputacion.[511] So that we may read the Text thus: He was made in the likenesse of men, took upon him the form of a servant and was made of no Reputacion. In the 1. we have the Humanity of our Saviour, in the 2nd his demeanour, while he lived here in our flesh, in the 3rd his Divinity.

We begin with the first of these. He who was [in the] form of God and thought it not robbery [to be equal with God], was made in the likenesse of men.

ἐν ὁμοιώματι του ἀνθρώπων and ὁμοιώμα, tho' it do frequently signify the outward appearance, externall habit and form of a thing, yet it doth include the inward Being and Reality of it, for ὁμοιώμα is all one with εἰκὼν, and that the Apostle opposeth to σκιά Heb. 10.1. Law had a shadow of good things to come not that very Image of things; And so the word is used, Gen 5.3. Adam lived 130 years and begat a son, κατά τὴν εἰκονα ὕτου, in his own likenesse so that by ὁμοἰω(μα), the likenesse of men, we must either understand the substance and reality of them, or else we must grant that Adam begat not a son, but the shadow and phantasm of a sonn. But if this word ὁμοιώμα, will not serve the turn, we have another word in the Text μορφή. He took [upon him the form of a servant] and this is not the same with μόρφωσις.

But μορφή κυρίως ἡ οὐσία (Phavorin). So Basil L.4. Cont[ra] Eunom[ius] τὸ ἐν μορφή φεȏυ ἐν οὐσία θεοȗ οὐ γάρ ἄλλο μορφή καὶ ἄλλο οὐσία. To be in the form of God, is to be of the same substance with God, for the Form is not different from the substance. So then he was made in the [likeness of men Phil. 2.7], i.e. so he really took our nature upon him, was made like unto us, sensible of cold, hunger, thirst, wearinesse, sorrow, Death.

---

511 Cp. with similarity in Nativity Sermon for 1618. Andrewes, Vol. 1, p. 205.

For further confirmacion of this, we have clear Text the Testimonies of the Fathers and the whole Church of God in all Ages.

1. Nature assumed is the seed of Abraham Heb: 2.16, seed of David Rom: 1.3. seed of woman, Gen: 3.15 and God's own son was made of a woman Gal: 4.4, and so was truly and really the fruit of her womb, Luc: 1.42. And if all this will not satisfy the eye of faith, see this truth with the eye of sense; Accompany him into the Desart, there, behold he was an hungred, Math: 4.2. Accompany him to the shipp, and there see him asleep, Math: 8.24. Accomp[any] him to Jacob's well and there see him sit down and wearied, Joh: 4.6. Nay accomp[any] him to Golgotha, and there behold him dead, Joh: 19.33. Now to be hungry, sleepy, weary, dead, these are not incident to the nature of God, but of man.

So in that he [was made in the likeness of men,] he really took our nature [upon him]. Neither did he take the substance of our Nature only, but all the properties also and qualities thereof; so that in the Dayes of his flesh, he was sub[jec]t to the same weaknesses which we find in our frail nature, and was encompassed with like Infirmities, Heb: 5.7. And yet here to prevent a mistake we are to remember; That as he took upon him, not an humane Person, but an humane Nature; so 'twas not requisite he should take upon him any personall Infirmities, as sickness, blindnes, lamenes and particular kinds of diseases, which are incident to some only, not to all men in generall, but those infirmities only which do accompany the whole nature of Mankind; such as hungring, thirsting, wearinesse, greif, paine, mortality; to these was he subject, and had his full share of them.

Now for the Testimony of the Fathers we have them with a full stream *ἡ γὰρ ἀναληφθεῖσα φύσις τουτο ἦν*, Theod[sius] Human nature was not in imagination or show, but truly assumed. And *μέγας θεὸς μικρόν βρέφος*, Basil: Behold I tell a wonder above all wonders, the great God was made a little child. And *qui regit sydera, ubera sugit*, Bern[ard]. He that governs the starrs, sucked the breasts of a woman; Lord Paramount of the whole world took upon him the form of a man servant. *Esurivit Christus qui omnes pascit* (Aug[ustine]). He was hungry who gives all creations food and nourishment. He thirsty, with whom is the well of life; He dumb before his Tormentors; who made both Deafe to heare and Dumb to speak. 'Twould be endles to repeat but the Tyth of what they have scattered up and down in their writeings concerning his Humanity.

Lastly for the consent of the ch[urch] we have it in 3 creeds universally received *πιστεύομεν εἰς ἕνα* Κύριον Ιησοῦν Χριστόν, *διὰ τῆυ ἡμετέραν σωτηρίαν σαρκωθέυτα καὶ ἐυανθρωπήσαντα.* [We believe ... in one Lord Jesus Christ ... who for us men and our salvation ... was incarnate ....and became man] So Nicene Creed. And *ἀδιαιρέτως, ἀτρεπτως, ἀσυγχύτως,* [Athanasius]; *γεννηθέντα ἐκ* Μαρίας *τῆς* (Παρθένου) [Born of the Virgin Mary]. In our Mediatour each nature remaineth intire in itself, and retaineth the properties agreing thereunto without any conversion, composicion, commixtion, or confusion whatsoever. So we have no reason to doubt of the Truth of this poynt that He [was made in the likeness of men]. We may with astonishment behold our Dust and Ashes assumed into the undivided unity of God's own Person; and admitted to dwell there as an Inmate under the same roof, and yet amidst those everlasting burnings [Is: 33.14], the Bush, i.e. our Nature in the Person of the Lord Jesus, to remain unconsumed.

But now 'tmay be demanded, why was it requisite that He should be made [in the likenesse of men], what necessity was there of it?

1. Bec[ause] the Work of our Redemption could not be performed without it. The businesse that our blessed Saviour had to doe; was to deliver the seed of Abraham, Gal: 3.16. And them he could not deliver except he destroyed death and him that is the Lord of [death and Divells], and them he could not destroy except he dyed (for such was Gods love to justice and hatred to sin, that he would not have his justice swallowed up with mercy, nor sin pardoned without such a propriacon). So then dye he must, and dye he could not, except he were mortall, and mortall he could not be, except he took our nature upon him, so 'twas, necessary that he should be made in the likenesse [of men] that he might become mortall, destroy death, deliver us.[512]

2nd. Man 'twas fit he should be, bec[ause] Man was the Party that by the Articles of the first Covenant was tyed to this obe-

512 This text reappears identical in 1605 Christmas Sermon. Ibid., p. 10.

dience; and 'twas requistite, that as by one man's disobedience many were made sinners, so by the Obedience of one man, many should be made righteous, Rom: 5.19. Now if our Redeemer had been only God, he could have performed no Obedience; the Godhead being free from all manner of subjection.

3rd. Our nature being alienated from the life and communion with God, it could not be better restored to that communion then by this assumption of our Nature to his in the same Person. This Reason is given by Irænaeus, Athan[asius], Cyrill and generally by [the] Fathers. And by this we may see what a great and gracious alteracion there is, between man's condicion before, and since the Incarnacion.[513] Moses tho' God's familiar, yet when he besought the Lord that he would shew him his glory, he received this answer. Thou canst not see my face, for then shall no man see me and live, Exod: 33.20. And Abraham tho' God's speciall friend, Father of the Faithfull, yet he held it a great matter, that he should take upon him so much, as to speak unto God; yea the very Angells thems[elves] (which are greater in power and might) are fain to cover their faces when they stand befor[e] him, Esa: 6.2. But now that our nature is so highly advanced, that our Mediatour is made man like unto ourselves, we may do that which Moses, Abraham and the Angells were afraid to doe, goe boldly unto thee throne of grace Heb: 4.16.

But now again it may be demanded, why in this flesh of ours thus advanced the fullnes of the Godhead should dwell Bodily? Why should God make choice of that habitacion to dwell in, when he thought it fit to publish the Gospell?

1. Because the Doctrine of the Gospell could not be published, but by the abrogacion of the Mosaicall Law, and Leviticall Priesthood; but 'twas not fit that those should be abrogated by any of Moses's fellow servants, but by one far above Moses; the son of God. This may be confirmed out of the 3rd to the Heb: v. 2, 6 where comparison is made between Christ and Moses; Moses was a servant in the house, but Christ a son and Lord; and therefore no marvell, if Moses give place to Christ, the Law to the Gospell.

2. Doctrine of the Gospell was to be received as Eternall and

513 The same remark of the Fathers appeared in the above sermon. Andrewes, Ibid., p. 14.

Immutable; and it makes much for the immutability of it, that was delivered by one, unchangeable. For if in him who was made in the likenesse of men, the Godhead had not dwelt when he thought fit to publish the Gospell; what might have hindered, but as the law of Moses gave place to the Gospell, so the Gospell might give place to a 3rd doctrine? But seeing Christ is the Author of the Gospell, 'tis called an everlasting covenant, Esa: 55.3. i.e. *respectu modi dispensandi;* Dispensacion of the Gospell, not like that of the Ceremoniall Law, to have an end, but this Covenant is the last, no 3rd to be expected. And therefore 'tis said Heb: 10.27 that if we sin wilfully after we have received the Truth, there remaineth no more sacrifice for sin but a certain fearfull looking for of judgment.[514] i. e. if there were a 3rd covenant to be expected then there were some hopes by that to make expiacion for what we commit against the 2nd; but there is no such thing to be expected, but a certain fearfull looking for of [judgment].

Lastly, it being the proper office of our Redeemer to be a mediatour betw[een] God and man 1Tim: 2.5, 'twas meet he should partake with both. And being before all Eternity consubstantiall with his Father at the appoynted time, he must be consubstantiall with his children; such a Redeemer such a Mediatour became us, Heb. 2.17. And thus much for the *ὁμούσιος* and *ὁμοιόνσιος*. That he who was in the form of God was made in the Likenesse of men; and the ends for which and Reasons why 'twas so behovfull.

Let us in the next place see what an high condescension 'twas in him, that he would be made like unto men. For what is man, but a thing of nought;[515] a vapour that appeares for a little while and then vanisheth [Jam: 4.14]; his time passeth away like a shadow, or a tale that is told [Ps: 90.9]; yea what is man in his prime, in his best condition that may be, but vanity, extream vanity, altogether vanity, Ps. 39.5. And that the great God, who hath scarcity of nothing, but fullnes of all things should be made in the likenesse of man, who is nothing but emptines and vanity? that he who

514 This quotation which in the Authorized Version is verse 26 seems to be a favourite text of Andrewes. For example in his Sermon on "Forgive us our debts", he adapts it. "If we willingly sin after remission 'there is no more sacrifice for sin'." Ibid., Vol. 5. p. 431.

515 This same sentiment is expressed in 1605 Nativity Sermon. Ibid.,Vol. 1, p. 5.

hath neither beginning of time, nor end of dayes should be like him, whose time passeth away as a tale that is told? What greater condescension can there be then this?

But yet further, Let us view his Humility by these Gradacions.[516] Consider 1. Person who was made in likenesse [of men]. 2. Person of whom. 3. Place where he was made in the likenes [of men].

1. How can a man be born when he is old? Can he enter the 2nd time into his mother's [womb, and be born?] Joh. 3.4. Children use to be born and old men to dy[e], but see here the contrary; the ancient of dayes is born Dan: [7.22], and not long after many thousands of children dye. God tells us by his Prophet Jer. 31.22 that he would create a new thing upon earth, a woman should compasse a man, and that woman a virgin too; here is one ridle[517] upon another, a virgin with child, nay a virgin to bring forth a man, and that man the ancient of dayes, and who had his beeing before, and gave a being to his Mother. Again it is not usuall for a King to be borne, for altho' those are born of Princes are borne to a Kingdome; yet not so soone as they are born, untill they come to maturity, they are so far from being kings over others, that they live in subjection, and differ little from servants, tho' they are lords over all [Gal: 4.1]; But he who took upon him the form of a servant, was born a King, Math: 2.2. Where is he that is born King of the Jewes? and Esa: 9.6 Unto us a child is born; unto us a son is given, and the government shall be upon his shoulder and his name shall be called, Wonderfull Counsellor, The mighty God, The everlasting father, the Prince of Peace. 3ly, Suppose the Majesty of all princes, kings, Monarchs in the whole world could be gathered together and united at once; and adde to this the glory, splendour and excellency of all Saints and Angells, and the whole quire of heaven; and all this in comparison to the Majesty of God would not make the magnitude of a Pismire.[518] Now this great God who measuereth the earth [Hab: 3.6] and sea, the sun, moon and starrs; who sustaines all things created, governs them without pain or weari-

516 Cp. with Ms. 3708, p. 13, and Brightman, p. 212.

517 Archaic form of riddle.

518 This is an old English word for *ant*.

nesse, insomuch that a leafe from a tree cannot fall to the ground without him. This is he who made hims[elf] of so small reputacion as to be made in the likenes of men.

2. Consider the person of whom he was made, a poore virgin, one who was so poore, that she had not swadling cloaths to wrap him in,[519] or a lamb to present in the Temple for him, but was forced to offer two young pigeons, Luc: 2.24. And yet he made choice of his Mother before he was born of her. Certainly if it were in the power of the sons of men to chuse their Mothers, obscure, mean and poor women should never bear; all would aim at an high and great extraction: But the Saviour of the world passed by all the great Potentates and sent his Angell to an handmaid of low degree Luc 1:52[520], to tell her that the Holy Ghost should overshadow her and he would be born of her. And here was a new thing under the Sun [Eccl: 1.9], that God should be born of a woman; that the Bl[essed] virgin should be both the Mother of her Father, and the Daughter of her son. Can the waters of the vast Ocean be comprehended in a little fountaine? Can such plenty of grain as may suffice the whole world be contained in a little garner, or the great globe of the sun take all its magnitude from a little starr? Yet here, he who is greater and brighter than the sun, vaster than the ocean, He who is the bread of life, sufficient to satisfy 100,000d worlds, was contained within the narrow bounds of a virgins womb.

3. Consider the Place, where he was made in the likenes of men. He did not chose the kingly Citty Jerus[alem] nor Tiberias, nor any other famous Citty, but a little abject, obscure Town Bethlehem Math. 2.1. Hear how the Prophet describes it, Mic: 5.2. Thou Bethl[ehem] Ephratah, little among the thousands of Judah, *non modo parva, sed parvula*, not only little but dimin[utive], little, so little, that 'twas not to be accounted one of a 1000d for the meannes of it, A sorry poor village; if it had not been for him that was born there, it had not deserved that Apostrophe the Prophet bestowes upon it, And thou Bethlehem – there 'twas he was made in the likenes of men. And there we must goe, not to the best house in

519 Cp. with Cosin's sermon for Epiphany 1621; Cosin, Vol 1, p. 9.

520 This should be 1.48.

Town, but a common Inne, and not to the best chamber, nay not to any chamber in the Inne, but to the stable, and to no choicer place in the stable, than the manger, there 'twas the world first saw made in the likenesse of men Luc. 2.7, where he had no hangings but cobwebs; no cradle, but a cribb, no attendancie but the poor dumb beasts;[521] And yet all this was of his own appoyntment and choice. Any [reason] why should he pitch upon Bethle[h]em to be born in? Fathers give these conjecturall reasons. 1. Bec[ause] Bethle[h]em was called the citty of David, and what fitter place for the son of David to be born in then the Citty of David?

2. Bethl[ehem], House of Bread; and what fitter place for him to be born in, who was the bread of life which came down from heaven, then the House of bread? 3. In a stable at Beth[lehem], a place for Beasts; to show unto us how that 1. Satan had gott such power over them that there was no room for him among men. 2. that men whom he came to save, were brutish in their understanding and like unto the beasts that perish.

And thus much of the 1st Degree of our Saviour's Humiliacion, that He would be made in the likenesse of men.[522]

2. Not only soe, but he became as the meanest of men, He took upon him the form of a servant. Form of a servant? Why, so he might take upon him the form of a glorified Angell, for they are servants, all ministering spirits, Heb: 2.14. And then what better are we for his humility? for he only redeemed that Nature which he assumed. Yea but to our comfort, the Apostle tells us that he was made in the likenes of men, he was made a little lower then the Angells, Heb. 2.7. Lower 1. in respect of Nature, bec[ause] he made him Man, so by nature mortall; 2. respect of Time, so to continue in that low condicion, but during his mortall life: So he took upon him the form of a servant in the likenesse, i.e. in the nature of men. And if we trace him from his cradle at Bethl[ehem] to his crosse at Golgotha, we shall find his whole life to have been but an hard Servitude.

2. Until the Age of 30 yeares he lived in great obscurity, the

---

521 This paragraph is very similar with text in 1615 Christmas Sermon. Andrewes, Vol. 1, pp. 157 –60.

522 Refer also to above sermon, p.160.

story of the gospell is silent concerning his condicion of life; yet dureing that time he lived in subjection. 1. to his Father to whom he was equal from all Eternity; he came to doe his will, Heb.10.9 and when he pray'd to be delivered from that sad hour of his Agony, 'twas in submission to his Father's will, Math: 26.39. And 2nd in subjection to his natural Parents, for he was subject unto them, Luc: 2.51. And the Heir differeth nothing from a servant so long as he is a child. Gal. 4. 1.

3. Servant in respect of Temptacions he was under; for if he had not been in the Form of a servant, the Tempter durst not have been so bold as to have put those questions to him, Math: 4.2. &c. And to have hurried him from one place to another, from the Wildernesse to a Pinnacle of the Temple; from a pinnacle of the Temple to an exceeding high Mountain; Here Darknes seemed to have gotten the upper hand of light;[523] He who dwelleth in that light, which no eye can approach unto, to be under the Powers of Darknes.

4. Servant in respect of all the crosses, miseries and afflictions of this life. He was so poor, that when the Foxes had holes, and the birds of the air had nests, the son of man, the saviour of the world had not where to lay his head, Luc: 9.58. And tho' he had some money in the bag, that was carried by his pursebearer, yet that was not enough to pay Caesar his Tribute, but he was forced to a miracle for it, Math. 17.27. How often was he in journeyings? in perills by his own Countrymen, in perills in the citty, perills in the wildernes, perills among false Brethren. In wearinesse and painfulnes, in watchings often, in hunger and thirst, in cold and nakednesse [2Cor: 11.26-7], so that he might say more truly then Jacob did, that the dayes of his pilgrimage were few and evill [Gen: 47.9].

5. Servant in respect of his own meniall servants; how did he rise from supper, not only to serve them, but to doe that most servile, the meanest office that might be, to wash their feet, Joh. 13.5.

Lastly, at his Death, he was not used only as a Servant but a bondslav. For Math: 26.15 Judas one of the 12, one that ate of

---

523 Cp. with Ms. 3708, p. 16.

his bread, nay one whom he had made steward of his house, yet this Judas sold him for thirty peices of silver (of our own money £3/15s), the exact price of a slave, Exod: 21.32. So that he who all his life time took upon him that form of a servant, was at his death bought and sold as a slave. Tho' he did many Miracles upon earth, yet this may seem to be the greatest miracle of all, that so great power of God could come wrapt up in so much infirmity of the flesh. And all this he did willingly, He made himself of [no reputation]. As God the Father from the beginning decreed this humility of his son, so the son hims[elf] was as 'twere of counsell against hims[elf] and conspired to his own humility. His Fathers will was so much his, as that I may say, his Father only did not forsake him, but he hims[elf] in a manner forsook hims[elf] for his willingness to be made of no reputacion, was such, that his passion which the Prophet call the Bruseing and travell of his soul, Esa: 53.11. He hims[elf] calls it but a Baptisme, Luc: 12.50. He came to his death, as to an holy dipping or washing something that would consecrate him; and to all his sufferings as to so many ceremonyes of honour.[524]

Indeed there are some Passages in scripture that seem to expresse a drawing back of our saviour, and a kind of Reluctancy to this great humility: but it we more warily consider them, they shew only a larg fear of the danger, not any close or dishonourable desire to avoyd any abasement or sharp encounter, Math. 26.37. 'tis said, he began to be sorrowful and very heavy; which words expresse a greatnesse, and weight of the danger with a just apphrension of it; not any dejection of spirit, but a solemn greif and sad oppression of it, such as may be seen in afflicted fortitude. And as for those few withdrawings and deliverys of hims[elf][525]- once from an intended stoneing Joh: 8.59, another time from a plotted precipitation, Luc: 4.29 these were not so much declineings of sufferings, as a reservacion of hims[elf] to a signall kind of death. And his very expireing at last, Joh: 19.30 was not of necessity but choice; for 'tis said, that he bowed the

---

524 Cp. with "His Passion, as He termeth it, a second baptism, a river of blood, and He even able to have been baptized in it, as He was in Jordan", in Good Friday Sermon for 1605. Andrewes, Vol. 2, p. 169.

525 Cp. with Ms. 3708, p.14 and Brightman, p. 212.

head and gave up the Ghost. Not bowing, bec[ause] he had given it up already, but bowing, because, he then would do it. None of the most innocent subjects that had sleep most at command, so slumbred when he would, as our saviour died, when he would, when 'twas his good pleasure so to doe. He expected that hour which could not compell him when it came; and he resigned his life, not to the law of humane nature, but to that deliberate and definite constitucion of God's eternall Decree and Order. So that his Father's foreknowledge and counsell asserted his birth and humility from casualty, His own Obedience, in making hims[elf] of no reputacion, exempted it from necessity; his expectacion of suffering freed it from immaturity; And his manner of suffering, not how, nor when his enimies would, but how and where and when hims[elf] pleased, vindicated it from the conquest of Malice. And thus his being made like unto men; his takeing upon him the form of a servant and being made of no reput[ation]: as they were foreknown and decreed, so obedient and voluntary. He made hims[elf of no reputation].

I shall conclude with this of the Apostle, Let the same mind [be in you, which was also in Christ Jesus, Phil. 2.5]. But alas! which of us will stoop a whit, or at all set our own to the sail for our brethrens sake? Nay if we be above them, neither then stoop so low, turn them out of house and home, suffer them to want and perish. Consider, if Christ had beene so unkind to us, we had ere thus perished in Hell. He disdained not to take on him, even the basest condicion of men, of a servant and for our sake to be poor; But how many of us with patience can bear our poverty? Doe we not often murmur and grudge against God as an unequall disposer of temporall Blessings. Do we not break out into intemperate language? Rather then we will want, we will steal, rather then starv, we will have out of the rich mans barnes; But know that unlesse Christ had been poor for thy sake, thou ere this had had thy portion with the Divell and his Angells. But

2ly, seeing our blessed Saviour came down from heaven, humbled hims[elf] so far as to make hims[elf] of no reput[ation] for us. Oh let not us swell with pride, but answer him with our humility. *Nunquam magis nomina facio quam cum dono.* (Seneca) I never oblige men more then by giveing. Who can swell under an obligacion? Who can withstand those everlasting burnings? [Is:

35.14] Who can rise up under that hand which is sealing his pardon? Who will not be his humble servant that will knock of his fetters, and set him at liberty? *Magus amoris amor*; love is the loadstone to draw on love,[526] even that love, which is the mother of Humility. And therefore we shall find that all the saints of God have ever bowed thems[elves] under the hand that raised them up; have been humbled with favours, never lower then when they have been in the 3rd heaven, bended most when they have been laden with benefits, like eares of corn in harvest, full and hanging down the head. And he that shall set hims[elf] seriously to this Christian exercise of humbling hims[elf] under God's mercys, shall certainly find the force and omnipotency of this vertue, and what wonder it can work in his soul. It is (saith the devout Schoolman) the most potent monarchie in the world, makeing us rich, by makeing us poor, makeing us strong, by makeing us weak, makeing us kings by makeing us servants, makeing us wise by makeing us fools, giveing up all things by leaving us nothing, laying us at Gods foot that we may sit in his bosome.

To conclude, let us rouze up our souls to a cheerfull retribucion of thanks. Let us offer up ourselves, our soules and our bodyes as a continual sacrifice of thanksgiveing unto him who hath done so great things for us, for our bodyes, our soules, Redeemed them from the Pit of Hell, from that brimstone and those scorchings which are kindled for the Divel and his Angells. What shall we render unto the Lord? [Ps: 116.12] Why, bec[ause] we are brought with a price [1Cor. 6.20], let us glorify him in our bodyes and in our spirits which are his. This should be our constant and continued practice here on earth, to stand as candidates for an Angel's place by glorifying God here in our earthly members, which is *προοίμιον μελλούσης ξωής*, a Prologue and Preface to that which we shall be and art hereafter. It was a phantasie which possessed many of the Heathen, that men after death should much desire and often handle those things which did most take and affect them when they lived. So Lucian bringeth in Priam's young son calling for milk and cheese and such country eates, which he most delighted in on

526 This is also quoted in the Lenten Sermon for the Fifth Sunday in April, 1596. Andrewes, Vol. 2, p. 99. Refer also to P.C.D., p. 109 and M.L.E., p. 39.

earth.[527] Even now (saith Maximus Tyrius)[528] doth Æsculapius[529] minister physick; Hercules[530] try the strength of his Arm, Castor and Pollux[531] are under sail, Minos[532] is on the bench and Achilles[533] in Armes.

This was but a phantasie, but a fiction: but 'tis is fair resemblance of a Christian in this respect, whose span is but a prologue to Eternity, a short and imperfect declaracion of that which he shall act more perfectly hereafter; whose life is grace, and whose Eternity shall be in glory, which is nothing else (saith a pious Author) but *gratia consummata nulla tenus impedita.* Grace made perfect and consumate, finding no opposicion, no temptacion to struggle and fight within. For tho' there will be no place for Almes, where there is no poverty, no use of prayers, where there is no want, nor need of patience where there can be no injury. Yet to praise and glorifie God are everlasting offices, tribute due to God's Power and goodnesse and wisedome which are as everlasting as hims[elf] to be

527 The youngest son of Priam was Polydorus who according to Euripides was sent with much gold for safe keeping by his mother, Hecuba to the Thracian king, Polymesta. At the end of the Trojan War the Thracian king aligned himself with the victorious Greeks and murdered Polydorus, mainly for his gold. Aeneas recalled how he discovered his grave shortly after he fled Troy. Virgill, *Aeneid*, Bk. 3.1.1.

528 This is probably Maximus of Tyre, philosopher and orator, who lived in the 2nd C. A.D. He is the author of 41 extant *Dialexeis* delivered in Rome in the time of Commodus. These presented philosophical themes, with an eye to their ethical implications. He frequently quoted from Homer and Plato.

529 He is a legendary physician and in Greek mythology the god of medicine. His healing cult became popular in Rome on Tiber Island in the 3rd century B. C.

530 He is the Roman equivalent of Heracles, the greatest of the Greek heroes. Many legends arose very early of his feats such as the killing of the Nemean lion, the captures of the stag of Cerynea and the mad bull of Minos. From the 6th C. B. C. he is worshipped as a god, especially at shrines such as Thasos. He probably is the earliest foreign god and cult to be received in Rome and was worshipped at the Ara Maxime.

531 These two in classical mythology were twins noted for their devotions to one anotherand were famous warriors. They are patrons of mariners.

532 He is perhaps an historical figure, but best known in Greek mythology who imprisoned Daedalus and Icarus on Crete.

533 Achilles was the hero at Troy by killing Hector, but he himself died when wounded in his ankle by Paris, the only vulnerable part of his body after his mother Thetis had held him by the ankles to bathe him in the river Styx to make him immortal.

rendered him here on earth in our spirits and in our bodyes and to be continued by us with Angells and Archangells in the highest heavens for Evermore. Amen.

SERMON TWO

AT EASTER

Introduction

This sermon was probably preached at Easter 1589. Victory is its theme but from the opening and other innuendoes it is not only Christ's victory over the cross but also England's victory over the Armada in the summer of 1588. If the Spanish attack had been successful the Reformed Church would have ended almost as soon as it had begun, stated Andrewes. So whenever he reiterated Christ's victory throughout the sermon, there is also the underlying sense of victory over Phillip II and thanksgiving of being freed from the tyranny of Roman Catholic Spain. Christ's victory gives us "our freedom" in His death and resurrection. He not only freed us "from the power of the grave" but also raises our bodies "to immortality". "He who had his *perigæum*, was brought low, very low, as low as Hell, had also his *apogæum*, rose again from the dead." By trampling down death He has enabled all to triumph over the grave. Christ died for the dead as well as the living, and as Andrewes indicated later to Cardinal Perron, for the unborn too.[534] Easter day therefore can be regarded as the birthday for all Christians as it marks the beginning of a new life, eternal life in Christ, and the assurance of the resurrection of our bodies.

When teaching on Christ's death, Andrewes stressed how important it was to believe that it was not only Christ's humanity that suffered at Calvary but also His divinity. Not to believe this

534 Ms. 3707, p. 148; Andrewes, Vol. 11, p. 20.

was to be guilty of the Socinian heresy. So he painstakingly indicated that He who died on the cross is the Son of God. "For tho' He died and His body was truly severed from His soul, yet His Divinity still remained unseparated from His body, and soul, so near and inseparable was that hypostacicall union." Once again he emphasised that Christ's death and resurrection are but the expression of His infinite love, compassion and mercy for us; "His sorrowes and sufferings, victory and triumph [were for] the good of us men and for our salvation." Indeed all was accomplished in union with the Father and the Spirit to make "a true Pascha".[535]

Although Good Friday wrought our redemption it did not assure us of eternal life. This was only achieved when Christ broke the bonds of the grave, which had been prefigured in Jonah, Daniel, Moses and Samuel. The Resurrection is "the stock which extends to almost every branch of Christianity" as it is the ground for our faith, salvation and justification. Without it we are all utterly lost, and therefore the Resurrection must be regarded as our comfort and as such should be worthy of constant meditation, stated Andrewes.[536]

Hence he suggested one way of meditating on Christ's Resurrection was to observe the fields and gardens at Easter time. Here new life is shooting up from the deadened earth. It is also seen in some creatures like the silkworms whose bodies are transformed. It could also be gathered by reflecting on some Old Testament figures such as Abraham, Enoch, David, and Job who had faith in a Saviour. Quoting St. Jerome, Andrewes declared that none had spoken more clearly of Christ's Resurrection than Job. So it is not surprising that those immortal words of Job, "For I know that my Redeemer liveth, and that He shall stand at the latter day upon the earth", featured as a text for another of his Paschal sermons in 1610 at Court.[537]

Once again this divine warned against those sins, which would make it difficult to share in Christ's triumph. Although Christ's gift at Easter is freely offered there were many whose sins

---

535 Ms. 3707, pp. 145, 148.

536 Ibid., p. 147.

537 Ibid., p. 149; Andrewes, Vol. 2, pp. 252-69.

of pride and vanity made it difficult for them to accept this free and blessed gift. These, Andrewes believed, preferred to rely on what they considered were their own sufficiencies rather than to accept this gift of grace from God. They even regarded themselves in a pharisaic way, as being holier and better than others. And so they glory in those things that we have received *gratis.* Andrewes advised that we shall never "trust in" Him until we "distrust ourselves".[538]

This led to Andrewes' next point, good works. He warned against seeing these as being an alternative to faith, when in fact they went hand in hand. They are the expression of faith and their fruits are from grace. Although by "our good workes ... we cannot deserv heaven, yet they qualify us for admittance thither." Nevertheless they must not be seen as meritorous and winning heaven as "even our best workes ... have a tincture of sin adhereing to them." It was also important that these good works glorify God as he stressed in a sermon in St. Giles in 1598 in which he admonished those who flounced their good works to seek their own praises and glory rather than to honour God and to be an example for others to imitate. He also censured those who decried good works by referring them to the parable of the tares and wheat when the former should not be separated from the latter until harvest time. His view on faith and good works was succinctly expressed in the twilight of his life. Good Friday is the day to bring death for sin, but "Easter to bring good works from the dead". Thus faith without works "is not imperfect, but stark dead." [539]

When preaching on the resurrection of our bodies, he touched on another of his favourite teachings throughout his life. The body as well as the soul must have its part in worship. "'Tis the soul that worships God, but 'tis the Body that lifts up the eye and bowes the knee to him." Both must be offered to God as he was to repeat in his Paschal Sermon in 1614 and in the Nativity Sermon in 1622 and as he had in his Seventh Sermon on the Temptation.[540]

---

538 Ms. 3707, p. 146.

539 Ibid; *Apos Sacra*, pp. 522-8; Andrewes, Vol. 3, pp. 83, 94.

540 Ibid., Vol. 1, pp. 262 – 3, Vol. 2, p.333, Vol. 5, pp. 554 – 5.

1Cor 15.27. But thanks be to God who giveth us the victory, through our Lord Jesus Christ.

In times of distraction, warrs and fightings when we have to doe with subtle and powerfull enimies, what better newes, then newes of a victory and that victory absolute, and that over no ordinary, but potent enimies, such as flesh and blood could not encounter with. So give me leave to bespeak you, as the Angells did the Sheapherds, Luc: 2.9 Be not afraid, for behold here are tideings of great joy, of a glorious Triumph, and a victory for that Triumph, and that victory on your side, for unto you is risen a saviour who is Christ the lord. He who had his *perigæum*, was brought low, very low, as low as Hell, had also his *apogæum*, rose again from the dead; with his own right hand, and with his holy Arm got hims[elf] and us the victory. He hath loosed the paines, and shaken off the fetters of Death and to our endles comfort hath put our enimies, sin and Satan, and the Grave to an utter and perpetuall foil. Death indeed for two dayes had power over him, He was cutt off out of the land of the living [Is: 53.8]; and by that blow the strongest constitucion of Religion was shaken, Christianity at an end, as soon as begun. This we may see in his Disciples, poor men, their faith was as weake as their fortunes; they remembred not what was often foretold, but were as apt to forget their Master's words as to forsake his Person. Their former *Tu es filius Dei* [the Saviour of the world], is comed now to an *ἠλπίζαμεν*,[541]we did hope that this had been He that should have redeemed Israel, Luc: 24.21.[542] And for the officious Matrons that prepared spices and oyntments after his buriall, their odors smell stronger of a funerall than a resurrection; the grave had devoured him; and for ought they knew, might have digested him;[543] they came to the sepulchre, not to see whether he were risen or no, but on purpose to imbalm him, Luc: 24.1 where instead of his body, they meet with an Angell, who encounters with their unbeleeveing thoughts, and

541 This text is repeated in Sermon Six.

542 Cp. with Easter Sermon for 1616 with its emphasis on hope, especially. "And who is he, that we might hope in him? That is *Jesus Christus spes nostra.*" Andrewes, Vol. 2, p. 375.

543 This idea also appears in the Sermon for Easter Day 1615, ibid., p. 357.

tells them that he is not there, but he is risen, according as he told them in Gailee. Tho' he was taken by wicked hands, crucified and slain [Acts 2.3.], yet he rose again the 3rd day; and by his riseing justified hims[elf] against death in sin and against death for sin, and so purchased for us, the 1st and 2nd Resurrection.

This Day then is both our saviour Christs and the Christian's birthe's day, for we are all begotten againe unto a lively hope, by the Resurrection of Jesus Christ from the dead, 1Pet: 1.3. Take away the day of his Resurrection, and the day of his Nativity and Passion are gone, yea and we are gone too, for if Christ be not risen, then is our faith vain, we are yet in our sins, [1Cor. 15] v.17. But St. Peter tells us of an *οὐ δυνατὸν κρατεῖσθαι*, Act: 2.24; that it was not possible that he should be holden of the paines of death. The Earth had swallowed such a morsell, as shee could not digest; and therefore David Ps. 114.6.[544] *ὠδινήσατο*, the earth travailed with him in her womb, was in pangs of pain and trouble, or (as others) cast into a fit of a shakeing Ague till shee was deliver'd of such a burthen. The sun in the Firmanent hid his face and hung all the world in mourning [Luc: 23.45]; the earth trembled, yea the very foundations shook and were moved, the whole frame of Nature was troubled to see the sufferings of the God of Nature.[545] The Divells roared, the graves opened [Math: 27.51-2]. Death threw down her weapons as vanquished, and he who was nailed to the crosse, the scorn and derision of Passengers, He who was imprisoned in the house of Death for 3 dayes and 3 nights broke from the prison of the Grave, shooke off the bands of Death, not only for hims[elf] but for us too; for now since his conquest, Death hath lost her terror, force and strength, nor shall the Grave hereafter be able to hold any of us, but every faithfull soul, may insult over Death and the grave and (with St.Paul) sing this *ἐπινίκιον*, O Death, where is [thy sting, O gave, where is thy victory], But thanks [be to God who giveth us the victory through our Lord Jesus Christ].

In the Text we have these 2 generall Partes, 1st a Benefit re-

---

544 A better reference is Psalm 147.17.

545 A similar description of nature in sympathy is found in the 1615 Paschal Sermon, Andrewes, Vol. 2, p. 356; and in the Passions Sermons for 1604 and 1605, Ibid., pp. 155, 173.

ceived Victory. 2. Duty to be returned, Thankfullnes. In the former generall we have observable

1. Author or donor of the Benefit, God.

2. Manner of it's conveyance, not by way of merits, but gift, thanks [be to] God who Giveth [us the victory].

3. Meanes of conveyance, Our Lord Jesus Christ.

4. Persons to whom 'tis conveyed, *Nobis*.

5. Benefit which is made to us, *νῖκος* and victory.

1. And who more fit to give us this victory, then he who is the giver of all victory, *Deus exercitum*. And therefore 1st He is able to doe it, for he can raise an Army with a word of his mouth, and that of vile despicable creatures, of locusts, caterpillars, cankerw[orms] and that a great, potent Army for so he is pleased to call it, Joel: 2.25. He did once make the cloudes his magasine and slew more with hailstones, then Joshuah and all Israel with the sword Josh: 10.11. When Gideon's army of 32000 were brought to 300 and that handfull to encounter with a very numerous army, which were like Grasshoppers for multitude [Jud: 7:12]; the Trumpetts cried before the Battell, the sword of the Lord and of Gideon, Jud: 7.20. 'twas the former that made the latter victorious by causing the Midianites to set every man's sword against his fellow, and so to become their own executioners. This God is he who can tear mountains with his voice, shake whole kingdomes with one breath, before whose presence all the Inhabitants of the earth are but as many grasshoppers [Is: 40.22], all Nacions of the world as the dropp of a Bucket Esa. 40.15. This is He, who by raising up his son from the Dead, hath given us this victory. Rabbins have a saying, that God hath 4 keyes which he delivers, neither to Angell nor Seraphin: Key of Raine, of Pestilence, Wombe, [and] Grave; these he keepes alwayes in his own immediate custody: so 'tis he alone that killeth and maketh alive, that bringeth down to the grave and bringeth up, 1Sam: 2.6. Yea, that bringeth down the Grave, that burieth the Sepulchre, and puts death itself to Death for so he promised, or rather threatned by his Prophet Hos: 13.14. O death! I will be thy death, O Grave I will be thy destruction. And what he promised, he hath punctually performed, all things are truly comed to passe, in the New Testament which were foretold in the old. St. Paul seemes to be no other then the prophet Hosea in his Formalities, haveing taken a degree in the Science of Christianity, who tells

us, that God hath raised up the lord Jesus and by him brought life [and immortality to light through the gospel] 2Tim: 1.10, not only life but immortality, such life as shall never be extinguished by death. 2nd, As God was able to give us the victory: so he was willing also, for He is a Father to us 1Pet: 1.3. Blessed be God who according to his abundant mercy, hath begotten us againe, in the first Adam he begot us to the enjoynment of this, in the 2nd he begot us againe, to the hope of a better life. And how did he this? of his own good will he begat us, Jam: 1.18. There was no motive, in us to occasion such as blessing, and therefore (Apostle) according to his abundant mercys he [hath begotten us again unto a lively hope], no one single mercy would serv the turn; for many defects were removed, many sins to be forgiven, many perfections to be attained, and therefore according to his manifold mercyes[546] [hath begotten us again unto a lively hope 1Pet1.3]. And God loved the world (Saviour) and what could he see in the world worth loveing? nothing but a world of sin to be seen; yea, the sin of the world was so great in St. John's time, that it was greater then the world, for the whole world liveth in wickednesse, 1John 5.19. So whatsoever God did for us he did it out of meer mercy and compassion, out of the bowells of a Father. And therefore Blessed be God (1Peter [1.3]). Thanks be to God (St. Paul) that [giveth us the victory. 1Cor:15.27]. And how did he give the victory? In that he raised up the Lord Jesus the 3rd day and shewed him openly, Acts. 10.40.

But stay, He raised [up the Lord Jesus], did not our Lord hims[elf] say that he hims[elf] would do it. Joh: 2.19, Destroy this [temple, and in three days I will raise it up], but when 'twas comed to doing, was he too weak to perform it? had he need of an help to doe it? Here the Socinian[547] desires no more to ground

546 This text is identical to that in Easter Sermon for 1616. Ibid., pp. 370 - 1.

547 A sect founded by Laelius and Faustus Socinus, two Italian theologians of the 16th C. There were eight principles that Socinians believed. 1. Scripture only is the source of truth. 2. The way of salvation was through knowledge and an holy life. 3. Knowledge of God, that He is the Supreme Lord of all things, but He is not a Trinitarian God. 4. Christ by His life and resurrection was raised to divine power. 5. The prophetic office of Christ. 6. The kingship of Christ. 7. The priesthood of Christ. 8. The church consisted of those who upheld these saving doctrines. Andrewes makes reference to to this heresy in other sermons. For example in 1615 Paschal Sermon. Ibid., p. 353.

his Heresy upon, to deny his Godhead, to find him worse then his word. But we are to know that he was not unable to doe it. He raised hims[elf] and he was raised too. For 1st if he was raised by the Father he raised hims[elf]: those two Persons make but one and the same God, Joh.:10.30. I and the Father are one, ἓν ἐσμέν, and whatsoever things the Father doth, these doth the son likewise, Joh:5.19. So if the Father raised him up the 3rd day, then the son also raised himself ἐγερῶ, I will [raise it up], (saviour) yet not so I, as if he meant it exclusively to the Father and the holy Spirit; for the sonne as he is God is one and the same with them both. Now this was a work of the Diety, and that *ad extra, et opera Trinitatis ad extra* [*sunt indivisa*]. But 1. Whether his Divinity raised his humanity, still he raised hims[elf] for those two Natures make but one person, one θεάνθρωπος, who had power to lay down [his life that he might take it up again], Joh. 10.17. The expression there is worth our observacion, I lay down [my life]. Now what we pay is due debt, what we lay downe is but a pledge, and may be taken up again at our pleasure. So at the conclusion of his passion when he cryed out, 'tis finished, and so gave up the Ghost, He gave not up the power of reuniteing his body and soul together againe; for tho' he dyed, and his body was truly severed from his soul, yet his Divinity still remained unseparated from his body, and his soul, so near and inseparable was that hypostacicall union, that even death could not unloose it; against the son of Mary it might have full power, but not against the saviour of the world; for a time it might destroy the man, but not the Mediatour; for so he still lived, even while the grave enclosed him, *vitâ Personae*, tho' not naturall. That ejaculacion which dropt from him in the extremity of his pangs, My God [why hast thou forsaken me, Math: 27.46] is not so to be understood, as if his God-head had forsaken him, But (as Master of sentences)[548] *tum se foris separavit Divinitas ut non adesset ad desensionem, sed intus non desuit ad unionem*; His godhead did then and ever accompany his manhood, but 'twas not always an helper, it never ceased to be present with our saviour, tho' it did not them aid him. Yesterday, the other day, and to day, on the crosse, in the grave, and at the resurrection, God was with

548 i.e.Peter Lombard.

him, God the Father for him God raised up the 3rd day; God the sonne, for as he suffered, so he rose again the 3rd day according to the scripture; and God the holy Ghost, for he hath an influence also upon the Resurrection. Ps: 104.30; when thou lettest thy spirit goe forth, thou shalt renew the face of the earth; All the 3 Persons joyned to make our Resurrection a true Pascha, a passage over from the Ægypt of this world to the land of promise.[549] And this they did for us, who had neither power, nor purity, nor perfection to work out our own recovery; to move compassion, much lesse to deserve or challenge it. No 'twas God's free bounty and goodnesse that conferred this benefit upon us; which leads to the 2nd Particular, the manner of conveyance, not by way of Merit, but deedy Gifts. Thanks [be to God that giveth us the victory through our Lord Jesus Christ].

2nd par[ticular]. But there is such an immoderate swelling, such a secret itching humour of vanity, wherewith men are generally possessed, that they will not accept of this benefit, by way of Gift, but of Merit and reward. Pride is a vice, which cleaveth so fast unto the hearts of men, that if we were to strip ourselves of all faultes, one by one, we should undoubtedly find that the very last and hardest to put of[f].[550] And therefore how doe we repine and quarrell, when anything falls out amisse to us, as if we had not deserved it; and how doe we undervalue and lessen Gods blessings as if they were not so much, or at least not more then we deserv. There was somewhat of this tympany in Our Lord's own disciples; Master (Peter) we have forsaken all [and followed thee]; what shall we have therefor? Math: 19.27. And I desire (Mother of Zebed[ees]) that these my 2 sonnes [may sit, the one on thy hand, and the other on the left, in thy kingdom], Math: 20.21. The Psalmist tells us that we are but dust; and how hard is it to keep down the wind of Pride from blowing up our dust! [Ps: 103.14]. If there be anything in us that makes us look better then our brethren, then presently we cry with those in the Prophet, Esa: 65.5 stand by thy selfe, come not near to me; for I am holier than thou. And so

549 Andrewes devoted a whole sermon at Easter 1612 on the "true Pascha". Andrewes Vol. 2, pp.290 - 308

550 Cp. with a similar view expressed by Hooker in his sermon on *The Nature of Pride*, Sermon III, Pt. 1.

we glory of those things which we have received *gratis* as tho' we had not received them. Who was it that made thee differ from another? Was it not thy Maker? Before thou had hadst a being, there could be nothing to move him to give thee a being but his own good pleasure. And ever since thou hadst a being, do but examine thy demeanour towards him, and thou wilt find nothing whereby thou canst any way oblige him. No alas! The best Saint in heaven must say with St. Paul, By the grace of God [I am what I am]; By grace you are saved through [faith; and that not of yourselves; it is the gift of God], Eph: 2.8. And as 'twere on purpose to confute all those who will be medling, and have an hand in the work of their salvacion, he adds v[erse] 9, Not of works, [lest any man should boast]. And again Rom: 11.6, If by grace, then 'tis no more of works, otherwise grace is no more grace. As for our workes, even our best works, do what we can they will have a tincture of sin adhereing to them; for there is not a just man upon earth that doth good [and sinneth not], Eccl: 7.20. So if we should receive according to our works we could expect no other wages but those of sin, eternall death, Rom: 6. ῶ [551]

Meritum meum miseratio Domini, (Augustine), my merit is God's mercy, and as long as he is rich in Mercy's, I cannot be poor in merits. Tho' the Heathens flattered thems[elves] with their *spendida peccata,* and out of love to their own deservings, called all their vertues ἕζεις, habitts, Qualities acquired by their own paines, care, industry; yet in the Gospell we find all Christian Graces termed by the names of δόσεις and χαρίσματα, gifts, which come down from the father of lights,[552] *Nunquam satis Christo confidemus nisi, de nobis penitus diffisi, nunquam in ipso nos satis solabimur, nisi in nobis, desolati simus,* we shall never truly trust in Christ; unles we altogether distrust ourselves, never receive sufficient comfort from him while we are of opinion we can have any from ourselves.

But here it may be demanded then, *cui bono*? To what end are good workes and dutyes of new obedience so strictly enjoyned? and why should we take any pains to suppresse the incursions and riseings of sin, and Christ good motions of piety and devo-

---

551 i.e. the last verse, v. 23.

552 This idea is also in the Second Sermon on Prayer, Andrewes, Vol. 5, p. 312.

cion? *Quis virtutem amplectitur;* take away all rewards, and all vertue and goodnesse will be neglected. In answer to this, we say, 1st That Good works are necessary, but not meritorious, 'tis our duty to be fruitfull in them, God commands and wee must obey, and this is the end of our Redemption, to serv [him day and night, Rev. 7.15], but when we have done all, we [are] unprofitable servants, [Luk: 17.10]. Yet 2ly we shall be rewarded if we continue in [them, Rom: 11.22]. Rev. 2.10, Be thou [faithful unto death, and I will give thee a crown of life]. But we are to know, 'tis his promise that engageth him, not our performances; He should be unjust, if he should not recompence the obedience of his servants, bec[ause] he hath promised so to doe, yet if he should look with a severe and observant eye, upon our most pious endeavours, and perfect obedience, as they proceed from us, he might find enough in them eternally to condemne us, for our righteousnes are [as filthy rags], Esa. 64.6. 3ly, Tho' by our good workes we cannot deserv heaven, yet they qualify us for admittance thither. For tho' God be very free and bountifull in bestowing his gifts, and gives farre more then we can deserv or desire; yet he is not prodigall, bestows them not promiscuously, without respecting who and what those men be that partake of his favours; the lewd, careles, licencious person, shall not have the same usage, with the sober vigilant pious soul. Every mansion in God['s] Kingdome shall be given to them only, for whom 'tis prepared [Joh: 14.2]; and who those be our Saviour tells us [in] Math. 25.34, Come ye Blessed of my Father, [inherit the kingdom prepared for you], for I was an hungry, [and ye gave me meat; I was thirsty, and ye gave me drink; I was a stranger, and ye took me in]; where he sheweth 1. that they are blessed, who are partakers of God's kingdome 2. what manner of persons they be for whom that kingdome is prepared, such as have faithfully served him by workes of mercy and dutyes of an holy life. So you see we must be carefull of our lives, conscientious in our wayes, perform good workes we must, but rely on them we must not; for when we have done all we can, we have not done so well as we should [Luk: 17.10] our Duty. That common saying of the Father is true, *Sunt* --- good deades may be the way to overcome our enimyes but they are not the cause of our victory, that we have only by our Mediatour. And so we pass to the 3rd particular, the meanes of Conveyance. Our Lord Jesus Christ, Thanks [be to God who giveth us the victory].

3rd par[ticular. Christ Jesus is the meanes by which are conveyed unto us all his Father's Mercys; and therefore after we have layd open our wants in our Prayers, we conclude all with this clause, Through [Jesus Christ our Lord] being confident that when we goe to him, in that name, he will both heare our desires and graunt our requests. He who is equall to the Father hath told us so; Joh: 15.16, Whatsoever ye [shall ask of the Father in my name, he may give it you]. Looke upon every Blessing God bestows upon thee, spirituall or temporall; and look again whose image and superscription it beares, and unlesse you hast it in and for Christ, tis but imaginary, not so much a reall blessing, as an illusory shadow, for God conveyes hims[elf] no[t] otherwise to us, but by him; of him and through him; and to him are all things, Rom: 11.36. So thanks be to God [who hath given us the victory, through our Lord Jesus Christ.]

The victory here principally meant is our freedome from the power of corruption, from rotting for ever in the Grave, and that is accomplished by our saviour's Resurrection, as the Apostle setts hims[elf] to prove clear through this chapter so that in vain may we hope to rise from death, unles he be risen; the proofe of that then must be of great moment, and nearly concernes us; for our saviours Resurrection is the stock which extends it self to almost every branch of Christianity. 1. on this our faith is grounded, [1Cor. 15.]14, If Christ be not risen then is our faith vain; 2. on this stock is engrafted the pardon of sins, v. 17, if Christ be not raised, ye are yet in your sins. 3. on this depends our justificacion, he died for our sins and rose again for our justificacion, Rom. 4. ῶ.[553] So if no Resurrection, no faith; if no faith, no pardon of sins, if no pardon of sins, no justificacion; if no justificacion, no salvation: So if no Resurrection, we are utterly lost, we have hope only in this life [1Cor: 15.19], and so [no eternal life]. But Christ is risen from the Dead, that is our comfort, a point requisite to be known, and worthy our meditacion. And to this end the holy Ghost hath prefigured it to us under types and shadowes, especially that of Jonah

553 i.e. the last verse, v. 25.

from the belly of the whale [Jonah 2.10], the deliverance of Daniel from the lion's Den [Dan: 7.10]; the drawing of Moses out of his cabinet of Rushes [Ex: 2.5], Samson's carrying away the gates of Gaza [Judges 16. 29], these (as interpretors) did prefigure his escape and return from Death, to be a deliverer of his People, and his leading captive Hell and the Grave. 2. We have many prophesies long before his Incarnacion, foretelling his resurrection; that by the Prophet, David. Ps. 16.11,[554] Thou shalt not [leave my soul in hell: neither shalt thou suffer thy Holy One to see corruption], and what David foretold was punctually and so a title fullfilled. The old Fathers, who lived before that fullnesse of time, in which he came in the flesh, dyed in this faith; they waited for the *Messias*, they looked for and relyed upon the promised seed. Our Saviour speakes of the times as high as Abraham, Joh: 8.56. And the Apostle Jude speakes higher of him, that Enoch the 7th, from Adam prophesied of this, [the Lord cometh with ten thousands of his saints] Jude v.14. And therefore certainly he was acquainted with the promise of Christ Jesus to redeeme the world which administers one strong refutacion of the Racovian Heresy;[555] for if Christ who was manifested in our nature, in the latter end of the world, was the redeemer of those who lived in the first ages of the world, then he was not a Saviour only (as they affirm) by his word and doctrine, or by the example of his life, sufferings and resurrection, but by his sacrifice and satisfaction; for how could either the personall teachings or example of Christ, reach to, or be conveyed up to them who lived so long before him? But that which is most remarkable, is that this light should shine so clear in the land of UZ, that Job a gentile should see it so clearly; for *nemo tam aperte de Resurrectione post Christiani, quam iste ipse hic ante Christiani* (Jerome) no man since Christ's time did ever speake so clearly of Christ's resurrection and his own, as Job here before his comeing; the Apostles did not apprehend it more evidently by the eye of sense, than he did by the eye of faith,[556] Job. 19.25, I know [that my

554 In the Authorized Version this 16. 10.

555 This takes it name from where the Socian Catechism was first published in Racov, Poland, 1605. A Latin version was sent to James 1 who had it publicly burnt in 1614. For more details refer to *Oxford Dictionary*, p. 1361.

556 This text reappears in 1610 Paschal Sermon with the same quotations from Jer-

redeemer liveth], my judgment is fixed, my faith is confirmed in this thing; 'tis as clear to me that my Redeemer liveth as if I had already seen him alive. 'Tis as sure to me that I shall rise again, as if I had been dead and were already risen, my faith makes this as evident to me now, as my experience shall hereafter. 3. We might produce same eye-witnesses of this truth, such as did eat, and drink with him after he was risen; such as were chosen purposely to testifye his riseing, a cloud of witnesses [Heb: 12.1], more than five hundred brethren at once [1Cor: 15.6]. 4. An Angell from heaven sent down to wait upon him at his rising, Math. 28.6. Lastly, his adversaries the Jewes,[557] who were not more sollicitious to conceal, then labourious to hinder a resurrection, they afford us some arguments to prove it. After they had crucified him and Joseph buried him, they set a watch, and they seal the sepulchre and suborn the souldiers to say, that he was not risen, but stollen away [Math: 27.28]. And so endeavouring to abuse the work with a lye; they confirm his resurrection. For let them be at charge to bribe the watchmen, and let the watchmen sleep so soundly that an earthquake cannot wake them, and then say his disciples stole him away, this poor shift is so far from shakeing it, it confirmeth our faith. For if they were asleep, how could they tell his disciples stole him away? Or if they did steale him, what could they take away? or if they did steale him, what could they take away more than a carcase?[558] He is risen, he is not here [Math.28.6]: if the Angel had not said it, yet the earthquake, the clothes, the grave itselfe did speake without an Epitaph; or if these were silent, yet where such strange impossibility's are brought in to colour and promote it, a lye, doth confute itselfe, and malice helpeth to confirme the truth. So being confidently assured of it we may say, thanks be to God [who giveth us the victory through our Lord Jesus Christ].

But stay, was not this victory got by his death and Passion? was not our Redemption compleately wrought upon the Crosse when he cryed out *consummatum est*, all [is accomplished Joh: 19.30]. 'Tis true we were reconciled by his death, but much more by his life,

---

ome. Andrewes, Vol. 2, p. 253.

557 Sermon Six repeats the slanderous work of the Jews towards Christ's death.

558 This reappears in Easter Sermon for 1608, Andrewes, Vol. 2, p. 234.

Rom.5.10. We were set at liberty by his death, the ransome was payd, the handwriting called in, and cancelled [Col: 2.14], but we had received no acquittance, captivity was not led captive [Eph: 4.8], till his resurrection. By that he did show hims[elf] to be lord Paramount, to have subdued death, for ever; and therefore when he rose, he brought not his grave-clothes out with him, as Lazarous did Joh: 11.44 but left them behind, as haveing no occasion to use them again, death haveing no more dominion over him; Or he left them for us to lye down in, to sleep awhile, and to rise us again, and reign with him; for his victory and Triumph belongs to us too; that's the next particular, Persons to whom this victory conveyed, *Nobis*. Thanks [be to God who giveth us victory through our Lord Jesus Christ].

4th par[ticular]. Indeed this was the end he aimed at in all his sorrowes and sufferings, victory and Triumph, the good of us men and for our Salvacion. His thirsting on the crosse was not for water, he is the well of life, but for man's Redemption; his riseing from the dead, was not for hims[elf]: for so there was no more need of taking us his life, then of laying it down; but 'twas for us men, that we might be freed from the power of the grave. If he our head be risen, then shall we his members rise alsoe; the Apostle takes it for an infallible consequence, and therefore joynes them both together as things of like certainty Rom: 8.11.

In further prosecution of this, we shall show 1.τὸ ὅτι that there shall and may be a Resurrection. 2. That the same body which is turned to Dust, shall be raised again, 3. that tho' it be the same for substance, yet much differing in Qualityes.

1. 'Twas the Apostle's Demaund to Agrippa Act: 26.8. Why should it be thought a thing incredible that God should raise the dead? It implies no contradiction, there is no impossibility in it, 'tis as easy for God to give life unto a dead body, as in the beginning to give that body a being out of nothing. For confirmacion of this, let us 1. hear what God sayes to us out of his word, 2. what he speakes to us out of his works.

1. Exod. 3.6. I am the God of Abrah[am], Isaac, Jacob and obs[erve] how our Saviour applyes this Text to prove a Resurrection. Math: 22.32. God is not God of [the] <u>dead</u> but the Liveing, yea, but how may the Argument be made good out of this place? Abraham, [Isaac and Jacob] are long since dead and buried. Yet

thus: God is said to be the God of Abraham, [Isaac and Jacob] after a more speciall and peculiar manner. And if we look upon them only in this life, they had their share of sorrowes and sufferings, nay a larger share than the wicked of this world; they had no settled habitacions, but were forced to sojourn, sometimes in one country, sometimes in another. Jacob gives an accompt to Pharaoh that the dayes [of the years of my pilgrimage were few and evill [Gen. 47. 9].[559] Now wherein was God, more the God of Abraham and Isaac [and Jacob] than of Pharaoh or Abimleth? if an eye be had to the things of this life; nay he may seem rather in an especiall manner to be the God of the latter than the former. And therefore[e] the difference not being in this life, it must needs follow, that there is another, and they could not be capable of any blessednesse in another life, if they should be kept continually under the power of death; it followes therefore again, that there must be a Resurrection that they must be restored to life, that God may show hims[elf] in an especiall manner, the God not of the dead but of the liveing. So Joh: 5. 28, 29. The hour is comeing, in which all that are in their [graves shall hear his voice]. Hour now is comeing, we know not how nigh; in the which all that are in their <u>graves</u>; not only such as ly[e] dead in their beds or coffins, but in their graves; not only such as have been there 3 dayes as Lazarous was, but 3,000 yeares, all that are any where in their graves, shall heare his voice, come forth and find a Resurrection.

2. Let us hear what God sayes to us concerning this point out of his works. Through the whole frame of Nature, especially this time of the yeare, what more visible then a Resurrection? when you goe into the your gardens you may learn this lesson from herbes and flowers: how do they decay and dye, and rise again and flourish? walk into the fields, see how the same corn that lay dead under the clod, sprouts forth, 1st the blade, then the ear, after that full corn [Mark 4.28].[560] Now say within thy self, if my withered flowers, if my dead corn find a Resurrection, then why not my dead body?[561] Again, looke higher, the Heavens declare [the

559 Andrewes had used this quotation in the previous sermon.

560 Cp. with similiarity of text in 1616 Paschal Sermon. Andrewes, Vol. 2, p. 379.

561 Cyril of Jerusalem in *Procatechesis* Lecture No. 4, Ch. 30 had used the example

glory of the Lord Ps: 19.1]. *Dies in noctem moritur,* ('tis Tertullian obs[ervation]) each night is but the last dayes funerall, and what's the morning but a Resurrection? We have many more emblemes of this in meane sensitive creatures, phoenix, flies, Grasshop[pers], silkwormes, which after they have beene changed into the formes of diverse other creatures, at last resume their own shape again. And tho' these instances may seeme Arguments rather persuasive than convinceing, yet upon due consideracion, they show a fitnesse in nature to rise; and under the power and providence of the God of Nature, from the raiseing of these low inferiour creatures, we may confidently conclude a likelihood and probability of raiseing that which beares his own image; shall man for whose sake other creatures find a Resurrection doubt of his own?

But 2. that the very same bodyes shall rise, that's the difficulty. Do not the Fowles of the Air devour some, Beasts of the field, othersome? And if we goe to the Graves can we find any difference in the mould of one body from the mould of another? What shall we say in this case? How shall the torn and scattered limbs be gathered together? How can the mixed dust be sever'd and so every soul be re-united to it's own body? This is but a seeming difficulty; and may thus easily be cleared: 1. Same matter and substance of every body remaines, tho' scatter'd in diverse and different places 2. Then we must either deny God's Omniscience, that he knows not the Partes of every Body, and in what places they are; or his Omnipotency that he cannot recollect and unite them; and to deny either of these is to deny God, for his Attributes are his essence. But in the next place, these Reasons may be given for the point, why it should be so

1. Our Bodyes were created to be companions with our soules, as in this life, so in that to come, and therefore they are washed in the Laver of Regeneracion, Eph. 5. 2,7.[562]

2. By our Saviours Ascension and sitting at God's right hand our flesh hath taken possession of glory, our Bodys being members of Christ's mysticall Body.

---

of corn as an illustration for the resurrection of the body. "He who raises the corn, which is sown for our sakes, as year by year it dies,- will He base difficulty in raising us up, for whose sakes that corn also has been raised."

562 A better reference is Titus 3.5.

3. There is no reason but that those very Bodys which with the soul have suffered persecutions and afflictions on earth, should with the soul be made Partakers of Glory in Heaven; those I say; for why should this body suffer famine, nakednesse, martyrdome, and another which suffered none of these inherit peace and happinesse? The proper residence of vertue and goodnesse is the soul, yet when shee would display that goodnesse, shee useth the Body. 'Tis the soul that worships God, but 'tis the Body that lifts up the eye and bowes the knee to him.[563] 'Tis the soul that is charitable, but the hand gives Almes. 'Tis the soul that is fed in the Sacrament, but the mouth that receiveth bread and wine; Nay if Persecution or marytrdome befall, then 'tis the body alone that goes to the stake, the soul can neither be fired nor famished: Now if the body be thus faithfull unto death, why should it be denyed a Crown of life [Rev: 2.10]?

But what (may some say) shall I rise with my weake sickly, torn, wearied, and unweildly Body? Shall I again be troubled with my gout, stone, strangury? Alas! 'tis my hope and comfort that I shall dye sooner (sooner better) and to be cured and acquitted of these paines, and must I once now reassume them, that I may reassume the same body?[564] Nay, blessed Lord, rather let my soul alone live with thee, but as for my body, be it far from me, let it for ever rest in the grave. Nay, but it shall not ever rest, but shall rise a glorious body, as free from diseases and corruption as thy soul, Neither botches, nor boyles nor the gout, nor the stone shall any whit torment it. Thy Saviour comes with healing in his wings [Mal: 4.2], and he shall raise it the same body indeed for substance, but for qualityes in a far more excellent condicion; the glory of this latter house shall be greater, then the glory of the Former [Hag: 2.9]. 'Twas sown in weakenesse, dishonour and mortality; it shall be raised in Power and honour and to Immortality [1Cor: 15.42-3].

And if so how cheerfully may every beleeving Christian desire with St. Paul to be dissolved, [For we know that if our earthly house of this tabernacle were dissolved, we have a building of God, an house not made with hands, eternal in the heavens 2Cor.

563 Cp. with that in the Seventh Temptation Sermon. Andrewes, Vol. 5, p. 555.

564 Cp. with that in the 1606 Paschal Sermon, Ibid., Vol, 2, p. 194.

5.1].[565] And when it shall please God to visit him with lamenesse or sicknesse or any other disease, and so to call him out of this world, he may boldly cry out with good old Hilarion,[566] *Egredere anima Egredere*, goe out ô my soul! Death is but a gaol-delivery, a goeing out of Prison, a shakeing off my chaines, a bringing home from banishment, a destruction of toyle, the sting of death is sin, and the strength of sin is the law [1Cor: 15.56]. But thanks be to God [who giveth us the victory though our Lord Jesus Christ]. Amen.

565 This text is also at the end of Sermon on *Thy Kingdom Come*. Ibid.,Vol. 5, p. 395.

566 Also known as St. Hilarion the New who was abbot of Pelecete c. 754.

SERMON THREE

AT EASTER

Introduction

This unfinished Easter Sermon was possibly preached a year on as there is yet another innuendo to the Armada invasion with Andrewes stating that both "danger" and "deliverance" were implied in "victory".[567] There is also a reference to Perkins' book, *Armilla Aurea*,[568] first published in 1590, and a year later published in English as *A Golden Chaine*. A full version of the Passion text can be had by reading the Good Friday Sermon for 1604.

Although this Easter Sermon has the same text and a similar theme of victory as the previous one, it is very different. Paul informed the Corinthians that, despite their doubts, Christ's Resurrection has given them victory over death, and the assurance of the resurrection of their bodies. Fifteen hundred years later, there were still many doubters who rejected this wonderful news of God's gift of eternal life. However Andrewes assured his auditors that this news of eternal life is the sweetest they could hear. "These thick clodds of earth shall be made glittering and glorious like so many starres of Light," when "death is swallowed up in victory."[569]

Yet the events of Easter Day revealed not only deliverance but

---

567 Ms. 3707, pp. 156-8.

568 This is subtitled "The Description of Theologie, contining the order of ther causes of Saluation and Damnation, according to Gods Woord."

569 Ms. 3707, p. 152.

also danger to our salvation. To save souls Andrewes laboured to show what is ahead for those who ignore Christ and His precepts. In imagery similar to that used in Lecture Ten, Andrewes warned that if we ignore the Resurrection we subject ourselves to our spiritual enemy and commander, sin, which is "powerfull, malicious, [and] tyranicall", and which knows no restraints. It continually breaks forth "like that of fire out of an oven", and comsumes all before. Another "enemy" we face is "the wrath of God" kindled by sin, and which is "like a consuming fire" demanding "vengeance", and results in our eternal separation. How horrible this wrath is could be gauged from Christ Himself who shrieked in agony from it on the cross. The "wrath of God" has his sub-officers: God's "law, our conscience [and] death". The law "proclaimes us as traytors" and punishes us with "a terrible sentence" carried out by His two executioners, consience and death.[570]

The place of execution is hell, which Andrewes depicted in vivid medieval imagery. It is a "bottomles, black Dungeon and Pitt of Hell where no sun to enlighten, no air to refresh, no water to cool; the fire indeed is perpetuall." It has no end, even after millions of years there is "no possibility of ease, ... they are as far from the end of their misery as beginning." It will go on for eternity. Even worse than this perpetual torment is to be "banished from the comfortable presence of God, the beatificall vision ... the unspeakable joy and happinesse of the heavenly Jerus[alem], the sweet society of glorious saints and Angells."[571]

The alternative is deliverance, a gift given to us through God's mercy, His "incomprehensible mercy"; "that boundles, bottomles fountain of all his favours; the best link in the golden chain of our salvacion, the whole and sole cause of all our happinesse." Once again Andrewes attacked predestination as he expressed this mercy in Anselmian terms of how Christ by His bitter and agonising death has discharged all our debts, and has won us "a great victory" over "God's wrath ... [and] over death" for all.[572] It is a gift for the "faithfull and penitent", and also for the impeni-

570 Ibid., p. 154.

571 Ibid., pp. 155-6.

572 Ibid., p.156.

tent sinner after he repents. That is why Andrewes preached so frequently on the need for *metanoia*.[573]

He concluded this sermon with his teaching on salvation. Although as intimated Andrewes disliked the Calvinist doctrine of double predestination, he nevetheless believed as clearly illustrated in this sermon that all would not inherit eternal life. Calvinists, such as Perkins, taught that God had foreordained even before creation and thus the Fall, those who were the elect and the reprobate (supralapsarianism).[574] In reply to this belief, in his Lecture on Genesis 2.16 Andrewes argued, "that the foreknowledge of God is no cause of any action, no more then our eyes, being open and seeing a man." Although "God gave Adam power and ability and freedom of mind" to obey His command he chose not to follow God's counsel and commandment, but his own desires. "Therefore man knowing God's will and yet willfully breaking it, is the cause of his own ruine, and God is justified" to punish him. And so it is man who makes himself a reprobate.[575] Thus "all faithlesse, disobedient, impenitent sinners" exclude themselves from Christ's victory. Nevertheless Andrewes preached, "We must be carefull in separating evill from good, untill the great day of separation, when God shall sever all evil from good for ever; for here God is a Fisher, and Common-wealths and Churches are as a Net, which hath in them good and bad together." On Judgment Day God will do the separating.[576] As is obvious in these lectures, Andrewes always impressed that if we wanted to be sure of eternal life we must persevere in being faithful to Christ until our dying breath.

Text 1Corinthians 15. 57.

---

573 Refer especially to his Lenten sermons.

574 Perkins taught that God did not give Adam persevering grace. Perkins,Vol. 1 p. 96.

575 *Apos. Sacra*, p. 186. Donne preached, "Christ saves no man against his will." "Christ beats his Drum, but he does not Press man; Christ is serv'd with voluntaries." Donne, Vol. 7, p. 156.

576 *Apos. Sacra*, p. 31. This was the same argument that Whitgift had used against Cartwright. Whitgift, Vol. 1. pp. 183 - 4.

Thanks be to God, who giveth us the victory thorow our Lord Jesus Christ.

This whole chapter is nothing else, but an earnest and grand assertion of the main and comfortable article of the Christian faith, touching the Resur[rection] of the Body; by some weakely questioned, by others obstinately denyed in the ch[urch] now planted in Corinth. Wherein the Apostles processe and Method is very accurate and artificiall. For 1st by way of preface he makes an entrance or preparacion to his future dispute, breifly repeateing and highly commending that Gospell or Evangelicall Doctrine, concerning the death, the buryall and Resurrection of Christ, which before he had preached and planted amongst them; intending by this skilfull insinuacion to gain credit or advantage to his own cause, prejudice and disparagement to his Adversaries. You have the preface in the 11 first verses. After which followes the Disputacion, where the main Conclusion is 1st propounded, then prosecuted. Propounded v.12. why say some among you that there is no Resur[rection]? Where under the angry demand Negative, this Affirmative is implyed. Doubtles whatsoever any among you say or think, there shall be a Resur[rection] of the dead. This conclusion in the rest of the chap[ter] he prosecutes according to the rules of Art, 1st confirming and fortifying his assertion with strong and effectual arguments, then vindicateing it from the exceptions and Cavills of seducers. The Arguments of confirmacion are drawn partly from Divine Testimony expresse and apposite to the Question in hand, partly from places of Reason, where of some directly prove and enforce his main conclusion, that it shall be a Resurrection: others from the Contrary Error deduce a number of absurd impossibilityes. Every error is fruitfull and multiplyes itself: for (Apostle) deny the Resur[rection] shake[s] this foundacion of Faith, straightaway the whole fabrick of Religion is endangered; the Right of Christ annihilated, the Faith of Christians deceived, their Hope defeated, their comfort abolished, their miseryes encreased, the Patience and constancy of Martyrs eluded, the very Doctrine of the Gospell, the vertue of Christ's death, the soules immortality, the punishment of the ungodly; all these will be disputed and questioned, and finally Epicurianism, Atheism and irreligion induced and established.

Sure Truth cannot be the Mother of such Monstrous and hatefull impietyes, all her issue is ever like hers[elf], fair and beautifull; and therefore these foul errors never spring from her womb, but were conceived of a lye, and 1st begotten by the Father of Lyes. All this at the v.35. Then from confirming the Apostle proceeds to confuteing, meeting with all objections and solving such knotty sophisms as were used by the Adversaryes to oppugne or intangle this evident Article of the Resurr[ection] where being occasioned to discourse of that admirable change and transfiguracion which shall be seen in the Bodyes of all holy men when the lord Jesus shall find alive on the Earth at his 2nd comeing: At length from that discourse, he slips into a sweete meditacion of our future happinesse of that glorious estate of the Saints in Heaven; surpassing all conceit and capacity; where (as the Apostle here witnesses) these dark Tabernacles of clay, these thick clodds of earth shalbe made glittering and glorious like so many starrs of Light; these base earthly bodyes, shall become spirituall bodyes and these weake ignorant soules, perfectly wise, just and holy like the Angells thems[elves]. And bring as 'twere once more rapt up into 3rd Heaven in this divine contemplacion, and in a sort, aforehand in acutall profession of his heavenly Glory, he lookes down and sees under his feet death and Hell his spirituall enimies aymeing at him and gapeing after him; but in vain, for shrowding hims[elf] under the wings of his saviour, and there takeing sanctuary as one now far enough above their reach, and out of all danger, he triumphantlly sings, Death is swallowed up in victory. v.54, and in an h[oly] scornfull derision askes v.55 O Death [where is thy sting,] O Grave, [where is thy victory?] And so much the more to amplify the comfort and honour of his Christian Triumph and conquest, v.56 he showes who those enimies are, how potent, how cruell, how terrible! viz. the Sting of sin and of Death, the Malediction of the law, the Wrath of God, the damnacion of Hell, all these vex the servants of God, with continuall hostility, but we need not much feare. For thanks be to God [who giveth us the victory through our lord Jesus Christ].

This is the connexion; the words are familiar and obvious, the sense plain without obscurity or ambiguity, and therefore further explicacion will be needles. The Partes in generall may be 2. 1. God's mercy to us. 2. Our Duty to God or what he bestowes upon us, He gives us victory; then what we owe unto him; we are to give thanks. Let us 1st Consider how mercyfull God hath been to us and then we shall more clearly apprehend, and more readily acknowledge how dutifull, how thankfull we should be to him [that] giveth [us richly all things] 1Tim: 6.17.

Every victory implies 2 things 1. Danger 2. Deliverance: So doth this in the Text. The Danger is implied, the victory expressed, and here set forth, 1st by the degree or measure of it, 'tis not only a freeing and secureing of us from our enimyes, not a bare escapeing from them with life &c. but a glorious triumphant victory. 2ly, by the subjects of this Deliverance, or the Persons deliver'd. US. 3ly, by the Author or cause of it which is either Principall or subordinate: the Principall, God; the subordinate, either inwardly moveing and inclineing him thus to deliver us, which was his own free Love and Mercy, not any good[ness] or desert in us, - or, outwardly occasioning and meritting Jesus Christ his death and Passion. Here's matter and Meditacion enough for the whole life of a Christian, a larg and plentiful harvest. It shall only reape some of the most eminent eares. And

1. To take a short view of our danger, when I consider the terrible Legions and armies of spirituall enimyes, which are continually encamped against our guilty soules: me thinkes we may as justly cry out, as those Isrealites did cowardly, who can stand before these sonnes of Anah [Deut: 9.2]. The leader and commander of these hostile Troopes is

1. Sin a most powerfull, malicious, tyrannical enimy; It raignes in our members Rom: 6.12. It fills the heart full of evill and madnesse Eccl: 9.3. It makes men implacable Rom: 1.31. No bounds, no limitts, no lawes will restrain or keep them in order. And therefore 'tis compared to a breakeing forth like that of fire out of an oven, Hos: 7.6 or of mire and dirt out of rageing sea, Esa: 57.20; In a word, If we would but spend some time to make ourselves acquainted with ours[elves] and beg of God to reveal the secret evills of our nature unto us to make us see, that treasure of iniquity, that Hell of heart, that Magazine of sin and mischeife that is there, we would adore that boundlesse mercy, that great victory, by which we are freed from this great evill, the dominion and tyranny of sin.

2. Next enimy the wrath of God, which at first was nothing

till our sinnes had kindled it, but now it devours and wasts like a consumeing fire, it cannot be quenched, but with the blood of innumerable soules. I tremble at the very mentioning of it. How dreadfull are these few words, <u>the wrath of God</u>. A consumeing fire [Deut: 4.24], a river of brimstone [Is: 30.33], a Roul of curses, a treasure of vengeance; an Hell of horror and darknesse, tribulacion and anguish [Rom: 2.9]; all these are but short periphrases to set forth the wrath of God. If there were no Death, no Hell, no Devill, this lake of fire [Rev: 19. 20], this one scorching flame were enough to make all sinners for ever infinitely miserable. Some of the Saints were but lightly touched with this flame, yet see how strangely they were affected and afflicted. Begin with David, when God did but frown upon him, and show him an angry countenance, he was poured out, [like water]; all his bones [are out of joint:] his heart [is like wax], Ps. 22. 32,38.[577] So Job that Pattern of Patience, in the extremity of his greif allmost forgetts hims[elf]; and in an impatient fitt expostulates with God, O thou preserver of men, why set me up as a mark [against thee, so that I am a burden to myself? [Job 7. 20]; a Butt to thine arrowes are in me [Job 6.4], the venome thereof lick up my blood, and the terrors of God fight against me, Job 7.20.[578] But above all other instances, that one wofull, rufull complaint of the son of God upon the crosse abundantly testifies, that of all tortures, pressures, anxieties, the Wrath of God is incomparably the most unsufferable. Stripping, scorning, spitting, smiteing, insulting, peirceing, dying, all these base injuries of those butcherly villaines, he quietly endured with meeke and lamblike patience: the flight of his weake and fearfull Disciples, the violence of those bloody and murtherous Jewes, the fury of spitefull and malitious Devills, all these little moved him; they could not extort so much as a word of sorrow from his mouth, much lesse a teare from his eye or a sigh from his heart;[579] But when once he began to wrastle with the wrath of his Father, when God began to lay upon him the iniquities of us all; not only

---

577 A wrong reference. In the Authorized version this is v.14 in this psalm.

578 The last part of this quotation is from Job, 6.4.

579 In the 1604 Passion Sermon Andrewes stated what moved him was the joy that was set before Him. Andrewes, Vol. 2, p. 161.

to neglect, forget, forsake him as a stranger, but to break, bruise, wound him as an enimy; this wrastling wrang from him pangs, teares; strong cryes, and bloody sweates; and lastly forced him to utter his greif in that sad and lamentable voyce.[580] [My God, my God, why hast thou forsaken me? Math. 27.46]. And how shall we stand under the fury of this wrath, which thus made our Redeemer to shake and stagger! how must we needs be confounded, to behold that angry face, which our innocent saviour could not see without horror and amazement! If such a valiant champian, armed with invincible courage and strength, did yet shrink under that heavy hand; If he who had the strength of a Diety to support him; the fullnesse of the spirit to sanctify and prepare him; the message of an Angell to comfort him; the Relacion of a beloved son to refresh him; the assurance of victory and glory to encourage him; yet notwithstanding all these abatements that the son of God should pray with strong cryes [Heb: 5.7] and bloody dropps [Luk: 22.44], and wofull conflicts of soul against the cupp of his Father's wrath [Luk: 22.42]; ô what a condicion will all sinners be in, who must stand, or rather everlastingly sink under the weight of that wrath, which amaz'd and made heavy unto death the soul of Christ hims[elf]? Sure it cannot chuse but sink millions and worlds of us guilty weaklins into irrcoverable perdition.

Here's danger, and misery enough, if we goe no further: but yet we have not discovered all our enimyes: These 2, Sin and the wrath of God (which we may call the Commanders) are attended with inferiour souldiers, officers and instruments all appointed for our pain. They are many. I shall name but 3. his law, our conscience, Death. The law of God proclaimes us Traytors, prosecutes us, with continuall threates and curses, arraignes, convicts us and finally gives a terrible sentence against us. Conscience and death are the 2 Executioners; Conscience begins the torment of a sinner, Death finishes and consummates it.

3. And 1st Law of God, like God's great Cannon or Ordinance, breathes nothing but fiery damnatory curses, maledictions and vengeance against all offenders; it batters and bruises the most obstinate, obdurate heartes, and makes them melt away with

580 Cp. with Ms. 3708, p. 16.

feare and sorrow. The very delivery of this Law upon Mount Sinai was little lesse than Death: looke into the story and see with what awfull Majesty, with what terror and astonishment it was proclaimed; there was fire and smoak and lightning, thunder, trumpetts; the M[ount] trembling, Moses quakeing, palenesse in the face of Israel [Jer: 30.6], the heavens and Elements all in an uproare, Ex.19.16 [and] Heb. 12.21. If it were thus terribly promulged,[581] how terribly shall it be exacted and executed. That 1st fire wherein it was delivered, was but terrifying, the last fire (wherein it's execution shall be required) consumeing. Fitly therefore doth the Apostle term it, a killing lettere [2Cor: 3.6], the ministry of condemnacion [2Cor: 3.6], for ever since our first transgression made us obnoxious, this Law without all pitty, speakes nothing but Death and damnation.

4. And when once this severe Judge hath past the fatall sentence, conscience and Death are straight ready to doe execution. Conscience is a fire kindled in our own bosomes, by the flashes of the Law, feeding upon the heart and bowells which (unles it be quenched with the sprinkling of Christs blood) is the very beginning of that fire which shall never have an end. 'Twas the opinion of Philo the Jew, and of Origen, that the paines of the damned in Hell were nothing else but the pangs of their conscience; howsoever it's generally confessed that the knawings[582] of this worm is the bitterest part of their torment. Spirit of a man [will sustain his infirmity], Prov: 18.14. Poverty, ignominy, sicknesse, fetters, racks, gibbetts, fires, wheeles, all these some stout and undaunted spiritts have not only endured but contemned: But make choice of the most stoicall, most couragious, most resolute, most fearless man, one whom nothing could ever tame or terrifye if once this worm of a guilty conscience begin to gnaw within him; if this fury set upon him, and sharpen her teeth against him; if his own heart with deaf and deep stroakes lash and launce[583] itselfe; then look upon the face of this guilty heart, and thou shalt see it pale and gastly; his speeches full of stopps and interruptions; his silence

581 Archaic spelling of promulgated.

582 i.e. gnawings.

583 It means "to spear".

museing, his eyes stareing; his motions unsteady and distracted, his mirth forced, his smiles heartles and faint: no musick can refresh him, no dainties cheare him, no company delight him, nothing can ease him; he suspects, he feares, he knowes not well what nor whom: He is weary of the day, weary of the night --- of others --- of hims[elf]: every shadow, every dream affrights him; he still tosses and turnes, yet still finds his tortures remediles. Fain would he stop the clamourous mouth of his conscience, but still it barkes and yells; fain would he smother his sin or at least, cast it behind his back, but still it will be before his face, he cannot look upon a stick or stone but they seem to upbraid him with his villany; the very birds and beasts seem to cry out upon him, and to say Thou art He. As in Plut[arch] we read of one Bessus, who confessed the parricide of his own Father being accused by none but chirping sparrowes,[584] And in Eccl[esiastic] story, Theodor[ic] i.e. Arrian king haveing cruelly martyred Sym[m]achus,[585]afterwards thought he saw his frowning face and grinding teeth in the gapeing Jawes of a fish upon his table. The worker of all this woe, and that which setts the conscience thus at odds with itself, makeing it peirce and prick so deepe, is the venomous sting of sin, which like a thorn lyes rotting and festering within, and so casts the con-

584 Related by Plutarch "As for Bessus ... he killed his father and long went unsuspected. At last, when he had come to dine at a certain house, he prodded a swallow's nest with his spear, knocked it down, and killed the nestlings." Those accompanying him asked, "'What is wrong with you, man? What is the meaning of such strange behaviour?' To this he answered: 'Why, haven't they all along accused me falsely and denounced me for killing my father?' The company was astonished at these words and reported them to the king. The truth was discovered, and Bessus suffered the penalty." Did Bessus expect "that the birds of the aire" would tell of his crime? Plutarch, *On the delay of the Divine Vengeance*, Ch. 8, lines, 553 – 4. This is also included in M.L.E., p. 33.

585 He was elected Pope in the late fifth century to oppose the concessions of his predecessor, Anastasuis II, to the Emperor and the Patriarch of Constantinople. However Theodoric refused to give his consent to this election, and instead accused Symmachus of simony and celebrating Easter on the wrong date. A council was summoned to deal with the charges, but on his way to attend Symmachus was attacked and refused to attend. In his absence the council endorsed his election but declared it had no power to deal with the charges. Consequently Symmachus found himself virtually a prisoner in Rome, and the respective supporters shed much blood as a consequence. Eventually Theodoric withdrew his opposition to Symmachus who devoted the rest of his life defending the Catholic faith against various heresies.

science into those endles, easles fits of sorrow. This is one part of our sins torment, the akeing and chafeing, and galling and gnawing of conscience.[586]

5. The other parte is Death. By which I mean not only this temporall, momentary, dying death, but especially that other Eternall, everlasting, everliveing Death,[587] wherein the wicked damned sinner is not only utterly and irrecoverably banished from the comfortable presence of God, the beatificall vision and fruicion of the 1st and cheif good; the unspeakable joy and happinesse of that heavenly Jerus[alem], the sweet society of glorious Saints and Angells, but further he is plunged into a River of brimstone, a place of hopeles, helples torture: where the scourge of God's reveng is most sharp and heavy; 1st upon his Body, then his soul. 1. In his Body, besides uglinesse, deformity, exquisite pain in every joynt and Article, this Death will afflict every sense with odious and horrible objects. His eye shall see nothing but what's terrible, amazeing apparitions of deludeing Devills, the ear heare nothing but shrikes and lamentacions and gnashings of Teeth; the Nose smell noth[ing] but unsavoury stenches; the tongue shalbe ever complaineing, never pittied, the whole Body ever boyling, never consumed. 2ly, For the soul, as the substance of it is much more pure and sensible then the Body, so the pain must needs be so much more intollerable; See this distinctly in every power and faculty. The understanding is stuffed with rebellious, impious blasphemous cogitacions; the Will with sensuall, bruitish, divellish motions; the Affections are vexed with implacable fitts of outrageious hatred, malice, envy, but above all the rest, the conscience then lashes and lyes on mortall and deadly stroakes upon the ever wofull and liveing, dyeing heart.

It were easy further to amplify the torments of this death many wayes as from the Adjuncts or Associates of the damned, from the circumstances. 1. of the Place, the noysome, loathsome, bottomles,

586 Cp. with Grotius, the sting of a gnawing conscience at the remembrance of ungodly and wicked actions, especially when "the houre of death approacheth unto the *wicked*, who doe then seeme more sensible of an *imminent judgment*; and this *gnawing worme* of conscience the most prophane wretches and wicked tyrants in the world could never utterly mortifie and destroy in them." *True Religion*, p. 71.

587 Cp. with text in Good Friday Sermon for 1605. Andrewes, Vol. 2, pp. 151 – 2.

black Dungeon and Pitt of Hell where no sun to enlighten, no air to refresh, no water to cool: the fire indeed is perpetuall, but the darknesse palpable, like that of Ægypt, such as may be felt Exod: [10.21].

Then of the Time, which is an endles duration, after 1000'ds and Millions --- they have no possibility of ease, they have not spent one minute of their Eternity, they are as far from the end of their misery as beginning.[588]

I have dwelt long upon our danger, that the comfort of our Deliverance might be more sweet and welcome. Yee see who are our enimies, how feirce, how cruell, sin, the wrath of God, the law of God, the fire of conscience, fire of Hell, but thanks [be to God, who giveth us the victory through our Lord Jesus Christ].

And here for more cleer and orderly proceeding, you must give me leave to invert the method proposed and to consider 1. Author of our Deliverance, 2. Measure, 3. Subjects.

God. The Principall cause and Author of our Deliver[ance] is God, the Lord of Hosts, the mighty one of Israel, who else could effect it? Alas, what are men, or what are Angells that they should grapple, and encounter with such fierce and furious enimies? No, the workeing of our freedome was a taske, far exceeding the feeble strength of any weak creature.

Giveth. But what moved God to this work of Mercy? Apostle here makes answer, his own Mercy was the mover not our desert; this delivery is not our purchase but his gift: God giveth --- that incomparable incomprehensible Mercy, that boundles, bottomles fountain of all his favours; the best link in the golden chain of our salvacion,[589] the whole and sole cause of all our happinesse. When we like vile rebells lay weltering --- when dead in sin and sensles of our misery; when the powers of darknesse were insulting over us, and triumphing in our ruine, even then the Father of mercyes out of meer pitty cast a compassionate [skirt over us Ezek: 16.8], he snatcht us like brands [Zech: 3.2.], he gave us a champion who subdued our enimies, loosed our bands, purchased our freedome. And

588 This description of hell is very similar to that in Lecture Ten.

589 This is a confutation of the teaching of Perkins' theology as set out in the *The Golden Chaine*, translated into English, a year after its publication in Latin in 1590.

Yet here we may not so extoll the mercy of God, that we forget his Justice; Compassion had the 1st hand in this victory, but satisfaction must have the next; his Mercy could not have releeved, unles his Justice had been satisified for us; so it was, God [who giveth the victory], yet 'tis in and through [our Lord Jesus Christ]. He is our victor, champian, strong-man who hath disarmed and foyled all our enimyes, perfectly appeased his Father's Wrath, fully satisfied the law, loosed the sorrowes of Death, led captivity captive [Eph: 4.8], triumphed over the powers of Darknesse. And which is strang, all this not by doeing so much as suffering; for interposeing hims[elf] in this spirituall combat, those wounds, those stroakes, that danger which was intended to us, he willingly endured and by endureing conquer'd. He was made sin for us, (Apostle) 2Cor: 5.21 i.e. as hims[elf] expounds the phrase, a curse for us, Gal: 3.13.[590] What meanes the curse of sin, but all the sorrows due to sin: He then that felt the curse, doubtlesse felt all those sorrowes, the terror of God's Wrath, Gods Law, all these at once, he suffered for us and subdued. He began to be troubled in soul, Joh: 12.27. To an agony, Luc: 22.44. To anguish of mind, deep distresse, Mar: 14.35.[591] To have his soul round about on every side environed with sorrow, and that to Death, Mat: 26.38 and this such as never heard of nor felt, Lam: 1.12, sorrow done [unto me, wherewith the Lord hath afflicted me], but Jerome and Chaldee[592]melted [me]. And truly it should seem by that fear[ful] sweat [which dropped] that he was scarce some furnace, the feeling whereof was able to cast him into that sweat and turn it into dropps of blood. But sorrow's of his soul unknown --- none ever have, nor shall suffer like. --- His soul like a scorched heath --- drops of dew of divine comfort. Powers of darknesse let loose to afflict him; the influence of comfort restrained to releev him; so in silence we may admire but all our word's not able to reach [Him].

So this our Sponsor or Surety hath fully discharged all our debt, crost the whole score, discomfitted all our enimyes, quitt us from all danger. He only hath done all, payd all, suffered all,

---

590 Cp. with text in Passion Sermon for 1605. Andrewes, Vol. 2, p. 175.

591 Cp. with text in Passion Sermon for 1597, Ibid., p. 123; and Ms. 3708, p. 16.

592 This was a term used for Aramaic passages in the Old Testament, which was used for dating from the time of Jerome.

which we should. He hath no partners, no companions, none in earth or heaven to share with him in this payment, in this victory. Woe were us, if hee had left but one Mite of our ransome to be payd; one of our weakish enimyes to be foyled by our own soules: And woe to them that botch up the unvaluable and infinitely precious sufferings of Christ, with the superfluityes of flesh and blood; and in this spiritual skirmish trust any whitt to their own strength. None but Christ that hath wrought for us such a great victory; his stripes [have healed us Isa: 53.5.], the shedding of his blood prevented the spilling of ours; his Death was to us quickening and restorative; his bitter passion our glorious victory.

Victory - And thus was our peace procured, our Eternall Redemption obtained; we are now not only safe but we may be secure; our enimyes are not only repelled or wounded, but destroyed and abolished and what fear, what danger can there be from a dead adversary. Our Champion hath not covenanted for some anxious truce, some doubtfull intermission of hostility, but hath given us an absolute freedome, a certain victory. A Victory

1. Over Gods wrath, he is now no more angry with us in earnest; all the fiery darts of his Indignacion were thrown at the precious heart of his Eternall son: our divine surety: So that now, if we tast or sip of that bitter cup, yet we come not neare the dreggs; and if sometime our insolence force him to take the rod into his hand, yet he layes on but gently strokes; and out of a tender fatherly affection, corrects for amendment, not for punishment or expiaion.

2. Victory over God's Law. The sharp edge of it is abated, the damnation sentence repealed; as it cannot save us; so it cannot condemne us. 'tis indeed still a schoolmaster[593] [Gal: 3.25] but like one without a rod, it teaches only without correction; it hath given over lashing and scourging, and now only gives excellent Lectures and lessons of Piety and Justice.

3. Over conscience: The streames of Christ's blood, have quenched that flame and drowned that worm; she that was a spitefull and revengefull fury, is now become a sweet and sure friend; her sower frowning countenance is changed into friendly

593 Cp. with that in P.C.D. (1650), p. 71.

smiles; her accursing tongue now excuses and plead's for us; her rough hand now lovingly embraces us; and will no longer be at odds with us if we be at peace with God.

4. Victory over Death. And 1st for the temporall dissolution of Body and soul, (*τὸν ἀθανατὸν ἐκθανάξωσε* Pelusiot.)[594] Christs death killed this death, according to that of the Prophet Hosea 13.14. O death, [I will be thy plagues: O grave, I will be thy destruction] so that now to us, it hath neither the nature, nor deserves the name of death; it may more properly be termed (Nazian[zen]) in his funerall oration for Cyprian[595] *πόθου πληώσις ἡ δέσμων λύσις*, the gate of Heaven, the aim of our desires, the ease of our burthens, looseing of our fetters, unloading of our baggage; and in Pelusiot's *προοίκιον ἀθανασίας*, a preface or Poem to imortality, a sweet night of rest after the tedious and toylsome day of this life; a quiet harbour after a storm and tumultuous navigacion; Like that cherubim at the entrance of Paradise, with one stroke admitting our soules to the fruicion of their endles felicity. And as the 1st death is thus sweetened to us so the 2nd is utterly subdued; our 1st Resurr[ection] hath sufficiently secured us from the 2nd death; our Redeemer hath bought off our torment with his own, and drunk so deep of that bitter potion, that he left not one drop for us. And tho' perhaps, sometime in some violent storm of desertion or temptacion, we be driven very near to the gates of Hell, so that we seem now falling into that fearful gulfe; yet in all this, our danger is rather imaginary then reall, and not so great in truth, as in our apprehension. Be the Tempest never so rough, the Anchor of hope still fastens our wavering vessels, and at length our cheif Pilot (who can command both wind and weather) sends us a gentle calme and serenity, and in the end brings us to the Haven where we would be. In a word, so long as our Head is in heaven, we may be sure, we cannot set our foot in Hell. So then 'tis manifest that in Christ we are more than conquerors [Rom:

---

594 St. Isodore of Pelusium died c. 450. He was an abbot, exegete and letter writer who supported the teaching of St. Chrysostom and opposed Nestorius and the monophysite, Eutchyes.

595 Probably this is Caesarius, brother of Gregory Nazianzen, who died in 369. Gregory of Nanzianus, Oration VII.

8.37] and therefore aptly doth the Apostle expresse the measure of our Deliverance by the name of victory.

Us. Our next enquiry will be after the subjects of this Deliv[erance], or what person they are that share in this victory. This Text answers in a word US. God giveth US ...

US not all, it is then a restraining particle and implies a double Limitacion 1. To us men, not Angells, then 2. To US faithfull and Penitent, not to prophane unbeleevers.

1. For the evill Angells if we may presume to guesse at a reason of their desperate mind; it seems bec[ause] their fall was willfull without suggestion, therefore 'twas irrecoverable without Redemption; whatsoever was the cause, the effect is certain that they all suffer the vengeance of eternall fire.[596] Christ did not suffer, nor satisfy for them, for he did not [take on him the nature of angels] Heb. 2.16. And the rule of Damascene[597] is sure and infallible. *τὸ ἀπρόσληπτον οὐ θεράπευτον.*

2. Men only partake of this victory but is it given to all men? No, to US, i.e. them that beleev and obey whom he purged to be a peculiar people, zealous of good workes [Tit: 2.14], to them that fear his name.[598] Mal. 2.4.[599] And therefore all faithlesse, disobedient, impenitent sinners, *qua talis*- none of this US in the Text to whom victory.

And thus having in some measure discovered Gods mercy to us in this victory, 'tis now time that in the last place we should reflect upon our duty to him.

596 Cp. with that in Christmas Sermon for 1605. Andrewes, Vol. 1, p. 13.

597 He was commonly known as John of Damascus or St. John Damascene, a Eastern theologian, who lived from 675-749. One of his famous work is *The Fountain of Wisdom*, which gives a summary of the teaching of the Fathers.

598 Cp. this with similar teaching in sermon on *Remission of Sins*. Andrewes, Vol. 5, p. 98.

599 In the Authorized Version it is verse 5.

SERMON FOUR

At Easter

Introduction

In this Easter Sermon there are again similarities with other Paschal Sermons of Andrewes. This one commenced with the women preparing their spices and ointment before the Sabbath began, and then their observing the Sabbath. Once it was over, at the first streak of light, they came to the tomb to anoint their Lord. He preached in a similar mode at Easter 1608, that although the women were anxious to embalm their Lord's body as soon as possible "yet not with breach of the sabbath. Their diligence leapt over none of God's commandments for haste. ... But [the sabbath] was no sooner over, but their diligence appeared straight. ... Not their own sabbath sleep - but 'before day-light' they were well onward on their way."[600]

This sermon also unveiled Andrewes's opinion on the dead; they were to be buried according to the rites of the Church and with love and they were to be remembered. Thus the Women's "Remembrance of the Dead is worth our observacion".[601] He also made this clear in his 1608 Easter day Sermon when he preached that Christ's burial and anointing was as an act of love. "Herein is love [which] ... continueth to the dead, as if they still were alive. And when I say dead, I mean not such as the dead hath left behind them, ... but I mean performing offices of love for the dead him-

600 Andrewes, Vol. 2, pp. 226-8.

601 Ms. 3707, p. 160.

self; to see he have a sepulchre to go to; not so to bury his friends, as he would bury his ass. ... To see he have one, and not thither to bring him, and there to leave him, and bury him and his memory both in a grave. Such is the world's love. ... All after Christ living, but go to His sepulchre who will, not we." In his teachings on the Eucharist Andrewes always taught it was not only for the living but also for the dead and even for the unborn.[602]

Andrewes' emphasis on the women observing the Sabbath reflected his teaching on Sabbatarianism. All through his ministry, beginning with his Catechetical Lectures in Pembroke Hall, Cambridge, he stressed that the Lord's Day is a day on which all physical and recreational works ceased, other than for works of mercy. It is a day to worship God and render praises and thanks to Him, and to partake of the Sacrament.[603] To do otherwise is to break the moral obligation of the Sabbath as reflected in this sermon. "Every thing is beautifull in it's season, the action is good and warrantable if no circumstance be wanting, but that which is lawfull, if done upon another day, may be sin and deserv death; if done upon the sabbaoth."[604]

Although Andrewes began this sermon with the events of that first Easter morn, most of it was devoted to the Passion, which was depicted in brutal and gory imagery. This covered Christ's agonising prayer and betrayal in Gethsemane, His cruel trial at Gabbatha, and His excruciating suffering at Golgotha. His description of the crucifixion was so vivid that one can almost feel the nails being hammered into his hands and feet, and the wreath of thorns being pressed into his skull. Such a nauseating description of Christ's sufferings was repeated almost verbatim in his 1604 Passion Sermon before James 1.[605] In both sermons he appealed to his auditors to see Christ's sufferings as a means for meditation, of which one way is through the medieval imagery of *liber charitatis*. "His wounds they are as windows, through which we may well see all that is in Him." And "For Christ pierced on

---

602 Andrewes, Vol. 2, p. 225, Vol. 11, pp. 19 - 20.

603 P.C.D., pp. 157-8.

604 Ms. 3707, p. 160.

605 Andrewes, Vol. 2, pp. 169-70.

the cross is *liber charitatis,* 'the very book of love' laid open before us." By contemplation before a crucifix, God's immeasurable love and mercy are conveyed to the viewer who sees Christ embracing even the most miserable sinner, as He wants to make all His and "heirs ... of the kingdom of Heaven". In return the viewer must "look upon thy crucified Saviour and Love him", and then show that love in "an holy life" and of "good works". Such a meditation should crucify all the sinful acts of our flesh, he suggested.[606]

Andrewes described Christ's conversation to Pilate on His kingdom in a similar fashion to his lecture on Christ's kingship. Both emphasised that Christ rules not through fear but by love over the "hearts and consciences" rather than the body of His subjects.[607]

This sermon also reflected his teaching on original sin as stated in Lecture Nine; we have all sinned, rather than "the collective guilt inherited from Adam 'in whom all sinned.'" We are all responsible for our sins. Hence it is our sins that caused Christ to die, and which continue to crucify Him. We therefore cannot blame the Jews, or Pilate or Caiaphas for His death. Indeed we are in the same position as David when Nathan said to him, "Thou art the man. 'Tis thou and He, and I, and every one of us, that put to death the lord of glory." Yet the wonderful news is that he "suffered such sorrowes in body, [and] in soul" "for our sinnes and our salvation". However Andrewes warned that for those who continue to "proceed in their wicked wayes ... there remaines no more sacrifice for sin" as expressed in Hebrewes 10.26.[608] He had also preached in this vein in the lecture, *And forgive us our debts* in the series on *The Lord's Prayer,*[609] given earlier in his ministry. Christ "bids us pray for pardon of our sins, putting no difference

606 Ibid., pp. 132, 178; Ms. 3707, p. 168. Welsby indicated that Bishop John Fisher had also preached with great effect on this window imagery in one of his Good Friday sermons. Welsby, p. 197. However there is no firm evidence to suggest that Andrewes knew this sermon. Fisher's sermons were not in Andrewes' library. Chambers, pp. 99 - 121.

607 Ms. 3707, p. 163.

608 Ibid., p.168.

609 These were first published in 1611 with the title *Scala Coeli.* On the title page the editor, Francis Burton, explained the purpose of these sermons, "the first six to guiding to the true Doore" and the rest "teaching how so to knock thereat that wee may enter."

whether they be penny debts, or talents; whether fifty, or a thousand; if we ask forgiveness, He tells us He is ready daily to remit them." But "'if we willingly sin' after remission, 'there is no more sacrifice for sin.'"[610]

Text St. Luke 24. 7.
The son of man must be delivered into the hands of sinfull man and be crucifyed and the third day rise again.

Tho' in the beginning of this Text, we meete with the sad, dolefull newes of our Saviours Passion, yet this chapter is the History of his glorious Resurrection. And to bring down the story to the Text, we must take notice of some officious Matrones, whose Piety tow[ards] God, and Remembrance of the Dead is worth our observacion. Text saith they prepared spices and oyntments and rested the Sabbaoth day according to the commandment, v. ῶ[611] For their ch[urch], God had sanctified the Sabbaoth day to be a day of rest, and therefore they would not prophane it to perform a ceremony; not breake a precept tho' to annoynt a saviour. Every thing is beautifull in it's season [Eccl: 3.11], the action is good and warrantable if no circumstance be wanting, but that which is lawfull, if done upon another day, may be sin and deserv death;[612] if done upon the sabbaoth. And therefore they rested the sabbaoth day. But as soon as the sabbaoth was over, very early in the morning they come to the sepulchre; An undertakeing in appearance but to little purpose; they might remember how the sepulchre was guarded, the door made fast, sealed up and a stone upon it, which they of themselves could not roll away, nor could they see who would do it for them; so but small hopes of comeing at the body which they intended to imbalm; Yet their zeal to the work made them not discouraged at the difficulties; they made tow[ards] the grave, where they found the passage cleared, the Guard removed, the stone rolled away, and the Body gone too, for they entred in

610 Andrewes, Vol. 5. p. 431.

611 i.e. Luke 23. 56.

612 Cp. with "There are many things which are good only in their times and places ..." in lecture on Genesis 1.11, 12, *Apos. Sacra*, p. 71.

and found not the body of the lord Jesus, Luc. 24.3.[613] So the provision they had made was but to small purpose, they might return the spices and oyntments to the places where they had them; his body instead of an embalming, had met with a glorious Resurrection. God had sent down two of his Angells from Heaven to wait upon his son, and as 'twere to hold by the Hangings, while he rose from his Bedchamber, the Grave. These Angells encounter with the unbeleeving thoughts of the devout matrones, and endeavour to reason them into a beleef of the Resurrection; you seek Jesus who was [crucified Mar: 16.6], beleev us, he is not here, or if not beleev us, come and see the place and beleev your own eyes; or lastly, if you distrust both us and yourselves, beleev him, whom you seek; you cannot but have better thoughts of him, then that he should tell you an untruth, and remember how he spake unto you when he was yet in Galilee, [Luc. 24] v.6. How he foretold that he should dye and how he should dye, the time and manner, and how long he should be under the power of death. Call to mind how that none of those things which have happened but were foretold, that by the determinate councell of God, for the salvacion of Mankind, he should be betrayed into the hands of sinners, accused, be[a]t, set at nought, slain, and revive again the 3rd day. And this is the very time, th' other day, the preparacion [Luk: 23.54]. He was taken down from the crosse, and entombed in this sepulchre, yesterday he rested in it, and this is the 3rd Day, early this morning, is the Sun of R[ighteousness] arisen [Mal: 4.2]. So once more, Remember how he spake unto you, when he was yet in Galilee, saying The son of man must be delivered into the hands of sinfull men, and be crucified and the 3rd day [rise again].

In the Text are observable these particulars 1. *Traditio*, the trecherous betraying or delivering up of our saviour. 2. Persons to whom he should be betrayed, sinfull men. 3. How they would use him after he was betray'd to them, they would do no lesse then crucifie him. 4. What should become of him after he was crucified, maugre all the power and malice both of men and Divells, he should not see corruption, but rise again. 5. Time, when he should rise again, the 3rd day. Lastly, the Person that should undergo

613 This text is very similar to that in the 1608 Paschal Sermon. Andrewes, Vol. 2, pp. 227 – 9.

this variety of changes, the Son of Man. This son of man must be delivered [into the hands of sinful men, Luc. 24. 7].

To begin with the 1st of these, the Treacherous betraying [of our Saviour]. No sooner had he done his Devotions in the Garden, and gathered together his Disciples, but behold a great multitude armed with swords and staves came to apprehend him, Math. 26.47. And one of his own Family must be hired to betray him. Judas is that man; one who had the most beneficiall office in his Family. He had trusted and honoured him with the Bursar's place, made him Treasurer of that little he had, as if he would purposely hire and keep him from that treason; yet that Judas play'd the perfidious Traytor, gott about him a company like unto himself, a multitude with swords and staves, a Band with clubbs and armes to attack his Master. And here we are to consider who they were that came, viz: scribes, Pharis[ees], high Pr[iest] and their servants, a band of souldiers, and elders of the Jewes; all which agreed upon it, and came with full consent that they might apprehend him; And they had no sooner seized him, but they condemned him presently; they made short work; their feet were so swift to shed blood [Rom: 3.15], that the next morning, very early, by breake of day they led him away and delivered him to Pilate; the Governor must be broken of his sleep, awakened before his hour, to hearken to their clamorous accusacions. In all hast they bound him, led him away, and delivered him to Pilate.

2. And now to carry on this sad Tragedy of our saviours Passion, we come to [the] next Act, the 2nd thing obs[erved] in the Text, viz. the Persons to whom he should be betrayed; where we shall present you with an unjust and timorous President, a mocking King, and Prophane souldiers; all conspiring the death of the King of the Jewes.

And for the better understanding of this, we are to consider what was the state and condicion of the Jewes at that time. A little before the birth of our saviour, subdued they were by the Romans, who takeing the government into their own hands appoynted them governours of their own. At that time Herod held the jurisdiction of the nothern parte, the hilly country tow[ards] Galilee, and Pilate was the Deputy in that rest of Jury; And therefore they delivered our saviour to Pilate, that he being the President might proceed against him; examine, arraigne and give sentence upon him. And in order hereunto, they framed an Inditement against him of these two heades, sedition and Treason.

1. A seditious person they charge him to be, stirring up the people from Galilee to this place, Luc. 23.5. Again, Disobedient, we found this fellow perverting the Nacion, and forbidding to give Tribute to Caesar v.2 when indeed there was nothing lesse true then either of these.

1. If to maintain the truth, defend the Law, to preach the Gospel to the poor, to heal the broken hearted, to preach deliverance to the captive, to set at liberty those who are bruised [Is: 61.1, Luk: 4.18]; if to preach and proclaim <u>all</u> these, be to be a seditious person, then the allegation cannot be denyed; for such a seducer he was, and no other end in seduceing he had. The first part then of the charge was a manifest aspersion; and the 2nd was a flat lye. For

2. How did he forbid the payment of Tribute who commanded it, confessed it a debt and paid it, Math. 22.21. And rather then Caesar should want his due, he sent Peter to the sea, to fetch so much money out of the mouth of a fish, as should pay for them both [Matth: 17.27]. And 'tis observ'd, that he wrought no miracle about mon[e]y, but that one, to pay Tribute etc. So he was no enimy to Caesar, in point of Tribute etc. neither ever had he any thought of an earthly crown. When the people sought for him, to make him a King, he conveyed hims[elf] away, and hid hims[elf] to prevent it, Joh. 6.15. Nay he would not by so much as a subordinate Judge, to divide the land betweene the two dissenting brethren, Luc. 12.14. Howsoever this last charge, because it reflected upon the person of Caesar, Pilate takes speciall notice of it; and upon this point he reexamines him, Joh: 18.33.[614] Art thou a King? To which our Saviour returnes this answer; Thou sayest that I am q.d. Altho' thou seest me sold as a slave, apprehended as a Theif, humbled like a servant; accused like a Malefactor, and defamed for rayseing tumults; yet know that I am a King. A king I am but not according to your apprehension; and a kingdome I have, but not such an one as your Master Tiberius governs; My kingdome is not of this world [Joh: 18.36]. You rule over the bodyes of men, but

---

614 This should be v.37 in the Authorized Version.

I over their hearts and consciences; you govern by your lawes, I by my Truth and gospell; your subjects obey for feare, mine for love; yours is an outward and temporall and perishing; mine a spirituall and everlasting kingdome. With this answer Pilate rested so fully satisfed, that he went out and said to the Jewes, I find no fault in him at all. And so he begins to think of some way to save his life. And 3 evasions he resolved upon. 1. He sends him to Herod. 2. He caused him to be scourged. 3ly, He putts it to their choice, whether they would acquitt him or Barrabbas. Behold here the Pattern of a wicked Judge! If his own conscience told him that Christ was blameles, then why doth he post him over to another Judge? why whipp him, and scourg him and put him onto the scale with Barrabbas? He should have interposed his power to have saved him, and not have deliver'd him to the will of them He knew to be his enimies.

But with the 1st order of Pilate, doubtles the Jewes were well pleased; for they presumed, that he would find no better usage at Herod's hands, then his, and so thither they cary him, and present him to that cruell, bloody king, Luc: 23.8.

And obs[erve] here 1st, how Herod was wonderfull glad at his comeing, for he was desireous of a long season to see him. Desireous to see him? who would not? Abraham, Moses, Patriarchs, Prophets, Angells, the whole world desired to see him! Not an house into which he enter'd, if they bad[e] him welcome, but he brought salvacion with him. But this was not it, that made Herod glad to see him, but meerly to satisfie his curiositie; For 2ly, he thought to have seene some miracle done by him; He had no better opinion of him, then of some magitian that being brought into the presence of a king, begins straitway to show his impostures. And 'tis probable this was the reason that tho' he asked many things, our saviour gave him no answer, made neither sermon, nor wrought miracle before him, as knowing his intentions to be vain, if not malicious, no way to be bettered or to profit by him. 3dly, Herod seeing him stand before him, as a meek innocent Lamb, tooke him to be weak and ignorant, and therefore he set him at nought and playd upon him, Luc: 23.11 as if he had been some worthlesse person. And his followers, his men of warr did he like; they scorn'd and derided, and play'd upon him at their pleasure. And when they were weary with their prophane sport, they clad him in a gorgeous coat, exposed him to contempt and scorn and returned him back to Pontius Pilate the president. The conclusion was, that Herod and Pilate were friends that day, tho' before enimies, yet they could agree well enough to put the Lords Anointed to death; Men of different and dissenting judgments yet soder[615] and unite when any mischeif is to be done to Christ or his members.

Well Pilate haveing received him again, setts on foot another project to save his life. At that Feast the Jewes had a custome; that the Deputy should release a Prisoner, whom they would. And he takes from hence an occasion to propose unto them Jesus and Barrabbas, two, so diametrically opposite for vertue and basenesse, that Gold and filth, a Diamond and Pebble, the sun and darknesse; heaven and Hell, are not more unlike, then Jesus and Barrabbas. Pilate did not Imagine that the Jewes could be so notoriously wicked as to preserve a murtherer, a Malefactor, one that was not worthy to live upon the face of the earth, before a just man, one that went about doing good. Yet they clamour presently, not this man but Barrabbas Luc: 23.21. And here (me thinks) I see Darknesse got the upper hand of light [Luk: 2.53], Jesus must be crucified and Bar[rabbas] released; th' one a murtherer, th' other a saviour, the one a stirrer up of sedicion, [the other] a Peacemaker; th' one who went about doeing good, [the other] mischeif; Jesus who probably healed some of those wounds which Bar[rabbas] had made; Jesus who commanded to sheath the sword, which Barabbas had so often drawn; Jesus the Saviour of mankind, Bar[rabbas] the destroyer of them, yet that must suffer and this must be freed. This is such an high Indignity, that the Prophet ends his sufferings with this Particular, He was numbered with the Trangressors, Esa. 53. ω̂ [616]

However Pilate would not yet consent to it; tho' an Heathen and a drowzy sinner, yet his conscience chaff'd and murmured within him; And to quicken it the more, his wife sends to him, that he have nothing to doe with that just man Math: 27.19. So he still cast about how to deliver him; and bethought hims[elf] of

615 Archaic form of solder

616 i.e. v. 12.

a 3rd way how to do it [Luk: 23.22], to scourge him and let him goe Mat. 27.26. And 'tis the opinion of Beda,[617] Eusthathius[618], Athenaeus[619]etc; that he was tyed to a Pillar and there scourged with a whipp, in which they tied certain huckle bones or plummetts of lead, with sharp thornes to the ends of the thongs to augment the pain. So twas a painfull servile and base punishment not inflicted on any but slaves and bondmen. And thus was the true king of Israel used, had his garments torn off him, as if he had beene one of the vain fellowes; and had his flesh torn with scorpions, when he was delivered into the hands of sinfull men.

After this they array him in a purple robe, put a scepter into his hand, and set a crown of thornes upon his head [Math: 27.28]; and that hand which set a crowne upon his head, knockt it down with a cane fast to his head; so that looke how many thornes there were, so many entrances through his skin, and so many slu[i]ces there were for his blood to issue forth; which gusht out and streamed as fast down his face in the Palace as it did down his back and shoulders at the Pillar. Nor was this all, but he endured cruell mockings, they bowed the knee in scorn and said, Hail [King of the Jews Math: 27.29]. In the mean time, some spitting in his face, others smiteing him, and on the head with that very reed, which they had just put into his hand instead of a scepter.[620]

And in this dresse was he brought forth to the people that they might sport and recreate thems[elves] with that wofull spectacle. And Pilate like your fellowes which show some vain sights, ushers it in with *Ecce Homo*. --- A man he is,[621] and can men do lesse then pitty so ruefull a spectacle? Alas! Here is but a stranger to me, but he is of your own flesh and blood, an Israelite, and will you not have compassion upon one of your own Nacion? Doe not your bowels melt to see him thus torn, thus mangled? Have you no

617 The English monk and scholar of the 8th C. His *History of the English Church and People* up until 729 has been invaluable for our understanding of that period.

618 He was bishop of Antioch from 324- 330.

619 He was a Greek writer in the early third century B.C.

620 Cp. with 1605 Passion Sermon. Andrewes, Vol. 2, p. 166.

621 Cp. with 1597 Passion Sermon. Ibid., p. 128.

regard? no remorse? no bowells? are you not men?[622] Behold the man [Joh: 19.5]! the man you have presented to me, scourged like a slave, drencht in his own gore, crown'd with thornes, scorn'd, buffetted, spitt on. Doubtlesse he will never affect more crownes, that hath felt this of thornes, the purple and reed will sufficiently teach him, that his person was not made to wear a Diadem, nor his hands bound with thongs, ordain'd to weild a scepter; Had he before any ambitious thoughts, by this time they are taken down from aspiring to kingdomes.

But neither that wofull spectacle of a man so cruelly used, nor Pilate's *Ecce* could any whit allay the malice of the Jewes. Dye he must, nothing could satisfie them, till they saw him breath out his last. And therefore in a rude tumultous manner, they cry again, crucify [him, crucify him Luk: 23.21]. A seditious person he was, and if he went about to save him, he was no friend to Caesar [Joh: 19.12]. With this Pilate was conquered; at the name of Caesar he shrinks, and will rather crucify 1,000d Christs, then be none of Caesar's friend. And so he delivered him up to be crucifyed.

And thus you see, how the Son of man when he came into the hands of sinfull men, was miserably used, hurried from place to place, posted from Judge to Judge, put over from torment to torment, from the garden to Annas, from Annas to Caiaphas, from Caiphas to Pilate, from Pilate to Herod, from Herod to Pilate again; cruelty walking the circle, and impiety now treading the Ring. His apprehending joyn'd to his Agony, his Accusacion to his apprehending that received by derision, derision by stripes, stripes by crowning with thornes. 'Tis not to be told what he suffered in his soul, when compassed round with sorrowes and distressed with feares, and that even to death; in his body when his cheekes were swollen with buffetting, his face defiled with uncleane spittle, his back torn with the whipp, his head pierced with the crowns of thornes; never did innocent man indure such a world of contumelies, such a complicacion of miseries.[623]

But this is not all, being delivered into the hands of sinfull men, they will not leav him till they crucify him, 'tis the last Act of this

622 Cp. with 1604 Passion Sermon. Ibid., pp. 140 –1.

623 In meditative form this is in Brightman, pp. 214- 8; Ms. 3708, pp. 15 –8.

Tragedy and the saddest that ever was presented; the Sun became pitch at the sight of it, the earth quaked, the Temple split, the graves opened, and the dead awaked at the sense of it [Math: 27. 51 -2]. And the son of man [must be delivered into the hands of sinful men and be crucified Luk: 24.7].

Be crucified. And here we shall consider 1. The place where, 2. manner and nature of that death, what 'tis to be crucified.

1. Place, Golgotha Math: 27.33 an unpleasant unsavoury place; unpleasant to the eye, for the skulls and bones of dead men; and unsavoury to the nostrills, for the heads, and putrified limbs of malefactors rotting in that place; 'twas the very sink of Jerusalem; a place for all filth and rubbish; thither was our blessed saviour haled with a cursed violence, spareing no disgrace or cruelty as they led him to it; and he watering the stones and pebbles in the streete with his own blood, so that they who did not see him, have traced him by his scattered blood from the Town-hall to the place of execution.

And there they crucified him, Math: 27.35. That kind of punishment of old was not in use amongst the Jewes, but borrowed from the Romanes; and of all other punishments 'twas the most painfull and most shamefull.

The word crucifie is applied to denote unto us, the tormenting and torturing of a man upon a frame of wood erected in the form of a crosse, where 1st He was miserably racked, his body drawn out to that length and breadth that you might view every joynt, count every ribb, number every bone in his body, read to that purpose, Ps: 22.17. They pierced my hands and my feet, I may tell all my bones, they looke and stare upon me. 2nd. In this great extremity he was nayled to the tree thorow each hand, thorow the palm of the hand, the union, meeting of the joynts and sinewes where we are most sensible, so that the wounds there could not chuse but be exceeding painfull. 3rd. There was a ledge of wood made to stand upon, not for ease but torment, that after they had stretched his body at large, as much as will and malice could devise, they might nayle his feet down to that board, fasten him at length, and keepe him in the same extremity of torment. This 'tis to be crucified. And thus our saviour hung 6 long houres upon the rack for our Redemption, for his passion began about that 3rd hour, Mar: 15.25 and twas the 9th hour before he gave up the Ghost, v. 34. And all that time he was in full and perfect sense, as appeared by his voyce, [v. 37]. He cryed with a loud voyce and gave up the ghost. And here, we shall not omit one passage of his enimies, full of spite and malice; 'Twas a custome of the Jewes, as of other people, to give wine to those that were condemned, and led to their execution, to comfort and revive their spirits, the better to enable them for the stroke of death; but such was their barbarous inhumanity, that to increase his miseries, instead of wine, they gave him vinegar mixed with gall to drink, Math: 27.34. And this not to hasten his death, or send him sooner into another world, but to continue him longer in those terrible paines, it being the quality of vinegar (as Naturalists obs[erve]) to stanch the effusion of blood; so least he should bleed too soon to death, they gave him that on purpose to prolong his torments. But contrary to their expectation, no sooner had he tasted of it, but the work was finished: presently he bowed his head and said Father into thy hands [I commend my spirit], and haveing so said he gave up the Ghost, Luc: 23.46.[624]

And thus after many Deathes we have brought our saviour to his death upon the crosse. Now *consummatum est* --- the last mite due for our Redemption is paid; and you have heard what a dear price he paid for it. What he suffered, is not for any tongue to tell, but his that felt it.

Now he that both done and suffered thus much for us, deserves and requires of us, often to repeate and seriously to meditate upon his sufferings; To what end were these passages written but for our Instruction and Meditacion? So let us leave the story and reflect upon our selves.

'Twould be of marvelous use to us for the rectifying our judgments concerning those proffures[625] which are at any time upon us to render them lesse weighty in our estimacion of them; if we would compare them, either with the intollerable weight of our sins or those incomparable, bitter sufferings of our ever blessed lord and Master Jesus Christ.

---

624 For similar text see Passion Sermons for 1604 and 5. Andrewes, Vol. 2, pp.143- 5, 169 -172.

625 That is, proposals for tasks, duties.

Consider him (Apostle) that endured [the cross], consider the dealing of sinners with him [Heb: 12.3], their undue and illegal proceedings against him, no just cause, no just proofes, but clamours and outcryes, rayling and spitting, buffetting, insulting, and all manner of contumelious and despitefull usage. Contradictions of all sorts, in all respects against his person, offices, doctrine, miracles, conversation, life and being. Doe but thorowly applyingly consider this, and then tell me whether it can be reasonable or allmost possible, for any of us to faint under our petty sufferings? what are we? the best of us, the greatest of us, to him? And what our sufferings, the worst of them, the saddest, the severest of them to his? so amidst thy sorest disasters consider him. ---

2. Whatsoever our saviour suffered in soul, [and] Body, from any persons, at any time 'twas for our sinnes and our salvation. And least we should forget this, the Prophet Esa[iah] tells us it 7 times over in one chap[ter], Esa: 53. He tooke upon him our greifes, our sorrowes; He was wounded for our iniquityes and broken for our transgressions, the chastisement of our peace upon him, with his stripes we healed.

The Lord laid on him the iniquity of US. All, every one of us, we were the men, who for our many sinnes, should have beene so dispised, so rejected, suffered such sorrowes in body, in soul, that should have been thus smitten of God, wounded, bruised.[626]

Let us examine and return a true verdict and it will appeare, that we were the men, that thus used the son of God. We and our fathers together, we and our friends together; we they, who gave him those wounds, we they, that so chastised him, so bruised him. We were principalls in the Murder; Judas, Caiphas, Jewes and Pilate instruments only to execute what by our sins we had effected.[627] There is not one of us here who had not a hand in his death; unlesse there be any that dare say his heart is clean. However we desire to putt it off from one to another; yet we had a hand in it as well as they. It may be, many will wonder, that they should be charged with so haynous a fact, as crucifying [the Lord of glory 1Cor. 2. 8], and every one be ready to ask me in the Disciples Lan-

626 Cp. with Passion Sermon for 1604. Andrewes, Vol. 2, p. 150.

627 This is also expressed in the above sermon. p. 151.

guage; Is it I? [Math: 26.22] Or another, is it I? Yet, as Nathan to David, Thou art the man [2Sam: 12.7]. 'Tis thou and He, and I, and every one of us, that put to death the lord of glory; Thou and I, as well as others, were the transgressors for whose sinnes, God hath smitten and wounded and bruised him. There is not an Oath we vainly take, but was as a thorn in his crown; not a leud action we commit, but was as a stripe on his back, no mischief we plot, but is as a spear that runs him to the heart. Every notorious habituall enormity indulged to against conscience, is a thorn, and a nayle and a spear yet to wound him. And if any be so wretchedly prophane, as still to proceed in their wicked wayes, let them hear their doome, 'tis an heavy sentence, Heb: 10.26. There remaines no more sacrifice for sin [but a certain fearful looking for] of judgment and fiery indignacion which shall devour Adversaryes. For if [those that despised] Moses law, died without mercy, of how much sorer punishment shall he be worthy, who hath troden under foot the son of God, counted the blood of covenant an unholy thing and done despite the Spirit of grace.

But if any will be crucifying, let them turn it upon another object; instead of crucifying Christ let them crucify their own flesh with the affections and lusts [Gal: 5.24].

And now 3. How many excellent contemplacions may we have upon this sad object, our crucifyed saviour? Let us looke into his body, we may easily doe it; his stripes are as lattices, and his wounds as so many windowes to let in our eyes.[628] Our friends will open their doores to us, that we may come in, their garners that we may fill our sacks, their cellars, that we may tast their wine, their purses to lend us money; but did you ever read of a friend that would open his whole heart, nay that would dye for another? The Apostle tells us, that for a good man, one will dare to dye [Rom: 5.7]; he would scarce do it, he would but attempt, assay, dare to doe it; but when we were enimyes, open professed enimyes, Christ dyed [for us Rom: 5.8]. We may look through the doore of his sides, and see his bowells of loveing kindnesse, heart of compassion, moveing and stirring, yerning upon us. And shall not our bowells move and stirr? can we for very humanity, be

628 Cp. with Passion Sermon for 1605. Ibid., p. 178.

lesse then compassionate towards him? Alas! but few, very few he sees, that are sensible of his sufferings, and that putts him in a passion still. He may to this day complain, as he did by one of his prophets, That men hide their faces from him, and esteeme him not, Esa: 53.3. And he may ask as he did by the prophet Jeremy, Is it nothing to you [who pass by Lam: 1.12]? Shall I shed all these teares? pour forth all this blood, sweat, bleed, dye, thus ignominiously, painfully, accursedly for you? And will you not pitty me for it; and will yee have no esteeme, no regard but by your continued crying transgressions, crucify me again, keep my wounds fresh and bleeding? I could not be at rest in heaven, till I had put my selfe into pain to ease you; and now that I have done it, will you not put yourselves to a little pain, compunction, contrition to ease me? 'Tis but your compassion I call for; that you would have pity upon yourselves; compassion upon your own soules; those soules whose redemption cost me so dear, will you sell them for a thing of nought? why will you be so cruell to kill yourselves, now after I have died for you?

Lastly, look upon thy crucified Saviour and love him. He loved thee first, cast an affection upon thee, when thou wast a stranger; nay not a stranger only, but an enimy, an enimy so stubborn, that thou stood out in rebellion; so poor, that thou wast exposed to the loathing of thy person, so contemptible that no eye pittied thee [Ezek: 16.5]; And yet when thou wast in such a case, he cast his skirt over thee [Ezek: 16.8] and made that the time of love. Then came he from heaven to make suit to our soules, and he was resolved to speed in his suit, or it should cost him all that he had. A man hath nothing more precious then his blood, and that he would and did spend to espouse us, *sic Deus dilexit,* if you aske me how much, I cannot tell. Christ so loved his enimyes, that he made them his friends; so loved sinners, that he made them just men, so the children of wrath, that he made them vessels of mercy [Rom: 9.23]; so loved the servants of sin that he would make them his brethren, so the children of darknesse; that he would make them members of his own body; so poor beggars, that he would make them his sonnes and heirs, heirs of a kingd[om], Heirs of the kingd[om] of Heaven; No reason can be given for it, but only *sic dilexit,* so God [loved the world that he gave his only begotten Son Joh: 3.16] and that's all.

But alas, how coldly do we answer his love? our love is more fervent to any pleasure, any profit, any vanity, then to him. If the same Question were put to us, that was to Peter, Simon son of [Jonas] love yee, your saviour? [Joh: 21.16]. Love yee the Lord Jesus? Love yee the son of God who [loves yee], you would with one voice reply, the lord knoweth, we all love him. Well then I hope, it is so, and shall only make this motion, That you by an holy life testify your love, by good works justify your love, that your love continue and encrease, and he will requite it with love againe; give you beauty for ashes, the oyle of gladnesse for the spirit of heavinesse; nay more he will give you hims[elf] and with hims[elf] all his riches and abundance, all his glorious promises, even glory and immortality, and eternall life.

SERMON FIVE

AT CHRISTMAS

Introduction

As already evident in Sermon One, Andrewes never ceased to be amazed at the mystery of the Incarnation, when the second person of the Godhead took our "unworthy" nature. In his 1605 Christmas Sermon at Court he expressed this amazement in the words of John *Chrysostom*, "'It casteth me into an ecstasy, and maketh me to imagine of our nature some great matter, I cannot well express what.'"[629] He believed that all Christians should be content to accept this act of God as one of the great mysteries of the faith which is the cause for celebration and makes "the feast great" as he declared in his Nativity Sermon for 1607.[630] In expounding and defending this great mystery he reiterated much of the contents of Sermon One, which later was repeated in the Court Sermon for Christmas day, 1611. They all defended the Chalcedonian formula against the various heresies on the hypostatical union in Christ. In this sermon he emphasised that "No one point of divine truth hath been either more subtilly opposed by heretiques, or more learnedly cleared by the great lights of the ancient ch[urch] than this of the Hypostaticall union." Hence he defined the Chalcedonian teaching that has always been accepted by the major Western and Eastern Churches.[631]

---

629 Ibid., Vol. 1, pp. 5-6.

630 Ibid., p. 32.

631 Ms. 3707, p. 173. Some of the Orthodox churches (Armenian, Coptic, Ethiopian

Andrewes again presented "the truth of his Humanity" to expose the heretical teaching of the Anabaptists, the modern Marcionites. Christ's body was real and true as ours are in all ways, except for sin. Even after His Resurrection Christ still possessed "a true Humane body". To support his teaching he quoted from the Fathers, this time Gregory Nazianzen, Damascene, Epiphanius and summarised it in the words of Irenaeus, "his Diety willingly permitted that his humanity should be afflicted."[632]

Not only did Andrewes in this sermon attack heretics but also theologians such as the Thomists who debated *ad infinitum* over the ways that God could have redeemed mankind. All that schoolmen needed to know, suggested Andrewes, was that man could not save himself. When God decided to rescue him from his misery, He chose to send His Son into the world to redeem him. All this was expressed in the allegory of verse ten of psalm eighty-five, *Mercy and Truth shall meet; Righteousness and Peace shall kiss one another* which Andrewes related in vivid imagery, much of which was repeated in the 1616 Christmas Sermon which took this verse as the text.[633]

This sermon also saw Andrewes preach on Christ's righteousness and man's unrighteousness, "there is not one righteous, ... we are all defiled and polluted, and must cry with the leper, unclean." We all must therefore go to our "High Priest " if we want to "be saved".[634] Righteousness, had been one of the doctrines much discussed by Reformers who claimed that Christ imputes rather than impartes His righteousness to us. It was this doctrine that changed Luther's life. Luther had always been obsessed with his own sins and despite whatever he did to rectify his life he believed he was a hopeless sinner, and thus unable to enter into a relationship with a righteous God. Then came his *Turmerlebius* (Tower experience). It all seemed so easy, he was made righteous through the righteouness of God through Christ who had died for our sins. Faith,

---

and Syrian) rejected the Chalcedon teaching on the two natures of Christ in one person (dyophysite), and believe one nature Christology (miaphysite).

632 Ms. 3707, p. 173.

633 Andrewes, Vol. 1. pp. 175-95.

634 Ms. 3707, p. 177.

and not good works was the glue to the union between the sinner and Christ. Hence being justified by faith alone and not good works, became Luther's cry. Andrewes also preached on Righteousness in a sermon at Whitehall in 1600. Here he declared that although God alone is righteous, the Son of God through His life and obedience to His Father has imputed His righteousness to us. Such preaching showed he shared the Reformers teaching of inherent righteousness, and therefore we can never merit righteousness. Without Christ's righteousness, our own righteousness is but "dung" and will not be sufficient on Judgment day when we face that "most dreadful place and time". A true righteousness is pure or as Chrysostom expressed it, it must not have "a spot in it", and therefore through the "spotless one" sinners receive Christ's righteousness as a gift. This, Andrewes stated had been the teaching of the Fathers such as Ambrose and Augustine, collated by Bernard as, "What can hinder us, but that we should 'use him and his righteousness; use that which is ours to our best behoof, and work our salvation out of this our Saviour.'" So in *Jehova justitia nostra* through Christ we are "justified", "forgiven" and prayed for, before the throne of heaven.[635]

Amidst all the controversy over a justifying righteousness amongst schoolmen, Andrewes insisted that the only thing needed was that "we must come to *justitia nostra Jehovâ.*" With this in mind he indicated that both Cardinal Bellarmine and Thomas Stapleton[636] were correct in using the term *imputation*. "The Church of Rome taketh this Name aright ... that Christ's righteousness and

635 Andrewes, Vol. 5, pp. 109, 112, 121, 125.

636 St. Robert Bellarmine (1542-1621), a Jesuit theologian and Cardinal who disputed with James 1 over the nature of the Church. James' *Triplici Nodo, Triplex* Cuneus or Apology *under Oath* came under attack from Pope Paul V who directed Bellarmine to respond to it. James had referred to himself as "a Catholic Christian" and one who reverenced the general councils of the early Church more than the Jesuits do. Bellarmine responded under the title *Responsio Matthaei Torti as librum, Triplici etc.* James in turn summoned Andrewes to reply. Accordingly he wrote *Tortura Torti* (1608) in which he raised three major issues: the Papal claim to supremacy, the dispensing power of the Pope and the Royal Supremacy itself. Bellarmine counter answered in his *Apologia* to which Andrewes responded in 1610 with *Responsio ad Apologiam.* In this work Andrewes more than anywhere else stated his belief in the real presence of Christ in the Eucharist.

Thomas Stapleton (1535-1598), a Prebendary of Chichester under Mary 1, later taught

merits are imputeth to us." However "in the positive justice", that is, "that part thereof which is meritorious for reward, there fall they into a fancy" as they "suppose 'a righteousness from God,' ... without the righteousness in Christ. ... So by this means shrink they up their Name, and though they leave the full sound, yet take they half the sense from it." They therefore ignore that in *Jehova justitia nostra,* there is forgiveness of sins, "to give us salvation", just as "in the Name of Christ" there is "a power for remission of sins" and "a power to save." It is only by Christ's absolution of our sins that we have "our righteousness". Hence "we have cause to blame them justly, for not contenting themselves with that which contented" Isaiah, St. John Baptist and the Fathers.[637]

Andrewes concluded with the old Patristic adage, that Christ became man in order that man may become divine, that is, Christ came to earth so that man could be lifted to heaven. So "for shame let us not live in our sins, seeing our Lord was born this day to dye for them." As we are "washed, healed, [and] freed" we should strive to sin no more, and show our thanks for a "free Pardon" by "a lively faith" which brings forth fruit. Otherwise we cannot claim such a pardon; "it belongs not unto thee". In other words good works are also necessary. Hence he concluded with another of his favourite teachings, *imitatio Christi.* "He is the great Exemplar and Pattern of holynesse and we ought to follow his stepps, tho' we cannot fill them." This is the Christian vocation.[638]

Heb. 2.17.
Wherefore in all things as it behooved him to be made like unto his brethren, that he might be a mercyfull and faithfull high Priest, in things, pertaining to God, to such reconciliacion for the sins of the people.

There is nothing in our Christian Faith not truly admirable; our Religion is a meer Tessae or mixture of marvells. But that which most exceeds all created capacity and comprehension,

---

at Louvain and Douai. He translated Bede's *Historia Ecclesaistica Gentis Anglorum* into elegant Elizabethan English.

637 Andrewes, Vol. 5, pp. 106, 118 - 9.

638 Ms. 3707, pp. 175, 178.

which is a pure absurdity and contradiction in Nature, and which forced the very Angells into astonishment, is that which Damascen calls *Πάντων καινῶν καινῶτατον* the only strang new thing under the sun, or (as St. Paul aptly termes it) *μέγα μυστήριον*; viz. that the word ... be made flesh, ... cover and cloath hims[elf] with flesh and blood, and 2 natures so infinitely distant meet and unite thems[elves] in one person. A Person in whom all the predictions and computacions, Accompts, Types, shaddowes, of Jacob's shilo,[639] Balaam's starr,[640] Esay's Imm[anuel],[641] Daniel's Messiah,[642] and Mal[achi]'s sun[643] are fully accomplished. A person, in whom the discipline and Tutorage of the law is ended, the Dayes and Date of the mosaicall Policy is finished. For Christ alone is the Truth of all Types, Body of all shaddowes, substance of both Testaments, end and aim of that law, whole and sole subject of the Gospell[644], so that all these wonderfull wonders were wrought by our Saviour's Incarnacion. In which mystery, both a distinct particular knowledge is requisite, and all ignorance and mistakeings are dangerous. And that's the reason why the Apostle doth here so continue and inlarg his discourse, upon a poynt so important, and as if he were loath to remove his Pen, or take off his thoughts from so pleaseing an Argument; he dwells upon it, resumes it again and again, dilates and amplifies it in different words, but all to the same sense and substance in the former verses and here in the Text. Wherefore in all [things it behooved him].

Words, but few, but matters rich and plentifull, where we are informed 1st How. 2ly Why, God became man or here we have 1. Truth and verity 2. Motives or end of our saviours Incarnacion.

For the truth of his Humanity. He did not only resemble us in some few more noble and excellent partes and faculties of our nature, but was made like unto us *κατά πάντα*, all Partes, Powers, Properties, even defects and infirmities naturall and incident

---

639 Genesis 49.10.

640 Numbers 24.17.

641 Isaiah 7.14.

642 Daniel 9.25.

643 Malachi 4.2.

644 Cp. with Nativity Sermons for 1609 and 10. Andrewes, Vol. 1, pp. 49, 75 – 6.

to all of us, were all in him; He was born week and feeble as we are, an infant of a span long [Lam: 2.19, 20], in great poverty, his Parents so poor, that his mother was not worth a lamb, Luc: 2. 24. He was obscurely brought up, increased in age, stature, wisdome; attained by degrees to his Perfection; was troubled like one of us with hunger, thirst, wearinesse, weaknesse, weepeing and heavinesse; He suffered, died and was buried [Creed]. All these and all the rest harmles accidents of our nature, he willingly undertook. In all he was like his brethren, like in all, both subtance and innocent qualities. Least the Marcionites of old, and Anabaptist should hence deduce their Error, That Christ had no true and reall, but only an Imaginary and phantasticall Body, bec[ause] he is said to be like [man], the Apostle to dash this fancy adds **κατά πάντα,** he had not only a shape and shaddow, or empty resemblance of our flesh, but every way, in all respects, in all things, like unto us only sin[645] (the shame and stain of nature) excepted.

But why was he thus altogether made like unto [us]? Text gives 2 Reasons in one word πρέπε. 1. Bec[ause] this was convenient, 2. Bec[ause] necessary.

'Twas convenient, *oportuit,* it behooved our Redeemer to be Incarnate. To question whether God by some other meanes, might not have wrought the reconciliacion of mankind is a needles and dangerous curiosity, Lombard, Aquinas[646] and their servants the schoolmen, are too audacious, boldy disputeing of the Power and Widsome of G[od], what he could, and what he might have done in his case. This is certain, that God can doe more, than any man can conceiv; but again, this is as certain, if other meanes were possible, yet of all others this was most convenient, that the wrath of G[od] should be pacifyed, the sin of man purged by the blood of him who is God and man. Nor could there be a more clear demonstracion of the boundles justice, mercy, truth, wisedome of G[od] then this. And therefore

2. *Debuit,* it was necessary Christ should be Man; for haveing

---

645 Gregory of Nanzianzus stated, "becoming for all men all things that we are, except sin." Oration XXX. Refer also to Nativity Sermon for 1605. Andrewes, Vol. 1, p. 9.

646 Peter Lombard's (1100 - 60) *Sentenses* was the standard textbook of Catholic theology prior to Thomas Aquinas (1125? - 74) *Summa Theologica.* These two were regarded as the "most influential mediæval teachers." Johnson, p. 341.

undertaken the charg of our great H[igh] Priest, to be the Ransomer and Redeemer of our souls, the Purchaser of our eternall peace and pardon, 2. vertues were of necessity required in him for the discharg of that high and honourable office, Mercy and fidelity; Fidelity towards G[od] in procureing his favour and working our reconciliacion; Mercy tow[ards] us his weak brethren, in releeving and commiserateing our infirmities. Now 'twas his Incarnacion that fitted and enabled him to the practice of both these vertues, that made him both faithfull and mercyfull. For neither could our H[igh] Pr[iest] have been faithf[ul] unles for our sinnes he had sacrificed his Body, and shed his blood, without which there is no remission [Heb: 9.22]; nor mercyfull[ness] unles the lively experience and sentiment of our miseries in hims[elf] had wrought in him a true and tender compassion tow[ards] us. Whereas now *non ignarus mali,* in that he hims[elf] hath suffered, being tempted, he is able to succour [them that are tempted Heb. 2.18].

This is briefly the sence and resolucion of the Text. Let us now see what may be collected for our Instructions.

And here the main point which this Text offers to our consideracion and expresseth *in Terminis,* is this, That our L[ord] J[esus] Christ, the eter[nal] Son of G[od] was truly made Flesh, a true entire Man in all things like unto his brethren.

Let us breifly take a distinct and particular view of the severall particulars in this Collection.

1. His Body was no aery Meteor, an empty phantasm, a meer shape or shadow, but a true Humane body, endured and informed with a humane and reasonable soul, and attended with all the essential and naturall properties both of body and soul, which are usuall and necessary consequents of our Humanity. For proof whereof we have.

1. The expresse Testimony of our Lord himself. After his Resurrection tho' his body was refined from all corruptible qualities, yet it remained still a true Humane body: his humane nature was then beautified with glory, but not abolished or annihilated. And therefore when he appeared suddenly and unexpectedly in the midst of his Disciples, Lest they should suspect him to be a Ghost or spirit without any quantity or bodily dimensions, he appeales unto their senses, (certain and infallible witnesses) and bids them

handle [me and see, for a spirit hath not flesh and bones, as yee see me have His body Luc: 24.39].

2. If he had not a true humane body, then he not out true Redeem[er],[647] he did not dye for us in truth, but only in conceit and opinion of by-standers, *καλά ... καλά Φαντάσματα* [beautiful (but) beautiful visions]. But this is confuted by the Prophet Esay 53.4,5. Surely he hath born our griefs and carried ô sorrows; he was wounded for [our] transgressions and bruised for [our] iniquities; chastisement [of our peace was upon him, and with] his stripes we are healed.

2. As he participates with us in a true humane body, so is this body informed with [a humane and reasonable] soul; He hath not a dead, livelesse body, nor is it quickened or animated by his Deity only (as Ar[ius] and Apollinarius conceited) my soul heavy [unto death Math: 26.38], Into thy hands [I commend my spirit Luc: 23.46], and in the same place *ἐξέπνευσεν*, gave up [the] Ghost, yeelded up [His spirit Math: 27.50]. Besides the 2 principall powers of reas[onable] soul, und[erstanding] and will are both affirmed of Christ. In his understand[ing], he increased in knowl[edg] and is ignorant of the last Day; his will was diverse from his Fathers, not as I will, but as thou [wilt Math: 26.39]. And indeed how could he be man without a reasonable soul, that gives a man both his name and being? How could he suffer death, that is a separacion of soul and body? How satisfie God's justice that required especially the punishment of the soul as the cheif offender?

Lastly, as Damascen and before him Nazian[zien] disputes; either he took our soul with our flesh or he left our soul under the wrath of God in the danger of Hell, for, 'tis a certain rule, *τὸ ἀπόοληπτον ἀθεράπευτον* that which Christ did not assume, he did not redeem, and therefore either he hath [our body and redeems it or he did not and did not redeem it] .

3. Our Lord in the state of Humiliacion stooped so low, as to take up our very defects and infirmities; Defects of body infirmityes of mind.

And 1. He took our bodily defects. By defects, we mean not any want, or diminucion of any Parts or members, (for the com-

647 Andrewes expands on this in his Nativity Sermon for 1611. Andrewes, Vol. 1 p. 90.

posicion of his body was most entire and absolute) but those miseries, sorrowes, and calamities which are in all us; as to suffer hunger, thirst, cold, wearinesse, labour, anguish and death itself. But yet here least we mistake, the Ancient Doctors help us with some necessary caveats; Christ tooke not our defects indefinitly and promiscuously, but only such as are εὔλογα πάθη (Epiphan[ius])[648] such as are decent, and not unbecomeing our nature. And again (as Damascen, and before him Euseb[ius], Bishop of Thessalon[ica]), in Photius[649] φυσικὰ καὶ ἀδιάβλητα πάθη, καὶ ἀναγκαῖα πάθη, naturall and in all inculpable. And to the same purpose, S. Basil well distinguishes φυσικὰ καὶ ἀναγκαῖα πάθη from such as are ἐκ κακίας κὰι προαιρήσεως μοχθηρὰ, necessary passions from such as are impure and perverse. And therefore 2 kinds of defects must here be excepted and excluded to which our Saviour was not subject.

The first kind are such passions as are not naturall, or common to all the posterity of Adam, but peculiar to some arising from some particular causes and sinnes; as diseases of diverse sorts, consumptions, Fevers, Leprosies, dropsies and the like. The 2nd kind are such defects as are vitious and sinfull as difficulty and indiposicion to good, prones and prophension[650] to evill. These are not generall innocent infirmities incident to all, but special and corrupt, befalling only some few by intemperance or some other occasion. And in these (pollucions rather than Passions) Christ not like his brethren: but in all the rest he was only with this difference, that all defects in us are necessarily contracted by sin, but in him voluntary. For as Irenaeus, *quiescente verbo homo patiebatur*, his Diety willingly permitted that his humanity should be afflicted.

Now secondly for Infirmityes of the mind or soul, the same restriction and limitacion, must again be repeated. Some Infirmities are naturall and generall to all, as to be born unlearned, indued

---

648 He was the fourth century bishop of Salamis who upheld the Nicaea Council and wrote the *Refutation of all the Heresies*.

649 As Patriarch of Constantinople in the ninth century he was involved with Rome in the struggle for Bulgaria. Photius accused Rome of trying to impose on the Bulgarians heresies such as the *filoque* clause, and of undermining the strict fast of Lent.

650 i.e. inclination.

with all naturall affections, love, joy, sorrow, hope, fear etc. all these were in our Redeemer; other proceed from some particular ill disposing causes; as to be born not only unlearned, but uncapable, foolish, dull, stupid, these not in him.

Again, Infirmities, some are faulty and tainted with sin; from these our Saviour was alltogether free, for he was holy [one of God, Mark 1.24] others are only miseries not sinnes or blemishes, as pure ignorance or nescience, fear, sorrow - all these he took upon him, and in all these was like [unto us] as appears thorow the whole story of his life in the gospell. See now the glorious Son of G[od] in all things made like [unto us]. But here least we err, we must so conceiv our Saviour to be like [us] in these weak affections that yet betw[een] his and ours, there is a manifold wide difference. For 1. all affections in Christ are Regular and orderly governed by sound judgment and Reason; lending allw[ays] to lawfull and good objects, but in us for the most parte, wild and exorbitant, rejecting the curb and counsell of Reason and rushing headlong into all [sin]. 2. In our Lord Reason, their seat and originall, in us they reside in the sensitive appetite, a brutish faculty and much depraved. And thus [the Word became] Flesh [and dwelt amongst us Joh: 1.14]. And mark how properly L[ord] Immanuel; for he is not only God for us, or God with us, but God one of us; God comed down in the likenesse of man amongst [us], and therefore he that hath none like hims[elf] in heaven or earth, hath yet made hims[elf] like one of us. He that was our Father is now also our brother *ὁμοιούσιος* and *ὁμούσιος*, same person like his Father true and perfect God in his divine nature, in his humane, true and perfect man.

If now you ask after the manner of this hypostaticall union and enquire how these 2 natures so distinct are united in this one person? I must 1. answer with J[ustin] Martyr, *σαφής ἔλεγγος ἀπιστίας τὸ πῶς περί θεοῦ λέγειν*. How and why, are 2 sawcy questions in divine mysteries where we are to beleev what we cannot comprehend. And the very Pagan Germans in Tacitus thought it *sanctius* and *reverentius de Deo credere quam scire*. A modest and silent veneration becomes us here better than any curious inquisicion.

No one point of divine truth hath been either more subtilly opposed by Heretiques, or more learnedly cleared by the great lights of the ancient ch[urch] then this of the Hypostaticall Union. The errors were principally 5. Some changed the one nature of Christ into the other; some confounded the 2 natures with their properties; others divided the person; others separated the natures, and lastly some affirmed them to be united only accidentally. Against these 5 dangerous errors the famous councell of C[h]alcedon (a venerable assembly of above 600 bishops) protested in 5 words, confessing in the name of the whole Christian catholique ch[urch] that the 2 natures to be united in his one person, *ἀτρέπτως, ἀσυγχύτως, ἀδιαίρετως, ἀχώριστως, οσιώστως*.[651]

1. *ἀτρέπτως*, unchangably, for the Word without any alteracion in hims[elf] was made Flesh; 2. *ἀσυγχύτως*, distinctly, without any confusion, either of Natures or properties or faculties; 3. *ἀδιαίρετως*, indivisibly, the manhood, not only assisted by the Godhead, but personally united to it; 4. *ἀχώριστως*, inseperably, the natures so neerly joyned, that our very thoughts cannot separate them, without dissolving the person. Lastly, *οσιώστως*, essentially, for the humane nature, is now a substantiall parte of the person, not an externall accompaniment, or adjunct, or like a vestment to be put off or on.

Take briefly, the summe of all in these 3 Proposicions; 1. Here is an union; or makeing of 2 one. 2ly, The things thus united, are the Godhead, as 'tis limited to the 2nd Person in the Trinity, and the manhood. 3. For the term of this union, these 2 are made, not one Nature, but one Person of the Mediatour.

The point is deep and difficult[652] and therefore requires so much the more diligent heed and attention; we are to look well to our thoughts, that they walk warily in this narrow path; betw[een] ignorance on the one side and error on the other.

Well now, what use of this point? 'Tis the usuall and generall *Quære*, what newes? And when we hear good newes we use to be merry and chearfull. I have told you such newes, as may well warm us all at the heart. 'Twas an Angell that told it as first, as was fitting. And he said withall, it was glad tideings of great joy

---

651 The Chalcedonian formula is a major part of the 1611 Christmas Day Sermon. Andrewes, Vol. 1, p. 91.

652 In the above sermon Andrewes listed these difficulties. Ibid., pp. 87-91.

to all [people Luc: 2.10]. But what is it? This day was born unto us Σώτηρ, [a Saviour Luc: 2. 11]. Tully confesseth all the Latine tongue cannot expresse the word, and I am sure no tongue can expresse the thing, the Mercy of this Saviour, the comfort of this salvacion. 'Tis enough that we feel and enjoy it tho' we cannot expresse it.[653]

Come then, this is the Day which the lord hath made, nay this is the Day in which the lord was made, letts therefore rejoyce [and be glad in it Ps: 118. 24]. But how shall we show our gladnesse? by riotting, drunkenesse, chamb[ering], wanton[ess Rom: 13.13].[654] Is this to be glad or frantick rather? Solomon calls such mirth madenesse, Eccl: 2.2. And Nazian[zen] Orat.38 (where he discourses excellently how Christians should celebrate this Festivitie) [ἀχ] λὰ πάντα μὲν Ἕλληοι παρῶμεν [but rather we should leave all such things to the Greeks].[655] If we should keep a Feast to Bacchus

---

653 Andrewes' sermon at Christmas 1613 expresses this theme of joy of a Saviour. Andrewes, Vol. 1, p. 64ff.

654 A similar comment is made at the end of the next sermon.

655 The full text from Gregory of Nanzianzus. "Therefore let us keep the Feast, not after the manner of a heathen festival, but after a godly sort; not after the way of the world, but in a fashion above the world; not as our own but as belonging to Him Who is ours, or rather as our Master's; not as of weakness, but as of healing; not as of creation, but of re-creation.

And how shall this be? Let us not adorn our porches, nor arrange dances, nor decorate the streets; let us not feast the eye, nor enchant the ear with music, nor enervate the nostrils with perfume, nor prostitute the taste, nor indulge the touch, those roads that are so prone to evil and entrances for sin; let us not be effeminate in clothing soft and flowing, whose beauty consists in its uselessness, nor with the glittering of gems or the sheen of gold or the tricks of colour, belying the beauty of nature, and invented to do despite unto the image of God; Not in rioting and drunkenness, with which are mingled, I know well, chambering and wantonness, since the lessons which evil teachers give are evil; or rather the harvests of worthless seeds are worthless. Let us not set up high beds of leaves, making tabernacles for the belly of what belongs to debauchery. Let us not appraise the bouquet of wines, the kickshaws of cooks, the great expense of unguents. Let not sea and land bring us as a gift their precious dung, for it is thus that I have learnt to estimate luxury; and let us not strive to outdo each other in intemperance (for to my mind every superfluity is intemperance, and all which is beyond absolute need), - and this while others are hungry and in want, who are made of the same clay and in the same manner.

Let us leave all these to the Greeks and to the pomps and festivals of the Greeks, who call by the name of gods beings who rejoice in the reek of sacrifices, and who consistently worship with their belly; evil inventors and worshippers of evil demons. But we, the Ob-

or Venus, some Idoll heathen God, we could not doe it in a worse fashion.[656] Let us rather joyn hearts and tongues with that Quire of Angells, Luc 2.[14] and bear a parte with them in that h[oly] hymn which they sang at the birth of [Christ] saying, Glory [be to God on high] who hath sent down the Prince of peace to earth, and so much testified his good will tow[ards] men [Luc: 2. 14]. And with Zachary, fall to our *Benedictus* [Luc: 1.67- 79], and with all the creatures in H[eaven] and E[arth], Rev: [5.1]3, say, Praise, honour, glory, Power be to Him that sits upon [the throne].[657]

The feast of our Saviour's Nat[ivity], not a single Festivall, [οὐ]κ ἁπλῶς ἁγία πανήγυρις Nyssen)[658] ἀλλ' ἁγία ἁγίων κὶ πανήγυρις πανηγύρεων; the most holy and most solemn of all the rest, being the originall of all others. And therefore the ch[urch] thinking it not meet to confine so great a Festivall to one Day, hath appoynted 4 Advent Sundays as 'twere to usher in this celebrity and to prepare and dispose us for it. But surely; if all our Dayes, all our yeares were wholly spent in rendring Thanks and Praise to our Incarnate Saviour for his Benefitts, our whole life would be too short for so worthy an exercise.

And we must take care that our Thanks be not only a labour of the Lipp; our best Thankfulnesse is our hearty chearfull, constant obedience; if we serv this Saviour in holynesse [and righteousness all the days of our life Luc: 1.75], for to this end was our Lord born, that we might be born again; and he came down to earth purposely, that he might lift up our soules and affections towards heaven. Let's therefore be Christians in earnest, deny ungodlinesse [and worldly lusts, we should live soberly, righteously, and godly Tit: 2.12]. By all meanes labour and study to be holy, harmles [undefiled, separate from sinners Heb: 7.26] that so at least we

---

ject of whose adoration is the Word, if we must in some way have luxury, let us seek it in word, and in the Divine Law, and in histories; especially such as are the origin of this Feast; that our luxury may be akin to and not far removed from Him Who hath called us together." Oration 38, v. 4 -6.

656 Cp. with text in 1613 Nativity Sermon. Andrewes, Vol. 1, pp. 132 -3.

657 Cp. this with appropriate text in Brightman, p. 119.

658 This is Gregory, bishop of Nyssa (c.330 - 95), the younger brother of St. Basil and St. Macrina. He was deposed by Arians and exiled for two years. He was a famous theologian, orator and writer. He also wrote a biography on Macrina.

may in some things be like unto him, who was like unto us in all things. For shame let us not live in our sins, seeing our Lord was born this day to dye for them.

And if sometimes severall frailties dropp from us, the Apostle tells us this for our comfort, that our faithf[ul] and m[ercifull] h[igh] Priest hath [made reconciliacion] for [the] sinnes of his people, which was the end or motive of his Incarnacion of which in the next place breifly.

St. Bern[ard] in one of his sermons[659] hath an elegant Fiction of a lovely Debate in Heaven, between the Mercy of God and his Justice about miserable Mank[ind] after the fall of Adam. I shall represent his thoughts in my own words, and keep to his ground, varying only the Descant. Thus it runs. After Adam by his Transgression hath offended his maker, and withall his Posterity lay weltering in blood, ripe for destruction, ready for Hell, the glorious Attributes of God were diversily affected with this calamity of man, so goodly a creature; And standing all together before the throne of the Alm[ighty] there waiteing his pleasure, the Mercy of God being nearest to him, had quickly espied his frowning countenance, and fearing an heavy sentence, with teares in her eyes, she hastily falls at his feet, and thus bespeakes him. Turn thine eyes (d[ear] Father) from this wretched man, and look a while upon me, thy loveing Mercy; I confesse (dread Soveraign) he is not worthy to be pitied: but is not thy Mercy worthy to be magnified? He hath forgotten to be dutifull, for he is a man, but canst thou forgett to be gracious [Ps: 77.9], who art a God? I deny not, he hath meritted the utmost of thine anger and justice hath reason to demand him, and thou canst not punish him beyond his desert: but shall not my teares quench thy flaming Indignacion? Shall it not be thy glory to passe by iniquitie? And will it not far better become thy Majesty to commiserate, then to reveng? What tho' the transgression of this wretch be infinite? (tho' it seemes to want one Degree, for 'tis not so bad as to despair of thy Mercy), but be it infinite, 'tis the more proper object for thy more infinite and boundles clemency. Thus Mercy prayed, and would thus have contin-

---

659 Sermon 1 Annunciation of the Blessed Mary. This sermon is the text for Andrewes' 1616 Christmas sermon in which he includes contents of Bernard's sermon. Andrewes, Vol. 1., p. 180ff.

ued; but Justice an angry Suiter, stepp'd in and thus interrupted her. Great Judg 'tis now my turn to plead, be not perswaded by this importunate Advocate my sister Mercy; Shee knowes thy tendernesse, and still she hopes thus to weep thee into pitty. I wish thee not to look upon the Malefactor, for can thy pure eyes behold such iniquity?

Nor do I desire that Mercy should be neglected: but her turn is past, and now mine succeeds. For did not Mercy move thee to crown with so many honours this thy unworthy creature? Didst not thou raise him out of nothing, to be little inferiour to the Angells, and set him over all the workes of thy hands?[660] Didst thou not plant in him a goodly Image of thine own Majesty, and leav him thy Leiutenant upon Earth dreadfull and venerable to all thy creatures? Didst thou not give him an easy law to try his obedience with power enough to do it; and didst thou not say, that Death and Vengeance should pursue his Apostacy? And were not all these acts of Mercy? Now then (L[ord]) hear mee thy Justice; and compare his contempt with all this thy courtesy. To requite thy favours he hath sinned, and how? I cannot name his wickednesse at once; 'twas not only Pride, or Presumption, or Ingratitude, or Luxury, or cruelty to his offspring, or Infidelity or Apostacy, but all these. And shall not the Judge of all the world do right? [Gen: 18.25] Mercy never suffers thee to punish the Innocent, and can Justice permitt thee to spare the guilty? Didst thou not justly pay the very like rebellion in those more noble spirits, who now are Devills, with utter and perpetuall rejection, and shall man escape? Tho' alas I delight not in his misery, but now if thou strike not, he will hereafter be bold to dare thee to thy face, and despise not only thy Justice, but thy Power and thy Truth and thy Wisedome, And think thee a week Idoll all made up of Mercy. This sharp oracion prickt Mercy at the heart, and with fresh teares shee answers:

Lord, Justice sayes true, for if man were Innocent he should not need thy Mercy. But suppose him worse (if that may be supposed) can his wickednesse equall or surmount thy pitty? Can he doe that which thou canst not pardon? Then should his malice be more infinite than thy clemency. Thy goodnesse indeed he richly

660 Cp. with text in Nativity Sermon for 1605. Ibid., p. 14.

tasted in his creacion; but he shall never feel thy Mercy, unlesse now thou send me to releev him in his misery. And hast thou no regard to thy tender Mercy, wilt thou never use mee? I did not deprecate the curse of Devills, I did not petition thee for their offence, for I saw it was personall, without suggestion, much more ingratefull and malicious; and 'twas fitt for Justice to chastise them; and besides that damned crew, thou hast yet here millions of h[oly] Angells left to serv thee. But shall Justice still prevail and exclude thy Mercy? Shall shee now again, by one weak wilfull man ruine all his poor posterity? Nay shall Satan thine enimy triumph in so rich a spoil, and rob thee at once of this whole most noble Tribe of all thy earthly creatures? This was his hope and aim when he seduced him. But who then shall be left on earth to serv thee? Who shall honour thy majesty, when the devill hath all mank[ind] under his obedience? Justice herself hath yeilded that shee delights not in man's misery. Pardon and pitty then (gracious Lord) and redeem this worm thy servant from that hellish Tyranny. For I resolve not to leav my suit, till thou hast graciously answered mee.

Here Justice again replyed, But canst thou (Lord) neglect thy Justice which is thy self? Canst thou forgett thy word, and not make good that comminacion: In the same day thou eatest [thou shalt] surely dye? [Gen: 2.17] 'Tis me thy Justice whom man hath wrought, and wilt thou put up this injury and not see me satisfied?

Whiles these 2 pithy Orators were thus pleading the Allm[ighty] heard them both with Patience; and beholding with equall favour somet[imes] the one, somet[imes], the other, as 'twere, *dubiis affectibus errat, et modo nescio quid similis crudele minanti vultus erat, modo quem misereri credere possis.* Tho' he seemed rather enclined to his Mercy, yet again lookeing upon his Justice *ἕτερος μὲν θύμος ἔρυκεν*. He was loath to disrespect her; At length the Love of God calls upon him, and prayes him to set his Wisedome on work to meditate a Peace betw[een] M[ercy] and J[ustice] and so to compose the controversy. Indeed this was appropriate work for God's infinite Wisedome; shee readily undertakes the task, and propounds to both Parties this Temperament; what if we could find some innocent Mediator, that would be content to suffer the punishment which man hath deserved, and to dye that he may live?

But where shall we seek him, in earth? 'Tis man that sinned; In Heaven? But which of the Angells hath either so much power, or so much charity, as to buy off man's Torments with his own? No he must needs be a Person of no lesse than Infinite Dignity; and he must be both man to suffer death and God to conquer it: and thus may both Justice be satisfied, and M[ercy] gloriously honoured.

Then Wisedome fixing her eye upon the etern[al] Son of God, who presently takes Wisedome at the word and looking upon his Father, he sayes, Behold here I am to doe [thy will Heb: 10.9]. fitt me a Body [Heb: 10.5]; for I resolve to be made Flesh, and to dispatch all this businesse. Hereupon M[ercy] and Justice straight wayes met together, they embraced and kissed each other.

And thus was Alm[ighty] God highly pleased, his Love, his Goodnesse, his Mercy, his Justice, his Truth, Power, Wisd[ome] all glorified and poor man reconciled and his sins purged.

And now you understand somewhat better the force of this word in the front of the Text, *πρέπει*, *debuit*, you see how convenient, how necessary 'twas in respect of God, in respect of us, that God should be born and dye for us; that Christ our M[erciful] and F[aithful] H[igh] Pr[iest] should make reconciliacion for sinnes ---. Every word allmost offers an Instruction but I will but touch and be gone.

1. Obs[erve] who it is that hath reconciled us to God? Even our faith[ful] H[igh] Pr[iest] --- who is justly named Esa. 9.[6] Prince of Peace, for chastisement of our Peace was [upon him, Is. 53. 5]. When we were at odds with God, 'twas he that set us even and made up the breach. When we lay all arrested by Gods law for the debt of our sinnes, Christ gave his word for us, who being our surety, paid our debt, cancelled our obligacion, fastened it to the tree, and crossed the black lines of God's debt-book, with the red lines of his own blood[661] [Col: 2.14]. Hee's the only valuable price, the only invaluable ransome of our soules; the true Purgatory or propitiacion for sin, the fountain opened to the House of David for uncleanenesse. Wash here, if thou wouldst be clean.

2. Our faith[ful] H[igh] Pr[iest] made reconciliacion for the sinnes [of the world], not for any of his own, that was needles,

---

661 Cp. with 1605 Passion Sermon. Ibid.,Vol. 2, p. 181.

for he was clean without sin, and that's his royall Prerogative. But for all others without exception, or exemption, we all gone astray like [sheep Isa: 53.6]; there is not one righteous, no not one [Rom: 3.10], we are all defiled and polluted, and must cry with the leper, unclean [unclean Lev: 13.45]. Not only all polluted with sin, but all polluted with all sin; at least in the propension and inclinacion of our corrupt nature. And therefore deny thy self, goe to this H[igh] Pr[iest] if thou wouldst be saved. For surely to the best of us belongs nothing but shame and confusion [of face Dan: 9.8] but in him we have plentifull Redemption. For

3ly Our M[erciful] H[igh] Pr[iest] hath purged the sinnes of his People. The sinnes, not one or two, this or that, but indefinitely without restriction or limitacion, the sinnes, all the sinnes of what number, of what nature soever; be they never so loud and crying, the blood of Christ cryes louder and obtaines a remission. Here's thy comfort, but learn thy Duty also.

Now thou art washed, healed, freed, sin no more, least a [worse thing come unto thee Joh. 5.14]. And remember this also, that altho' the Gospell proclaimes a free generall Pardon, yet it belongs not unto thee, unlesse thou take it and apply it; Tho' the blood of Christ be a soveraign Potion, yet (as Prosper[662] speakes) *si non bibitur non medetur*; if not drink it, not doe thee any good. Thou hast no benefit by Christ, unles by a lively Faith, with old Simeon, thou hugg him in thine Arme [Luc: 2.25], and canst say with Thomas [my Lord and God Joh: 20.23], and with St. Paul [the son of God] who loved me [and] gave hims[elf] for me [Gal:2.20]. And thy faith is not lively, unlesse it be fruitfull, unlesse it work thee to a serious and solid Piety, to a constant and universall obedience; to an hatred of all sin, and love of all vertue. For faith is lame unlesse it have 2 hands, with one to take Christ into the soul, with the other, to give up the soul unto Christ. And if thou wouldst have him to be thy Jesus, thou must make him also thy lord; for he saves none but those that serv him. So remember this,

662 His full name is Prosper Tiro, a monk of Aquitane who lived 390 – 455. A contemporary of Augustine whose teaching he defended fiercely, especially in Marseilles where Pelagianism was rife. He wrote three books in defence of Augustine's teaching. His lasting memorial lay in the canons of the Council of Orange 529, which were based partly on his *Epigrammata*.

and walk as becometh the Dignity of thy h[oly] calling. Be not *Christiani noisi macula*, the stain and dishonour, the blotch ulcers of the Christian name; *μάθε πολύ σεαυτὸν αἰσχύνεθαι*, Revere thy selfe, consider thou art a Christian, and say shall such a one as I am, do any thing unworthy the honour, unbecomeing the excellency of so h[oly] a calling.

Again, if it behooved this our H[igh] Priest to be made like unto us; then certainly it highly concerns us to be made like unto him; especially in holynesse; He is the great exempler and Pattern of holynesse and we ought to follow his stepps, tho' we canot fill them. This very end of his comeing into the world of his being made like unto us, was a designe of holynesse; that we might serv him without fear in holinesse [and righteousness before him all the days of our life Luc:1.75]. The Doctrine which he taught was a mystery of Godlinesse. He the teacher of it was pure holy, undefiled; and no man can rationally hope to be like unto him in glory hereafter, who endeavours not to be like unto him in purity and holynesse here.

Give me leave to conclude with that of St. Aug[ustine]. *Ad illam pertinuit propter non nasci, ad nos propter illum renasci*; 'Twas our saviour's love to be born for us; and 'tis our duty to give him birth for birth and to be born again in him. Let this day then be that happy epoch of our new birth; so shall we make this day a Festivall in Heaven, God the Father will blesse this day, bec[ause] upon it he getts new children, God the sunne, will blesse this day, because upon it he getts new brethren: God the Holy Ghost [gets] new Temples. And who would not Feast the blessed Trinity; hence the holy Angells clap their wings, for the[re] is joy in heaven over one sinner that repenteth [Luc: 15.7]. All the Inhabitants of heaven will triumph at our new birth, be glad spectators of our growth in Christ, rejoyce to see us of the same mind, every day liker and liker to him, till we grow to ripenesse and maturity, to be perfect men in Christ Jesus [Col: 1.28], and being made like unto him [Luc: 20.36], at last be *ισάγγελοι*, equall to the Angells; and with Angells and Archangells and all the company of heaven cry aloud saying:

Salvacion, honour, power, thanksgiveing be unto him that sitteth upon the throne and to him that was made like unto us, even to the lamb for evermore. Amen [Rev: 7.10,12].

SERMON SIX

At Easter

Introduction

In this sermon there are also similarities with the other Easter sermons. Andrewes' emphasis on the Resurrection as the core of our faith is reminiscent of Sermon Two, whilst the description of the women coming first and early to the tomb is similar to that in Sermon Four and the beginning of the 1608 Paschal Sermon at the Jacobean Court. "These women ... were last at His Passion, and first at His resurrection; stayed longest at that, came soonest to this, ... to anoint Him."[663] There are also links with the 1609 Easter Sermon as both contained details of the "five sundry time [Christ] appeared ... this day".[664]

This sermon also revealed some of Andrewes' other interests in life - science, nature and the cosmos with his reference to Copernicius' discovery that the earth revolved around the sun.[665] This is not surprising with his own theological belief that the earth is submissive to the heavens, and so unlike the Papacy he had no hesitation in believing that Copernicius was correct.

In comparison with the previous sermon with its intense theological discussions, this Easter sermon is more descriptive. Some time is spent again on the sacrifice of Christ that had al-

663 Andrewes. Vol. 2, pp. 222 – 4.

664 Ibid., p.238. In this 1609 Easter Sermon, Andrewes took Christ's appearing before the disciples from St. John's account (20.19).

665 Amongst his closest friends were the likes of Francis Bacon.

ready been foreshadowed in Abraham's willingness to sacrifice his son, and in the Passover itself, whilst Our Lord's resurrection was pre-empted by Job and Deutero-Isaiah. Andrewes depicted Christ's triumph over the last enemy, death, that "wages of sin" as "a fatall overthrow". He trampled "down death by death" and brought life to those in the tombs, and for all those after who accept Christ as their Lord.[666] Thus Christ has won victories over all our enemies, and ideally there should be no more enemies. However Andrewes suggested that this has not been the case. No sooner had Christ conquered death, than a new enemy arose, infidelity. It was seen in the women when they first saw the empty tomb, in Peter and the Apostles when Mary Magdalene told them "He is risen", and in the two disciples who travelled to Emmaus.[667] Our blessed Lord had to reveal Himself before them, and then to all the disciples in order to make them believe that He had risen just as the Scriptures had foretold.[668]

Andrewes reiterated that the "resurrection is the stock which extends itself to allmost every branch of Christianity", as he had in Sermon Three. The resurrected Christ is indeed our God, as seen in His descent from heaven, and in the manifestations of his works on earth, as well as in His death and resurrection. It is only He "who wrought out a righteousness for us", and sent the Holy Spirit to dwell in us.[669]

It is also obvious that as well as St. Luke's account of the resurrected Christ appearing before the disciples, Andrewes also drew on Paul's words, that the "the great foundacion of our Faith, Hope [and] Expectation" is that the Son of God "died for our sins and rose for our [salvation]". This must always be the Christian's

666 This is very similar to the Orthodox Pascha troparion: "Christ is risen from the dead, by death hath He trampled down death, and on those in the graves hath He bestowed life."

667 In his 1607 Paschal Sermon at Court he stated that "Emmaus signifieth 'a people forlorn;' all that are at *sperabamus* have lost their hopes, are said to go thither; and thither we should all go, even to Emmaus, but for the hope that breathes from the verse [i.e. *But now is Christ risen from the dead, and become the first fruits of them that slept*]." Andrewes, Vol. 2, p. 208.

668 Ms. 3707, pp. 180, 185.

669 Ibid., p. 185.

hope, and in that hope is also the belief that our own bodies will be raised on the Last Day. Thus the Resurrection signifies new life, new hope, new everything, and therefore there is more to Easter "than three dayes idlenesse and a plentiful dinner". His sermon finished on a great note of triumph that the vision we have of our resurrected bodies will be "an everlasting Jubilee".[670]

Luke 24: 38 - 9.
And he said unto them why are ye troubled? and why do thoughts arise in your hearts? Behold my hands and my feet that it is I myself: handle me and see for a spirit hath not flesh and bones, as yee see me have.

By the Resurrection of our saviour (of which this chapter is both an History and Demonstracion) the Powers of the Grave are shaken, and the last enimy that shalbe destroyed, even Death herself is become mortall. We read indeed of some foyl shee was put to by former assaults, as when Elijah rescued the widdowe's son, 1Kg. 17.22, and Elisha by prayer released the Shunammite's child, 2Kg.4.34. But those being led captive againe to the grave, and brought down to dust and corruption were no abatement of the power of death, but rather a lustre to her strength, for opposicion adds glory to the conquerour. Only now by the Resurrection of our saviour, Death received a fatall overthrow; Christ raised from the dead, can die no more, and in him all mankind are made victorious. As by the transgression of the first Adam, sin, and death which is the wages of sin, seazed upon all [Rom: 5.12, 6.23]: so by the obedience of the 2nd we have a freedome from the sting of death and the strength of sin [1Cor: 15.56]; in the former we all dye, in this we must all live again; the first Adam gave a being and force to death and this a Destruction. So that with St. Paul, we may insult over Death and the grave and sing this ἐπιύκιον, O Death, where is [thy sting? O grave where is thy victory? 1Cor: 15.55]. And now is not all yet finished? The last enimy is utterely foyl'd, Death [1Cor. 15.26]; and can there remain any enimy beyond the last? Yes, the strangnes of the victory has raised a new controversie, and mankind is now as much threatned by

670 Ibid., pp. 185, 189.

Infidelity as formerly by Death; *olim vitio, nunc remedio laborat*, the Remedie is so admirable, that it confounds the Patient, and makes health itself appear but fabulous. 'Tis true Christ is risen from the dead, but who beleeves our report? [Rom: 10.16] Even the Disciples thems[elves] did not remember, what was often foretold, but were as apt to forget their master's words, as in his distresse to forsake his Person. The officious Matrones prepare sweet odors and spices [Luc: 23.56], and their ceremonious piety, made them rise very early in the morning, 'twas scarce light when they were for the Sepulchre.[671] An undertakeing in appearance but to little purpose; the door, they might remember was made fast, a great stone upon it, roll it away they could not, nor could they see who would do it for them; so 'twould be an hard matter to come at the body of Jesus which they intended to imbalm. Yet they made tow[ards] the grave; true piety is not, presently heartlesse upon every rub; to be withstood doth not so much quench, as inflame true zeal; 'tis the glory of a Christian, to meet with and yet not to be discouraged at difficulties. So on they goe and found the passage cleared, the stone rolled away. God had dispatched Harbingers from above. 2 Angells, who with an easy diligence had commanded the Place, removed the guard, and rolled away the stone.[672]

So they entred in, but found not what they looked for, the Body of their Lord, [Luk. 24] v.3. No, small hopes to find the liveing among the dead [Luc: 24.5]; the Angells encounter with their unbeleeving thoughts, and that with such a speedy officiousnesse that they made answer before they were questioned; we know; you seek Jesus that was crucified [Math: 28.5]; Beleev it, He is not here, but is risen: or if you will not beleev us, beleev him, Remember, how he spake unto you when he was yet in Galilee, [Luc: 24] v.6. With this they departed satisfied, and told it to the eleven, but their words seemed to them as idle tales, and they beleeved them not, [Luc: 24] v.11. Strang that the very Apostles should so soon turn Infidells, and make no more account of the Resurrection then

---

671 Cp. with previous sermon, and the 1608 Paschal Sermon. Andrewes, Vol 2, pp. 222-4.

672 This description of the women coming to the tomb with their spices and ointments is told at greater length in the Paschal Sermon for 1608. Ibid., pp. 222 – 251.

an idle tale. Yet Peter withdrew hims[elf] from the rest, and desirous to satisfie his distrust, ran to the sepul[chre] where he saw all those things which were before the ensignes of Death, now become the trophies of a Resurrection, the grave clothes folded up and layd by thems[elves], a true tho' silent witnesse of his conquest, so he departed full of wonder and amazment and had a conflict within hims[elf], between beleef and distrust.

After that he hims[elf] appeared to two of the 70, that went to Emaus, a little village 60 furlongs from Jerusalem. And the Evangelist is copious in setting down what happened in that journey; upon what occasion our saviour joyned hims[elf] unto them, what he taught them, how he was known of them, and with what care and faithfulnes, the relacion was carried to the rest of their brethren. The only Newes then stirring both in and about Jerus[alem] was concerning the Resurrection, the strangenesse of it, such a kind of Resurrection, as had filled all the witnesses of it with fear and astonishment. And this was the subject of the Disciples' discourse in their journey to Emaus, [Luc:24] v.14. Whereupon our saviour hims[elf] drew near, heares them give the relacion of it, and expressing their own doubtfulnesse concerning the truth of it. And he first checks their distrust and then fully informs them, finds them both story and faith to beleev it, [Luc:24] v.27, and made hims[elf] known unto them, not only by discourse, but by breakeing of bread; and when he had done this, he vanished out of their sight, [Luc:24] v.30. The 2 disciples were so glad and full of this good news that they could not for joy lodg that night in Emaus, but tho' very late, yet they returned to Jerus[alem] to impart it, [Luc: 24] v.33. They knew no newes could be more welcome to the disconsolate Disciples then to heare of their master's Resurrection. The two tell it and the Eleven hear it with a great deal of passion, greadinesse and content. And just as they were telling of it, in comes the lord hims[elf], stands in the midst of them and thus salutes them. Peace be unto you, [Luc: 24] v.36. A salutacion very suitable to the Persons to whom he spake; for they had need of peace haveing no peace with God, whom they had so greatly provoked; nor peace with men, for they were shutt up, environed and beleageured with their enimies, nor peace with thems[elves], for they were in fear, dark, night fear; the house was to them as their grave, the door as the grave-stone, and they even buried in fear, that God and man had forsaken them.[673]

And tho' the salutacion was comfortable yet the suddain apparition of such a person, that he should come in the doores being shutt, at that time of the night, without the least noyse, this did so amaze and terrifye them [Luc 24:37], that they were *inter spem metumque dubii;* jealous of their own senses, and supposed what they heard was but the voyce of a spirit, and what they saw, not a reall body, but some aery phantasm. And therefore to rectifie that mistake and to put it out of all controversie, that it was his very self, the same body raised that was crucified, He exposeth hims[elf], to their senses, Handle and see me; why are ye troubled, and why do thoughts arise in your hearts. Behold my hands and my feet, that it is I myself, handle [me and see, for a spirit hath not flesh and bones, as yee see me have [Luc: 24. 38 –9].

In the text we have observable these particulars.

1. An expostulation, why are yee troubled etc.

2. A Declaration, 'tis I, even my self.

3. Proof of it; and that 1st by sense, Behold my hands and my feet, handle me and see. 2ly, by Reason. I am no spirit, for a spirit hath not etc.

From the first of these the expostulacion, we may draw these conclusions 1st, that the best of men are subject to passions and perturbacions, why are ye [troubled? Luke 24.38]. 2. That our saviour was a discerner of the Intents and thoughts of the heart; He did not only look upon but look into his disciples, why do thoughts [arise in your hearts? Luke 24. 38].

1. Passions and pertubacions are indelible characters of our humane nature, and to blot out these would be to destroy Humanity. To quit a man of troubles and distractions, is so to consider him intellectuall, as to forget that he is sensible. Elijah was subject to Passions and infirmityes, Jam: 5.17. And so was Moses, he did exceedingly fear [and quake], Heb: 12.21. And St. Paul, he groned to be delivered from the Body, Rom: 7.24. And how often did David call upon his soul, why so troubled? So the best of God's servants, Elijah, Moses, David, St. Paul, yea our saviour hims[elf],

---

673 Cp. with text in Pashcal Sermon for 1609. Ibid., p. 245.

was often troubled; How did he mourn, and weep over Jerusalem? Luc: 19.41 and groan in spirit, Joh:11.33. And was greived for the hardnesse of [their hearts], Mar: 3.5. 'Tis the condicion of all here below, to be subject to vexacion and trouble. Copernicus[674] his opinion is here most certainly true, the earth turnes about, only heaven stands still; only there is true rest to be had. Who is then here that complaines not, either of Asa's gout, [1Kg: 15:23, 2Chron: 16.12] or Job's unsavoury breath [Job 17.1], or Naaman's leprosy [2Kg. 5.1, 27], or Hezekiah's boyle [2Kg: 20.7, Is.38.21], or Solomon's vexacion of the creature? [Eccl: 1.14]. None can be found but sometimes one thing or other will molest, and trouble them. And why then should our saviour find fault with his disciples? Why are yee troubled? Why, who could chuse but be troubled of such an apparicion? to see one breake in upon them, in the dead of the night, the door and inletts being all shutt, there expose his naked, wounded body, and bespeak them unawares, when they never dreamed of him? Might they not be terrified at such a voyce and troubled at such a vision? Yes doubtlesse they might; And therefore 'twas not the passion they laboured under our Saviour reprooved, but their Infidelity; *vitium vetat non vitam;* 'tis not the passion he checked but the perturbacion; they fear, and so he rebukes them not, but they fear where no fear is, they used not the meanes to prevent and remove their fear. Upon the very 1st Day of his riseing, He appeared 5 severall times to Mary Magd[alene], Mar: 16.9. To the women comeing from the sepulchre, Math: 28.9. To the 2 that went to Emaus, to S. Peter, and now to the 11 and the rest that were gathered together.[675] And yet not withstanding that they had been so often told of his Resur[rection] and saw his body and heard his voyce which they could not but know, *vox hominem sonat,* yet, they did suspect his Resurrection. And therefore he justly checks, their doubtfull and distrusting thoughts.

Besides *διαλογισμοὶ ἀναβαίνουσι*, they were such thoughts as rose in their hearts, and 'tis St. Aug[ustine's] observacion *cogitationes istae terrenae sunt si enim caelestes essent in cor descenderent,*

---

674 In 1530 Copernicus proposed his theory that the planets revolved round the sun, which opposed the Roman Catholic view that the earth was the centre of the universe.

675 These five appreances appear in the 1609 Sermon. Andrewes, Vol. 2, p. 238.

non ascenderent; the thoughts of their hearts, were earthly, sensuall, for if they had been heavenly, they would not have risen out of the heart, but descended into the heart. They did not lift up their hearts, but let them lye poreing upon things below; and so their thoughts savoured of the nature of the soyl. Their former, *tu es filius Dei,* --- the saviour of the world [Math: 16.16], is now comed to a poor ἠλπίζομεν, we hoped indeed, that this had been he which should have [redeemed Israel] but we are disappoynted of our hopes[676] [Luc: 24.21]; Pilate hath condemned him, souldiers crucifyed him, Joseph buried him, and for ought we know, the grave hath devoured and consumed him; and then might he not justly expostulate with them, why are you thus troubled, and why do such thoughts as these arise in your hearts?

Once more, why are yee troubled? Such is the condicion of humane nature, *ut nec morbum ferre possumus nec medicum*; neither can we away with the disease, nor indure the Physitian, neither bear the wound, nor beleev the cure. Apostles could not be ignorant, how it behoved Christ to suffer [Luc: 24.26], and how necessary it was in respect of thems[elves]; without his Resur[rection] they were utterly lost, both as to their spirituall and temporall condicion. The world could not but hate them for their master's sake, who was accounted no better then the Prince of Devills. And being lost in this world, what ground had they for their hope of any comfort in another? Take away the Resurrection, and what is there in Christian profession, that might invite a wiseman to embrace it? Christ's birth was mean and despicable, his life exposed to scorn and contempt, his death shamefull and accursed. Now what inducements are these to move any to trust in him? what encouragements to leave and follow him? were it not irrational to expect life and immortality from one that lyeth under the dominion of death? To hope for eternall happinesse, by one that is perished? To looke for redemption from sin, Hell and the Grave, by a crucified saviour? so all their comforts are vain and empty, all their hopes dead and fruitlesse, their Religion sunk and gone, a meer delusion, without a Resurrection. And therefore well might our saviour say, why are yee troubled? I tell you the best newes

676 Cp. this thought with the theme of 1616 Pashcal Sermon with its theme of hope. Ibid., p.364ff.

that ever came to the world. 'Tis I, even myself, [handle me, and see,[Luc: 24.36].

We say *Quod volumus facile credimus;*[677] and therefore, me thinks, their thoughts should have been wholly taken up in informing thems[elves] in those very scriptures which pointed out his Resur[rection] in the Law of Moses, the Prophets, and the Psalmes. But bec[ause] that is ever best known, which is most doubted oft; therefore never was any matter carried with more scruple and slownesse of beleef, with more rubbs and doubts and difficulties then was this of Christ's Resurrection. Mary Magd[alene] saw it first, and shee reported it, but they beleeved her not; The 2 that went to Emaus reporteth it, neither could they be beleeved. Diverse women together saw him, came and told the Disciples of it; but they made light of it, it seemed to them ὣς λήρος [what nonsense]. Well, all the Disciples saw him, and even seeing, looking upon him, they doubted, and were troubled. Afterwards when the heat of this truth began to warm their hearts, and they were put out of all doubt, they told it but to one of their company who happened to be absent, Thomas, and you may hear how peremptory he was, Joh: 20.25.[678] He will not beleev, not he, unlesse he might not only see with his eyes but feel with his fingers, and put in his hand into his side; and all this he did, before he would preach Christ risen from the dead. Now, 'tis St. Aug[ustine's] observacion upon the place *valde dubitatum ab iis ne dubitaretur a nobis,* all this doubting was by them made, that we might be out of doubt, not troubled, have no grudgeings, nor no contradicting thoughts ariseing in our hearts against this truth. And thus much of the 1st conclusion, that [the best men are subject to passions and pertubations] and Christ did reprove, 1st the distrustfull thoughts, 2ly, the earthly, thoughts of his disciples; and 3ly suffered them to doubt to confirm us.

2. Con[clusion]. That our saviour is a discerner [of the thoughts and intents of the heart Heb: 4.12]. And this makes for his Diety. For only God is χαϊός [good]; neither man nor Angell can look in the labyrinthes and fathome the depth of the hearts, but only

---

677 It means "we believe easily what we want to".

678 Cp. with 1606 Paschal Sermon. Andrewes, Vol. 2, p. 190.

he that made it. And that our saviour did this, we read in the text, why do thoughts [arise in your hearts?] And Luc: 9.47 He perceived the thoughts of their hearts, and Math: 9.4 as soon as any bad thoughts arose in the hearts of the scribes, He discovered them, why think yee evill [in your hearts? Math: 9.14]. To multiply more Testimonies to this purpose would be but needlesse, Let us proceed to show.

1. That the *nomen tetragrammaton*,[679] the incommunicable Name Jehovah, is attributed to him Jer: 23.6. In his dayes Judah shall be saved, Israel shall dwell safely, and this is his name, whereby he shall be called, Jehovah our Righteous[ness]. Now that Jehovah is the proper and peculiar name of the only true God, we read Exod: 3.13, a name as far significant of his nature and beeing, as we are possibly enabled to understand; yea, so far expressive of God, that as the thing signifed, by it, is incomprehensible, so many have thought the very word itself to be ineffable. This Name God appropriates to hims[elf], in an eminent manner, Exod: 6.2, 8 and the Etymologie of it notes 1. the ὁμοιοὐσια, the Beeing which God hath of hims[elf]. 2. the dependency which all other creatures have of him. So that he whose name is Jehovah is the only true God.

2. We have his own word for it, Beleev me, that I am in the Father and the Father in me [Joh: 14.11]; and so, that I and the Father are one, Joh.10.30. And hear, how he commands his Disciples to Baptize all nacions in his name, Math: 28.19. And when he was dying on the crosse, hear how he disposeth of Paradise as his own Inheritance, Luc: 23.43. And when he spake to the People, he made no such preface as the Prophets did, thus [speaketh the Lord of hosts, Hag: 1.2], but like the lord hims[elf], I say unto you, *vox non hominem sonat*.

3. We have his ubiquitie and Eternity for it. He was in Heaven and upon Earth at once, Joh: 3.13. None hath ascended up to Heaven, but he that descendeth, even the son of man which is in Heaven. And his goings forth were from everlasting or the dayes of Eternity Mic: 4.2.[680] So that he had simply no beginning, for *nunquam erat quando non erat Eternitas.*

---

679 It means "the four letter name" for God.

680 It should be 5.2.

4. We have his works for it, for to omit those many works which did shew forth thems[elves] in him, his giveing eyes to the blind, and leggs to the lame, eares to the deaf [the dead are raised up and the poor have the gospel preached unto them [Math: 11.5]. To rise again from the dead, by his own power, is a work only peculiar unto God, and that he did. How lordly did he speak it, Joh: 2.19, Destroy [this temple, and in three days I will raise it up], a godlike speech, and proper only to the King of Heaven; the power of men and Angells could not promise so much. There is not the highest of men, that if he but lay down his Head on his pillow to take a nap, can certainly resolve to rise at what hour he pleaseth, no this is only his Peculiar who neither slumbers nor sleeps [Ps: 121. 4].

Let us take heed therefore of entertaining any such unworthy thoughts of our saviour as may rob him of his Diety. For us that fly to him as one that suffered for our sinnes and made satisfaction to the Justice of God for them; who wrought out a righteousnesse for us; who quickens us when we are dead, and sends the holy Ghost to dwell and abide in us, and is hims[elf] present with us, 'tis impossible we should ever have the least consolacion in our flying for refuge to him; unlesse we have this grounded persuasion concerning his eternall power and Godhead.

The great foundacion of our Faith, Hope, Expectacion lies in this, that He who redeemed us with his own blood, is the sonne of the living God; which if he had not been, he could not have performed the work he had to do for us. And bec[ause] he hath such a peircing eye, as to look into our hearts, to spye out our thoughts and intentions; we ought to watch over our hearts, and to see that we have truth and integrity in our inwards parts; that we do not double and dissemble with him, draw nigh unto him, with our lipps only [Is: 29. 13], give good words with our mouthes, but curse with our heartes; if so, he will spy it out, and reproove us as he did the Apostles, why do such thoughts [arise in your hearts]? And thus much of the expostulation, why are ye troubled?

We proceed now to the declaracion, 'Tis I, even myself.

2. Declaracion. And this is the main poynt observable in the Text, Our saviour's Resur[rection], a Fundamentall poynt of Divinity, so termed by the Apostle, Heb: 6.2 not laying again the foundacion of Repentance from dead works and Resur[rection]

of the dead. And so 'tis necessary that this ground be surely layd, otherwise all the rest of the building will surely fall.[681] The proof of this then is of great moment and nearly concerns us; for Christ's Resur[rection] is the stock which extends itself to allmost every branch of Christianity.

1. On this is our faith grounded, 1Cor:15.14. If Christ be not risen, then is our faith vain. 2. On this the pardon of our sinnes, v.17, If Christ not risen, then yet in your sinnes, 3. On this our Justificacion Rom: 4.10.[682] He died for our sins [1Cor: 15.3] and rose for our [salvation], so if no Resurrection, no Justificacion and if no Justificacion, no Salvation. But we hear him here become his own Herauld, proclaiming his own Resur[rection] tis I mys[elf]. And after he was risen from the dead, He told his Disciples, that his riseing again the 3rd day, was foretold in the scriptures; and he promised out [of] those scriptures; the laws of Moses, Prophets [and] Psalmes [Luc. 24.44-6].

1. This was foreshewen, in the story of Isaac wherein his sacrifice or suffering was acted. For from the time that God commanded Isaac to be offered, Isaac was a dead man, but the 3rd day he was released from death. And the Text tells us expressly, that 'twas the 3rd day, when Abraham came to Mt. Moriah, and had his son (as 'twere) restored to him again, Gen: 22.4, which circumstance of time, had it not been for some mystery, had not needed to have been observed. For had there been nothing intended, but that naked story, what did it concern us to know, whether it were the 3rd or 5th day, that Abraham came to Moriah. And the Apostle applyes this release of Isaac from slaughter as a type and figure of the Resur[rection], Heb: 11.19. By faith Abrah[am] offered up Isaac, and he received him from the dead in a figure.

2. This was typified also by the law of sacrifices which were to be eaten before the 3rd day, some were to be eaten the same day they were offered, but those that were deferred the longest, as the Peace offerings, were to be eaten before the 3rd day, Levit: 17.18.[683] The 3rd day, if any sacrifice were eaten, 'twas not accepted for an

---

681 Cp. with text in 1607 Paschal Sermon. Andrewes, Vol. 2. p. 209.

682 It should be 3.24 -5.

683 It should be 7.17.

atonement but accounted an abominacion. To note unto us that the sacrifice of the Messiah (which those sacrifices did typify) was to be complete and finished that 3rd day by his riseing from the dead: and therefore the type was to be finished within that time, beyond which time 'twas not accepted for atonement of sin, because then 'twas no longer a type of him.

3. We have propheticall Texts of script[ure] fortelling his Resur[rection] in generall Job: 19.25 I know that my Redeemer [liveth], my Judgment is fixed, my faith is confirmed in this thing, 'tis as clear to me that my Redeemer [liveth], as if I had allready seen him alive. So in that famous prophesy Esa: 53.10 He shall see his seed and prolong his dayes and the pleasure of the lord shall prosper in his hand. And Zach: 12.10 they shall look upon, or see him whom they had formerly peirced; therefore he was to live again after they had peirced him.

4. In the Psalmes we have not only his Resur[rection] foretold, but the very time thereof determined, tho' not in expresse termes, yet by necessary consequence, Ps: 16.10 thou shalt not leave my soul [in hell] nor [shall thou suffer thy Holy One to see corruption] i.e. the messiah shall have a Resur[rection] before his body see corruption; and then the 3rd day at furtherest; for τῇ τρίτῃ ἡμέρᾳ, (glossary) the Body naturally [on] the 3rd day begins to tast corruption. This we may gather by the story of Lazarous; when our saviour comanded the stone to be rolled from his grave, Martha his sister answered Lord, by this time he stinketh, [for he hath been dead four days] Joh: 11.39. And for this cause 'twas that our saviour undertook not the raiseing of Lazarous from the dead, till he had layen 4 days in the [grave] least the Jewes might have slaundered the miracle, if he had done it sooner, and said, that Laz[arus] was not dead but swooned. 'Tis a Rule given by the Masters of Physick, that such as are troubled with Apoplexies, fallings sicknesses, and such like diseases, should not be buried till the expiracion of 72 hours, that is 3 dayes and 3 nights; In which space of time, they say the humours of them make their revolucion, begin to stop, and give over their motion. Now if a Body may be kept so long unburied, 'tis supposed it may be kept so long uncorrupted (if no corruption begin before death) but longer it will not continue. And therefore when we read so often in the Gospell, that our saviour should rise again the 3rd day; the h[oly]

Ghost in those expressions, reports not so much the number of dayes as that fullfilling of the prophesie, that is his body should not see corruption, but should rise before the time, that dead bodyes do ordinarily begin to corrupt; it should suffer a disjunction, but not a dissolucion. Indeed the Body of our saviour did not lye 40 houres, 2 full dayes in the grave; for he was crucified the 6th hour of the preparation of the Sabboth, the 9th hour gave up the ghost, late in the evening was taken down and buried; so he rested in the grave, the night that belongeth to the Sabboth, together with the day and night ensueing it; and in the morning of the 1st day of the week, he rose again: so that his body was not in the heart of the earth much above 36 houres, and therefore could not see corruption.

And to justify that of our saviour, Math. 12.40 [so shall the] son of man be 3 dayes and 3 nights in the heart of the earth:

1. We must take part of a day for the whole; 2. Reckon (as the Jewes did) the evening and the morning but for one naturall day; so counting still the precedent night with the succeeding day. This order of reckoning the night before the day was common and usuall with the Jewes and they have warrant for it out of Gen: 1.5, 8, So if we count the night past with the day following then the text is clear, He was 3 dayes and nights [in the heart of the earth Math: 12.40].[684]

Thus much for declaration of our saviour's Resur[rection] as 'tis poynted at, in the law of Moses, the Prophets and Ps[almes].

2. 'Tis I, even myself, if we do but goe unto the grave, that will turn Evangelist, and tell us so, we cannot write upon it, *hic jacet*, but *Resurrexit* and 'tis no more τάφιος but τάφος.[685] And if we view the place, 'tis as full of Christ as ever it was; only thus, formerly, 'twas the place of his death, now of his Resurrection. And in it we have an ocular Demonstracion, Mar: 16.6, Behold the Place where they layd him; If you will not beleev mee (Angel) beleeve your own eyes; Behold the place where they had made

---

684 Andrewes used this same outline of time in the 1617 Sermon at Easter in Durham cathedral. Andrewes, Vol. 2, p. 393.

685 i.e. "no more *grave* but a *wonder*".

him sure enough (as they thought).[686] The grave was in a Rock, no danger of underminers below ground, with a great stone, upon him, and a seal upon it, and a strong guard upon that, no fear of robbers above ground. And yet behold, in spite of the malice of the Jewes, and the vigilancy of the souldiers, and the power of death, he has broken thorow all and has indeed cozened those Ravens, which croaked over his carkcasse when he was dead, and called him cozener, Math: 27.63. He had told them he would rise again and they were afraid he would be as good as his word, and therefore take such care to prove thems[elves] lyers, and supererogate to their own damnation.

Behold the place! Why what's there to be seen? enuff both to convince the Jewes calumny and the womens Infidelity; to prove against the Jewes he was not stolen away and against the women, who came to seek him, that he was not there. There they might see his winding-sheet; He was up in the morning and had left his bed-cloathes behind him; No Theif would have been willing to have forgone such a purchase, 'twas fine linen [Mar: 16.46], the weight but small, the worth much. Besides, say the Robbers would, I see not well how they could steal his body, and leave the cloathes, for they were glued to his body with mirrhe, which is tenacious and therefore no easy matter to divide [Joh: 19.39-40].

Again, Behold the Place, and in it the Napkin which was tied about his head, very curiously folded up together and laid by in a place by itself [Joh: 20.7]. It is not probable they that came to rob the grave, would take so much leisure, as to make up the cloathes. Fear and hast are the continuall attendants upon all theevish actions; Let them ask their Barrabbas, if he were to steal a Jewel would he stay to unfold the Paper that it is wrapt in?

But where were the souldiers all the while? the sturdy watch, that guarded the sepulchre? ô sayes the Jewes they were asleep, and then even then 'twas; that his Disciples stole him away. But observ here, how they run into absurdities, for if they were asleep how knew they who stole him away, how knew they 'twas his Disciples; And if they did know how were they asleep?[687]

---

686 Cp. this with similar text in 1608 Paschal Sermon. Andrewes, Vol. 2, p.233.

687 Cp. this similar text in 1608 Paschal Sermon. ibid., pp. 233-4.

But say they were, what likelyhood his disciples should venture for his dead corps; to break through so strong a troup of armed men, to steal him away after death, when they had so shamefully, forsaken him in his lifetime? His Disciples stole him away! Why? one of them had betrayed him, another foresworn him, all the rest run away from him; and now why should they venture their lives for him when he has lost his own? *Cui bono*? is a question (as the orator tells us) very materiall in actions of this nature; to what purpose should they steel him? what benefit should they reep by so doing? There was certain dangers in the undertakeing such an enterprise, no probable certain benefit, in acheiveing it; was it to free his body from the scorn of his enimyes that they should not insult upon this dead lyon? Lest those *quondam* children, after they had slain the lamb of God should tear him too? This indeed might cary some color, were it not that his body was out of their custody now, it was now in his friends hands, (Jos[eph] of Ar[imathæa] and Nic[odemus] two Potent men), both able as Rulers and willing as disciples to protect him from all scorn and Insolence. The permission of his enimyes reached no further but to the guarding of the sepulcher. Or was it convey him away in private and give out amongst the people that he was risen from the dead, and so get credit to their doctrine by this lying miracle? This indeed was the thing, the Jewes feared; but mark I pray you how groundlesse. 1st very improbable that the Disciples ever would give out such a report, had it not been true; secondly, allmost impossible, they should persuade the people to the beleef of it.

1. Improbable that they would, for condsidering he had told them before, that after 3 dayes he would rise again; had he deceived them in this poynt, they would never have trusted him more, never have undergone those many persecutions and cruell deaths for his sake, never had endured to be afflicted, tormented, hated of all, every where spoken against, chased from city to city for his names sake, who himself had been false to them.

2. Tho' they would yet 'tis scarce possible they should persuade other generally to the belief of Christ's Resur[rection] had it not been true. For where-withall should they doe it? Considering 'tis a thing very improbable to reason in itself, that a dead man should rise; there must be some strong outw[ard] motives to draw others to the beleef of it; as outw[ard] Est[ate] and pomp,

noblenesse of birth, largenesse of meanes, Power of Rhetorique, multitude of witnesses etc. But the Disciples of all the world, were most destitute of all these externall helps; they were but poor fishermen, meanly descended, and as meanly accommodated, all their wealth but a staff and a wallet; no great number, since Judas' death not a full dozen;[688] and for their learning and Rhetorick, no great clerkes here, but week, ignorant men; all the strength of their Arguments, lay in the truth of them; that indeed was such, as they durst seal it with their dearest blood, and durst professe it before all the world. And God set his seal to it too, the many miracles that he wrought by their hands in the confirmacion of their doctrine; and by this meanes, first planted his church, and brought many nacions in a few yeares to the acknowledgement of the truth of the Gospell and the Resurrection of Christ; which has now continued for about 1600 years and ever got ground upon Infidelity; tho' miracles ceased long ago, and indeed he were a miracle that would require one now. He is scarce a man that will question the truth of that story, which so many Kingdomes, for so many ages, have constantly professed, the Resurrection of Christ.

As for ourselves, if we had no other Resurrection sermon but this dayes solemnity for allmost 1600 years, it were enuff to leave us inexusable. This is the day which the lord hath made, let us rejoice and be glad in it, (David Ps: 118.24). Nay more, this is the day which made the lord, which proved him to a lord indeed. He was before but in the form of a servant, poor, vile, despicable; but on this day he appeared like himself, the lord of glory; trampled and triumphed over all his enemies, the very last enemy which was death. In memory of which his Triumph, his church hath set apart this day, with its seconds for the celebracion of the solemnity.

But that's not all; there is more required to the keeping of Easter, than three dayes idlenesse and a plentifull dinner. The Intention of the Primitive Church was with humility and thankfulness, to celebrate the memory of Christ's Resurrection allready past; and the certain hopes of our own to come. For his Resurrection is but the pawn and earnest of our's; as he died and rose again, so by the mercy of God, and vertue of the same must wee: God, who

---

688 Andrewes overlooks that Matthias was chosen by the Apostles to take Judas' place before Pentecost which was only fifty days after Easter.

is able to perform it, has said it, has promised it; and if his bare word may not be taken; he has given us an earnest, the more to assure us of it, the Resurrection of his son; He died and rose again, therefore it is not impossible for us to do so; The same power that raised him, can do as much for us, and not only can but will do it. For if we beleev that Jesus died and rose again, even so they also which sleep in Jesus [1Thes: 4.14] will God bring with him; And this beleef, this faith will melt us, this liquifaction will transform us, and this transformacion unite us to Christ, and this vision will be our exultacion, and this exultacion an everlasting Jubilee. In a word, this will quit us of all uncertaintyes, lead us thro' all difficulties, and by these meanes we shall attain to not *ἀνάβασιν*, a bare, but *ἐξανάβασιν*, a full resurrection which no death, no evill shall follow, a Resurrection to Eternity of life, of bliss and glory.

APPENDIX

Features of MS. 3708 and Some Thoughts on Andrewes' Preparation for Holy Communion

Ms. 3708 is an edition of Andrewes' Prayers transcribed by Gilbert Sheldon,[689] for the Shirley family whose chaplain he was, prior to the death of Sir Robert Shirley in the tower in 1656. As Sheldon left the household after preaching the funeral oration for Sir Robert, this manuscript must have been transcribed before 1656.

What is important about this manuscript is that it is quite independent of any other devotional publications of Andrewes during the seventeenth century, although it shares common text with six of those publications. These include:

1. The Greek manuscript copied by his secretary, Samuel Wright, with a Latin text written by an unknown hand parallel to the Greek (Part 1). This was published in Oxford, 1675. This is basically the version printed in Oxford for the Library of Anglo-Catholic Theology in 1853 under the hand of Dr. John Barrow, Principal of St. Edmund's Hall. There is much common material with the Latin.

2. A Latin text printed from papers in the possession of Richard Drake who owned the copy text of Part. I, which he translated from the Greek and published in 1648 with the Latin as Part II.

689 The handwriting is identical to that of Sheldon's letter to John Barwick, dated 10th January, 1653, now in St. John's College Library, Cambridge.

In the edition of 1675 and subsequent ones, the second part remained quite distinct from the first, and for such a long time it was thought that Andrewes' Devotions consisted of one part in Latin and another in Greek, emphasised in the nineteenth century when John Mason Neale translated the Latin in 1844 and John Newman the Greek in 1875, and afterwards the two translations were combined in one edition. A third of the text in Sheldon's transcript is found in Part II.

3. The Manual for the Sick, edited by Drake in 1648, from a copy "under the fair hand" of Andrewes' amanuensis (probably Samuel Wright). In the preface he commented how he found "in Latin, annexed with the Manual for the Sick" prayers for Holy Communion. So consequently these were printed as part of the Manual for the Sick. Ms. 3708 has twelve pages of English in common with the Manual, which in Sheldon form part of the preparation for communion. It is clear from Sheldon's transcription and from Laud's *Eucharistia* that Drake mistakenly printed part of a *Preparation for Communion* with *the Manual for the Sick*. Such confusion resulted from the fact that Andrewes wrote for his own use, and left few or no headings. The headings in manuscript collections and the original editions are the work of scribes and editors.

4. The Latin text of the Appendix to David Stokes' *Verus Christianus* published in Oxford, 1668 from papers given him of "several hands", and reprinted in the 1675 edition of *Preces Privatæ*.

5. Laud's *Eucharistia*, written before 1643, incorporated passages known from the Manual in English, and from Part1 (i.e. Latin from Wright's Greek) and Part 2 in Latin. Laud's Eucharistic devotions began where Sheldon's transcript commenced: *Quaecumque ab infantia usque ad momentum hoc* ... and ends with communion prayers. The passages Laud has used follow the same order as in Ms. 3708 but on a smaller scale. Parts in common are found in L.A.C.T. edition of Laud's Work, Vol. 3, pp. 72 – 5, and in Ms. 3708, pp, 1, 2, 21, 22, 36, 37 and 61. Although there are similarities in arrangement Laud's text it is independent of the Sheldon manuscript, and manifests that he used a Latin and English text of a preparation to communion similar to that by Sheldon but not identical with it.

As already stated the Sheldon version is independent of any

other surviving manuscripts and has many additions and omissions in comparison with them. Such variations are indicative of Andrewes' reworking of his texts. All texts reveal a reshuffling of lines, sentences and indeed whole sections. Sheldon's manuscript manifests how Andrewes sought the same meticulous care in private devotion as he did in worship in his private chapel. The best evidence that the Sheldon's manuscript is a faithful transcript of Andrewes' text is in its excellence of movement from line to line and from section to section.

With the discovery of the Sheldon transcript we now know that the *Preces Privatæ* was not only in Latin and Greek. It is an evolving work in English, Greek, Latin and Hebrew that has been reworked and rearranged many times. Much of the text appears in a very different arrangement in F. E. Brightman's translation of *The Preces Privatae of Lancelot Andrewes*, (London, Methuen, 1903).

It also proved that Andrewes did have a definite Preparation for Communion in his Private Devotions. One of Brightman's criticisms of the Preces was that only a small proportion was devoted to such a preparation. But this was not Andrewes' fault, but that of Drake who mistakenly confused two separate texts and as a result printed part of the Preparation for Communion in *A Manual for the Sick*. [690] Sheldon's transcription of Preparation for Communion is the only manuscript that has the Preparation for Communion as a whole and it thus forms the longest sequence known amongst Andrewes' devotional writings. The next longest is the cycle of prayer for seven days.[691] Much of the contents of this Preparation reflect the outline in the Prayer Book Exhortation before making one's Communion of self-examination and confession, amendment of life and reconciliation with others, an act of faith and thanksgiving for Christ's act of sacrifice for sinners. All this is held together by a sequence with a series of echo-like refrains, which act to divide the movements, and to recall earlier moments in a changed context. The sequence turns and turns itself, not unlike how Andrewes spoke of Repentance in his Ash Wednesday sermons as "a kind of circling".

---

690 Brightman, lii; Brightman, *Manual*, pp. 38ff.

691 Brightman, pp. 40 – 101.

The refrain:

Vellem, si plus.	I wish it were more
Metuo, ne.	I fear it should be.
Doleo quod non.	I am sorry it is not
Gauderem, si.	I would be glad if. [692]

This refrain links with a marginal comment Andrewes made in his notes on the Prayer Book against the General Confession "That desire to be penitent, wish they were, would be glad if they were so, fear they are not enough; are sorry they are no more."[693]

In the first appearance of the refrain, what is suggested of penitence is applied to hope, expressed in words from the psalmists:

In tegmine alarum	Ps. 36. 7	Under the cover of wings
In umbra	Ps. 57. 1.	In the shadow
Spera in Deo	Ps. 42. 11	Trust in God
Sub pennis.	Ps. 91. 4	Under the feathers.[694]

The second appearance links a vision of glory with an act of penitence. Andrewes' general intercession ends with the plea that he, and all those for whom he prays and indeed all the people of God, may come into the kingdom, stand there in righteousness and be filled with the glory. Thus in the refrain the emotional gradient is downwards:

Cuperem ut	I wish it might be
Gauderum si	I would be glad if
Metuo ne	I fear it should be
Doleo quod non.	I am sorry it is not. [695]

The third and last time the refrain appears is near the end of

692 Ms. 3708, p. 9; Brightman, p. 130; *Preces Quotidianæ*, p.367.

693 Andrewes, Vol. 11, p. 367.

694 Ms. 3708, p. 9; *Preces Quotidianæ*, p., 367.

695 Ms. 3708, p. 22.

an act of penitence, expressing a most personal unworthiness, characteristic of Andrewes.[696] He reflects that his sorrow is not enough:

Doleo enim utcunque	I do grieve somewhat
Metuo quidem ut satis	I fear it is not enough
Cuperem ut magis	I wish it were more
Gauderem si magis	I would be glad if it were more
Doleo quia non magis.	I grieve it is not more.[697]

There are indeed many such sequences in the *Preparation*. Another example is the actual preparation in order to be worthy to receive the Sacrament. Two main strands meet on page 8 – the one expressing thanksgiving for Christ's sacrifice and hope of redemption, and the other an acknowledgement of one's own unworthiness

Dignus es Domine Deus	Lord God you deserve
accipere laudes	praise
et gratias	and thanks:
Quem ego peccator	And I, a sinner
non sum dignus invocare	have no right to call on you
nec vel nominare	even to name
nec in corde cogitare:	or think of you:
Te invoco, adoro	call out to you, I worship you.
Te toto cordis affectu	with all my love,
nunc et in sæculum	I bless you now
Benedico.	and always will.[698]

The last four lines are repeated from the act of adoration on the first page of the sequence. The echo signals the end of the first movement of the *Preparation*: a hymn of praise enclosing prayers for grace. It completes a circuit. The other refrain looks forward, across the meditation on the life of Christ, to a bitter self-examination.

---

696 e. g. in the introduction to the lectures.

697 Ms. 3708, p. 31; *Preces Quotidianæ*, pp. 377-8.

698 Ms. 3708, p. 8; Brightman, p.196; *Preces Quotidianæ*, p.366.

Totus ergo confuses	totally ashamed
Nec dignus nominare	unworthy to name you
Nec invocare	or call on you
Nec in corde cogitare	or even to think of
Nomen Tuum …	your name …[699]

Out of the deep trough of humiliation, the echo recalls, in muted form, the wholehearted hymn of praise.

The Preparation begins with a prayer for forgiveness of all those sins committed from infancy until that very moment, known or unknown, in sleep or awake before making one's Communion.[700] Next comes a prayer of adoration addressed to the Trinity: *Pater bone/ Fili pie/ Spiritus benigne,*[701] followed by intercessions for the Church, deliverance from spiritual enemies and for grace.[702]

As intimated the first part of the Preparation is mostly penitential, interspersed with hymns of praise, acts of faith and hope and meditations on Christ's sufferings, including the *Anima Christi,*[703] and a vivid account of those sufferings.

Caput spinis coronatum
arundine impactis
Oculi lacrimis suffusi
Aures conviciis oppletae
Os felle potum et aceto
Facies sputis foede illita
Dorsum flagellis exaratum
Collam cruces onere depressum
Manus, pedesque extensi et clavis suffixi
Cor lancea perforatum
Corpus lacerum et squalidum
Sanguis copiose manans undique
Pectus moerore turbatum

---

699 Ms. 3708, p. 27; Brightman, p. 158; *Preces Quotidianæ*, p. 374.

700 Ms. 3708, p. 1; Brightman pp. 134-5; *Preces Quotidianæ,* p.326.

701 Ms. 3708, p. 1; Brightman p. 198; *Preces Quotidianæ*, p. 358.

702 Ms. 3708, pp. 2-5; Brightman, pp. 170, 247, 253-4; *Preces Quotidianæ*, pp. 358-9.

703 Ms. 3708, p. 10; Brighman, p. 93.

Anima tristum et Agonizantem
Vocem Eli Eli.[704]

The sequence in English opens with an act of trust.

O Lord thou knowest whereof we be made; thou remembrest
we are but dust, but filth, frayle flesh, but a wind
that passeth away, and cometh not againe.
Remember Lord what my substance is.
O Lord consider my complaint for I am brought very low
Let my present misery more prevayle to stir compassion, then
my sinfull life past to provoke thine indignation
O Lord God how longe wilt thou be angry with thy servant
that prayeth?
Behold I shew unto thee the lowliness of a poore supplyant,
shew not to me the rigour of a fearfull judge.[705]
Not for O Lord, not for us, not for any thinge of ours.
But
1. for thy selfe thine own selfe
2. for thy name, for the glory of that name.
3. for thy faythfullnes and truth.
4. for thy mercyes thy many great and wonderful mercyes.
5. for thy sonne our mediatour
blessed spirit our comforter.[706]

The next paragraph has two acts of trust, concluding with an act of confession

O deliver not thine owne inheritance into the will of the
enemy.
Lord carest thou not that I perish?
I am thine, O save me
Behold O Lord how that I am thy servant
I am thy servant and the sonne of thy

704 Ms. 3708, p. 11; Brightman, p. 216; *Preces Quotidianæ*, p. 312.

705 Ms. 3708, pp. 36-7; Andrewes, Vol. 11, p. 187; Laud, Volume 3, p. 74.; Brightman, *Manual*, pp. 62-3.

706 Ms. 3708, p. 37. Laud's version has this paragraph in Latin. Vol 3, p. 89.

handmayd, thy unprofitable wastfull
servant, yet thy servant
thy unkind lost child, yet thy child.
Though I have not reteyned the dutye and kindness of a sonne, yet doe not thou cast from thee the kindness & compassion of a father.[707]
Lord I have not denyed thy name, but confessed it ever, and in the confession of it, and invocation thereof I desire to spend my last breath.
O Lord I have prepared my heart to seeke thee, though not accordinge to the rule of thy sanctuary.
O Lord I believe, helpe my unbeleife.
O Lord I freely forgive, whomsoever I have any thing against
O Lord I have patiently borne whatsoever thy hand layeth upon me for my chastisement
O Lord I come unto thee weary and heavy laden, thou hast bid me come, thou hast promised him that cometh to thee that thou wilt not cast him out.[708]
I have sinned but I hide it not
excuse it not, like it not.
I will confesse my wickedness and be
sorry for my sinne.
My confusion is dayly before me, and the
shame of my face hath covered me.[709]

What follows next is a long sequence of confession based on the Ten Commandments.

1. I have touchinge thee O Lord been full
of rovinge imaginations & evill
thoughts.
I have not studied to seek & know
thee as I ought.
Knowinge thee I have not glorifyed thee nor

707 Ms. 3708, p. 38; Andrewes. Vol. 11, pp.187-8; Brightman, *Manual*, p.63.

708 Ms. 3708, p. 38; Andrewes, Vol. 11, p. 189; Brightman, *Manual*, p. 57.

709 Ms. 3708, p. 39; Andrewes, Vol. 11, p. 205.

beene thankfull to thee accordingly.
I have doubted of thy promises & not
trusted to thy helpe.
I have made flesh mine arme &
hoped for prosperitye rather from
man then from thee.

2. I have neglected invocation &
adoration, and not performed it
with the duty and reverence that I should.
I have not beene thankfull
especially not for thy chastisements.
I have not worshipped thee in
spirit & in truth.
I have beene more carefull of the
outward ceremoniall part of
thy worship, then of the inward
& spirituall.
I have drawne neere to thee with my
lips, but my heart hath beene
farre from thee.

3. I have not spoken of thy name
with due regard.
I have not given occasion to others
to sanctifye thy name, but
rather by my evill life, it hath
beene evil spoken of.
I have not duly reverenced, and
regarded those thinges, whereon
thy name is imprinted.
I have with rash oaths and eager
execrations oft abused thy holy
name.

4. I have not brought to thy publike
service the care & reverence
that became me.
I have not spent the days

consecrate thereto in holy exercises.
I have upon no sufficient cause
absented my selfe from thy holy
assemblies.
I have upon those dayes intended
mine owne private business.
I have been content in them with the
use of the meanes alone, without
any practise at all.

5. I have not so reverently spoken
nor so dutifully carryed my
selfe, towards some as thou hast
placed over me, as was meet I should.
I have not so carefully prayed
for them as was requisite.
I have not opposed to those who have
unreverently spoken of them,
chiefly of those who had in
government touchinge my soule.

6. I have not wished and procured
the good of my neighbours as I
should, but rather maligned, beene
angry and quarrelled with them
& sought revenge upon every light
iniurye.
I have not had that compassion on the
poore that I should, nor ministered to
their necessityes.
I have not defended them against the
wronge of others as I might.
I have not reioyced in the good
successe of my neighbour,
but envyed his wellfare.

7. I have not possessed my vessell
in holiness & honour, nor
preserved it from pollution as

the Temple of the Holy ghost should be.
I have not eschewed the occasions of
lust, nor made that covenant with
mine eyes that I should.
I have suffered my fancye to wander
too licentiouslye.
I have not brought under my body
nor kept it in subiection with
such abstinence as I should.
I have more studiously intended &
with more cost my flesh then my
spirit.
I have not so kept mine eares and
tongue as I should.

8. I have not beene content with mine
own estate, but wished an
higher
I have not beene so exact in
payinge & dealinge with those I
have dealt withall as in iustice
I was bound.
I have by undue meanes interverted
mine own use that which
was not mine.
I have not of that whereof I had more then
enough beene willinge to part
with to the releefe of the needye.

9. I have not beene so studious of
speakinge the truth as I should.
I have desired to seeme and to be
reputed more then I was.
I have not had that care of the good
name of my brother, as I was
bound.
I have not so hated flattery as I should.
I have not so stood and defended the
truth as was meet I should.

10. I have beene full of wandrings
desires, wicked affections, unlawfull
concupiscences, evill suspicions &
surmises, immoderate lusts touchinge
my neighbour, and that which is his.[710]

Next comes an expression of unworthiness in a prayer before receiving the Sacrament, separated from the last sequence by a pleading not found in any other publication.

O remember not the sinnes and
offences of my youth. Ps. 25.7.
For youth & childhood are
but vanitye. Eccl. 11.10.[711]

Lord I am not worthy thou shouldst
come under the sordid roof of my dwellinge.
For it is wholly desolate & ruinous,
neyther canst thou (within me) have
a fit place where to repose thy
head. Math. 8.8.
But as thou didst vouchsafe to rest
in the stable & manger of bruite
beasts. Luc. 2.7.
As thou didst not disdayne to be
entertayned in the house of
Simon the Leper. Math. 26.6.
As thou didst not forbid the Adulterous
sinner (my likenes) to draw
neere and touch thee. Luc. 7.39
Nor didst abhorre her impure and
prophane mouth.
Neither the theife confessinge thee
on the Crosse Luc. 23.43
Vouchsafe also to receive me

---

710 Ms. 3708, pp. 39 –57; Andrewes, Vol. 11, pp. 213-6; Laud, Vol. 3, p. 88; Brightman, *Manual*, pp.38ff.

711 Not in any other published collection. Ms. 3708, p. 57.

An outworne wretched and
most unworthy sinner.[712]

The last part of the English sequence has three Communion prayers, the first reflects the *anamnesis* in the Canon; the second is a prayer to be engrafted into Christ's body through the Sacrament and the third to abstain from sin to allow the efficacy of the Sacrament.

In the presence of thy Sacrament
we therefore O Lord, even we
Remembringe the savinge passions
of thy Christ
His life-givinge Crosse
most precious death
three dayes burial
resurrection from the dead
Ascention into heaven
Session on the right hand of God the Father
Glorious and fearfull cominge againe.
Lord we beseech thee
That with the pure testimony of our conscience
receivinge part of these thy holy thinges
we may be united to the sacred body &
bloud of thy Christ.[713]

Let me so receive these mysteryes that
I may become worthy to be ingrafted
into thy bodye (which is the church)
That I may become one of thy
members, and thou my head,
That I may remayne with thee &
thou in me
That now not I in myselfe
but thou in me and I in thee
may forever continue

712 Ms. 3708, pp 58-9; Brightman, p. 121.

713 Ms. 3708, pp. 59-60; Brightman, p. 123.

in an insoluble bond of love.
Wash out the staines of my old and fresh sins
Neither let any sinfull spot abide
where so pure sacraments have entred.
Through this Sacred mystery
which I heere call upon to my aide
Bury me (alreadye dead to this world)
with thee in thy grave.[714]

And receivinge this sacrament worthily
Let us procure Christs dwellinge in our hearts
and be made the Temple of thy holy Spirit.
Even soe O Lord
Neither make any of us guilty
of the reverend & heavenly mysteryes
Neither feeble and weake in mind or bodye
for the unworthy receivinge of them.
But grant that to the latest gaspe
we may worthilye entertayne
The hope of these Holy Sacraments
of thine.[715]

The remainder of this Preparation for Communion reverts to Latin, followed by prayers for other times in the Liturgy: the Offertory and Post- Communion.[716]

Any new edition of Andrewes' *Preces Privatæ* will need to accommodate this manuscript in Lambeth Palace Library.

---

714 Ms. 3708, p. 60; Drake's version in Vol. 11, p.335.

715 Ms. 3708, p.60; Brightman, pp. 123 –4.

716 These can be found in Brightman, although the order is a little different in places, pp. 121- 4.

Printed in the United States
141339LV00003B/42/A